The Sociology of Katrina

Perspectives on a Modern Catastrophe

Edited by David L. Brunsma,
David Overfelt, and J. Steven Picou

ROWMAN & LITTLEFIELD PUBLISHERS, INC.
Lanham • Boulder • New York • Toronto • Plymouth, UK

ROWMAN & LITTLEFIELD PUBLISHERS, INC.

Published in the United States of America
by Rowman & Littlefield Publishers, Inc.
A wholly owned subsidary of The Rowman & Littlefield Publishing Group, Inc.
4501 Forbes Boulevard, Suite 200, Lanham, Maryland 20706
www.rowmanlittlefield.com

Estover Road
Plymouth PL6 7PY
United Kingdom

Copyright © 2007 by Rowman & Littlefield Publishers, Inc.

British Library Cataloguing in Publication Information Available

Library of Congress Cataloging-in-Publication Data

The sociology of Katrina : perspectives on a modern catastrophe / [edited by] David
L. Brunsma, David Overfelt & J. Steven Picou.
p. cm.
Includes bibliographical references.
ISBN-13: 978-0-7425-5929-5 (cloth : alk. paper)
ISBN-10: 0-7425-5929-7 (cloth : alk. paper)
ISBN-13: 978-0-7425-5930-1 (pbk. : alk. paper)
ISBN-10: 0-7425-5930-0 (pbk. : alk. paper)
1. Hurricane Katrina, 2005—Social aspects. 2. Disasters—Social aspects—Louisiana—
New Orleans. 3. Hurricanes—Social aspects—Louisiana—New Orleans. 4. Disaster
relief—Louisiana—New Orleans. 5. New Orleans (La.)—Social conditions—21st
century. I. Brunsma, David L. II. Overfelt, David. III. Picou, J. Steven.
HV6362005.N4 S63 2007
303.48'5—dc22   2007005905

Printed in the United States of America

♾™ The paper used in this publication meets the minimum requirements of
American National Standard for Information Sciences—Permanence of Paper
for Printed Library Materials, ANSI/NISO Z39.48-1992.

This book is dedicated to
the victims and survivors of Hurricane Katrina
all those dedicated to make New Orleans
a better place for all who inhabit it

The editors each dedicate this book to:

From David Brunsma:
"To my Hooky-Dook Henry"

From David Overfelt:
"To my mother, Tamara Rapier, for being a constant source of inspiration"

From J. Steven Picou:
"To my grandchildren"

Contents

List of Figures

List of Tables

Preface

David L. Brunsma

On August 29, 2005, Hurricane Katrina hit the Gulf Coast with a vengeance, logging in as one of the most devastating, costly, and deadly storms in the history of the United States—the disaster that is Katrina is ongoing. The hurricane created the largest internal U.S. diaspora of displaced people as the result of a natural disaster in American history. However, this disaster, the preparation for it, the media and governmental framing of it after landfall, the deaths and evacuation of survivors, the recovery efforts, and the reconstruction efforts of affected cities and neighborhoods within cities laid bare the staunch sociological, demographic, racial, classist, political, and institutional issues of inequality, racism, classism, and "development" in the United States. Thus, this disaster has renewed and made more critical important discussions about disaster research, media constructions, the role of the military, national preparedness and homeland security, institutional failure and reconstitution, questions of the status quo before and after disasters, poverty, racism, labor issues, and a whole host of other issues central to understanding the past, present, and future of the U.S. social structure. This volume is devoted to understanding these complex webs.

Throughout 2005, we—David Overfelt, Judith Blau, and myself—were busy putting together the 2006 annual meetings of the Southern Sociological Society to be held in New Orleans, Louisiana. The theme for that conference, "Diaspora," was chosen long before Katrina hit; however, the theme took on a whole new meaning once the hurricane had struck—a new meaning indeed. The membership of the society pulled together, and ultimately we created an energetic and amazing conference comprised of a subset of some 20 special Katrina-related sessions with some 80 original and pertinent sociological analyses of the Katrina disaster. The Southern Sociological Society was the first association to hold a major conference (in March 2006) in New Orleans after the horrific disaster. The catastrophe of Hurricane Katrina has forever left its mark on this conference—one that will not soon be forgotten, nor should it be. In this conference, we provided, wherever possible, opportunities for faculty and students of New Orleans' departments of sociology to gather and share their experiences of facing and surviving Katrina. Numerous community activist groups (e.g., Community Labor United and NOHEAT), New Orleans community members, as well as affiliates of prominent New Orleans institutions were on-site to add their voices to our discussions. We also had a silent auction (organized by Sociologists for Women in Society, South and the Local Arrangements Committee) to benefit those of our colleagues and students who have been affected by the hurricane—including an on-site muralist, Turbado Marabou, who created a fantastic thematic mural to both commemorate the theme of the conference and the situation in New Orleans post-Katrina. All these facets of this program make it unique indeed.

The conference was heavily populated with original and cutting-edge research pursuing the events before and after Katrina through critical sociological lenses. This volume brings together the best of those papers through the original contributions of some of the top disaster researchers in the United States and beyond. The importance of this collection of chapters cannot be overestimated. No one can deny the crucial importance that interdisciplinary teams of critical scholars have in providing social scientific analyses to increase public awareness and understanding of the plethora of issues surrounding Katrina as a public disaster. It has become clear to us that the Southern Sociological Society has the most fantastic set of scholarship on Katrina and that this scholarship needs to be made available to everyone—not only those who attended these meetings. Thus, we sought to edit and publish a volume of the best of these papers. You now hold the fruits of that labor in your hands. All the royalties from this volume go to the Disaster Relief Fund of the Southern Sociological Society.

It is impossible for us to thank all the people who made the conference as well as this volume possible—so we will not attempt to do so in full. We do especially want to thank Judith Blau and the Southern Sociological Society, the departments of sociology at Missouri and South Alabama, as well as our families. We intend this volume to be useful across the undergraduate, graduate, and scholar lines as well as of great interest to a much wider lay readership. The issues dealt with in this volume will be relevant for decades to come, for the world will see more catastrophes of this enormity with more frequency, and the impacts on populations will become increasingly more devastating.

Foreword

Kai Erikson

Most of the disasters that sociologists have known something about and drawn on in their own research have been fairly small in scale. A number of the disasters alluded to in the chapters of this volume, for example, are of that kind. They occurred in obscure places with names like Buffalo Creek, Centralia, Cordova, Love Canal, Northridge, Red River, and Three Mile Island. If we know the names of those places at all, it is almost sure to be a consequence of what happened there: a flood, an underground mine fire, an oil spill, a toxic contamination, an earthquake, another (very different) flood, or a near meltdown.

The scale of those events has allowed us to imagine that we can sometimes see a disaster whole, that we can really fathom it, wrap our minds around it. I have been in that position myself and know the feeling, justified or not, that I had it in my grasp.

No one will ever get that feeling with Katrina. It was (and is) so immense that it will be impossible for us to take its full measure. The area impacted by Katrina (and her unruly partner, Rita) was 90,000 square miles, roughly the size of Great Britain. The number of people displaced by it is turning into one of the largest population shifts in the history of this country. The number of people who appear to have been damaged in one way or another by it has now reached epidemic proportions. It was, as the old folk song goes, a mighty storm.

More to the point, however, we will never be able to take the true measure of that disaster because it is still in motion, still taking form. We call it "Katrina" because it came to public attention as a hurricane, but the story of Katrina is not one of winds and waves and storm surges or even of collapsed levees and collapsed institutions. The story of Katrina is what those winds and surges did to the persons and communities caught in their path, and the dimensions of that occurrence are only now emerging in enough detail to begin the process of understanding. "Katrina" exploded into being in August 2005, but it does not have a defined location in the flow of time. As the chapters in this volume make clear, what we mean by "Katrina" began long before the storm of that name began to take shape, and it will be an ongoing event for a long time to come. The storm is not over.

The only way for us to ever acquire an understanding of Katrina, then, is to come at it from many different vantage points—to chip away at it, to probe this detail and then that one, to try this way of approaching it and then that one, until all those fragments of information and insight begin to form a picture, like the tens of thousands of tesserae that together make up a mosaic. Science often works that way.

That is the process that this collection of chapters begins. It's an impressive start.

All the social scientists whose work appears in this volume would probably agree that the disaster we have decided to call "Katrina" is one of the most important events of our time. If judged by the number of lives it took, Katrina does not qualify as the worst disaster to visit our land. That distinction belongs to the Galveston hurricane of 1900 that swept more than 6,000 people to their deaths. If judged by the number of evacuations it precipitated, other events rank higher. But Katrina stands alone nonetheless. It was the most *destructive* disaster in our history when one considers the amount of harm it did, and it was the most *instructive* when one considers the potential significance of the knowledge that can be drawn from it.

It is crucial for us to come to terms with Katrina not only because the information we acquire in the process will contribute in some abstract way to our store of knowledge but also because it serves as a window into a number of urgent realities.

First, we need to understand Katrina in order to be able to contribute to a just and reasoned restoration of New Orleans and devastated portions of the Gulf Coast. I mean *restoration* here in two senses: restoring both the physical setting itself and the persons who lived in it to a condition of relative well-being. This does not mean that the aim of rebuilding should be to create a replica of what was. But it does mean that we need to learn what damage Katrina actually *did* to the places and people it slammed into before we can participate in an informed process of repair. In the absence of information of that kind, restoration plans are likely to be based on the proposals of political operatives with strategic advantages to press, architects with theories to put to the test, developers with other fancies dancing in their heads, and a host of others.

Second, as a number of authors note in what follows, Katrina had the effect of seeming to peel away the surfaces of the American social order, providing a rare glance at the inner workings of race, class, gender, and perhaps age in these United States. The national spotlight focused harshly on those issues when the news media first began to report on life in the civic centers and on the streets and housetops of New Orleans during the crisis, and even though the spotlights now shine elsewhere and the media have turned to other matters, it would be a terrible mistake if social scientists did the same.

Third, information gathered in the wake of Katrina may be vital in helping the country prepare for that stark inevitability, *the next time*. When seen through a social science lens, Katrina almost ranks as a perfect storm. It was responsible for what is now beginning to look like an unprecedented volume of traumatic injuries. It was responsible for what is in the process of becoming one of the most (and in all likelihood *the* most) disruptive relocations of people in the history of the nation. And it was responsible for a number of severe problems both for those communities that lay in the path of the storm and for those communities that offered refuge to the persons who fled it. To complicate all that, officialdom turned out not to have any useful ideas about how to respond to such an emergency. It is fashionable (and, of course, quite accurate) to decry the failures of those who were in positions of responsibility at the time, but the more urgent questions have to do with the failure of whole systems rather than the shortcomings of particular individuals.

Experts are close to unanimous in predicting that the future will bring a sharp increase in the number and severity of catastrophic events resulting from the following:

* The rampages of an ever more turbulent natural world
* The miscalculations of an ever more restless human world
* The ways in which the human population has situated itself across the surface of the earth
* Deliberate acts of terror (a newcomer to this dread listing as far as the American experience is concerned)

Knowing is far and away our surest line of defense against the harm that can be done by such events. Katrina supplies a remarkable opportunity to learn at least a part of what we will need to know in order to deal with that grim future. If I were in charge of Homeland Security, I would commission hundreds of research projects along the lines of the ones presented in this volume for just that reason.

In that sense, Katrina may be unique in the opportunity it offers to learn about the anatomy of modern disasters and about ways to prepare for them. And it is by definition unique in the opportunity it offers to truly understand what happened to the people who still suffer its effects.

I will certainly not claim to be a disinterested witness here, but I would suggest that the field of sociology is in a particularly good position to undertake such an inquiry. This is true for many reasons, far from the least of them being that Katrina cannot be visualized usefully as a natural disaster that blew across the horizon from a point out at sea and slammed into human settlements, even though that is how it got its name. As many authors in what is to follow note in one way or another, "Katrina" is the name we have given to a series of events and happenings that are largely of human invention. The settlements in Katrina's path were of human construction. The openings Katrina took advantage of to reach New Orleans and other vulnerable parts of the coast were of human construction. The susceptibilities of the persons victimized by Katrina were of human construction. And virtually everything that followed was a product of human hands or human imaginations.

In that sense, Katrina can be best understood as a collision between a natural force (itself of human construction to the extent that global warming or something of the sort can be said to have been involved) and what turned out to be a strangely vulnerable social order. The true contours of Katrina cannot be learned from studying the intensity of its winds or the fury of its surges. They can be learned only from studying the other party to that collision—the ways in which humankind created the physical and social landscape the storm landed on and the way in which persons and institutions responded to that crisis. That way of telling the story is a sociological one.

The chapters to follow, then, are a beginning of something important.

Introduction

Katrina as Paradigm Shift: Reflections on Disaster Research in the Twenty-First Century

J. Steven Picou and Brent K. Marshall

> In order to understand the manufactured uncertainty, lack of safety and in-
> security of world risk society is there a need for a paradigm shift in the so-
> cial sciences?
>
> —Ulrich Beck (2006, 331)

The answer to this question, recently posed by Ulrich Beck (2006), requires a theoretical analysis that goes beyond traditional conceptualizations in the disaster research literature. In this chapter, we restrict our focus to disaster research and perspectives that have emerged primarily from the disciplines of sociology and psychology in the United States over the past 50 years. This scope of inquiry is significantly more narrow than would be required to address Beck's important question. Nonetheless, we concur with his observation that "Hurricane Katrina was a horrifying act of nature, but one which simultaneously, as a global media event, involuntarily and unexpectedly developed an enlightenment function which broke all resistance" (Beck 2006, 338). In short (consistent with Beck's broader dictum), we suggest that Katrina as a sociological event requires a paradigm shift in disaster research and a reorientation and redirection of important research themes throughout the broader discipline of sociology.

Hurricane Katrina was a "destabilizing event," a disaster that invites sociological inquiry and forces a rethinking of the nature of risks that characterize modern catastrophic events. As such, current disaster typologies, research on disaster impacts, and strategies for implementing timely community recovery need to be recast in terms of Beck's declaration of Katrina's enlightenment

1

function. The chapters in this volume expand sociological perspectives in the disaster literature, providing alternative views and analyses of the consequences of the most destructive hurricane in the history of the United States.

On the morning of August 29, 2005, Hurricane Katrina made landfall on the Gulf Coast, just east of New Orleans and about 80 miles west of Mobile, AL. The incredible wind speeds (135 to 175 miles per hour) and storm surge (20 to 32 feet) that were generated over the 90-degree-plus water temperatures of the Gulf of Mexico created a hurricane that approached a "worst-case" event (Clarke 2005, 2006). The catastrophic damage unleashed by this dynamic meteorological and technological disaster resulted in the death of over 1,800 people, caused flooding and/or structural damage to 2.5 million residences, and displaced between 700,000 and 1.2 million people (Gabe, Falk, and McCarty 2005). What followed was the largest forced migration of the American population since the Dust Bowl in the 1930s. The economic impacts of Katrina may reach $300 billion, far surpassing Hurricane Andrew ($35 billion) in 1992 as the most costly "natural disaster" in U.S. history (NBC Nightly News 2005). Considering the global reach of the mass media and the 24/7 news cycle, the horrific images of the death and damage caused by the recent spate of worst-case events—Hurricane Katrina, the 9/11 terrorist attacks of 2001, and the Asian tsunami of 2004—forces an enlightened reflexivity, where risks of the twenty-first century undermine ontological security. It is abundantly clear that disasters, experienced either directly or indirectly via the media, will be pervasive features of social life in this century (see chapter 1 in this volume).

As the destruction initiated by Katrina continued to ravage residents of the city of New Orleans for over a week, it became obvious that this catastrophic event was something more than a "traditional" natural disaster (Hartman and Squires 2006; Quarantelli 2005). As the levees breached and floodwaters inundated 80 percent of the city, the failure of engineered, human-made levees revealed a critical second characteristic of Katrina's catastrophic impacts, that is, the failure of human technology and the collapse of an engineered levee system designed to protect residents. Indeed, the "complexity" of Katrina does not end with the failure of levee technology (Silove and Bryant 2006). Katrina was also a massive contamination event, with oil, pesticides, fertilizers, and numerous other hazardous and toxic wastes being contained in the floodwaters and migrating throughout New Orleans, St. Bernard Parish, the lower Ninth Ward, and the Lakeview area (Frickel 2005). Furthermore, that the dire consequences of a category 3, 4, or 5 hurricane for the city of New Orleans was repeatedly predicted by engineers, emergency management specialists, sociologists, and other scientists (see Laska 2004) points to the fact that the context of blame for the death and destruction caused by Katrina included a host of anthropogenic sources. Ostensibly, politicians and policymakers at all levels failed to act on the predictions of physical and social scientists. These early untoward forecasts went unheeded, revealing a manufactured failure that eventually resulted in an inept and ineffective response effort by all levels of government.[1]

Most sociologists would agree that Hurricane Katrina was different in many complex ways. In this chapter, we attempt to highlight the nature of this "Katrina difference" in terms of past conceptualizations of disasters in the social science literature. Over the years, disaster researchers have maintained a contentious discourse on the significance of distinguishing "natural" disasters from "technological" disasters (Erikson 1994; Freudenburg 1997; Quarantelli 1998), the former being framed as "acts of God," where the application of the traditional disaster stage model is appropriate and timely recovery and rehabilitation reflect an "amplified rebound" for impacted communities (Drabek 1986). The latter involves human error and technological failure and, when combined with toxic contamination, results in a never-ending cycle of secondary disasters and chronic psychosocial impacts, ultimately resulting in a "corrosive community" (Erikson 1976, 1994; Freudenburg 1997; Picou, Marshall, and Gill 2004). Figure 1 graphically depicts these two traditional models and the lack of timely community recovery for technological disasters. The "technological disaster model" provides an important sensitizing perspective for further elaborating sociological characteristics that reveal the "anomaly" that Katrina poses for future social science research on disasters.[2]

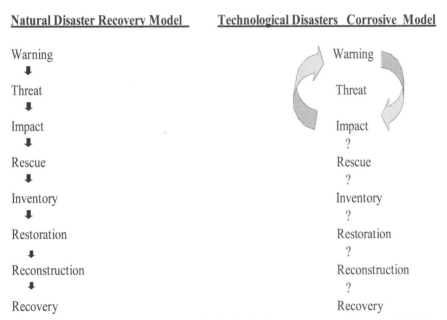

Figure 1.   Traditional Natural and Technological Disaster Stage Models (modified from Couch 1996)

CONCEPTUALIZING DISASTERS: A REVIEW

In this section, we briefly outline several themes in the disaster research literature and discuss the distinction between four types of disasters—natural, technological, natural-technological, and terrorism. All four are currently viewed as separate types of disaster events. In the past, disaster researchers, emergency management responders, government agencies, and the legal system all recognized that disasters could be classified as either natural or technological (Cuthbertson and Nigg 1987). Research by social scientists since the late 1940s has documented that natural disasters (hurricanes, earthquakes, and floods) are acute, life-threatening events that primarily destroy the "built" and "modified" environments (Fritz 1961). Prevention and recovery for this type of destruction has focused on revising and improving construction and engineering codes and developing sophisticated warning technologies in meteorology and seismology while concomitantly developing emergency response plans and facilitating natural disaster recovery through an "amplified rebound" (Drabek 1986; Kreps 1989).

For natural disasters, there is political and societal consensus that (1) a disaster occurred, (2) there are legitimate victims, and (3) rescue, restoration, and recovery should be "automatically" supported by federal, state, and local governments as well as voluntary relief organizations (Dynes 1998; Picou, Marshall, and Gill 2004). Natural disasters usually have short-term disruptive social consequences, and community recovery is most often described as therapeutic (Barton 1969). The outcome of the therapeutic community includes timely community recovery, and often there are significant improvements in the engineering and construction of the built and modified environments (Drabek 1986; Mileti, Drabek, and Haas 1975).

On the other hand technological disasters, that is, human-caused toxic events, involve the breakdown of technological processes and systems, in turn impacting vulnerable human populations (Couch and Kroll-Smith 1985). Technological disasters often leave the "built" and "modified" environments relatively intact while severely and permanently contaminating the "biophysical environment" to the extent that communities are uninhabitable (Chernobyl) or contaminating ecological systems to the extent that communities receive irreparable cultural and socioeconomic damage (*Exxon Valdez* oil spill). Catastrophic technological failure and the massive contamination of the biophysical environment produce a series of debilitating processes that plague victims and their families for decades (Baum and Fleming 1993; Edelstein 1988; Erikson 1994; Freudenburg 1997; Gill and Picou 1991; Kroll-Smith and Couch 1993; Picou and Gill 2000; Picou and Rosebrook 1993). A recent comprehensive review of 130 disaster studies in the United States, conducted by Fran Norris and colleagues, revealed that victims of technological disasters are more likely to experience severe and long-term social, physical, and mental health problems than are victims of natural disasters (Norris et al. 2001). Indeed, victims of mass violence disasters, such as terrorism, were found to be the most severely impacted (Norris et al. 2001).

Furthermore, numerous studies conducted on technological disasters by social science researchers demonstrate that anger, conflict, posttraumatic stress, depression, and loss of trust in responsible institutions characterize many survivors (Freudenburg 1997; Green 1996; Norris et al. 2001). Unlike natural disasters, many aspects of technological disasters are "contested disasters," and there is an effort to identify "principle responsible parties." Typically, in the aftermath of technological disasters, a legal discourse emerges, restoration and recovery are postponed, and the payment of damage claims are deferred well into the future (Hirsch 1997). During this period, victims suffer. For example, although a jury awarded victims of the *Exxon Valdez* oil spill $5.3 billion in 1993, the "principle responsible party" has managed, through high-cost, strategic-legal maneuvering, to stall payments for survivors for over 13 years (Marshall, Picou, and Schlichtmann 2004; Picou, Marshall, and Gill 2004). In short, technological disasters produce (1) a contested discourse regarding who was responsible; (2) chronic social disruption, anger, mental health problems, and the loss of resources for victims; (3) delayed restoration and recovery for impacted communities; (4) ambiguity of harm; (5) sociocultural disruption; and (6) litigation stress (Freudenburg 1993, 1997, 2000; Marshall, Picou, and Schlichtmann 2004; Picou, Marshall, and Gill 2004).

Numerous studies suggest that most technological disasters result in the emergence of a "corrosive community," that is, a consistent pattern of recurring chronic impacts to individuals and impacted communities (Couch and Kroll-Smith 1985; Erikson 1976, 1994; Freudenburg 1993, 1997; Kroll-Smith and Couch 1993; Picou, Marshall, and Gill 2004). From this extensive literature on technological disasters, Picou and associates identified three corrosive processes that produce the emergence and persistence of corrosive communities (Marshall, Picou, and Schlichtmann 2004; Picou, Marshall, and Gill 2004). First, there is uncertainty regarding the mental and physical health of victims (Arata et al. 2000; Baum and Fleming 1993; Freudenburg and Jones 1991; Green 1996; Picou and Gill 1996, 2000). Second, victims often blame governmental and organizational systems for failure, and a general loss of trust in government agencies, corporations, and other responsible organizations emerges (Couch 1996; Freudenburg 1993, 1997, 2000; Marshall, Picou, and Gill 2003). Finally, protracted litigation ensues (Marshall, Picou, and Schlichtmann 2004; Picou and Rosebrook 1993), extending chronic psychosocial stress, delaying community recovery, and interfering with independent research on impacts conducted by both physical and social scientists (Ott 2005; Picou 1996a, 1996b, 1996c).

We have suggested elsewhere that Hurricane Katrina could be conceptualized as a natural-technological, or "na-tech," disaster (Picou and Marshall 2006). In a na-tech disaster, a natural disaster *directly* or *indirectly* releases hazardous material into the environment (Showalter and Myers 1994). The likelihood of na-tech disasters in the future is on the rise because of "increases in the number of natural disasters, as well as increases in population density in disaster-prone areas and technologic and industrial expansion" (Young, Balluz, and Malilay 2004, 5). The amount of hazardous materials discharged during past natural disasters is unknown, and as a result, the long-term health effects of exposure are uncertain (Young, Balluz, and Malilay 2004). First responders, governmental agencies, and volunteer organizations are trained to respond to the short-term problems associated with natural disasters, while the long-term problems associated with technological disasters are rarely part of a long-term response program.[3] Young et al. (2004) note that hazmat releases can result directly from a natural disaster (dioxin from forest fires) or can result from unintentional disruptions (Katrina's impacts on oil refineries) or through purposeful recovery actions (pumping polluted water into Lake Pontchartrain). Hazmat releases from Hurricane Katrina were both unintentional and purposeful, possibly resulting in massive ecological contamination and human exposure.

As a natural disaster, Katrina was a monster meteorological event that literally obliterated the built and modified environments along a 90,000-square-mile area of the central Gulf Coast and destroying the homes of 700,000 people (Crowley 2006). As a technological disaster, Katrina was a massive, complex contamination event. Hazmat releases ranged from oil spills (from Mobile Bay to coastal areas west of New Orleans) to the creation of "toxic gumbo," that is, the bacteria-infested, hazardous floodwaters that engulfed the city of New Orleans (Frickel 2005). It has been documented in Louisiana that ten major oil spills resulted from Katrina's devastation. These major spills collectively released over 8 million gallons of oil into the environment (see Table 1). The U.S. Coast Guard reported that an additional 134 minor oil spills (less than 10,000 gallons) occurred in Louisiana. Oil spills were also reported in Mobile Bay and the Gulf of Mexico, suggesting that the total amount of oil released by Katrina's devastation may never be known. Nonetheless, the 8 to 9 million gallons of oil estimated to have been spilled by Katrina's fury establishes the "Katrina Spill" as the second-largest oil spill in the history of North

Table 1. Location and Amount of Oil Released from Hurricane Katrina Damage

Facility and Location	Spill (gallons)
Murphy Oil, Meraux, LA	1,050,000
Chevron Empire Terminal, Buras, LA	1,400,000
Bass Enterprises, Cox Bay, LA	3,780,000
Shell, Pilottown, LA	1,070,000
Dynegy, Venice, LA	24,822
Sundown Energy West, Potash, LA	13,440
Sundown Energy East, Potash, LA	18,900
Bass Enterprises, Point a la Hache, LA	461,538
Shell Pipeline Oil LP, Nairn, LA	136,290
Chevron, Port Fourchon, LA	53,000
Total	8,007,990

Source: http://www.laseagrant.org/hurricane/archive/oil.htm; see also Pine (2006) for more information on Hurricane Katrina's oil spill impacts on the coastal ecology.

America. The 1989 *Exxon Valdez* spill was the largest and was estimated to be 11 million gallons (Picou, Gill, and Cohen 1997).[4]

As refurbished pumps moved the contaminated flood waters out of the city to Lake Pontchartrain, the slow and inevitable migration of biotoxins had to eventually find their way to the Gulf of Mexico. Toxins such as benzene, lead, formaldehyde, hydrocarbons, dioxins, and other chemicals also leached into the soil and homes of survivors. These hazardous toxins will invariably pose long-term contamination risks to the local ecology as well as health risks to returning residents. The actual occurrence of this contamination and the physical health risks posed by this type of exposure to the survivors of Katrina will be debated endlessly by social scientists, toxicologists, epidemiologists, public health experts, and, of course, attorneys. Countless lawsuits, including a number of class-action suits, have been filed because of oil spills, levee breaches, the flooding caused by the Mississippi River–Gulf outlet, and other Katrina-related deaths and damages.

Independent of objective exposure to toxic chemicals, this emerging adversarial legal discourse will generate uncertainty, dread, and despair, which in turn will produce acute mental and physical health problems (Marshall, Picou, and Gill 2003; Picou, Marshall, and Gill 2004). Furthermore, the long-term consequences of Katrina contamination for ecosystems and ecological processes may never be accurately determined (Pine 2006), and the numerous lawsuits will invariably extend corrosive social processes and delay community recovery (Marshall, Picou, and Schlichtmann 2004; Picou, Marshall, and Gill 2004). Nonetheless, Katrina's impacts go beyond this na-tech scenario, and we elaborate on this point later.

The characteristics and impacts of catastrophic natural and technological disasters, as well as hybrid na-tech events, are relevant for understanding the risk and social consequences of modern terrorism (Marshall, Picou, and Schlichtmann 2004). Furthermore, Marshall and associates (2004) have suggested that although the initial damage and social impacts of the 9/11 terrorist attack manifested many similarities to natural disasters (Webb 2002), there were also social impacts similar to technological disasters that are directly applicable to the 9/11 attack and, most important, future catastrophic acts of terror. These similarities include (1) the role of government and recreancy, (2) the consequences of litigation, and (3) mental and physical health problems (Marshall, Picou, and Gill 2003, 78).

Following the 9/11 attack, the public mobilized, but the Federal Emergency Management Agency (FEMA) was criticized by many who complained about the unequal distribution of funds being unequal and that low-income areas, like Chinatown, were being ignored (Chen 2002). Indeed, critics also argued that minority and poor neighborhoods received disproportionately less aid than that accorded to the more wealthy Manhattan neighborhoods (Chen 2002). As the Democratic representative of Manhattan, Carolyn B. Maloney, stated, "Thousands of people have lost trust in the agency [FEMA] because of the prior rejections and false promises the first time around" (quoted in Chen 2002, 1). This form of blame on anthropogenic sources, endemic to terrorist events, has been echoed ever since by the survivors of Hurricane Katrina. In fact, not only has FEMA been criticized, but so has the Army Corps of Engineers,

Technological Disasters	Terrorist Disasters
1. Reckless Act of Death & Destruction (Profit-Driven).	1. Purposeful Act of Death & Destruction (Politically Driven).
2. Principle Responsible Party.	2. Responsible Individual/Organization.
3. Weak Preventive/Response System in Place—Incubation of Increasing Risk.	3. Weak Preventive/Response System in Place—Incubation of Increasing Risk.
4. Health Threats Associated with Ecological Contamination and Exposure, e.g. dioxins.	4. Health Threats Associated with Purposeful Exposure, e.g. anthrax, and generated toxic materials.
5. Loss of Control of Technology.	5. Destructive Control of Technology.
6. Chronic Mental Health Impacts.	6. Chronic Mental Health Impacts.

Figure 2.   Similarities between Technological and Terrorist Disasters

Homeland Security, state government, local government, and numerous other organizations, agencies, and groups involved in the response to Katrina's impacts in New Orleans and throughout the Gulf Coast region.

Numerous lawsuits have also been filed against insurance companies, chemical companies, and even the Army Corps of Engineers. These protracted legal battles will result in long-term (10 to 15 years) mental health impacts as well as delayed community recovery. Furthermore, physical health problems emerged after 9/11 and have continued over the past five years (Farnam 2006). First responders have suffered elevated rates of cancer, and hundreds have been disabled by various types of illness. Katrina victims, especially first responders, have also been beset by increased mental health problems and the complete lack of mental health infrastructures to respond to the growing social and psychological needs of survivors (see chapter 12 in this volume). Furthermore, in a manner similar to 9/11 survivors, the emergence of the "Katrina cough" signaled a host of respiratory problems directly associated with the piles of contaminated debris, hazardous dust, and widespread molds attached to the remaining built and modified structures in the impact area (see chapter 12 in this volume).

In summary, Figure 2 provides a comparative listing of similarities between technological disasters and acts of terrorism. Indeed, these similarities highlight the fact that technological, na-tech, and terrorism all manifest similarities in damage potential that portend serious long-term mental and physical health risks to people and communities. Furthermore, these risks become increasingly relevant for understanding the diverse consequences of Katrina. This new understanding must overcome the resistance of the inertia of previous sociological approaches to disasters and establish Beck's "enlightenment function" for future social science inquiry (Beck 2006, 338).

CHARTING NEW DIRECTIONS

Previous a priori classifications of disasters as either natural, technological, na-tech, or terrorism are possible analytically and perhaps were cogent when such large-scale disasters first became apparent. We suggest that typologies, although serving a heuristic purpose, limit and divert attention from the more critical task at hand, namely, the identification of processes that tend to be either "therapeutic" or "corrosive" or some combination of the two (Marshall, Picou, and Schlichtmann 2004; Picou, Marshall, and Gill 2004). The therapeutic processes identified by natural disaster researchers and the corrosive processes identified by technological disaster researchers may be present in the aftermath of any disaster event. With a primary focus on timely individual and community recovery, innovative emergency response and postdisaster intervention programs must be developed to include an array of techniques that *enable* therapeutic processes and *constrain* corrosive processes. These programs should be long term and based on a participatory model that maximally involves survivors (Picou 2000).

While we recognize the important contributions of pre-Katrina disaster research and the historic utility of disaster typologies, we suggest the need to move beyond the limitations imposed by simple a priori classification schemes (Marshall, Picou, and Gill 2003). We make this claim for three reasons. First, some disasters historically perceived as natural are increasingly viewed as anthropogenic. For example, with the growing scientific consensus regarding the anthropogenic underpinnings of global warming, the distinction between geological disasters (earthquakes and volcanoes) as natural and meteorological disasters (hurricanes, tornadoes, and floods) as anthropogenic, scientific veracity aside, may become increasingly salient across political, legal, and social dimensions (Marshall and Picou, in press).

Second, even though the disaster itself may be perceived as an "act of God" or "act of nature," the subsequent severity and duration of chronic impacts may be ascribed to anthropogenic factors (Erikson 1976; Freudenburg 1997; Picou, Marshall, and Gill 2004). More broadly, if all aspects of the environment are increasingly perceived as befouled by human activity, the responsibility for causing a "disaster" may be ascribed to industry or government, and the responsibility for the severity and duration of the disaster ascribed to government for (1) not enforcing regulations, (2) not being prepared for disasters, and (3) not responding in a manner required by law and expected by the victims. Such claims are clearly evident in the wake of Katrina.

Third, another reason for a less rigid classification scheme is the recent aftermath of two large-scale disasters (the 9/11 terrorist attacks and Hurricane Katrina) that clearly cannot be characterized as either natural or technological or as na-tech. For instance, as previously noted, short-term response by victims, disaster researchers, governmental agencies, and volunteer organizations to the 9/11 terrorist attacks were similar to response patterns observed in the aftermath of natural disasters. However, processes identified in technological disaster research as causing collective trauma and impeding timely community recovery emerged within a year after the attacks and continue today (Marshall, Picou, and Gill 2003). Further, there are aspects of the 9/11 terrorist attacks that render it unlike other disasters, such as the motives behind the attacks, the disaster scene as crime scene, and postdisaster anxiety related to future attacks (Marshall and Picou, in press).

Hurricane Katrina produced maximum damage to the built and modified environments, contaminated the biophysical environment, caused widespread mortality, produced serious physical health impacts for survivors, endangered severe mental health impacts, and relocated a massive segment of the population from the impact area. This "worst-case" disaster combines, in a synergistic fashion, the damage potential for all "types" of past disaster events (Clarke 2006). That is, natural forces, technological failure, ecological contamination, the response failure of human institutions, and the massive displacement of people have all interacted to amplify and exacerbate the severity of the impacts to the human community. Indeed, this worst-case synergism continues to negatively affect survivors, as corrosive social processes generate ongoing secondary disasters that exacerbate pre-Katrina inequalities and agitate post-Katrina politics (see chapter 8 in this volume). This shift in the conceptualization of disasters identifies the changing nature of risk in the modern world and refocuses sociological inquiry. Worst-case catastrophes invite a broader sociological understanding of the organization of social vulnerability, resiliency, manufactured uncertainty, and socioenvironmental policy in "risk society" (Beck 1992, 2006).

BARRIERS TO POST-KATRINA RECOVERY: CHRONIC CORROSIVE PROCESSES

Quite possibly, New Orleans and the Mississippi Gulf Coast will never completely recover from the catastrophic impacts of Hurricane Katrina (see the postscript in this volume). A major indicator of Katrina's destruction to the built environment is that in Louisiana alone, insurance companies paid $14.5 billion in claims during the first year after the storm, and many claims have yet to be processed (Scott 2006).[5] Specifically for the New Orleans metropolitan area, all sectors of non-form employment have experienced serious decline,[6] and the return of manufacturing, especially smaller manufacturers (food processors), had not occurred in the year since Katrina (Scott 2006). Even more serious, construction employment in the New Orleans metropolitan area has not rebounded, as in other metropolitan areas along the Mississippi Gulf Coast, reflecting an anomalous pattern following a natural disaster (Scott 2006, 12).

There is also lingering uncertainty in Louisiana regarding how the resettlement Road Home program funds will be utilized by hundreds of thousands of former New Orleans residents who are still displaced.[7] As Scott (2006, 13) has noted, these funds may be used to "(1) return and rebuild in New Orleans, (2) leave New Orleans but rebuild somewhere else in the state, or (3) rebuild in some other state". Given the complexity of the Road Home program and the necessity for displaced residents to reestablish residential, social, economic, and personal security in a timely fashion, the two options of leaving the New

Orleans metropolitan area appear to be the most advantageous to former residents. However, this scenario would only continue to delay recovery in terms of failing to reestablish the pre-Katrina population, economy, and culture of New Orleans in a timely fashion.

Community recovery also implies and requires the establishment of a vast range of resources for returning residents. Population return not only involves the movement of people but also includes the reestablishment of physical, cultural, economic, educational, familial, interpersonal, and personal resources. In short, in addition to physical capital, social and cultural capital must be created for a sense of community to emerge (Chamlee-Wright 2006; Dynes 2006). This therapeutic process is a prerequisite for recovery. However, given the multiple forms of damage that Katrina survivors have experienced, it appears highly likely that the long-term evolution of corrosive social cycles, at numerous levels, will significantly hinder the recovery process. Most important for recovery, the prospects for the city of New Orleans achieving "restoration" of the built and modified environments, which are critical achievements in the traditional natural disaster stage model, appear limited (see Figure 1). An in-depth evaluation of the potential for community recovery in New Orleans provided by Kates and associates (2006) resulted in the following opinion for the achievement of the "restoration" stage in New Orleans:

> Restoration—repairing what is repairable in the infrastructure of urban life— began in the second week. But the forced out-migration and low rate of return complicates the calculation of restoration. The result is that much repairable, but population–dependent, infrastructure has not been restored or used. Most services for which there is data available (electricity, gas, public transportation, schools, hospitals and food stores) are functioning at less than half of pre-Katrina capacity. (14656)

The prospects for "reconstruction" and ultimate community recovery are also bleak. By 2008, the New Orleans metropolitan area will only have 41 percent of the jobs that existed before Katrina (Kates et al. 2006). Throughout the Gulf Coast, 278,000 workers were displaced, and a year later 100,000 households still remained in FEMA trailers (Lotke and Borosage 2006). Furthermore, only 60 percent of the pre-Katrina population in New Orleans will return by 2008, resulting in an approximate maximum population of 279,000 residents (Kates et al. 2006). Essentially, this is a 35 to 40 percent reduction in the pre-Katrina population. The fact that 150,000 to 160,000 homes and apartment complexes were destroyed or damaged beyond repair means that by not achieving restoration in a timely manner, recovery for the New Orleans area will be denied well into the future. Public services and the local community infrastructure of New Orleans are functioning (one year later) at less than 50 percent of pre-Katrina capacity. Only 17 percent of city buses are in use, while only half of all streetcar and bus routes are available to residents (Liu, Mabanta, and Fellowes 2006). Gas (41 percent) and electrical (60 percent) services have been slow to be reestablished for residences and businesses, and "less than one-third" of all public schools were operating 12 months after Katrina (Liu, Fellowes, and Mabanta 2006, 6).

Given that medical care, educational services, public transportation, and other critical infrastructure capacities have not been restored will invariably create a social context that manifests collective trauma and corrosive social processes for residents. The rapidly rising crime rate, including homicides and post-Katrina domestic violence, may be the most significant deterrent to returning residents (Konigsmark 2006).[8] Furthermore, insurance companies have proposed a 31.7 percent increase in premiums for residential dwellings and approximately a 140 percent increase for commercial establishments. These drastic rate increases will serve as an additional impediment for the return of former residents.[9]

Research on technological disasters document the psychosocial dynamics of chronic disaster impacts. In contrast to the "natural disaster recovery model," the "technological disaster corrosive model" specifies a continuous and expanding cycle of distress for survivors of catastrophes that are human caused, that involve toxic contamination, and that necessitate anthropogenic (legal) resolution (see Figure 1). Erikson's research on the long-term "collective trauma" experienced by victims of the Buffalo Creek dam collapse and his analytical-comparative expansion of this concept as a "new species of trouble," which results primarily when survivors lose their "sustaining community," provides the basic model for understanding the future of communities impacted by Katrina (Erikson 1976, 1994). In Erikson's (1994) words,

> The mortar bonding human communities together is made up at least in parts of trust, respect and decency and, in moments of crisis, of charity and concern. It is profoundly disturbing to people when these expectations are not met . . . now they must face the future without those layers of emotional insulation that only a trusted community surround can provide. . . . But the real problem in the long run is that the inhumanity that people experience comes to be seen as a natural feature of human life . . . their eyes are being opened to a larger and profoundly unsettling truth that human institutions cannot be relied on. (239)

The residents of the communities ravaged by Katrina witnessed three major failures by human institutions: (1) the failure to prepare, (2) the failure to respond, and (3) the failure to rebuild (Lotke and Borosage 2006). We are now witnessing the failure to rebuild, and if past studies of technological disasters tell us anything, we should expect the emergence of corrosive communities and the expansion of corrosive social processes well into the future (Freudenburg 1997; Picou, Marshall, and Gill 2004).

The concept of the "corrosive community," introduced by Freudenburg (1997), focuses on the breakdown of the social fabric in communities impacted by technological disasters. Expanding on Erikson's seminal insights on collective trauma (Erikson 1976), corrosive communities emerge in the post-disaster phase of technological disasters (Baum and Fleming 1993; Erikson

1976; Freudenburg 1993, 1997, 2000; Freudenburg and Jones 1991; Green 1996). The defining characteristic of social corrosion is a "consistent pattern of chronic impacts to individuals and communities" (Picou, Marshall, and Gill 2004, 1496). This long-term pathological trend is characterized by the breakdown of social relationships, the fragmentation of community groups, family conflict, loss of trust, litigation, and the use of self-isolation as a primary coping strategy (Arata et al. 2000; Freudenburg 1997; Picou, Marshall, and Gill 2004). There is also a lack of sympathetic and empathetic behavior for survivors from nonvictims, and both resources and support capabilities from local, state, and federal institutions decline over time. These processes result in the continued deterioration of the social organization and culture of impacted communities, and residents experience group and interpersonal conflict as well as severe psychological problems.

Figure 3 provides a graphic representation of corrosive social cycles that emerge in corrosive communities. This dynamic process involves recurring threats, warnings, and secondary disaster impacts. Because most of the corrosive social processes that occur have anthropogenic causes, with survivors assigning blame to various responsible parties, this pattern of blame results in loss of trust in traditional institutions (Erikson 1994; Freudenburg 1997). For example, in the aftermath of Katrina, various government agencies, such as FEMA, local and state governments, and the U.S. Army Corps of Engineers, were blamed for inadequate responses to the disaster. In addition, 16 months after Katrina, insurance companies, politicians, police, agency subcontractors, contractors, neighbors, relatives, and others involved in initial reconstruction activities are regularly blamed for causing secondary disasters for survivors. This recurring "blame game" was manifested in political elections, the reorganization of the New Orleans levee board, and many intraparish conflicts that still linger in Katrina's wake. These corrosive cycles, or processes, pervade all dimensions of the social world, that is, at the social structural, cultural, intergroup, interpersonal, and personal levels of analysis.

Table 2 identifies specific forms of collective pathology that Katrina generated and from which corrosive social cycles may emerge. These negative social impacts were identified from a content analysis of newspaper articles published about Katrina in the *Mobile Press Register* from September 1, 2005, to August 1, 2006. Most likely, these problem areas are synergistic; that is, they are connected and magnify and amplify each other across all levels for survivors. For example, experiencing a death in the family, displacement, the destruction of your home, the breakdown of family relationships, and losing neighborhood and familial social networks are associated with cycles of anger, domestic violence, loss of trust, mental health problems, and spirals of resource loss that result in new threats, warnings, and impacts through the postdisaster period. An in-depth consideration of all the Katrina-induced negative outcomes documented across all social levels addressed in Table 2 goes well beyond the scope of this chapter. Nonetheless, modern catastrophes establish an avalanche of new risks for disaster survivors. Social scientists should focus

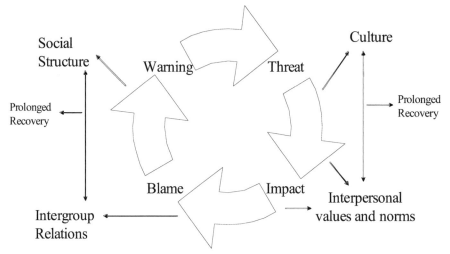

Figure 3. The Corrosive Social Cycle

Table 2. Summary of Social Structural, Cultural, Interpersonal, and Personal Impacts Documented for Katrina

Social Structure	Cultural Impacts
Massive displacement of over 1.7 million people	Loss of quality of life
35,000 people rescued (approx.)	Loss of cultural values
1,800 dead (approx.)	Decline in community cohesion
FEMA/Homeland Security delayed responses	Strained community relations
Loss of housing	Cultural uncertainty
Loss of financial resources	Loss of cultural socialization
Institutional failure	Loss of "sense of place"
Loss of tax revenues	Social conflict over cultural values
Loss of infrastructure	Loss of cultural resources (music, art, artifacts)
Collapse of federal government, state government, and local government support systems	Loss of meaning of life
Increased criminal behavior	
	Looting and loss of salvageable resources
Massive public recreancy	
Loss of medical and social services	
FEMA fraud	
Interpersonal	Personal
Loss of social, neighborhood and family networks and resources	Death
Loss of trust in agencies and organizations responsible for protecting resident	Injury
Social conflict between people who received FEMA aid and those who did not	Severe mental health impacts
Uncertainty regarding both immediate and long-term future	Anger
Mental health services overstressed	Anxiety

(*continued*)

Table 2. (*continued*)

Interpersonal	Personal
On-going agency and organizational corruption	Depression
Absolute disruption of daily norms and expected behavior	PTSD
Massive collective trauma	Suicide
Relocation to other regions of the United States	Domestic violence
Family conflict based on evacuation needs	Homicide
Divorce	Drug dependency
Loss of trust between relatives and friends	Alcoholism
Loss of resources due to evacuation	Child abuse
Lack of infrastructural support for evacuees needs	Feelings of helplessness and betrayal
	Collapse of family networks
	Self-isolation
	Avoidance
	Long-term income loss spirals
	Disruption of educational socialization
	Decline in children's grades
	Family conflict
	Children's mental health impacts
	Fear of being left alone
	Fighting with other children
	Loss of personal, family, economic, housing and civic resources
	Litigation, stress
	Conflict at K–12 schools

Source: Content analysis of *Mobile Press Register*, September 1, 2005, to August 1, 2006.

research efforts on these amplified risks, using traditional conceptual approaches as tools for better understanding disasters and their consequences in the modern world. The conceptualization of corrosive processes as the primary mechanism by which community recovery is denied and the continuing source for the emergence of chronic secondary disasters provides an initial point of departure for developing creative therapeutic interventions (Picou 2000).

ENABLING RECOVERY:
THERAPEUTIC INTERVENTIONS AND PROCESSES

Therapeutic interventions are most commonly a component of initial, short-term responses that are supportive and that recognize the needs, both material and nonmaterial, that characterize victims of natural disasters. Most often, such enabling processes reduce the levels of risk that threaten residents of impacted communities by providing resources, security, health care, and, in general, the restoration of financial, physical, social, and cultural capital. The

American Society of Civil Engineers (ASCE) has provided a list of critical actions that need to be taken to provide basic flood security for residents of New Orleans from future severe hurricanes. In addition to making "the protection of public safety, health and welfare at the fore-front of our nation's priorities," the ASCE recommended (1) making the levees survivable if overtopped, (2) strengthening or upgrading the flood walls and levees, and (3) upgrading the pumping stations (American Society of Civil Engineers 2006). These types of engineering achievements would definitely benefit residents of New Orleans by reducing the risk of flooding and offering residential security.

Most therapeutic responses occur at the interpersonal and intergroup levels and involve the collective mobilization of civil society. Countless private citizens from New Orleans and the Gulf Coast have volunteered both time and resources to initiate a regrouping of their neighborhoods and communities. Chamlee-Wright (2006) has identified and documented four basic strategies that private citizens who returned to their devastated neighborhoods have used for regrouping and reestablishing a collective identity and restoring social capital.

The most prevalent pattern observed for returning residents of New Orleans and the Mississippi Gulf Coast was "mutual assistance" (Chamlee-Wright 2006, 9). In contrast to direct external aid, "mutual assistance is a strategy by which storm survivors support one another by exchanging labor, expertise, shelter, child care services, tools and equipment, and so on" (Chamlee-Wright 2006, 9). The overwhelming destruction that residents of the Katrina-impacted communities found when they returned created an immediate, acute sense of helplessness. Survivors and evacuees, on returning to their neighborhoods, were clearly traumatized and distraught as they appeared in the media, pointing out and discussing the shattered remains of their homes. Often, only the foundation of the residence was visible, and people simply cried and repeated over and over that "there is nothing left, everything is gone." The critical point for initiating recovery resides with the question, Where do we start? Mutual assistance is the starting point for solving this dilemma because of three important reasons:

> First it is a source of material support. Second, it serves as a credible signal that friends, neighbors, relatives, employers and employees are committed to participating in the recovery process. Third it helps restore the social fabric of community that was torn apart by the storm. (Chamlee-Wright 2006, 9)

Other forms of therapeutic responses that facilitate regrouping and the mobilization of social capital include "charitable action," "commercial cooperation," and "entrepreneurial leadership" (Chamlee-Wright 2006). Charitable action was apparent throughout the New Orleans and Mississippi Gulf Coast areas in the months following Katrina's landfall. Religious groups, college students, philanthropic organizations, and volunteers from throughout the United States and many foreign countries traveled to the hurricane-ravaged area to offer materials, skills, resources, and time to survivors (e.g., see Jonsson 2006; see also chapter 6 in this volume). This form of therapeutic aid is highly visible and provides survivors with some semblance of "hope" in what is often defined as a "hopeless" postdisaster context.

Commercial cooperation, like mutual assistance, (1) provides essential material support; (2) helps to coordinate expectations by signaling commitment to a neighborhood or community; and (3) lays the foundation for the redevelopment of place-based social capital" (Chamlee-Wright 2006, 22; also see chapter 9 in this volume). The fact that Wal-Mart stores in New Orleans, Slidell, Biloxi, and Waveland, Mississippi, opened weeks after the storm, offering essential goods, provided survivors with a sense of hope that somehow they had turned around the sense of desperation and loss that was so prevalent after the storm. Finally, "entrepreneurial leadership" involves the establishment of commitments by local government boards and agencies to reopen schools and resume a host of public services. However, as Chamblee-Wright (2006) has noted, failure to deliver on such commitments, such as missing a projected date for providing garbage pickup, can result in loss of trust and generate anger among survivors.

These brief examples of therapeutic social processes also reveal that both corrosive and therapeutic processes can coexist and interact throughout the postdisaster collective context. Although Dynes (2006) has noted that social capital is the "primary basis" for emergency response, it is also apparent that social capital regrouping is critical for long-term neighborhood and community recovery. In this regard, corrosive social processes provide a formidable challenge to both therapeutic processes and long-term community recovery. Sociological research should address these competing processes in future disaster research.[10]

KATRINA AS SOCIOLOGICAL ENLIGHTENMENT: OVERVIEW OF CHAPTERS

Returning to the admonition of Ulrich Beck that organized the theme for this introductory chapter, Katrina sent shock waves throughout the sociological community. Katrina's destruction of the built and modified environments and toxic contamination of the local ecology rekindled numerous themes in environmental sociology, including global warming, environmental justice, and relationships between the human community and toxic biophysical environments. Population specialists and demographers were reawakened to migration patterns that have produced many vulnerable, highly populated communities near our coastline. Sociologists who study social stratification and race relations found issues of racism and inequality publicly visible in the wake of Katrina's wrath. Disaster researchers observed the failure of emergency response, and sociologists who study political and organizational behavior became students of institutional failure and malfeasance and bureaucratic ineffectiveness. Social psychologists observed personal and collective trauma, while the rhetoric of the media intrigued and sensitized many to the "communication society." Criminologists and collective behavior specialists became fixated on examples of criminal behavior, from looting to white-collar crime. In short, Katrina reawakened the sociological imagination for many and provided an enlightenment signal that reintroduced the need for understanding modern risks and promoting a more public sociology that is relevant to the social challenges that will confront society in the twenty-first century.

The chapters in this volume provide an initial step in this direction, covering a wide range of sociological issues and addressing a variety of sociological topics through multiple perspectives. Part I addresses the "framing of Katrina" through media outlets. Chapter 1, by Dynes and Rodriguez, demonstrates the irrational, exaggerated, and oversimplified nature of the media's portrayals in the post-Katrina South. The authors find, through an analysis of the frames used by the media, that much of the coverage was based on rumor and inaccurate assumptions, a highly deceptive situation for the average viewer. Tierney and Bevc pick up this framing discussion in chapter 2 and utilize both a historic description of the military's role in disaster response and a current description of the frames broadcast by the media post-Katrina in order to give us a greater understanding of the increasing role of the military in domestic disaster response. The authors posit that this role expansion has been encouraged through the exaggeration of post-Katrina crime and the contemporary application of militarism as an ideology. Frailing and Harper round out this framing discussion in chapter 3 with a quantitative historical comparison of looting rates surrounding the three most intense hurricanes to hit New Orleans. The authors assert that the increases in this antisocial behavior are largely associated with the socioeconomic changes that have transformed not only New Orleans and the Gulf Coast but the greater United States as well. Hurricane Katrina is seen as a unique event that highlights the already high rates of crime and the larger political, social, and economic context in which crime occurs.

Part II focuses on the evacuation experience of Katrina survivors. In chapter 4, Haney, Elliott, and Fussell analyze post-Katrina evacuation strategies, the reasoning behind strategy selection, the outcomes of these strategic choices, and the resulting emotional responses by utilizing a joint survey conducted by the Gallup Organization and the Red Cross. The authors argue that interpreting disaster response through a framework of roles, responsibilities, resources, race, and religion provides us with very important insights that can be useful to policymakers and disaster researchers. In order to continue expanding our understanding of evacuation experiences, Barnshaw and Trainor utilize a triangulation approach in chapter 5. Locating the experiences of evacuees in the larger context of sociostructural limitations, the authors argue that social capital, in the form of networks, may or may not be converted into resources useful to Katrina survivors. Bringing attention to the experience of evacuation from the perspective of those who helped the evacuees, Holcombe uses chapter 6 to focus on the responses of religious organizations in Houston, Texas. Through interviews with a variety of congregation leaders, the author demonstrates that religious organizations play an important role in disaster response by utilizing and expanding already existing social networks and community relief programs.

Part III focuses on issues related to recovery and reactions to the storm. Macomber, Rusche, and Wright explore the patterned reactions of racially diverse college students in chapter 7, making an effort to demonstrate the racial divide among American student thinking about class, race, and racism. In the end, the authors argue that the perceptions of the effects of Hurricane Katrina vary drastically by race and that this conclusion has important sociological implications for white thought at all levels of the social order. In developing a discussion of the changing nature of place perception in a postdisaster environment in chapter 8, Miller and Rivera argue that, in this suddenly disorganized location, the perceptions and attachments to place are dramatically altered. This unsettled nature of the disaster-destroyed place creates possibilities for positive social change because of the forced exposure of contemporary social and political problems. Trying to understand some of the localized implications of Katrina in chapter 9, Kleiner, Green, and Nylander utilize community-based research in East Biloxi, Mississippi, to both illuminate the important challenges for the community and bridge the gap between services and information during the totalizing experience that was the aftermath of this disaster. This proactive methodological approach allows the authors to connect emergent knowledge with community needs and to make recommendations for local development and redevelopment plans. Bringing this discussion of reaction and recovery to the broader, theoretical level in chapter 10, Capowich and Kondkar embark on the development of an axiomatic theory of cultural creativity as a phenomenon that emerges from local neighborhood social structures. The authors use these theoretical insights to make some recommendations for the future planning process of New Orleans.

Finally, part IV focuses on post-Katrina institutional change in education, health, and population. Addressing the broad institutional effects of Hurricane Katrina, Esmail, Eargle, and Das use chapter 11 to connect various literatures, discuss the impacts of disasters in general, and move into the many dimensions of education on which Hurricane Katrina had an influence. The authors argue that, in the wake of this disaster, there have been both losses and opportunities for the institution of education. Shifting to a different institutional area, Kutner discusses the impacts of Hurricane Katrina on health and the health care system in chapter 12. Through a demonstration of the effects of disasters across a broad range of sociological dimensions (from the individual to the institution), the author discusses the needs for the future of health care in the areas impacted directly by Katrina and the rest of the nation that remains largely unprepared for health care emergencies. Chapter 13 develops a discussion of patterned changes in the labor market of New Orleans over a large span of time. Donato, Trujillo-Pagán, Bankston, and Singer offer a detailed explanation of the historical patterns of immigration and the immigrant labor market in order to illustrate that the new post-Katrina immigrant labor market is becoming institutionalized. Clarke's postscript, "Considering Katrina," provides a synthetic closing to this volume that identifies salient issues and important questions for the ongoing catastrophe we have come to know as "Katrina."

NOTES

Portions of this chapter were supported by the National Science Foundation (OPP0002572) and the Alabama Center for Estuarine Studies and the U.S. Environmental Protection Agency (R-827072-01-1). The authors acknowledge the technical support provided by Carol Naquin and Linda Burcham. The contents are the sole responsibility of the authors and do not reflect the policy or position of the National Science Foundation, the Alabama Center for Estuarine Studies, or the U.S. Environmental Protection Agency.

    1. One notable exception to this claim was the immediate rescue efforts of the U.S. Coast Guard. The response of the Coast Guard was self-directed and spontaneous and was not inhibited by bureaucratic indecision. For more information on bureaucratic failure during Katrina, see Tierney (2005).

    2. The primary theoretical framework for the natural disaster stage model is structural-functional (Kreps 1989), while the ecological-symbolic theoretical perspective organizes the technological disaster corrosive model (Couch 1996; Kroll-Smith and Couch 1993).

    3. For an exception to this practice, see Picou (2000).

    4. However, some estimates by the state of Alaska suggest that actually 24 million to 36 million gallons of oil was spilled by Exxon in Prince William Sound. For more information, see Ott (2005, 4–10).

    5. Most recently, a federal judge ruled that for tens of thousands of flooded businesses and homes in New Orleans, insurance companies were liable for damages because policies did not explicitly rule out "man-made" flooding. State Farm and Hartford insurance companies were absent from this initial ruling because their policies excluded flooding "regardless of cause." Obviously, appeals will be forthcoming. For more information, see Treaster (2006).

    6. The one exception to this trend was the mining sector. For more information, see Scott (2006).

    7. The Road Home program was created by Governor Kathleen B. Blanco, the Louisiana Recovery Authority, and the Office of Community Development. The program is the largest single housing program in the history of the United States. Displaced Katrina survivors who owned a primary residence that was "destroyed" or suffered "major" or "severe" damage (FEMA) are eligible to receive up to $150,000 in compensation. Survivors who failed to have proper insurance receive a 30 percent penalty. For more information, see http://www.road2la.org/la-hurricanes.

    8. These increased crime rates, as well as the fact that 16 months after Katrina the New Orleans police force was 250 officers below pre-Katrina staffing, also represent a serious impediment to former citizens returning to the city. In contrast, the Mississippi Gulf Coast and other impacted inland areas of Mississippi appear to be achieving some progress toward restoration and reconstruction. Nonetheless, a year following Katrina, over 96,000 Mississippi residents were living in approximately 36,000 trailers and mobile homes (Chamlee-Wright, 2006).

    9. Indeed, the future racial composition of post-Katrina New Orleans will also be drastically altered. The city will be not only significantly smaller in population size but also "more white and Hispanic, more affluent, more tourism-entertainment oriented than its pre-Katrina reality" (Falk, Hunt, and Hunt 2006, 115). In addition, Lotke and Borosage (2006) note that in New Orleans, 54 percent of pre-Katrina residents were white and that 68 percent of post-Katrina residents are white. In the year following Katrina, the median household income in New Orleans rose from $39,793 to $43,447. These projections clearly reveal the race-based negative social impacts that will extend well into the future and continue to divide American society. For an excellent account of this racial divide, see Herring (2006); also see chapters 7 and 13 in this volume.

    10. Along these lines, it is interesting to note that Chamlee-Wright's research revealed that providing help to neighbors and friends was the second most frequently cited means of coping for emotional problems following Katrina (therapeutic process). However, the primary coping strategy was alcohol consumption (corrosive process). For more information, see Chamlee-Wright (2006).

I

FRAMING KATRINA: CONTEXT AND CONSTRUCTION

1

Finding and Framing Katrina: The Social Construction of Disaster

Russell R. Dynes and Havidán Rodríguez

In September 2005, the major programmatic themes and news headlines generated by the media, but particularly television, centered on hurricanes, specifically Hurricane Katrina and, later, Hurricane Rita. These themes have provided graphic glimpses of the human toll and suffering that such disaster events can have. However, in drawing these pictures, television stations have also conveyed irrational and exaggerated information (many times based on rumors or incorrect information based on unverified data) focusing on both human loss and physical destruction. The aftermath of such hurricanes is bad enough without such inaccurate exaggerations.

All disasters are not equal. Just as disasters are a quantitative leap over routine community emergencies, it is hard to compare Katrina to any other recent U.S. hurricane. The Galveston hurricane[1] might be the closest parallel, but not many commentators can go beyond superficial comparisons. In addition, Galveston was in 1900 and was not covered by television. Thus, the images of desolation and destruction as a consequence of this storm did not reach the international community with the speed and intensity of Hurricane Katrina.

Katrina impacted an extensive geographical area of the United States, approximately 90,000 square miles, or about the geographical area of Great Britain. The combined impact of high winds, rain, storm surge, distressed levees, and flooding created conditions that affected and disrupted the lives of hundreds of communities and millions of people. Further, there was a significant loss of life, extensive or total destruction of property, disruption of lifeline services, and the sources of livelihood (including employments) were significantly impacted, if not totally lost. Help from nearby communities was difficult to come by since they were in similar circumstances. The scope of the impact made dormant political divisions important. Katrina crossed state lines, parish boundaries, ideological positions, and activists' concerns. It also separated extended families and disrupted, if not severed, community, government, and industrial activities and functions. These effects were exacerbated by a lack of an adequate and coordinated response at the local, state, and federal levels.

FRAMING KATRINA

Katrina was the first hurricane to hit the United States to the accompaniment of continuous (24/7) television coverage. Certainly, Hurricane Andrew (1992) had considerable television coverage, but that was before competitive 24-hour cable coverage was available. In social science terms, television constructed the frame of meaning to which audiences and decision makers came to understand Katrina. For some along the coast, personal experience with Katrina might have helped. If you were on Dauphin Island or in Moss Point, Biloxi, in Bay St. Louis, north or south of Highway 10, in Kenner, or in a bar on Bourbon Street, the storm was slightly different. However, for most, the reality of the storm came through television networks. Even for "victims" who lost electrical power, if it came back, the coffee pot and the television were the first appliances back on so that one's own experiences would be understood and confirmed in the context of the information provided by the media.

Of course, television had considerable advantages in framing the storm, but it also framed distortions that we will address later. The advantage of television as an informational source is its visual imagery, usually backed by musical effects. People believe what they see, especially when it is considered "live." When the season started, it was not clear whether Katrina would be a one-night special or the beginning of a new prime-time series. However, Katrina, like any new series, had a lengthy and colorful promotion called weather reports. After the long prelude, monitoring the wind speed and its direction, the impact of Katrina was slowly revealed. Generating facts about the consequences of the disaster's impact in many different locations takes time. Consequently, factual information about the impact was much less in terms of "airtime" than on the available time that television has to program. Given the disparity of time and few facts, television tends to draw on common cultural assumptions (including myths) about what will happen. These assumptions include extensive damage, death, and injury; concern for children, the ill, and the elderly; forecasting mental health trauma; the absence of authority; extensive looting; and the incompetence of government and the inevitability of social disorder. Essentially, a state of chaos and anarchy was defined for the vast television audience. These assumptions and others framed the details of what came to be known as "Katrina."

With new technology, including split screen, individual segments can be magnified; that is, feeds can also be combined from several states within one screen. Programming formats to retain viewer attention suggest that the most dramatic stories in the last segment will be elaborated on in the next. Reporters also have the independence to create their own stories (Wenger and Quarantelli 1989), and dispersed film crews have latitude to find their own stories, ask their own questions, and develop their own special vocabularies, such as being surrounded by "toxic soup," missed by snipers, or unable to find representatives of the Federal Emergency Management Agency (FEMA). When one network had a "hot" story, other networks soon appeared on the same scene.

Over time, however, New Orleans became the feature presentation, and the rest of Louisiana and Mississippi became very minor themes. Certainly, because of the breaks in the levees and the flooding, the helicopter rescues, film clips of looting, and angry crowds at the Superdome and the Convention Center, it was vivid television drama and suspense. Many viewers would have fond recollections of New Orleans, and television personnel could find some high dry ground there. So New Orleans became the center of operations for the media regarding Katrina. Its mayor and police superintendent were available for interviews, but New Orleans was presented as a disorganized city on the brink of collapse, less from the storm than from its residents. On September 2, *The Army Times* (newspaper) reported that "combat operations are now underway on the streets. . . . This place is going to look like little Somalia. . . . We're going to go out and take the city back." "This will be a combat operation to get this city under control," was the lead comment by the commander of Louisiana National Guard's Joint Task Force. Now, after the storm has subsided, the story of Katrina can be told in a more precise and accurate manner.

FRAMING THEMES

Certain programmatic themes emerged in the television coverage, identified here as finding damage, finding death, finding help, finding authority and finding the bad guys.

Finding Damage

Certainly, television excels in presenting damage. The graphic images of destruction (i.e., houses obliterated by the storm, hotels and other industries all but destroyed, and cars and boats swept away by the forces of nature) are used to highlight the devastating impacts of "mother nature" and to captivate and retain the audience's attention. Often, however, it is difficult to place that damage either in a particular geographical location or in a meaningful social context. In certain ways, that lack of context can enhance concern as well as sympathy. It allows viewers to use their own imagination to project the meaning of such losses for those people who live in the area or to the home owners of what is now not salvageable. Electronic technology can enhance the images and provide views from all angles. The levee system and the canals in New Orleans provided outlines of the destruction of neighborhoods. The media expended considerable efforts and financial resources in "capturing catastrophe" through extensive and diverse (both quantitatively and qualitatively) visual imagery.

Finding Death

From the very beginning of the hurricane impact and with the onset of flooding in New Orleans, there were predictions of the death toll. The mayor of New Orleans predicted the figure at 10,000, and there were repeated statements that FEMA had ordered 25,000 body bags. Several days into the flood, there was repeated visual evidence of bodies in the flooded area and continuous allegations that such conditions pose serious health risks. However, the Pan American Health Organization has reviewed the research of the epidemiological risks of dead bodies in disaster situations and concluded that dead bodies seldom constitute health risks and suggest that the anxiety that leads to the inept removal of bodies often destroys information necessary for identification (Pan American Health Organization 2004). In such cases, family members are unnecessarily exposed to a second episode of unresolved grief.

As of October 15, the death toll in Louisiana was declared to be 972 and in Mississippi 221. In Louisiana, the search for bodies was recently declared complete, but the state has released only 61 bodies and made the names of only 32 victims public (*New York Times*, October 5, A1). This raises the question whether predictions regarding the total death toll in the early response period have any value. Although Katrina has one of the highest death rates in U.S. hurricane history (recent estimates put the death toll as high as 1,846), it is still significantly lower (10 percent) than the projected number publicized. This raises questions about why these projections were released and reemphasized by the local government. Perhaps it was to speed up efforts to provide assistance and disaster relief aid from the state and federal levels. This can also reflect the inherent difficulties and problems with estimating the death toll immediately following disaster impact. It is noteworthy that in past disaster events, initial death estimates could be quite low, particularly in impact-isolated areas of developing countries. This was certainly the case with the 2004 Indian Ocean tsunami, for which initial estimates suggested several thousand dead and now the actual figure comes closer to 300,000.

Finding Help

In the immediate postimpact period, reporters often asked those they were interviewing whether they had received any type of help or aid, often inquiring directly if FEMA had been there. In every disaster, the first to help (the "first" responders) are actually neighbors, family members, and other community members. Most persons (including reporters) do not think of such usual assistance as help; rather, "help" is someone they do not know. More recently, the term "first responders" has come into vocabulary to describe police, fire, medical, and other emergency management personnel. Perhaps that terminology has created the expectation for "victims" to anticipate that a first responder would be at their house "quickly." Nevertheless, "true" first responders are also community members who have been impacted by the same events but who are characterized by altruistic behavior in their response to these disaster events.

In addition, television coverage early in the response period revealed tremendous confusion about the role of FEMA on the part of both television reporters and those they interviewed. This problem was exacerbated given the inadequate response and performance of FEMA and the Department of Homeland Security bureaucracy in the initial stages of the response process. There was also an initial tendency to describe FEMA as the organizational location for a national 911 phone number; if hurricane victims called, someone would allegedly respond to their needs and provide the necessary assistance. This misunderstanding regarding the role of FEMA in assisting state and local governments among state and local officials, as well as by victims, added to the perception of the lack of help.

The perception of the absence of help in the face of overwhelming need, combined with bureaucratic finagling, can persuade members of a national television audience of the need to volunteer—to come to the disaster locale to help remedy that lack of help. At times, they can fill a need. On the other hand, at considerable personal expense in time and money, volunteers may arrive days later to find they are not needed or that they are not welcomed by government personnel at the scene. Just as victims might need helpers, helpers also need victims. Frustrated helpers are often prime candidates for television interviewers, accusing government bureaucrats of preventing their involvement while emphasizing their skills and their sacrifice as well as their conviction that they are needed.

Certainly, there may be a lack of knowledge by victims about the help that is available within a community and the location where information might be obtained. It is also possible that some victims will have much higher expectations about the nature and/or scope of help that will be available. Many will discover that the type of home-owner's insurance on which they have paid on for years will not cover their losses as they had long expected, nor will a reimbursement be quickly forthcoming. The long-run problem of "finding help" will be a topic of conversation in town councils, state legislatures, in Congress, and in the media for years to come.

Finding Authority

First of all, let us admit that the issue of authority in disasters is complex. Part of the complexity centers on the relationship among political jurisdictions and the understanding that current political officials have of that relationship. This is further complicated by the fact that officials of the U.S. political system come and go after elections, but disasters do not happen on that schedule. In fact, for most political officials, every disaster is their first in office. Historically, in the United States, responsibility for dealing with disaster response is located at the local level. If the demands are too great for the local community, the responsibility to assist the "locals" is assumed to involve the state. If state resources are not sufficient, the federal government is expected to provide additional resources. There are certain events (e.g., a terrorist attack) that are not respectful of local or state boundaries, and in those cases federal assistance can be predicted to be necessary. In addition, for such situations, federal resources and personnel are often prepositioned. As such, this creates the expectation that resources will be made immediately available to be used by local and state officials.

With the long lead time to Katrina, some television reporters were already on location interviewing local officials who usually expressed their expectation that FEMA would be immediately available. The same conversations were repeated in other localities, but the director of FEMA, also appearing in the media, seemed equivocal about assuming total responsibility; that ambivalence, in time, led to his replacement and eventually his resignation. Appearing before a congressional committee after his resignation, Michael Brown asserted that one of the problems with the response to Hurricane Katrina was that local officials in Louisiana were "dysfunctional," thus trying to shift the blame away from the federal government and, in this case, FEMA.

In addition to the problems of legal authority among different levels of political units, the notion of authority has been complicated by the adoption of a "command-and-control" vocabulary by some emergency management organizations. In a disaster with diffuse impact such as Katrina, the notion of having command and control is self-delusional. However, in the reorganization of FEMA and its inclusion in the new Department of Homeland Security, a standardized organizational system identified as the "Incident Command System" was administratively decreed as normative for disasters in the United States. There are elements of that notion that have considerable utility. For example, the notion of a command post as a location for coordinating the activities of the multiple organizations that will become involved in a disaster response makes sense. However, the idea that this is the location of someone who is commanding those organizations in their activities and is in control of the incident is out of touch with the reality and the events that are taking place.

The media's constant question as to "who's in charge?" seems to be based on what might be called the "Oz Theory of Authority," with apologies to Max Weber. The Oz theory is that behind some curtain there is a wizard. It is the media's responsibility to pull back that curtain to reveal the wizard commander. Perhaps the best advice is that if the question is answered by persons identifying themselves as being in command, the person being interviewed does not understand the complexity of the response. A response to a disaster such as Katrina is complicated and involves coordination and extensive communication, a complex task accomplished by many different groups and individuals. The decision making necessary is decentralized and usually made at levels much lower in the status hierarchy implied by the command-and-control model (Dynes and Aguirre 1978). In other words, there is no curtain and no wizard, simply a very complicated mosaic of individuals and organizations with skills, resources, energy, the capacity to improvise, and the knowledge of the impacted community. Merging their knowledge and energy in a coordinated effort is the real wizardry.

Finding the Bad Guys

Probably the most dramatic "evidence" of social chaos assumed to be created by Katrina was centered on New Orleans. The city was heavily populated by poor African Americans[2] who lived in areas that were initially flooded. They were directed to go to the Superdome, where assistance would be available. The photographic opportunity to show "mobs" of residents located together provided the backdrop for repetitive stories of looting, rape, murder, sniping, and roving gangs preying on tourists. Such stories introduced the next time segment with an implication that it would continue as the major programmatic theme. Such rumors were also promulgated by the New Orleans Police Department and other local officials; they were even presented as facts by local officials on *The Oprah Winfrey Show*. There were stories of piles of bodies in the Superdome and outside the Convention Center, where bodies were stored in basement freezers. One of the consequences of these stories was the diversion of security forces to follow up on such reports when they were needed for other critical duties. In addition, as the climate of fear increased, some emergency management service personnel refused assignments, citing their own apprehension.

While it is common for rumors of looting and all kinds of antisocial behavior to emerge in most major disasters, the volume and persistence of such rumors on television in Katrina was unparalleled. The staff of writers from the *Times-Picayune* provided a major critique of those stories in their September 26 issue. Among their stories, they quoted the Orleans Parish district attorney pointing out that there were only four murders in New Orleans in the week following Katrina, making it a "typical" week in that city, which annually recorded 200 homicides.

When the Louisiana National Guard at the Superdome turned over the dead to federal authorities, that representative arrived with an 18-wheel refrigerated truck since there were reports of 200 bodies there. The actual total was six; of these, four died of natural causes, one from a drug overdose, and another had apparently committed suicide. While four other bodies were found in the streets near the Dome, presumably no one had been killed inside as had been previously reported. There were more reports that 30 to 40 bodies were stored in the Convention Center freezers in its basement. In truth, only four bodies were recovered, and just one appeared to have been slain. Before this discovery, there had been reports of corpses piled inside the building.

In reference to reports of rapes during the six days that the Superdome was used as a shelter, the head of the New Orleans Police Department sex crime unit indicated that he and his officers lived inside the Dome and ran down every rumor of rape and atrocity. In the end, they made two arrests for attempted sexual assault and concluded that the other incidents rumored never happened, although it is important to note that rape is generally underreported in nondisaster times.

In reference to claims of looting, similar observations can lead to quite different conclusions. Is the person sifting through debris a friend or relative or a looter? Is the person pushing a grocery cart full of clothes someone flooded out of his home trying to save what few possessions he had left, or is the cart filled with looted materials? Are claims of looting at times used to inflate future insurance settlements? Again, rumors of looting are common for all disasters, but valid cases are rare. Some valid cases of looting can involve security forces brought in to protect against looting.

It does seem to those who have studied disaster behavior over a long period that the rumors of antisocial behavior were particularly virulent in New Orleans. Certainly, media coverage facilitated that impression. On the other hand, New Orleans has always had a reputation as the place for "hedonistic behavior," particularly among some religious observers, in part because of its repute for Mardi Gras. Perhaps, for many television viewers, it was a short step from the "Big Easy" to the "Big Mess," thus lending public credibility to the stories disseminated through the media.

FRACTURED FRAMES

There were many frames that were briefly mentioned on television but never became a focal point of stories. While there was preoccupation with death, there was less concern for the possibilities for suffering. Asking a victim who has lost family members or their entire possessions how they feel evokes sound bites that are neither cathartic nor reflective. They may evoke the initiation of a longer period of suffering, that is, the consequences of being a victim. But that longer period will be of little interest in future programming. Loss of jobs, economic security, and familiar neighbors, along with possible relocation and the initiation of a journey into the unknown, are seldom captured in a short response. Furthermore, the transition from being a victim to being a survivor will not be newsworthy to prime-time audiences, nor will the rediscovery of racism and poverty that flooded the television screens. Much of the flood damage seen was difficult to differentiate from the dilapidation of substandard housing. The loss of fragile resources was more hurtful for those who had little to lose. The lack of resources also created the inability to evacuate easily and efficiently. In addition, many of the medical problems experienced by evacuees had little to do with the hurricane itself but were the result of the quality and availability (or lack thereof) of health care services before the hurricane (see Rodríguez and Aguirre 2006).

There were other views that were difficult to visualize. One could not see the historic depletion of wetlands along the Gulf Coast that for centuries had cushioned the effects on coastal areas. Nor could one easily see the quality of building codes and their previous enforcement or the abundance of manufactured homes in certain coastal areas. It is also noteworthy that there has been a significant movement of the U.S. population toward high-risk coastal areas. Population density in coastal (high-risk) regions continues to increase, sometimes at a higher rate than the noncoastal populations. Currently, coastal counties constitute about 17 percent of the landmass (excluding Alaska) in the United States, but 53 percent of the U.S. population (153 million people) live in these areas. In addition, the coastal population increased by 28 percent from 1980 to 2003, and 10 of the 15 cities with the highest population counts are in coastal counties (see Crossett et al. 2004). Such population movement results in more building in desirable coastal areas. Further, in some coastal areas, gambling has become a major economic sector. When Hurricane Camille hit Biloxi in 1969, there were no casinos to be blown across the highway. But in 1991, Mississippi approved permanently docked riverboats, allowing the growth of casinos linked to a rapid expansion of the tourist/gambling industry in its three coastal counties. These floating casinos proved to be buoyant in Katrina's storm surge. While that bet was lost, post-Katrina construction will put gambling on firmer ground.

CONCLUSION

Hurricane Katrina was an event of catastrophic proportions, resulting in an extensive loss of life and property and human suffering—problems that were greatly compounded by significant deficiencies in government preparedness and response at all levels. Nevertheless, now that the waters have receded, we must realize that the images of chaos and anarchy portrayed by the mass media were based primarily on rumors and inaccurate assumptions. Some of these were supported by official statements by elected officials. This view of the drama of disasters is assumed to be another version of "reality television." Now, less attention is given to the hundreds of thousands of displaced who have been uprooted from their communities and their loss of economic livelihood. The efforts for reconstruction are not likely to appear in prime time any time soon.

Katrina occurred in the context of radical changes in the structure of U.S. federal emergency management. FEMA had lost its independent status and ready access to the president in a morass of 22 agencies combined into the Department of Homeland Security with its focus of international terrorism. FEMA lost power, active programs, authority, and many skilled personnel as a result of the reorganization. Many of the top people in the Department of Homeland Security had had little experience with domestic natural disasters. Many of these personnel were concerned with tightening national borders, not respecting local differences. It was easy to accept the media view that Katrina was the southern version of 9/11 and that New Orleans was "Baghdad South," needing law, order, and the military to quell the urban chaos.

There was a tendency to see every consequence as a result of Katrina. However, victims, without resources and in need of help did not have those resources before Katrina. Many damaged houses were only dilapidated before. The devastated health care infrastructure in the region was already on life support before Katrina. External authority was not a solution for decades of economic deprivation. With little knowledge or experience with the range of local disasters, it is likely that top government officials increased their limited knowledge of disaster response by watching television and distrusted reports from their knowledgeable employees on the ground.

A final question might be asked as to why the media framed disasters in terms of the themes described here (i.e., finding damage, death, help, authority, and the bad guys). The answer to this question must be put in the context of the role and functions of the media generally and following disasters specifically. During the aftermath of a disaster, the media have generally been characterized as "conveying inaccurate, biased or sensationalistic information" (Rodríguez et al. 2006) that significantly impacts how governments, organizations, and the general population perceive and respond to disasters. Actually, Dynes (1998) argues that the media define what is a disaster. As argued by a number of colleagues, although the media can play a critical and positive role following disasters, they also tend to provide biased, exaggerated, and inaccurate information that overplays human loss and suffering and physical destruction (see Fischer, 1994; and Pérez-Lugo, 2001; Rodríguez et al. 2006). As Mileti (1999) has argued, this portrayal of disasters and their aftermath result in both decision makers and the general public (those impacted by the disaster agent and not) reaching incorrect conclusions about the event thus impacting the decision-making process.

Nevertheless, in the world of the media, this is the type of news that is perceived as "newsworthy" in order to "captivate" the audience, to increase the number of viewers, and to impact its ratings. It is in this context of a media frenzy that the previously mentioned frames are particularly important. Therefore, the so-called experts (including elected officials and other government representatives) are interviewed and asked to provide data, information, and opinions (but mostly opinions) on the physical, social, psychological, and economic impacts of the disaster agent. As the case of Hurricane Katrina clearly illustrates, many of these "experts" are uniformed individuals providing "facts" that are based on inaccurate or incorrect information, portraying a state of chaos and anarchy in which antisocial behavior prevails in the impacted communities. However, these issues are not surprising to disaster scholars and researchers who have studied the role and impact of the media following disasters. Katrina is just another reminder on how the media (in their search for ratings) can serve to inaccurately promulgate a state of uncertainty and destruction while neglecting emergent prosocial behavior characterized by altruism, cooperation, and social cohesion (Rodríguez, Trainor, and Quarantelli 2006).

NOTES

This article was initially posted on the Social Science Research Council website "Understanding Katrina: Perspectives from the Social Sciences" in October 2005. For more general information on the media in disasters, see Quarantelli (2002) and Scanlon (2006).

1. The Galveston hurricane (or better known as "the storm") devastated Galveston on September 8, 1900. A category 4 hurricane, it is estimated that this storm resulted in over 6,000 deaths, primarily in the Galveston area, and over 3,500 homes were completely destroyed. This storm has been recognized as the "deadliest natural disaster" in U.S. history.

2. According to 2004 data provided by the U.S. Bureau of the Census, 68 percent of the population in the city of New Orleans was African American (compared to 12.2 percent for the United States), and 23 percent of all individuals in the city were living below poverty (compared to 13.1 percent for the United States).

2

Disaster as War: Militarism and the Social Construction of Disaster in New Orleans

Kathleen Tierney and Christine Bevc

Following the terrorist attacks on September 11, 2001, the U.S. government significantly restructured and altered the manner in which the nation prepares for and responds to large-scale natural disasters. In the response that followed the landfall of Hurricane Katrina, more than 63,000 National Guard and active military personnel were deployed to assist in the response and recovery efforts of the Gulf region. Beyond routine tasks, such as search and rescue and the delivery of relief supplies, military personnel also operated outside their traditional areas of responsibility and were armed with loaded weapons to deal with socially constructed threats of "urban insurgents" and charged with restoring order. The Katrina catastrophe provided the justification for U.S. leaders to push for the militarization of disasters, even though the idea has many opponents and the rationales for expanding the role of the military are questionable. We present the necessary background for understanding the military's present involvement in disaster management. Most important, we discuss how the framing of the victims of Hurricane Katrina, particularly with respect to the manner in which they were framed in media and public discourse, supported greater militarization of disasters and influenced subsequent government actions.

BACKGROUND: CIVIL DEFENSE, EMERGENCY MANAGEMENT, AND MILITARY AUTHORITY

In the United States, the management of disasters has long been intertwined with war-related concerns. Present-day institutions and policies related to disaster management were originally rooted in Cold War civil protection challenges, especially those associated with the threat of a nuclear attack. Particularly in their early history, "civil defense" programs focused on ways of preparing and protecting the public in the event of a nuclear war.[1] Because of their fundamental ties to nuclear war planning, before the formation of the Federal Emergency Management Agency (FEMA) in 1979, many disaster-related programs were the responsibility of entities such as the Office of Civil Defense (a Defense Department agency) and later the Defense Civil Preparedness Agency.

During the period just before the creation of FEMA, the doctrine of "dual use," or the notion that planning and response activities should be directed toward both war and natural disasters, continued to influence how emergency management issues were framed. Even as late as the 1980s, many domestic emergency management activities, such as the Crisis Relocation Program established under President Reagan, still tilted toward nuclear war concerns. The Crisis Relocation Program, a plan for relocating large populations in the event of an actual or threatened nuclear war, was opposed by many communities and was never fully implemented (May and Williams 1986). Ideas concerning comprehensive emergency management and all-hazards planning were not introduced into U.S. policy discourse until the late 1970s (see National Governors Association 1979). These ideas gained increased traction after the formation of FEMA, and they were well institutionalized by the time the Cold War ended (for accounts of the early history and almost continual reorganization of federal disaster and civil defense programs, see Drabek 1991; Kreps 1989; Waugh 2000).

By the end of the 1990s, comprehensive emergency management and all-hazards planning were official FEMA policies and were implemented broadly throughout the United States. The field of emergency management was on the way to becoming recognized as a profession, as indicated by the existence of certification programs; the initiation of specialized emergency management programs in universities, colleges, and community colleges around the country; and the development of textbooks for the emergency management field (see, e.g., Haddow and Bullock 2003; Waugh 2000; for discussions on educational goals for emergency management programs, see Thomas and Mileti 2003). While past military service had once been seen as a sufficient credential for holding a position as an emergency manager, newer conceptions of "core competencies" associated with positions in emergency management were much broader, including personal, interpersonal, and political skills; knowledge of public policy and public finance; and a variety of technical skills associated with assessing and managing hazards (Blanchard 2003). In short, by the early twenty-first century, emergency management was no longer conflated with preparedness for war, and the field was on the way to being recognized as a distinct profession. As Waugh (2000, 52) puts it, the transformation "from air raid warden to certified emergency manager" was complete.

At the same time, even as the field of emergency management moved away from earlier associations with military institutions and toward both greater concern with a broad range of hazards and greater professionalization, the U.S. military continued to play a role in responding to domestic disasters. The concept of military assistance to civil authorities (MACA) was invoked during community crises, such as disasters and episodes of civil unrest, and was later strengthened through the assignment of disaster missions to the Department of Defense (DOD) in official documents such as the Federal Response Plan and the National Response Plan (NRP), which is the framework currently used to manage domestic disasters, incidents of national significance, and catastrophic events (Department of Homeland Security 2004).

The increasing involvement of the military in activities related to hazards and disasters can be seen as part of a broader trend toward redefining the role of the military in supporting U.S. policies and plans. After the Cold War came to a close, the early 1990s saw the expansion of the role of the military beyond its war-making mission, as the concept of "operations other than war" (OOTW)—including such activities as assisting with the "war on drugs," providing disaster assistance, and peacekeeping—began to be reflected in official military doctrine. The use of the military for these types of missions was consistent with what Janowitz (1960) termed the "constabulary" conception of the military as a force that can be used for multiple functions other than war (Reed and Segal 2000).

The terrorist attacks of September 11, 2001, ushered in a further broadening of the role of the military in domestic crisis management. In the new policy environment following the 9/11 attacks, the United States is defined as "at war" with terrorism. The war on terrorism encompasses not only actual warfighting operations in other states, such as Afghanistan and Iraq, but also monitoring, detection, deterrence, and law enforcement strategies focusing on individuals and groups that use or seek to use terrorist tactics both abroad and in the United States. The use of the "war metaphor" to describe U.S. antiterrorism initiatives has led to an elevation of the role of military institutions in such programs. This broader reliance on the military has taken a variety of forms. To support the war on terrorism at home, the U.S. Northern Command (NORTHCOM) was established after 9/11 for the broad purpose of "homeland defense."[2] The Posse Comitatus Act, which forbids the use of the military in domestic policing operations, is continually being reexamined. The protection of U.S. borders is increasingly framed as a military function—although the use of military forces for this purpose could violate the Posse Comitatus Act. The "total information awareness" data-mining program, which targeted U.S. citizens for surveillance, was established within the Defense Advanced Research Projects Agency. While that program was exposed, discredited, and supposedly dismantled, there is a widespread belief that elements of the program are still operational (O'Harrow 2005). Military resources were deployed in the hunt for the Washington area sniper, the Salt Lake City winter Olympics, and other domestic "missions," including Republican and Democratic national conventions. The use of military forces in these ways greatly expands the concept of "operations other than war." (For a more detailed discussion on the use of military resources in missions within the United States, see Dunlap 1999; Healey 2003; Johnson 2004). In short, the post–Cold War years—and in particular the period since the 9/11 terrorist attacks—have been marked by increasing support for military involvement in a variety of activities that would normally be carried out by other entities (e.g., the Border Patrol and local governments), including activities that arguably constitute domestic policing.

Following the formation of the Department of Homeland Security (DHS) and the absorption of FEMA into that much larger bureaucracy, all preparedness for extreme events was recast to be consistent with the war on terrorism. While DHS now claims in the aftermath of Hurricane Katrina that all its activities with respect to "consequence management" were consistent with the all-hazards approach, that was not the case; programs, budgets, the kind of personnel who were put in charge of various initiatives, and DHS rhetoric all signaled a myopic bureaucratic focus on the terrorist threat (Tierney 2006). This institutional myopia, together with the use of the war metaphor, again encouraged mission creep, as defense and defense-related entities, rather than agencies like FEMA, were seen as possessing resources and skills that were critical for domestic civil protection in the post–9/11 context. National weapons laboratories, such as Sandia and Los Alamos, were sought out for their modeling and simulation capabilities as well as for their expertise with respect to nuclear weapons that might be used in domestic terrorism. Preparedness, training, and drills increasingly centered on strategies for dealing with terrorist attacks and weapons of mass destruction—and were increasingly managed by military and quasi-military entities. For example, the California component of the large-scale, 2004 "Determined Promise" terrorism exercise, which involved collaboration among numerous local, state, and federal agencies, was designed and coordinated by the Center for Asymmetric Warfare, an anti-terrorism entity affiliated with the navy under a contract from NORTHCOM, rather than by civil society entities with knowledge in the areas of training and exercises. As during the early days of Cold War civil defense programs, military and defense expertise is increasingly seen as a qualification for leadership positions in homeland security.

With high-level U.S. officials preoccupied with fighting the war on terror, military assets came to be viewed as a critical resource for managing domestic crises of all kinds, creating new opportunities for military institutions. For example, while formally adhering to the MACA doctrine, which emphasizes that military assets can be deployed only on request from civilian authorities, the NRP also gives military officials "immediate response authority" (IRA) to protect lives and property on the request of civilian authorities, without seeking approval through the DOD chain of command (Milliman, Grosskopf, and Paez 2006). Designed primarily for terrorism and attacks using weapons of mass destruction, rather than disasters, the NRP also allows the federal government to initiate operations on its own during catastrophic events in which such action is considered warranted.

The new provisions in the NRP, together with the Hurricane Katrina experience, have now created the possibility of preemptive federal and military mobilization for major crises, including natural disasters. During Hurricane Wilma, for example, federal DHS officials and military commanders from NORTHCOM pushed for a military deployment to Florida and Homeland Security Secretary Michael Chertoff sought to designate a Coast Guard official as the "principal official in charge" of the Wilma response and recovery effort. These efforts were rebuffed by Florida's emergency manager and by Governor Jeb Bush. Admiral Timothy Keating, the head of NORTHCOM, takes the position that military personnel on active duty should have broader autonomy in responding to and managing disasters (Block and Schatz 2005). Not surprisingly, the White House report on lessons learned from Hurricane Katrina also recommends a wider expansion of military authority in large-scale and catastrophic events, including recommendations that "DOD should develop plans to lead the Federal response for events of extraordinary scope and nature" and that "DOD should revise its immediate response authority [discussed previously] to allow commanders, in appropriate circumstances, to exercise IRA even without a request from local authorities" (White House 2006, 94.) In other words, under certain conditions, the military would be authorized to act on its own, rather than in support of civilian decision makers, in managing large-scale domestic crises. The White House report also envisions an expanded role for the National Geospatial Intelligence Agency and the National Security Agency in responding to U.S. disasters.[3]

We argue here that, like the terrorist attacks of 9/11, Hurricane Katrina may serve as a "focusing event" (Birkland 1997) leading to more fundamental changes in the manner in which large-scale natural disasters are managed. More specifically, we argue that the social construction of the Katrina catastrophe serves to support initiatives that seek to give the military even greater authority in future events. We discuss various ways in which the Katrina catastrophe served to bolster claims that the military is the only institution capable of acting effectively in the context of extreme events of national significance. We further argue that expanding the role of military institutions in disaster management as well as public acquiescence in such changes are consistent with a growing acceptance of the ideology of militarism that pervades both U.S. culture and national security doctrine. The following discussion focuses on how public officials and the media framed the government response to Katrina as the domestic equivalent of war. We also discuss the manner in which narratives concerning the hurricane supported the notion that the military was the only institution that would be capable of effectively managing major disasters and catastrophic events. This chapter concludes by exploring the implications of these changes for emergency management policy and practice.

THE VICTIMS OF HURRICANE KATRINA:
FROM URBAN RIOTERS TO ENEMY INSURGENTS

New information that continues to come to light provides empirical justification for labeling intergovernmental response to Hurricane Katrina—and in particular the federal response—as one of the worst leadership debacles in U.S. history. Legislation and policies developed following the 9/11 attacks had expanded the authority of the federal government and the president in responding to "incidents of national significance" and "catastrophes" (Sylves 2006). Yet even with ample forewarning and explicit guidance from the scientific community on what would likely happen when the hurricane made landfall, the president and the federal government failed to act decisively to mobilize resources before the hurricane struck. It was widely understood within the scientific, engineering, and emergency management communities that a large hurricane striking New Orleans would be a catastrophic event. The public now knows that President Bush was directly told of this imminent threat by Max Mayfield, the head of the National Hurricane Center. Yet Bush, DHS Secretary Chertoff, and other high-ranking federal officials made no changes in their schedules before and even after Katrina ravaged the Gulf region. Many key high-ranking Washington officials were not in the U.S. capital but were traveling or on vacation during the preimpact and impact period. The president decided not to cut his vacation, change his official itinerary, or return to Washington when the hurricane struck. DHS Secretary Michael Chertoff did not declare Katrina an "incident of national significance" until August 30, the day after the hurricane's landfall in the Gulf region.[4] The day that declaration was made, Chertoff was at a meeting at the Centers for Disease Control and Prevention in Atlanta, discussing the avian flu threat.

With so many officials away from Washington, with the communications infrastructure in the impact region essentially destroyed, and with so much uncertainty regarding the extent of the hurricane's impact, actions taken by government agencies in the days immediately following Katrina's landfall were guided primarily by rumors and by what was being shown on the mass media, particularly television news. Indeed, recent reports indicate that key individuals in charge of the Homeland Security Operations Center—a high-tech facility that is charged with situation assessment and decision support in major national emergencies—chose to act on the basis of news reports rather than eyewitness accounts regarding what was occurring in New Orleans as the levees began to fail. Seeing tourists in the French Quarter on CNN, Center officials concluded that Katrina's impacts were not as severe as those earlier warnings had projected.[5]

It appears that those who should have assumed leadership during the Katrina catastrophe were so blindsided by the fully predictable flooding of New Orleans that they failed even to cobble together a coherent message for the public. On returning to Washington three days after Katrina struck, for example, the president stated on *Good Morning America* that "I don't think anybody anticipated the breach of the levees"—a statement that was patently untrue. Other official statements regarding the hurricane showed a similar lack of awareness of the severity of the disaster and of what was actually happening in the areas that bore the brunt of Katrina's destruction.

In contrast, however, the media began to develop its own message immediately after the flooding of New Orleans began, as various media outlets centered their reporting around frames that were based on mythological thinking about disaster-related behavior, rumor, and erroneous statements made by local and federal officials. As we discuss elsewhere (Tierney, Bevc, and Kuligowski 2006), shortly after Katrina struck, media reports began to converge on a series of images that were presented as typical behaviors being undertaken by disaster victims in New Orleans. Those images highlighted social breakdown, lawlessness, and violence. New Orleans was depicted as a "snakepit of lawnessness and anarchy," and victims fighting for survival in unimaginably traumatic circumstances were characterized as criminals and "marauding thugs." Rumors concerning overwhelmed public safety agencies, the rape and murder of disaster victims, and armed criminals and gang members bent on taking advantage of the disaster became standard fare on nightly news programs. Since individual media accounts increasingly use other media reports as sources, reports coming from diverse sources—based more on hearsay than on actual observation or eyewitness accounts—were similar enough that they seemed credible. At the same time, the social responses described in news reports—looting, violence, and the use of firearms—were very different from behaviors that typically occur following disasters and resembled more closely behavioral patterns associated with civil unrest. Nonetheless, for both the general public and key decision makers, the Katrina disaster in New Orleans was framed as an episode of civil unrest.

Within days after these initial reports, the "civil unrest" frame was replaced by new reporting that began to characterize the events in New Orleans as the equivalent of war—and, more specifically, the urban insurgency the U.S. military currently faces in Iraq. News accounts quoted officials as saying that "we are fighting a war on two fronts," and public safety agencies that dispatched their workers to New Orleans worried that they were sending them "off to war." Indeed, military deployments following Katrina were so large that New Orleans did begin to resemble a war zone. Within five days after the hurricane, the number of National Guard forces and soldiers had tripled the size of the deployment following Hurricane Andrew. In all, an estimated 63,000 National Guard and other military troops were deployed to the Katrina impact region, with most military resources devoted to New Orleans (Government Accountability Office 2006). Television images continually showed armed military and other public safety forces traveling around the flooded city in boats, carrying out postdisaster search-and-rescue activities in ways that were indistinguishable from urban "search-and-destroy" missions.

Consistent with the "war zone" characterization, media reports also stressed the notion that the large military presence made hurricane victims feel safer and that order was being maintained only because so many armed and uniformed personnel were present.[6]

Throughout the Katrina crisis, official and media narratives stressed the notion that a catastrophe as large as Katrina could be brought under control only by the use of military assets. President Bush, for example, lauded the military as "the institution of our government most capable of massive logistical operations on a moment's notice" (Burns 2005). A navy officer was quoted as saying, "This is a significant disaster and a huge undertaking, and somebody's got to coordinate all of it . . . Nobody else had the ability to bring everyone together" (Associated Press 2005a).

Many of the military personnel that were sent to the impact region had previously been deployed in Iraq, Afghanistan, and other wars. In Alabama, for example, all the major National Guard units assisting in the Katrina response had already served in Iraq (Tyson 2005). These personnel viewed the situation in the impact region as comparable to those in which they had been involved overseas. After rescuing trapped residents from their rooftops, a navy helicopter pilot commented that conditions in the disaster area are "overwhelming compared to the man-made disaster I just came from . . . it's much uglier" (Kaczor 2005). An army reservist was quoted as stating, "This right here is utter devastation . . . that over there [in Iraq] was a walk in the park" (Apuzzo 2005). One soldier headed to the New Orleans area reportedly stated that he "didn't think he'd be going back to Baghdad so soon" (Schlesing 2005). National Guard personnel began referring to the impact region as "the zone," which is military jargon for dangerous areas (Purpura 2005). The combat experience gained in Iraq was characterized as "coming in handy," as National Guard personnel compared the devastation of the Gulf Coast with conditions they had experienced in "supporting the war on terror in Iraq" (Jafari 2005). In their efforts to deal with the socially constructed threats associated with looters, "marauding thugs," rapists, and other miscreants, military and police agencies sought backup from Blackwater USA, ArmorCorp, and other contractors that were also operating in Iraq. Similar to the situation in Iraq, there was little discussion of how long the military would occupy the Gulf Coast region. In a statement consistent with the current administration's position on Iraq, one National Guard officer stated that "we will be there . . . for as long as they need it" (Brown 2005).

MEDIA FRAMES AND GOVERNMENT RESPONSES

Once the media coverage of lawnessness, anarchy, and war began to die down, media organizations themselves were among the harshest critics of post-Katrina reporting (see Dwyer and Drew 2005). Unfortunately, those critiques began to appear only well after the event. In the early days after Katrina struck, media reporting and images of anarchy served to justify the manner in which disaster response operations were carried out. For example, within three days after Katrina made landfall, the governor of Louisiana and the mayor of New Orleans suspended lifesaving operations in New Orleans and ordered emergency responders to concentrate on arresting looters and deterring crime instead—an order that may have amounted to a death sentence for stranded victims in desperate need of rescue. Dusk-to-dawn curfews and statements that armed force would be used against those suspected of lawbreaking no doubt had a chilling effect on local self-help efforts. Victims and evacuees in dire need were characterized as unruly elements requiting strict policing and were treated as such.

As the situation deteriorated in the impact region and the Katrina response began to be characterized as wholly inadequate, the federal government moved decisively to militarize the management of the catastrophe. The director of FEMA, Michael Brown, was initially praised by the president but later singled out for his poor performance, called back to Washington, and then forced to resign. After attempting to federalize and militarize the response—a move that was rejected by Louisiana's governor—Bush sent Army Lieutenant General Russel Honoré to the region two days after landfall and put him in charge of Joint Task Force Katrina, the entity charged with coordinating military operations throughout the impact region. After Brown's departure, Vice Admiral Thad Allen, the Coast Guard's number three officer in command, was put in charge of coordinating the federal response to Katrina.[7] Honoré in particular was framed by both the administration and the media as the ideal person to restore public order in New Orleans. Referred to in the media as the "ragin' Cajun" and a "John Wayne dude," Honoré was characterized as possessing both the authority and the know-how to mobilize military resources to restore order and deliver services to victims.[8]

Not only were more military personnel involved in the Katrina response than had ever been mobilized for any other U.S. disaster, but their missions were also much broader. Those missions spanned relief-related tasks such as search and rescue, supply distribution, the transportation of evacuees, the provision of shelter, traffic management, debris removal, and repairing levee breaks, but, more important for this discussion, their assignments also included assisting local law enforcement agencies, enforcing curfews, and providing security at facilities such as the Superdome and the Astrodome. During Katrina, the tasks assumed by the military pushed the boundaries of legality to such an extent that at one point the army brought in some of its own judge advocates to clarify the "rules of engagement" for soldiers (Schlesing 2005). Policies were developed for the issuing of ammunition to military personnel, with less ammunition given than is typical during combat operations. However, outfitting military personnel with combat gear and firearms had never even been contemplated in modern U.S. disasters. Neither the Stafford Act nor the NRP envisions the use of the military in a law enforcement capacity. That type of mobilization contravenes both the Posse Comitatus Act and DOD directives.[9]

Some narratives even centered on the notion that Katrina was not unlike the enemies the military faces in war. For example, General Russel Honoré, the man referred to in the media as an "icon of leadership" and "man of action" (Neumeister 2005), described Katrina "as an enemy that pulled a 'classic military maneuver,' speeding toward land with overwhelming force, surprising and paralyzing the city and countryside and knocking out communications, electricity, water and roads in 'a disaster of biblical proportions'" (Neumeister 2005). Thus, nature itself was recast as an "intelligent enemy" like al-Qaeda bent on exploiting weaknesses in the nation's defenses. Under Honoré's leadership, the response to Katrina came increasingly to be treated as a military campaign (Miller 2005).

WHY NOW? THE BROADER CONTEXT

A recent report by the Government Accountability Office (2006) indicates that the DOD and the National Guard were not prepared to respond to Hurricane Katrina, although many of the deficiencies identified stemmed from problems with implementing the NRP. The report also notes that the military is currently overtaxed and that there are inherent tensions between requirements associated with war-fighting missions abroad and those associated with providing support during U.S. disasters. The report goes on to recommend more training and greater military involvement in disaster response (Government Accountability Office 2006). With National Guard, reserve, and regular military forces so overtaxed because of the war on terror and in a time when the military is experiencing significant recruiting difficulties, why is there so much support for expanding the responsibilities of the military in disaster response? Why are civil society institutions—the institutions that are legally charged with reducing disaster losses—now seen as not being up to the task of managing incidents of national significance? What forces appear to be driving the move toward greater military participation in disaster response decision making?

First, it should be noted that military involvement is a contested topic, with various stakeholders weighing in on different sides of the issue. In its *2005 National Action Plan on Safety and Security in America's Cities*, the U.S. Conference of Mayors came out in support of assigning a greater role to the military in disaster response and recovery (U.S. Conference of Mayors 2005). However, most U.S. governors oppose the idea (Associated Press 2005b). Legal experts argue that existing laws and authorities, such as the Stafford Act, the Posse Comitatus Act, and the Insurrection Act both restrain and permit military involvement in a variety of disaster-related tasks, even to the point of permitting domestic law enforcement under some circumstances. For example, if invoked, the Insurrection Act (originally intended to quell domestic uprisings) would grant military personnel the authority to act in a law enforcement capacity. President Bush considered invoking the Insurrection Act in Louisiana but, in what has been described as a political move, decided not to do so, thus avoiding a clash with Louisiana's governor (American Bar Association 2006). At the same time, as discussed earlier, changes are underway that would appear to permit the military to more easily act on its own in response to an incident of national significance or a catastrophic disaster event.[10]

Some argue that the military itself does not wish to have a deeper involvement in responding to disasters (American Bar Association 2006; Banks 2005). Yet at the same time, it is clear that NORTHCOM, which was established specifically to protect the homeland, does see disaster response (and other activities, such as responding during an avian flu pandemic) as among its responsibilities, as indicated by both official statements and its efforts to launch a response during Hurricane Wilma, even without a request from the state of Florida.

Other critics of proposals to involve the military more directly in managing disasters raise additional issues. One legal scholar (Banks 2005) notes that the federal government already has all the authority it needs under existing statutes and plans (e.g., the Insurrection Act and the NRP) and that there is no need to request further authorizations. That analyst also raises other criticisms, such as the fact that moves in the direction of greater military control contravene American values—values that see the military as an important resource but one that should always be subject to civil authority—as well as that trends toward the federalization and militarization of disasters are inconsistent with the federal system of governance itself. One of the strengths of that system is that responsibility is vested in those who have a great deal to lose if they do not perform effectively, namely, local and state political leaders.

Civil-sector emergency managers at the city and county levels—those with whom the military would presumably work—appear to be confused and uncertain with respect to the involvement of the military in disaster operations. One key finding from a 2004 survey was that even though the military is seen as having important resources to provide, emergency managers have little information on how MACA is supposed to operate and function in disaster situations (Milliman, Grosskepf, Paez 2006). Some emergency managers were not even familiar with the concept. Even when emergency managers had worked with the military in an actual disaster response, they still expressed a lack of understanding of MACA doctrines and principles (Milliman, Grosskopf, and Paez 2006).

Based on scholarship in economics and other fields, there is also some question whether a stepped-up federal and military involvement may have perverse effects, for example, by creating a "Samaritan's dilemma" in which expectations regarding federal intervention and military assistance may cause lower levels of government to become less vigilant about hazards management (Harrington 2005). This principle does not seem to operate with respect to individual and household decisions regarding disaster mitigation and preparedness—primarily because people discount the personal consequences of future disasters, and when they do think about disasters, they do not think in terms of long time horizons. However, the situation may be different for subfederal government entities.

From the point of view of both effectiveness and fiscal responsibility, it seems hugely inappropriate to consider mobilizing military forces from outside a community to carry out functions that community residents and local and state public safety agencies are better able to do on their own, such as lifesaving and rescue activities. Numerous studies on collective responses to disasters, conducted all over the globe, have consistently shown that most immediate lifesaving activities are carried out by neighbors, friends, family, and even total strangers who rush to provide assistance when disasters strike (Tierney, Lindell, and Perry 2001). The emergent groups that form following disasters are more effective than outside sources of aid, precisely because of their understanding of the community and its residents (Aguirre et al. 1995). Indeed, lifesaving activities did begin immediately after Katrina struck and were undertaken by both residents in the stricken areas and public safety officials, such as firefighting personnel from neighboring jurisdictions (Rodríguez, Trainor, and Quarantelli 2006). Both research and the Katrina experience itself argue for greater "civilian" involvement in disaster response activities rather than greater engagement on the part of the military.

Considering all these criticisms, it seems puzzling why the pressure to militarize disasters should be so strong. Many military institutions are reluctant to take on new missions, and the notion of "disaster as war" undermines civil society institutions. Military deployments are extremely costly, and such deployments may well not meet critical challenges, such as saving lives. Moreover, extensive involvement in OOTW—and now in disasters—may well undermine the military's sense of mission and its war-fighting capability. Nonetheless, steps are currently being taken to expand the role of the military in disaster management. We take the position that this is occurring not because of any evidence that the military will be effective in new disaster-related missions but rather because such involvement is consistent with the current ideological climate—a climate of militarism that places ultimate confidence in institutions based on the use of force (see also Tierney 2003; Tierney, Bevc, and Kuligowski 2006). Seen from this perspective, the elevation of the military as the only institution that "has the ability to bring everyone together" or that is capable of moving resources to disaster stricken areas[11] reflects current cultural assumptions regarding the superiority of that institution over others.

We do not argue here that the military has no legitimate role in disaster operations. Such an argument would be groundless, given the assets and expertise the military can provide in addressing the challenges associated with extreme events. Indeed, MACA and OOTW doctrines allow the military to contribute in important ways to disaster response effectiveness. Rather, our concern is with the manner in which post-Katrina developments are indicative of the expansion of *militarism as an ideology* guiding government practice. For this, we draw on the work of Chalmers Johnson (see, in particular, Johnson 2004), which argues that militarism and the imperial ambitions that it supports are the basis of U.S. activities in a variety of policy domains. Militarism, as opposed to the military as an institution, is the belief that military personnel and resources, as well as the martial values associated with military institutions, such as masculinity and the belief in demonstrations of force, are crucial to the existence of the United States as a nation. Johnson (2004) observes that "one sign of the advent of militarism is the assumption by the nation's armed forces of numerous tasks that should be reserved for civilians" (24) and that military involvement in domestic policing activities is a reflection of this trend. The hegemony of militarism as an ideology has been strengthened by the war on terrorism, which is rhetorically constructed as a war without boundaries—and seemingly without end (Cunningham 2004). That hegemony is further bolstered by the rhetoric (and reality) associated with the concept of the United States as an imperial power (but on the military–society tensions produced by imperial claims, see Morgan 2006).

In a review of classic scholarship on militarism, Van Tuyll (1994) discusses values, attitudes, and behaviors associated with militarism as a "cultural complex." Those cultural elements include reverence for symbols of military power, the glorification of "warriors," the dominance of military needs over other elements of public policy, and the broad diffusion of military ways of thinking and acting throughout society. Positive attitudes and emotions toward militaristic virtues and the value of "masculinist moral capital" (Stempel 2006) pervade American social life, from sport to corporate culture to political discourse. A consistent element in U.S. culture, militarism, and the cult of masculinity with which it is associated have become even more deeply entrenched in the context of the war on terror (Ehrenreich 2002; Kellner 2002; Klocke 2004).

Official narratives hold that, just as sanctions and diplomacy failed to resolve the nuclear threat posed by Iraq, civil society institutions have also proved themselves incapable of managing catastrophic disaster events. Thus, military officials such as Honoré and Allen were "the men for the job" following Hurricane Katrina—even though they lacked the knowledge of disaster law, policies, and procedure that reside in agencies like FEMA and state and local emergency management organizations.

Discourses of militarism and hypermasculinity associated with the "war on terrorism" thus provide ample justification for militarizing disasters—even if greater military involvement will do little to enhance response effectiveness and even if such involvement causes the costs associated with disaster mobilization (including those associated with hiring military contractors) to rise. Hurricane Katrina showed the shape of things to come, as one of the nation's greatest catastrophes was recast as an episode of civil unrest and urban insurgency.[12] Future efforts will likely be directed even more toward managing "problem populations," such as the poor and people of color, as uniformed forces seek to maintain order at any cost. Such strategies will be applied both to disasters and to other perils, such as avian flu, with future consequences that we can now only begin to envision.

NOTES

1. Civil defense programs in the United States actually date back to World War I, but the development of civil defense and disaster programs is more appropriately traced to the Civil Defense Act of 1950 and to Public Law 81-875, the Disaster Relief Act, also passed in 1950, which was the statute that formally authorized federal assistance to states and local governments in the context of disasters. Current disaster programs are governed by the Robert T. Stafford Emergency Assistance and Relief Act (the Stafford Act), which was passed in 1988.

2. NORTHCOM's jurisdiction includes the United States, Mexico, Canada, and Cuba, even though those other nations were not consulted before NORTHCOM was "stood up." Prior to 9/11, the United States never found it necessary to establish a military command with jurisdiction over the U.S. mainland—much less most of the North American continent (Johnson 2004).

3. Military, intelligence, and security agencies had already begun to take an interest in disaster management well before the occurrence of Hurricane Katrina. During the mid-1990s, in an initiative known as the Global Disaster Information Network, a broad mix of agencies, including the DOD, the Central Intelligence Agency, the National Security Agency, the National Aeronautics and Space Administration, the National Oceanographic and Atmospheric Administration, and others, worked together to identify ways in which military, intelligence, and other high-technology "assets" could be applied within the context of disasters (see Global Disaster Information Network 1997).

4. The concepts "incident of national significance" and "catastrophe" are elements in the Federal Response Plan. Chertoff's declaration was the first use of the "incident of national significance" designation for any disaster.

5. The DHS describes the Homeland Security Operations Center (HSOC) as "the nation's nerve center for information-sharing and domestic incident management," but it is also clear that HSOC's focus is on terrorism-related events, not natural disasters. Why its much-vaunted data collection and fusion capabilities were not used during the immediate pre- and postimpact periods is a topic for further study. Matthew Broderick, head of the DHS Operations Directorate and the HSOC, resigned effective March 31, 2006, following the House of Representatives report on Katrina, which singled him out for failing to inform high-level officials of Katrina's devastating impacts.

6. Some victims—primarily whites—no doubt did feel more secure as a consequence of the use of military force following Katrina. However, minority groups felt otherwise and complained about their treatment at the hands of military and public safety agencies.

7. FEMA has long had a system for predesignating federal coordinating officers (FCOs), who generally have many years of experience in managing federal response operations. Rather than using experienced FCOs, the president chose Admiral Allen to manage the Katrina operation and required FCOs in the impact region to report to Allen. William Carwile, a veteran FCO who had been put in charge of the Katrina response for Mississippi and who had struggled to inform the administration that Katrina's impacts were truly catastrophic, resigned his post and left government service shortly after Katrina.

8. A native of Louisiana himself, Lieutenant General Russel Honoré attempted to characterize the military's presence in New Orleans as much more of a humanitarian relief effort than law enforcement operation, seeing the latter as the role of the police (Bluestein 2006; CNN.com

2005). Although Honoré did order National Guardsmen and active-duty troops to hold their weapons down rather than upright (as if on patrol) (CNN.com 2005), his very presence and the large-scale military response to Katrina dramaturgically represented the disaster area as a war zone and communicated the notion that the Katrina response would have been unmanageable but for the military.

9. For example, see DOD 3025.1 Section 4.5.4, which describes the types of assistance the National Guard can provide, including assistance with rescues, evacuation, and the repair of damaged infrastructure. The directive specifies that these tasks can be carried out on the request of the governor of an affected state. See also DOD Directive 5525.1

10. Just how they would respond is another question. Even under such circumstances, current law would restrict the role of the military to non–law enforcement functions—unless, of course, the Insurrection Act is invoked in the context of a disaster.

11. It is inarguable that the military have specialized skills and resources, but the responsibility for the movement of resources and supplies during disasters is formally assigned to the U.S. Department of Transportation (DOT), a 110,000-person civilian agency that either controls or has some degree of influence over the entire transportation infrastructure of the United States. The DOT's role in disasters has been clear since the development of the Federal Response Plan in the 1980s. In the NRP, the DOT is responsible for Emergency Support Function (ESF) #1, "Transportation." The DOD is involved in ESF #1 only in a support role.

12. This idea continued into the long-term recovery of New Orleans when reelected Mayor Ray Nagin requested the National Guard return to the city (Reckdahl 2006). In mid-June, National Guardsmen returned to help local law enforcement patrol local neighborhoods following an increased number of homicides in the city (Reckdahl 2006). On the first anniversary of Katrina's landfall, the New Orleans police force remained depleted, and the National Guard remained in place, supporting local law enforcement with no exit date set (Saulny 2006b).

3

Crime and Hurricanes in New Orleans

Kelly Frailing and Dee Wood Harper

The physical devastation they cause notwithstanding, historically hurricanes have an even greater negative consequence for the most vulnerable populations in the impact area. Storms in the British colonies in the 1600s and 1700s killed hundreds of slaves. Aid collected for hurricane victims was typically given to and retained by the wealthy in storm-prone areas, extending the suffering of the poor. Unfortunately, this trend continued in the 1800s and 1900s in cases in which hurricanes struck the United States (Mulcahy 2005). Of course, the city of New Orleans is no stranger to hurricanes. Since its establishment in 1718, the city and its surrounding area has been hit by 13 hurricanes, and this does not take into account other damage the city incurred over time because of Mississippi River flooding. The first hurricane struck in 1722 and destroyed New Orleans. The city experienced subsequent hurricanes in 1778, 1779, 1780, 1794, 1812, 1831, 1893, 1915, and 1947 as well as Betsy in 1965, Camille in 1969, and Katrina in 2005 (Magill 2005–2006). The three storms under consideration in this chapter are the biggest, most powerful that have hit New Orleans. Moreover, sufficient data are available so that comparisons can be made.

This chapter reviews pre- and postcrime problems in the city of New Orleans following these three storms. The 1947 hurricane impacted New Orleans on September 19. At that time, acting governor Emil Verret mobilized the National Guard, which arrived the day after the storm. The bulk of the 3,000 refugees in the city were French-speaking bayou residents who stayed in the Municipal Auditorium. The Red Cross was stationed at New Orleans City Hall, and its staff assisted the National Guard. Despite an initially low estimation of damage, two areas of the metropolitan area, New Orleans East and Metairie, flooded on September 21 because of levee breaches and the overflow of Lake Pontchartrain. Postal delivery trucks provided rescue services, but some refugees were stranded after the flooding. The remaining floodwater was pumped back into the lake on September 29 and 30. A total of 11 people died in Orleans Parish as a result of this hurricane (*Times-Picayune* archives, September 20, 21, 22, and 30 and October 1, 1947).

Hurricane Betsy hit New Orleans on September 10, 1965. Nearly half a million people evacuated in advance of the storm, which many deemed the worst in 50 years. Governor John J. McKeithen asked President Lyndon Johnson for disaster assistance, and the National Guard arrived in the city on September 11. At the requests of three members of Congress from Louisiana, one of whom was Senator Long, President Johnson made a personal visit to New Orleans that same day. Betsy's floodwater began to recede in earnest on September 12. Of the 25 dead in Louisiana, 10 were from Orleans Parish (*Times-Picayune* archives, September 11, 12, and 13, 1965).

On August 29, 2005, the tidal surge of Hurricane Katrina caused the failure of the levee system, resulting in approximately 80 percent of New Orleans being flooded. Much of the city remained underwater for two weeks. With law enforcement occupied with search and rescue and the National Guard not deployed for nearly a week, law and order collapsed. Some grocery stores opened their doors, freely giving people food and water. Some stores, including those selling liquor, pharmaceuticals, and firearms, did not open their doors yet had their merchandise taken.

In the months following the hurricane, looting of damaged and unoccupied homes continued to be a problem. To give context to the high level of criminality following the storm, we examined macrosociological features of the city over the approximately 60-year period between the unnamed hurricane of 1947 and Katrina. These features included changes in population, in racial and household composition, in industrial and labor force characteristics, and in burglary rates.

Looting to a greater or lesser extent has been reported following all natural disasters. Yet a persistent notion that exists in the natural disaster literature is that looting is a myth or at least that prosocial behaviors far outnumber criminal behaviors. The primary objective of this chapter is the explanation of the variation in looting behavior for the three storms that impacted New Orleans for the years 1947, 1965, and 2005. Over the years, the disappearance of jobs has contributed to increased concentrated poverty, which is linked to a subculture of violence, which, in turn, is related to neighborhood variations in violent crime (Harper, Voigt, and Thornton 2003). We suggest that these socioeconomic changes underlie high rates of looting (residential and commercial burglaries) in the aftermath of Hurricane Katrina when contrasted to the two previous storms. We use burglary as a proxy for looting because looting did not exist in the Louisiana criminal code until 1993 (RS 14:62.5). This does not mean that the behavior now referred to as looting did not occur after the 1947 hurricane or after Betsy, but with no name in the criminal code for looting, police reports referred to what is now called looting as burglary following the 1947 storm and Betsy. Even with the criminal charge of looting in existence for Hurricane Katrina, police used a special code, "21K," after the storm when reporting losses that may have been caused either by the storm or by looting or burglary, in essence putting burglary and looting on par with each other. Using burglary as a proxy for looting also allows us to compare pre- and post-storm behavior across the three hurricanes of interest.

LITERATURE REVIEW

Natural disasters vary in the extent of their devastation and subsequent patterns of crime. For example, an earthquake estimated to measure 7.9 on the Richter scale hit Japan's Kanto region in September 1923. In the week that followed, rumors about Korean uprisings started in the most isolated and devastated areas and quickly spread throughout Japan. The end result was the torture and murder of about 2,600 Koreans living in Japan at the time (Ishiguro 1998).

Contractor fraud, in which contractors accept money up front for home or property repair they do not start, do not finish, or do shoddy work on, happened to 5.6 percent of people with damaged property following a tropical storm in Houston, Texas, in 2001 and to 3.4 percent of people with damaged property following flooding in the San Antonio, Texas, area in 2002. The victims of contractor fraud from both cities were more likely to be female, older, and college educated (Davila, Marquart, and Mullings 2005). Federal benefit fraud has also occurred after natural disasters, in particular after Hurricane Katrina. By October 2005, the Hurricane Katrina Fraud Task Force had charged 36 people in 17 separate cases with hurricane-related fraud. By February 2006, 212 people had been charged in 173 separate cases with hurricane-related fraud, representing a nearly 500 percent increase in the number of people charged with fraud. The majority of hurricane-related prosecutions since October 17, 2005, involve fraud to obtain emergency benefits from the Federal Emergency Management Agency and the American Red Cross (U.S. Department of Justice 2006).

In contrast to what the disaster literature argues and with other types of crime notwithstanding, looting may be the most common crime to occur in the wake of natural disasters. It followed the earthquake that struck San Francisco in 1906 (Morris 2002); the flood caused by Hurricane Agnes in Wilkes Barre, Pennsylvania, in 1972 (Siman 1977); the flood that devastated Buffalo Creek, West Virginia, in 1972 (Erikson 1976); and the earthquake that struck Tangshan, China, in 1976 (Zhou 1997). Furthermore, looting did occur in the wake of the devastation of New Orleans by Hurricane Katrina in August and September 2005.

Nevertheless, there is a widespread notion in the literature that looting is virtually nonexistent in the wake of natural disasters, such as hurricanes or earthquakes, though it does occur during civil disturbances, such as riots. In a paper contrasting the features of the two types of situations, Dynes and Quarantelli (1968) cite a review of natural disasters done by the Disaster Research Center at Ohio State University that found extremely low verifiable rates of looting after 40 natural disasters in the United States. They also suggest that what looting does occur after natural disasters may be due to a continuation of a civil disturbance, such as that which occurred in Chicago after a heavy snowstorm in early 1967. They conclude that looting during civil disturbances in American cities in the 1960s was an attempt at a redistribution of property.

The same researchers later expanded their argument by adding that looting during civil disturbances is almost always done by local residents in full view of others and with their support, while looting after natural disasters (what little of it there is) is committed by outsiders and strongly condemned by locals. During a civil disturbance, the right to property becomes collective instead of individual, and therefore, taking property, or looting, becomes normative. Looting in these circumstances is construed as a way to send a message of protest against the conditions that facilitated a civil disturbance in the first place (Quarantelli and Dynes 1970).

The reports of looting in New Orleans after Hurricane Katrina were ubiquitous, almost to the point of being inescapable. Newspapers, the Internet, and especially 24-hour cable news networks reported widespread looting beginning shortly after Katrina's landfall. In a study of the emergent behavior following the storm, researchers point out this fact and acknowledge that antisocial behavior occurred in New Orleans. However, they take care to characterize Katrina and its aftermath as a "catastrophe" and not as a "natural disaster," which they contend allows for both prosocial and antisocial behavior to emerge, and that the former was far more prevalent than the latter. One data collection during a quick study in the New Orleans metropolitan area after the storm included 150 interviews, participant observation, and document review; areas of focus included hotels, hospitals, neighborhood groups, rescue teams, and the Joint Field Office. All focus groups had improvisation in common, and even though their responses were reactive to needs that developed, those responses were overwhelmingly prosocial in nature and included activities such as rescuing those stranded by the storm and acquiring food and clean water (Rodríguez, Trainor, and Quarantelli 2006).

THE PRESENT STUDY

The disaster research literature provides little more than speculation regarding the underlying causes of antisocial behavior, focusing almost exclusively on individual motivation or crowd behavior. There is no systematic quantitative research that places looting behavior in the larger sociological context. We believe that variations in looting behavior can be understood comparatively by examining rates of looting before and after each disaster event in the context of macrosocial change. We contend that in conjunction with the demographic changes in New Orleans over the past 60 years, there have been significant negative economic changes in the city that created the context in which the high rate of looting that followed Hurricane Katrina may not have been entirely surprising. As the review of the following literature reveals, others have found a positive association between measures of relative deprivation, the lack of well-paying jobs, and crime, even without the triggering mechanism of a catastrophe.

A number of studies have investigated the relationship between crime and economic variables in the United States. One such study was a review of research that utilized time-series analysis of the relationship between crime and economic indicators over time. The examination of 10 studies revealed that both unemployment and decline in labor force participation are associated with higher crime rates and that nonparticipation in the labor force was more strongly associated with crime than was unemployment (Freeman 1983). Another study found that even after controlling for other sociodemographic variables, unemployment rates were an important determinant of property crime rates at both the individual level and the aggregate level (Raphael and Winter-Ebmer 2001). It is important to draw a distinction between unemployment and labor force participation. Those people who are out of work but actively seeking work are unemployed. People who are not working and not seeking work are not participating in the labor force. Some census tracts in the poorer neighborhoods in New Orleans have labor force nonparticipation rates as high as 80 percent for people 16 years of age and older (U.S. Bureau of the Census 2000).

From 1963 to 1987, jobs in different industries and different occupations within those industries were found to favor the college educated and females (Katz and Murphy 1992). Similarly, declines in employment over roughly the same span of time were found to negatively affect less educated males and males working in low-wage jobs most severely (Juhn 1992). Freeman (1996) has maintained that as the demand for unskilled male labor fell from the mid-1970s through the 1990s, there was an increase in the supply of males for crime. For males first committing crime, joblessness and inequality were associated with higher crime rates. That is, males continuing their criminal activity found that it was more lucrative than legitimate work. They also believed they would not be caught and did not experience a stigmatizing effect of incarceration if they were apprehended.

Finally, Gould, Weinberg, and Mustard (2002) examined both unemployment and wages and attempted to explain the inverse relationship between crime and labor market prospects for young men in the 1980s and 1990s. They found that both unemployment and low wages were significantly associated with greater crime and that low wages are more strongly associated with crime than unemployment. These associations held even when controlling for individual and family characteristics.

This body of research reveals that, in general, unemployment and low wages are associated with increased crime rates. As we will show, a substantial portion of the population of New Orleans has experienced high levels of unemployment, and the only significant job growth in the city has been in low-wage service-sector jobs in the past four decades. Most of this job growth has occurred in the food and hotel service subsector of the New Orleans economy, which often pays less than the minimum wage.

METHODS AND DATA SOURCES

In an effort to create an accurate picture of New Orleans and the sociodemographic changes that residents have experienced over the past 60 years, we employed a variety of data sources. To obtain information on changes in population and in racial and household composition, we used U.S. Bureau of the Census data for Orleans Parish (New Orleans) only and not those for the New Orleans standard metropolitan area, which includes five contiguous parishes (counties). We also used census data to calculate historical unemployment rates and median family income in 1950 constant dollars. The Bureau of Labor Statistics was our source of unemployment rates immediately before and shortly after Hurricane Katrina.

We employed County Business Patterns data not only to look at major industry changes over time in New Orleans but also to compare these changes to other large southern cities. Finally, we obtained information on burglaries—the crime we employ as a proxy variable for looting—from police reports found in historical issues of the *Times-Picayune* newspaper, microfilm archives of which are maintained at the Historic New Orleans Collection's Williams Resource Center and at the main branch of the New Orleans Public Library. These proved sufficient for information from which to calculate historical burglary rates, as did the information on burglaries published in the *Times-Picayune* some months after Katrina. Because the electronic records of the New Orleans Police Department were compromised during the storm, we obtained pre-Katrina burglary information from a former Loyola University New Orleans criminal justice graduate student whose position with the police department gave her access to that information.

The following tables present data reflecting changes in the social and demographic features of New Orleans that help clarify variations in the burglary rate for the three hurricanes.

After growing in the 1950s and 1960s and after peaking in 1967 at 675,000 residents (Division of Business and Economic Research 1967), the overall population of New Orleans proper fell by about 190,000 and in 2000 reached its lowest point in almost 40 years. Various estimates place the population of New Orleans before the storm between 432,000 and 454,863 (Liu, Mabanta, and Fellowes 2006; *Times-Picayune* archives, 2006). During this roughly 40-year period, the white population decreased by over half, and the African American population more than doubled, reflecting a higher fertility rate[1] and the depopulation of rural areas of Louisiana and of neighboring Mississippi[2] (Caplow, Hicks, and Wattenberg 2000). As also seen in Table 3.1, New Orleans became a majority African American city by the 1980 census.

Data from the U.S. Bureau of the Census are certainly available for 1940, and the argument could be made that they should be included here and in our analyses to better describe New Orleans before the unnamed hurricane of 1947. However, we believe the unemployment rates for that year were confounded by the Great Depression, an event not unique to New Orleans. The universality of the Great Depression's effects on the country stand in contrast to the changes specific to New Orleans, as we will demonstrate.[3]

As is evident in Table 3.1, the percentage of female-headed households more than doubled between 1960 and 2000. The variable female-headed household is a well-known indicator of the poverty in a given area, and in one study, it explained one-third to one-half of urban crime (Glaser and Sacerdote 1999).

As a majority African American city, unemployment data for African Americans becomes an important indicator for understanding the city's overall economic well-being. The unemployment rate for African Americans has been consistently high in New Orleans since 1950 (see Table 3.2). Since 1960, African American unemployment rates have at least doubled those of whites and were nearly six times higher in 1990. In 1994, New Orleans had the dubious distinction of being the "murder capital" of the United States with 424 homicides and an overall unemployment rate of 9.5 percent, with African American unemployment rising above 15 percent (Bureau of Labor Statistics 1994; Federal Bureau of Investigation 1994).

Table 3.1. Orleans Parish Population, Race, and Percent Female-Headed Households, 1950–2000

	1950	1960	1970	1980	1990	2000
Population	570,445	627,525	593,471	557,515	496,938	484,674
White population	387,814	392,594	323,420	238,192	173,305	136,241
% White	68.0	62.6	54.5	42.5	34.9	28.1
Black population	182,631	234,931	267,308	308,039	308,364	325,216
% Black	32.0	37.2	45.0	55.3	62	67.3
% Female-headed household	NA[1]	16.2	21.6	29.8	38.4	41

[1] Not available.

Source: U.S. Bureau of the Census (1950–2000).

Table 3.2.   Orleans Parish Unemployment by Race, 1950–2000

	1950	*1960*	*1970*	*1980*	*1990*	*2000*
Unemployment rate	6.0	5.5	5.7	7.0	12.4	9.4
White unemployment rate	4.9	3.9	4.1	4.0	3.0	3.6
Black unemployment rate	8.6	8.7	8.3	10.1	17.8	13.1
White-to-black unemployment ratio						
White	1.0	1.0	1.0	1.0	1.0	1.0
Black	1.8	2.2	2.0	2.5	5.9	3.6

Source: U.S. Bureau of the Census (1950–2000).

The ratios of African American to white median family income in Table 3.3 deserve comment. At no time in New Orleans since 1950 did whites have less than double the household income of African Americans. When viewed with data presented in Table 3.2, it becomes clear that as the city's African American population grew to become the majority, there was no growth in suitable jobs; thus, residents were unemployed at high rates. For those who did earn an income, that income remained stagnated and low. Taken together, these economic factors have generated severe economic inequality in the city.

To help explain these low incomes, we examined the types of jobs that have been available in New Orleans, going back to the year before Hurricane Betsy. Unlike the information in the three previous tables, which was obtained from the U.S. Census and therefore limited to census years, the industry data are available for additional years during the time span under consideration.

Table 3.4 clearly reveals that there has been a remarkable loss in higher-wage jobs, especially in the manufacturing industry sector, in New Orleans since 1964. Moreover, the jobs created in the wake of this loss are low-wage jobs, primarily in the service industry sector. There was an almost 200 percent gain in food and hotel service jobs (a subcategory of the service sector), the lowest-paying jobs in the city.

Of course, New Orleans is not unique in its loss of manufacturing jobs. A cursory inspection of most other cities in the United States reveals a similar

Table 3.3.   Orleans Parish Median Family Income in 1950 Constant Dollars by Race, 1950–2000

	1950	*1960*	*1970*	*1980*	*1990*	*2000*
Median family income	2,267	3,206	4,677	4,644	5,170	4,646
White median family income	3,143	4,394	6,961	6,241	7,472	8,829
Black median family income	1,391	2,018	2,392	3,046	2,868	3,594
Black-to-white median family income ratio						
Black	1.0	1.0	1.0	1.0	1.0	1.0
White	2.3	2.2	2.9	2.1	2.6	2.5

Source: U.S. Bureau of the Census (1950–2000).

Table 3.4. Orleans Parish Changes in Percent of Employees by Industry, 1964–2003

	Mining	Construction	Manufacturing	Transportation/ Utilities	Trade	Finance/ Insurance/ Real Estate	Services	Food/Hotel Services
1964	2.8	7.8	17.3	15.5	28.0	8.2	20.0	6.2
1965	2.7	7.9	18.2	14.5	27.8	8.0	20.3	6.4
1966	2.8	9.0	17.0	15.2	27.4	7.8	20.4	6.3
1970	3.2	6.0	14.6	15.9	27.6	8.7	23.8	6.3
1980	4.4	5.3	10.2	15.7	25.1	8.0	30.5	11.6
1990	3.3	3.0	7.8	10.1	24.4	8.0	43.0	13.5
2000	1.5	3.5	4.5	6.4	13.0	6.8	44.6	16.3
2001	1.9	3.2	4.4	6.6	12.3	6.8	44.2	17.3
2002	1.7	3.0	4.0	5.3	12.3	7.2	44.7	17.9
2003	1.1	3.0	4.0	6.5	11.7	7.3	45.9	18.4
Percent change	−60.7	−61.5	−76.9	−58.1	−58.2	−11.0	+129.5	+196.8

Source: U.S. Bureau of the Census, County Business Patterns, Louisiana (1964–1966, 1970, 1980, 1990, 2000–2003).

Table 3.5.   Percent Changes in Employees in Industries, New Orleans, Houston, and Atlanta, 1964–2003

	Mining	Construction	Manufacturing	Transportation/ Utilities	Trade	Finance/ Insurance/ Real Estate	Services	Food/Hotel Services
New Orleans	−60.7	−61.5	−76.9	−28.1	−58.2	−11.0	129.5	196.8
Houston	−50.0	−26.9	−58.7	−39.0	−35.7	8.8	139.1	67.4
Atlanta	−71.4	−41.4	−80.0	−45.3	−53.8	9.8	136.8	95.8

Source: U.S. Bureau of the Census, County Business Patterns, Georgia, Louisiana, and Texas (1964–1966, 1970, 1980, 1990, 2000–2003).

trend. However, New Orleans is unique in the astronomical growth of the percentage of employees in its food and hotel service jobs when compared to the two cities often mentioned as regional competitors, namely, Atlanta and Houston (Table 3.5).

All three southern cities arrayed in Table 3.5 experienced a decline in the percentage of those employed in higher-wage jobs, particularly those in manufacturing. Nevertheless, New Orleans experienced the greatest overall loss in all industry categories and the greatest gain in low-wage food and hotel service jobs.

The widespread destruction of the storm has made data acquisition difficult for both 2005 and 2006. In August 2005, the pre-Katrina population of New Orleans was estimated at 454,863; the population as of February 2006 has been estimated at 181,400, for a loss of nearly 275,000 people (Liu, Fellowes, and Mabanta 2006). The unemployment rate for New Orleans through August 2005 was 6.6 (Bureau of Labor Statistics 2006). The current unemployment rate remains unknown. Nevertheless, it is important to know that before Hurricane Katrina, New Orleans was still experiencing population loss (including the African American population) and high levels of African American unemployment with growth only in low-wage jobs.

DATA ANALYSIS

To show how our data merge, we employed a time-series analysis using linear regression and curve fitting. As noted previously, time-series analysis is a technique to examine the changes in variables over time and has been used in a variety of studies, including many reviewed by Freeman (1983), in a study of minimum wage and youth crimes (Hashimoto 1987), and in studies of protest (e.g., Aflatooni and Allen 1991; Lichbach 1985). Curve fitting produces a mathematical model of the data that can compactly contain and represent its primary properties. Furthermore, the equation of a line provides a valuable tool for predicting, or forecasting, future values of the dependent variable and for interpolating between measured variables. We used Statistical Package for the Social Sciences (SPSS) to model summaries for five variable pairings: population and manufacturing jobs, white population and manufacturing jobs, population and food/hotel jobs, white population and food/hotel jobs, and African American population and food and hotel jobs.

RESULTS

Using SPSS curve-fitting analysis tool, we examined the relationships between the five pairs of variables mentioned previously from 1950 through 2000. Table 3.6 shows the results of the analysis of these pairings. The R^2 value for each pairing is high, at least .92, and the relationship between each pair of variables is significant at .01 or better.[4]

Table 3.6. Results of SPSS Curve-Fitting Analysis of Five Variable Pairings

Variable pairings	Model Summaries Equation	R^2	F	df1	df2	Significance	Parameter Estimates Constant	b1
Population and manufacturing jobs	Linear	.960	71.92	1	3	.003	424,961.25	11,678.62
White population and manufacturing jobs	Linear	.996	833.61	1	3	.000	14.77	2.73
Population and food/hotel bobs	Linear	.920	34.43	1	3	.010	694,052.26	–13,175.11
White population and food/hotel jobs	Linear	.959	70.31	1	3	.004	77.83	–3.09
Black population and food/hotel jobs	Linear	.949	55.74	1	3	.005	24.46	2.68

As the independent jobs variables changed over time, the three dependent population variables changed with them. Table 3.6 reveals five interrelated trends:

1. As manufacturing jobs declined, so did the population of New Orleans.
2. The growth in availability of food and hotel service jobs also contributed to the decline of the city's population.
3. As manufacturing jobs disappeared, the white population of the city declined.
4. The only real job growth in the city occurring in the food and hotel service sector also contributed to the decline of the white population in New Orleans.
5. The increase in the availability of food and hotel service jobs is associated with the growth of the city's African American population, which occurred in terms of both percentage and raw numbers.

These structural changes in New Orleans, over time, helped establish and perpetuate the disadvantage of the majority of the city's residents. Given this statistical evidence, we now turn to the looting rates surrounding each of three hurricanes that struck the city. As noted earlier, there was no official charge of looting in the criminal statute in the state of Louisiana until 1993 (RS 14:62.5). We chose residential and commercial burglary as the proxy variable for looting. By doing so, we were also able to determine the prestorm burglary rate for each of the three storms under consideration.

The burglary rate before Katrina was more than three times that in the month preceding either of the other two hurricanes. The increase in the burglary rate during the month after Hurricane Katrina was more than four times that of the increase after either of the other two storms. Furthermore, the burglary rate after Katrina was calculated using only those losses that could definitely be determined to be burglaries. A majority of the poststorm losses reported to the police were coded as "21K," which indicated that the loss could have been due either to the hurricane or to looting. Therefore, the post-Katrina burglary rate may actually be much higher than what is reported in Table 3.7.

Table 3.7. Orleans Parish Burglary Rates per 100,000 in the Month before and after Hurricanes

	Burglary Rate in the Month Before	Burglary Rate in the Month After	Percent Increase
Unnamed 1947 hurricane	13.9	27.0	94.2
Hurricane Betsy, 1965	7.8	9.0	15.4
Hurricane Katrina, 2005	48.9	245.9	402.9

Sources: Times-Picayune archives, August, September, and October 1947; August, September, and October 1965; and February 7, 2006; NOPD source contact, February, 2006.

Both before Katrina and especially in its wake, the burglary rate was high. In the macrosociological context of New Orleans, with its declining population, high rates of unemployment, and low wages (if working at all), neither of these numbers should be a major revelation. Hurricane Katrina simply intensified and worsened the story of deprivation and crime, which had for many years plagued New Orleans.

DISCUSSION

The effects of the long-term negative socioeconomic changes documented for New Orleans were evident in the city's burglary rate before Katrina when compared to those of earlier hurricanes. Further, these changes—the economic decline of the city, the disappearance of higher-wage jobs, and growth only in low-wage service jobs—resulted in a large population of people trapped in abject poverty. These socioeconomic circumstances directly contributed to the unusual pattern of looting in the post-Katrina period.

We have already highlighted the disappearance of higher-wage manufacturing jobs and the simultaneous large increase in the service sector, particularly low-wage food and hotel service jobs. Given the location of New Orleans near the mouth of the Mississippi River, the changes in the availability of water transportation jobs over time deserve some consideration. With a two-mile berth, the Mississippi River Terminal Complex of the Port of New Orleans is the longest linear wharf in the world. More than 100,000 ships and barges with 10.5 million tons of general cargo pass through the Port of New Orleans each year, and these numbers do not take into account the cruise ships that also pass through the port (Port of New Orleans 2003). Water transportation services jobs, which are higher-wage manual labor jobs that include dockworkers, stevedores, and marine cargo handlers, have declined in New Orleans in large part because of the containerization of shipping. The number of employees in water transportation services jobs increased between 1964 and reached their peak of 12,764 in 1970. They then fell precipitously, for a 78.1 percent decrease in water transportation services employees between 1980 and 2003 (County Business Patterns, Louisiana, 1964, 1965–1966, 1970, 1980, 1990, 2002, 2003). Marine cargo handling, a subcategory of water transportation services, also mirrors this pattern. The number of employees in this subsector increased between 1964 and reached a peak of 12,141 in 1970. The number of marine cargo handlers then declined 80.7 percent between 1980 and 2003 (County Business Patterns, Louisiana, 1964, 1965–1966, 1970, 1980, 1990, 2002, 2003). These industry changes may not be as remarkable as those described previously. However, before containerization, the Port of New Orleans was a critical source of higher-wage manual labor jobs, which, over time, have been lost to residents.

While our research links changes in crime rates to economic change, particularly in employment and employment opportunity, the changes in the population of New Orleans were not solely the result of declining job opportunities. In the late 1960s, the interstate highway system was developed, and in the early 1970s, schools in New Orleans were integrated. Both of these developments facilitated and contributed to "white flight" to the suburbs, resulting in a population decline for the decade of 37,000 (U.S. Bureau of the Census 1970, 1980). In the 1980s, New Orleans experienced the "oil bust," an economic recession causing the oil industry in the area to restructure, resulting in the closing of company offices in New Orleans and moving many jobs to Houston and other locations. The result was a loss of about 25,000 related jobs (at middle-class income levels) and 65,000 residents for the decade, including a decline in the African American population (County Business Patterns, Louisiana, 1980, 1990; U.S. Bureau of the Census 1980, 1990). A more comprehensive explanation of the impact of socioeconomic change on social disorganization and crime will necessitate taking into consideration these events in terms of population change and subsequent economic opportunity and how such changes set the stage for the breakdown of law and order in the aftermath of hurricanes. Our analysis of the breakdown of law and order is only one part of a larger, more complex contextual, spatial, and temporal problem. For example, the functioning of the city's criminal justice system leaves much to be desired, and it commands little respect from the population of the city as a whole.

CONCLUSION

We discovered that the reaction of agencies of social control varied with each storm and may have served to repress looting or allowed it to happen. For example, while the levee system did not totally collapse after these earlier storms the way they did after Hurricane Katrina, there was significant flooding in the city after both the 1947 hurricane and Hurricane Betsy in 1965. As mentioned previously, the National Guard was in the city the day after the 1947 hurricane and the day after Hurricane Betsy in 1965. By contrast, during the first four days after Hurricane Katrina, the New Orleans Police Department was completely focused on search and rescue and could not address looting until the fifth day. The army, the National Guard, and police officers loaned to the city from other municipalities did not start arriving in New Orleans until the fifth day after the storm. During this four-day period, anarchy reigned. But what is instructive here is that property crimes before Katrina were already substantially higher than the pre- and poststorm rates for the comparable storms. We believe that it was not just the lack of social control that facilitated post-Katrina looting, then, but that it was the confluence of the lack of social control and the historically evolving socioeconomic conditions experienced by the poor of New Orleans long before the storm hit the city that resulted in significant looting. We do not wish to intimate that hurricanes and crime have a simple relationship, nor do we wish to suggest that race in any way explains crime. We acknowledge that these connections are complex and contain elements we have not fully addressed here. What we have endeavored to provide is a view of New Orleans over time that gives some context for what occurred following these hurricanes.

That said, the future of New Orleans is still in question. We believe there are two interrelated factors that, if thoughtfully considered and planned for during this rebuilding period, could improve the city. The first factor is housing. Well over half of New Orleans residents rented before Hurricane Katrina. Since the storm, rental rates have significantly increased throughout the city because of limited availability. If those renters who were displaced during Katrina have not returned over a year since the storm, it is difficult to imagine how they can ever return.

Not returning is certainly due, in part, to the lack of rental units and higher rents but also to a second factor: available jobs. While there has been an increase in wages and in bonuses for some food and hotel service jobs (especially jobs with national chains), many retail businesses have not reopened, and of those that have, some may fail because of the smaller population and customer base in the city. As mentioned previously, it is estimated that there were less than 200,000 New Orleans residents as of February 2006 (Liu, Fellowes, and Mabanta 2006). With a reduced population that has to pay considerably more for housing, less money is available to support retail businesses.

However, the larger issue is that because there have not been recently (nor are there now) any major corporations investing in the city, people who may otherwise want to return or who want to relocate to New Orleans cannot. This is especially true for those displaced New Orleans residents who, during their prolonged evacuation, may have found higher-wage jobs in other urban areas that have a more diverse labor market. An important strategy for city officials to repopulate and rebuild New Orleans would be to actively recruit corporations to the city, perhaps by providing incentives to create job opportunities for returning evacuees. If this and other strategies are not effectively employed, the city of New Orleans will experience a long and agonizing recovery.

EPILOGUE

Reports written since the one-year anniversary of Katrina do not contain much promise. The estimated September 2006 population of Orleans Parish is 187,525 (Liu, Mabanta, and Fellowes 2006). Race estimates of the population put whites at 82,048, or 43.8 percent, and African Americans at 86,917, or 46.3 percent (Louisiana Health and Hospitals/Louisiana Recovery Authority 2006). September 2006 estimates show the labor force is down to 137,752 from 204,476 before the storm. At no time since Katrina has the labor force exceeded 140,500. The unemployment rate in Orleans Parish has been increasing since July 2006 after falling nearly every month since November 2005 (Liu, Mabanta, and Fellowes 2006). Sixty-two percent of residents of Orleans Parish are home owners (Louisiana Health and Hospitals/Louisiana Recovery Authority 2006). Taken with the pre-Katrina rental rate, this information indicates that renters are in fact not returning to or coming to the city. Those who do live in Orleans Parish are struggling—10.6 percent are below between 100 and 200 percent of the poverty level, and 35.3 percent are below more than 200 percent of the poverty level (Louisiana Health and Hospitals/Louisiana Recovery Authority 2006).

These numbers indicate that recovery efforts thus far have not met their goal of improving opportunities for people in New Orleans. Still conspicuously absent are attempts to recruit companies that could provide jobs that would allow people to live in New Orleans permanently and productively. The time to take advantage of Katrina's upheaval and make significant, positive changes, especially in this area, is fast disappearing. It is a further disservice to the people of New Orleans for officials to allow this opportunity to slip away.

NOTES

1. Orleans Parish families with own children under 18:

Year	Black	White
1960	27,446	51,603
1970	37,797	35,978
1980	37,871	30,985
1990	42,994	14,602
2000	43,221	10,780

Sources: U.S. Bureau of the Census (1960–2000).

2. African Americans living outside Orleans Parish five years before the census who subsequently moved there:

Year	Different Parish/County	Different State
1960	9,725	5,324
1970	23,027	532
1980	34,073	22,826
1990	14,765	18,459
2000	23,631	10,527

Sources: U.S. Bureau of the Census (1960–2000).

3. Orleans Parish in 1940:

Population: 494,537
White population: 344,775
Percent white: 69.7
Black population: 149,762
Percent black: 30.3
Unemployment rate: 19
Unemployment rate, white: 15.5
Unemployment rate, black: 26.4

Source: U.S. Bureau of the Census (1940).

4. There is a danger of autocorrelation when making use of any statistical procedure involving time, including time-series analysis. However, there is no reason to assume that our variables should have changed together as they did over time. Further, our choice of analysis avoided common pitfalls of regression, including not analyzing a large number of independent variables to artificially inflate our R^2 values and multicollinearity, which is said to exist when independent variables are strongly related. Signs of multicollinearity include incorrect regression coefficient (b1) signs and regression coefficient values that are not significantly different from zero, neither of which were present in our analysis.

II

EXPERIENCING EVACUATION

4

Families and Hurricane Response: Evacuation, Separation, and the Emotional Toll of Hurricane Katrina

Timothy J. Haney, James R. Elliott, and Elizabeth Fussell

Meteorologists warned Gulf Coast residents of the threat posed by Hurricane Katrina three days before it made landfall, and the subsequent responses of those in the storm's path varied widely: some residents evacuated in their own vehicles before and during the voluntary evacuation period announced two days before the storm's landfall, others waited until a mandatory evacuation had been declared less than 24 hours before the storm's impact, and yet others chose to "ride out the storm," either in their homes or in local shelters, tempting fate and risking bodily injury or death. Complicating understanding of this decision-making process is that the fact that many families chose a combination of these strategies, with some members staying while others evacuated to safer destinations.

We contend that in order to understand these dynamics, attention must be paid not only to the objective threat posed by Hurricane Katrina but also to the perception of this threat by residents, their respective social roles and responsibilities, physical and financial resources, racial identity, and ties and religious faith. In this chapter we investigate these factors, focusing specifically on issues of evacuation timing, family unity, and the emotional response of those who experienced the event.

This line of analysis is relevant not only to those in charge of disaster planning but also to citizens in general who wish to make sense of the disgraceful yet highly selective images that filled media outlets following Hurricane Katrina's impact. These images and accompanying stories highlighted the drama of rooftop evacuations, the plight of thousands stranded at the New Orleans Superdome and Convention Center, family separation (Swerczek and Powell 2005), and failed government response. While these stories bear witness to the tragedy that unfolded, ultimately they represent extreme cases. The typical experience of families living in the path of Hurricane Katrina was much less dramatic and much more successful than those illustrated in the popular media, thanks in part to the evacuation strategies employed by residents themselves. Here we present a typology for identifying these strategies and outcomes and then advance and empirically test an analytical framework for understanding who was more likely to actualize each type, thereby helping to empirically clarify one of the worst disasters and mass evacuations in U.S. history.

A second goal of this chapter is to explore how Hurricane Katrina served as a stressor for various segments of the population and to what extent evacuation strategies exacerbated or mitigated the stress imposed by this natural, social, and technological disaster. Many New Orleanians anecdotally suggest that the stress created by Hurricane Katrina will linger in New Orleans for years to come. Although psychologists find themselves split on whether everyday events or large-scale catastrophes reveal more about manifestations of stress, many, such as Hobfoll (1989), now believe that the value of catastrophe research lies in the ability to isolate the stressor in question (something that cannot always be accomplished with inquiry into everyday stressors) while simultaneously observing the different ways that affected persons experience the associated stress. Following Hobfoll's logic, we examine correlates of current, short-term, and long-term indicators of stress triggered by Hurricane Katrina to determine whether particular evacuation strategies raise or lower postdisaster stress.

TYPES OF RESPONSE: EVACUATION TIMING AND FAMILY UNITY

The evacuation responses of Gulf Coast residents in the face of Hurricane Katrina must be contextualized in recent history and the regularity with which hurricane warnings occur. Katrina posed a familiar threat to families in the region. In the five years preceding Hurricane Katrina, New Orleanians had experienced four hurricane-related evacuations: of Dennis in 1999, Isidore and Lily in 2002, and Ivan in 2004. None of these warnings resulted in the level of destruction typically forecasted and popularly imagined. As with most hurricanes, the threat posed by Hurricane Katrina was identified well in advance of impact, providing residents days to define the situation and to make decisions about how to respond. Hurricane warnings were widely disseminated through the mass media and numerous local media outlets, so nearly all residents in the region knew of the threat well in advance of the storm's arrival. Stated concisely, warnings about Hurricane Katrina were familiar, amply provided, and widely received. In the case of Katrina, what differed was the level of destruction that occurred.

From the perspective of policymakers, the ideal response to a slow-onset threat such as Hurricane Katrina is full and early evacuation by entire families so that they can provide material and emotional support to members as they

Household Family Members Stayed Together During Warning, Evacuation, and Dislocation Period?	Individual Evacuated Prior to Disaster?	
	Yes	*No*
Yes	(1) "Evacuate in Unison"	(4) "Stay in Unison"
No	(2) "Evacuate by Division"	(3) "Stay by Division"

Figure 4.1.   Evacuation and Family Structure

remove themselves from harm's way and recover from any disruptions that might ensue. This ideal scenario, although rarely achieved, points to two key decisions residents make: when to leave and with whom. Heuristically and for the purposes of the present study, Figure 4.1 defines a simple two-by-two typology of the four logical combinations of these dimensions, highlighting whether an individual evacuated in advance of the storm (yes/no) and whether his or her family stayed together throughout the warning, evacuation, and dislocation period (yes/no).

The first cell of Figure 4.1 represents the policymaker's ideal, *evacuating in unison*. This type of response not only removes the most people from the threatened region but also conforms to the observation that, socially at least, disasters are very similar to other major life events, such as weddings, christenings, and funerals. They are times when family members come together, affirm primary bonds, and help one another cope (Drabek 1986; Drabek et al. 1975; Weine, Muzurovic, and Kulauzovic 2004). Disaster scholars assume that most families prioritize such togetherness in the evacuation process and evacuate only when the entire household is assembled (Mawson 2005). However, other considerations can—and often do—enter the decision-making process. For example, prior experience with hurricane warnings leads many to believe that the costs of evacuation are greater than the risks associated with staying (Perry, Lindell, and Green 1981; Perry, Green, and Mushkatel 1983), especially if evacuation means lost time from work, accrued expenses from travel and lodging, and substantial damage to property that could have been avoided or mitigated by staying behind. For the elderly and the infirm, evacuation itself can be riskier than remaining at home or in an institution in the storm's path. These considerations counter the ideal of family togetherness and trigger a set of complicated decisions governing who will stay and who will leave.

If these decisions lead to a strategy in which some family members evacuate while others stay, the result is one of two complementary types, depending on the individual involved (see cells 2 and 3 in Figure 4.1). One type of response is *evacuating by division*, in which the observed individual evacuates in advance of the threat but without all of his or her family members; the alternative involves *staying by division*, in which the observed individual is the family member who stays behind as others evacuate. As Zeigler, Brunn, and Johnson (1981) document, these types of individual response are part of a general strategy in which family members decide to divide in the face of threat, often with women and children in the household evacuating and men staying behind to protect property, make repairs, and report to work. Such a strategy affirms that family unity is just one of many concerns triggered by a slow-onset threat such as Hurricane Katrina and that decisions about who stays and who evacuates are informed by a number of factors, including social roles and responsibilities that vary across individual family members.

Finally, cell 4 in Figure 4.1 identifies a strategy in which all household members of the family stay in the threatened region to face the storm together. This is the policymakers' worst-case scenario because it means that evacuation rates will be lower overall and because it requires that subsequent search-and-rescue operations could involve multiple trips into the same treacherous, postdisaster environment.

PREDICTING TYPES OF RESPONSE: THE R-5 FRAMEWORK

We contend that the type of response an individual pursued in the face of Hurricane Katrina depended on at least five factors, which we call the "R-5" framework. These factors include risk perception, roles and responsibilities, resources, race, and religion. We maintain that each factor contributed to individual decisions about whether to evacuate and how to organize the evacuation of other household members of the family and that later these decisions influenced the degree of stress experienced after the event. Next we outline this framework and use it to develop hypotheses for predicting both family evacuation strategies and variation in stress levels experienced in the storm's aftermath.

R1—Risk

As prior research documents, evacuation decisions are directly related to the projected path of such threats (Johnson 1985; Peacock, Morrow, and Gladwin 1997). When initially identified as a threat to the Gulf Coast, Hurricane Katrina presented an extreme risk, widely forecasted to be the most powerful storm to endanger the region in decades. However, the threat posed by this storm was not evenly distributed across its projected path. Because most of the city of New Orleans lies below sea level, its residents faced a "double threat" of hurricane-force winds and rain coupled with severe and sustained flooding if the local system of pumps and levees failed, as events eventually exposed. Although not all New Orleanians fully appreciated this elevated risk at the time, many did. Assuming a positive correlation between risk perception and evacuation, we hypothesize that New Orleanians perceived a higher risk from the storm than others in the projected path and consequently were more likely to evacuate, all else being equal. Whether this correlation altered the calculus of decision making regarding "evacuation in unity" versus "evacuation by division" remains an empirical question.

As for stress, prior research indicates that one way in which disaster victims cope with postevent stress is by reinstituting familiar roles and routines (Prinstein et al. 1996). For many New Orleanians who experienced the worst-case scenario, such return to familiar roles and routines was, at best, difficult. Gill and Picou (1991) find that the distance someone lives from the epicenter of a technological disaster has a significant and positive effect on perceived risk. Accordingly, we expect that, on average, New Orleanians were likely to experience higher levels of stress than other residents of the affected region, as New Orleanians were more likely to have lost homes, jobs, family, and friends and were often unable to return to the city to view the damage inflicted. In contrast, residents of other areas, even those in the severely devastated parts of coastal Mississippi, were usually able to return to their communities, assess the damage, and reconnect with friends and neighbors in the aftermath of the storm. From this perspective, residence in New Orleans indicates not only higher perceived risk but also higher levels of stress associated with the realization of that risk.

R2—Roles and Responsibilities

The second set of factors in our framework highlights the social roles and responsibilities, or expectations, associated with parenthood, gender, and employment. Prior research finds that parents of dependent children are more likely to evacuate in the face of risk than those without children because they feel a heightened sense of responsibility not only for their own safety but also for that of their children (Johnson 1985). However, research also informs us that gender divides parenthood into distinct roles for mothers and fathers. In times of crisis, these roles may be subsumed by a general sense of parental responsibility so that mothers and fathers make the same decisions about when and how to evacuate. However, crises might also serve to amplify traditional gender roles, encouraging women and children to evacuate to safety, while men stay behind to secure property, assist others, and report to work if the threat fails to materialize. Enarson and Scanlon (1999) find that adults often fall back on these traditional gender roles during disasters and that women are more likely to prepare for disasters than men. Consequently, women, particularly mothers of young children, are more likely to evacuate, while men, including fathers of dependent children, are more likely to stay behind.

Along these same lines, we also expect employment to have an important but ambiguous influence on evacuation decision making. On the one hand, we know that the employee role brings with it financial resources and that these resources are important in times of evacuation because they help individuals and families cover the costs of fuel, lodging, and associated costs of dislocation. On the other hand, the role of employee can be tenuous, especially in service-sector jobs where employers often invest little in their workers and generally view them as expendable. In these cases, employment might serve as an anchor that keeps employees close to home for fear of being fired for missing work because of evacuation, especially if the (recurrent) threat does not fully materialize. From this perspective, we might expect individuals who are employed to be less likely to evacuate with their families than those who are not employed, all else being equal, thus increasing the likelihood of family separation during and after evacuation.

These same factors may also influence levels of postdisaster stress, as individuals become less able to manage their social responsibilities as parents, spouses, and/or breadwinners. In particular, parents are likely to feel more stress than individuals without children since they must protect and care for dependents in addition to themselves in a time of great uncertainty. Those in the labor force may also feel heightened stress as a result of lost opportunity, lower or no pay, and possible unemployment in the wake of disaster. Prior research, however, indicates that such stress may vary by gender since women experience more disaster-related unemployment and more demands to care for their family than men, both of which may increase the stress they experience (Enarson and Scanlon 1999). Relatedly, prior research also indicates that gender differentiates how people manage stress. Thoits (1987), for example, finds that women generally report more stress when exposed to uncontrollable stressors, such as a natural disaster, while men report more stress after exposure to controllable stressors. Furthermore, traditional patterns of women's greater emotional involvement and men's emotional detachment may influence their reports of stress (Kessler and McLeod 1984). Therefore, we expect that gender may override other basic roles and responsibilities associated with parenthood and employment when it comes to reports of postdisaster stress.

R3—Resources

In addition to risk, roles, and responsibilities, an individual's physical and financial resources are likely to influence the likelihood of evacuation because evacuation can be both exhausting and expensive. This consideration suggests that individuals with more resources, in terms of income and perhaps physical ability as measured crudely by age, may be more likely to evacuate than lower-income and less able counterparts (Drabek 1986; Elliott and Pais 2006; Johnson 1985). Furthermore, prior research indicates that lower-income individuals and those with less education typically report higher levels of risk perception (Pilisuk, Parks, and Hawkes 1987), which may result from a belief that their position in society does not afford them control over their lives, especially in times of disaster (Flynn, Slovic, and Mertz 1994).

Beyond affording opportunities to avoid disaster, resources can also become sources of concern before and after a disaster. Arata et al. (2000) found that resource loss accounts for nearly one-third of the variance in anxiety symptoms after disaster. Similarly, Freedy et al. (1994) found that those experiencing higher levels of resource loss during a 1991 earthquake also experienced mild to moderate elevations in psychological distress, controlling for other important predictors. Again, these findings underscore the possibility that although financial resources can facilitate particular evacuation strategies, they can also become a source of stress, especially for those with few but important physical assets to protect.

With these findings in mind, we hypothesize that elderly and less affluent residents are less likely to evacuate than their younger, wealthier counterparts, all else being equal. Similarly, those with more resources will be better able to realize their preference for staying together as a family unit and for minimizing the risk of separation. By utilizing their resources to stay together, we expect that individuals from wealthier families are also better able to reduce their vulnerability to stress and therefore report lower levels of it once the threat materializes.

R4—Race

As sociologists frequently explain, race is a social construct that can influence everything from an individual's sense of self to institutional processes of response (compare Molotch 2005). In the context of Hurricane Katrina, we expect that race operated through the dynamics of social networks to shape individual evacuation strategies (Hurlbert, Haines, and Beggs 2000) and that such networks tend to be homophilic, with network members sharing salient traits, particularly race (McPherson, Smith-Lovin, and Cook 2001).

Consequently, individual response to the threat posed by Hurricane Katrina is likely to have been influenced by the interpretation of warning information among those who were most similar to themselves, helping to explain some of the racial divide already observed in individual responses to the disaster (Elliott and Pais 2006). Furthermore, these racial differences are rooted in a lengthy regional history of oppression and inequality in the Gulf South (Elliott and Ionescu 2003). As Bullard (1983) finds, such oppression places racial minorities disproportionately close to environmental risks, thereby influencing not only levels of exposure but also the resources needed to process and adjust to such exposure. In this vein, prior research shows that even when white and black Miami-Dade residents lived in the same evacuation zone for Hurricane Andrew, blacks were less likely than whites to evacuate before the storm's landfall (Peacock, Morrow, and Gladwin 1997).

The underlying principle of homophily suggests that social networks are also stratified by class, and in New Orleans race and class are tightly entwined so that those with the fewest resources in their networks are also the least able to mobilize such resources to evacuate early and keep their families together

(Fussell 2005). Such race- and class-stratified social networks may also differentiate how individuals experience stress after a disaster. In the case of Hurricane Katrina, its disproportionate impact on the black community is likely to have increased both the individual and the collective stress of the event among African Americans in the region, similar to the cumulative stress documented by Erikson (1976) in his study of whites in the Appalachian town of Buffalo Creek, West Virginia, following the massive flood of 1972.

R5—Religion

Although prior research has spent a great deal of effort debunking the conceptualization of hurricanes, tornadoes, and floods as "acts of God" rather than as socially culpable events (for reviews, see Kreps 1984; Quarantelli and Dynes 1977; Steinberg 2006), less attention has been paid to how people's belief in God influences their response to such threats (Kroll-Smith and Couch 1987). We move beyond this "act of God" framework to hypothesize that residents expressing deep religious faith are less likely than others to evacuate because they are more ideologically inclined to leave their fates in God's hands (compare Turner, Nigg, and Paz 1986). A competing hypothesis, however, is that religious faith correlates strongly with church attendance and that church congregations serve as vital social networks that aid in the evacuation process, particularly evacuation in unison, as academics and public officials encouraged in the wake of Hurricane Ivan in 2004 (Laska 2004).

As for stress, we hypothesize that regardless of its correlation with early evacuation and/or family separation, strong religious faith is likely to support individual spirits in the wake of disaster, thus reducing stress and helping to put events in perspective. Next we describe the data used to assess this and prior hypotheses about evacuation timing, family separation, and the emotional toll of Hurricane Katrina.

DATA

Roughly one month after the storm, the Gallup Organization teamed with the American Red Cross to conduct a telephone survey of 1,510 randomly selected Hurricane Katrina survivors, ages 18 and older (Gallup Poll no. 2005-45). This sample was drawn from a database of over 460,000 Katrina survivors who sought sustenance, housing, health care, relocation assistance, and/or family reunification services from the American Red Cross as a result of the storm and subsequent flooding.

Gallup took several steps to ensure the representativeness of this sample. First, it conducted a pilot survey to determine the usefulness of the Red Cross lists for contacting survivors and for assessing the responsiveness of those contacted. Next, using results from this pilot survey, Gallup refined its survey administration in several ways. For sampled survivors lacking phone numbers, it conducted reverse number searches on the addresses provided. Interviewers sought updated contact information, including cell phone numbers, for those who could not be reached at their reported phone numbers. In addition, Gallup extended its field period to 10 days to include up to nine contact attempts (September 30 through October 9, 2005), increasing its final response rate to over 90 percent. On completion, no geographic or other weighting corrections were deemed necessary by the survey's primary investigators.

The resulting data set is the best available for our purposes, but it is not without potential bias when trying to generalize from the Red Cross population to the population of the entire affected region. For example, all else being equal, one might expect wealthier survivors to have been less likely to register with the Red Cross than poorer survivors given their greater personal resources and the stigma attached to receipt of charitable assistance among those who could afford to help themselves (Fothergill 2003). However, a couple of factors help to minimize this bias. First, survivors registered with the Red Cross not just for material assistance but also to alert friends and family of their safety and whereabouts during a time when regional telecommunications systems were crippled and intraregional phone calls were difficult. Second, many survivors registered with the Red Cross not to obtain help but to give it and in so doing were asked to register with the local chapter if they were from the affected region. (Each of the authors falls into one or more of these categories.) The end result is that some bias may be present in generalizing to the entire survivor population, but this bias is likely to be smaller and less systematic than might otherwise be expected.

To gauge this assumption empirically, we compared race, gender, age, home ownership, and income distributions for Gallup respondents from the city of New Orleans with data available for the city of New Orleans in the 2000 census. We chose this spatial comparison because it provided more reliable spatial boundaries and estimates than comparisons made across the entire affected region. Results (not shown) suggest that the Gallup survey oversampled women in the affected region by a rate of roughly 5 percent and oversampled blacks, non–senior citizens, and non–home owners by roughly 15 percent. Results also indicate that the average household income among respondents in the Gallup survey is approximately 14 percent lower than that recorded by the 2000 census. These comparisons suggest that minorities and less affluent residents were indeed more likely to be sampled by the Gallup survey than whites and more affluent residents. However, they also indicate that this bias is not extreme and that the sheer number and diversity of respondents in the Gallup survey is sufficient to estimate accurately basic social differences in human responses to the storm. The fact that we statistically control for many of these differences in our regression analyses further minimizes this bias, leaving us with reasonably conservative estimates for respective factors under investigation (compare Winship and Radbill 1994). Variable descriptions and the characteristics of the sample are reported in Table 4.1.

Table 4.1. Variables for Analysis, with Means and Standard Deviations (N = 1,510)

Variable	Description	Mean	Standard Deviation
Evacuation response	1. "Did you evacuate your house or apartment before Hurricane Katrina hit your local area, after it hit, or not at all?" 2. "Were you separated for at least a day from family members you had been living with?"		
Evacuate in unison	Evacuated before and experienced no separation	32.3	0.47
Evacuate by division	Evacuated before and experienced separation	35.1	0.48
Stay by division	Evacuated after (or not at all) and experienced separation	15.6	0.38
Stay in unison	Evacuated after (or not at all) and experienced no separation	17.0	0.36
Stress levels			
Current stress	As a result of Hurricane Katrina, to what extent are you *currently* experiencing each of the following: (a) trouble sleeping, (b) feelings of anxiety, and (c) feelings of depression? (Each coded 0 [none] to 4 [a great deal], summed, and divided by 3 to preserve original scale); n = 1,475	2.01	1.17
Short-term worry	How worried are you about what will happen to you in the next few months? (0 = not, 3 = very); n = 1,503	1.89	1.03
Long-term worry	How worried are you about what will happen to you in the next five years? (0 = not, 3 = very); n = 1,469	1.67	1.02
R1: Risk (residential location)			
City of New Orleans	New Orleans (Orleans Parish) resident	25.6	0.44
Other area	Resident elsewhere in the Katrina-affected Gulf Coast region	74.4	0.44

R2: Roles and responsibilities

Gender/parental status			
Mothers	Women with own children less than 18 years old	32.1	0.47
Childless females	Women without own children less than 18 years old	28.5	0.45
Fathers	Men with own children less than 18 years old	20.3	0.40
Childless males	Men without own children less than 18 years old	19.1	0.39
Employment status	"Did you have a job immediately before Hurricane Katrina hit?" (1 = yes; 0 = no)	68.0	0.49
R3: Resources			
Age (physical)			
Senior citizen	65+ years of age	8.6	0.28
Non-senior citizen	18–64 years of age	91.4	0.28
Household income (material)	Natural log of midpoints: <$10K, $10K–$19K, $20K–$29K, $30K–$39K, $40K–$49K, $50K–$74K, $75K–$99K, $100K+	10.1	0.84
R4: Race/ethnicity	Self-reported; one response only		
White		41.6	0.49
Black		52.4	0.50
Hispanic		4.3	0.20
Asian		1.7	0.02
R5: Religious faith	"What, if anything, has helped you to get through this difficult emotional time?" (1 = "prayer" or "faith/spirituality/Jesus/God"; 0 = other)	26.6	0.44

RESULTS

Evacuation Response

Descriptive statistics in Table 4.1 show that two-thirds of Red Cross respondents interviewed in the Gallup survey evacuated well in advance of the storm. Among those who did not, nearly half stated that they did not evacuate because they did not believe the storm would be as bad as it turned out to be. In fact, nonevacuees were five times more likely to cite this reason than a lack of money or transportation, and less than 5 percent cited a lack of proper warning for failure to evacuate. These findings counter the common claim that a lack of resources and access to transportation accounted for the relatively high rates of nonevacuation. While these factors may have influenced how individuals processed and presented their rationales for staying, it seems clear that prior experience reduced rather than amplified the perceived threat posed by Hurricane Katrina and that this dynamic played a key role in individuals' decisions to evacuate or not.

As for types of evacuation and nonevacuation, popular images and reporting from New Orleans and the Gulf Coast after the storm and subsequent levee failures reinforce the belief that those who stayed were more likely to experience family separation than those who evacuated. This perception was based on emergency response procedures that haphazardly divided kin in order to streamline rescue and relocation efforts after the disaster. Again, however, findings from the Gallup data challenge this simplistic interpretation. Descriptive statistics in Table 4.1 show that during the month following Hurricane Katrina's landfall, about half of all respondents reported being separated for at least one day from a family member with whom they were living before the storm. Moreover, this fraction is higher, not lower, among those who evacuated before the storm (52 percent compared with 48 percent among nonevacuees).

These patterns offer an important corrective to popular understanding of individual responses to the threat posed by Hurricane Katrina and, by extension, how residents of frequently threatened areas tend to respond to slow-onset threats. Next, we investigate the extent to which specific factors in our R-5 framework illuminate variation in these types of response using multinomial regression to predict each of the four types of response identified in Figure 4.1. For estimation purposes, the policymaker's ideal, evacuation in unison, serves as our reference, or comparison, category. Significant predictors of evacuation responses appear in Table 4.2 (full regression results appear in the appendices), and the low pseudo-R^2 statistic of 0.04 indicates that, overall, there were very modest differences explained by the R-5 framework because the majority evacuated before the storm. The results show which factors contributed to the differences that are observed in the survey results.

Table 4.2. Statistically Significant Predictors of Evacuation Strategies (p < .05)

	Compared with Evacuating in Unison	
Evacuated by Division	*Stayed by Division*	*Stayed in Unison*
Black (increases odds by 1.40)	Childless male (increases odds by 2.18)	*New Orleans resident (decreases odds by 4.44)*
Employed before hurricane (increases odds by 1.28)	Father (increases odds by 1.97)	Childless male (increases odds by 1.65)
	Religious faith (increases odds by 1.62)	Black (increases odds by 1.57)
	Employed before hurricane (increases odds by 1.56)	*Household income (decreases 22%)*
	Black (increases odds by 1.52)	
	Household income (decreases 58%)	

Note: Significant predictors are ranked in descending order of relative effect. Nonitalicized font references positive effects; italicized font references negative effects. Dichotomous variables are listed with odds ratio; continuous variables are listed with percentage increase or decrease. See Table A2 in the appendices for full results, including nonsignificant findings.

Beginning with our first factor, perceived risk, results indicate no significant difference in the evacuation behavior of New Orleanians and other residents in the affected region, with one exception. Although, statistically speaking, individuals from both areas were equally likely to spurn evacuation warnings and to keep families together, those who pursued this strategy outside the city limits were four times more likely to stay together after the storm hit than those inside the city limits (exp[1.49] = 4.44 times more likely, to be exact). Residents of the Gulf Coast who gambled and followed a strategy of "staying in unison" were able to keep their families together after the storm hit; those in New Orleans were not.

Turning to the factor of social roles and responsibilities, we find that gender exerted the strongest and most consistent influence on individual evacuation response. Consistent with prior research, we find that men in the region were about twice as likely as women to stay behind as other family members evacuated (fathers, exp[.68] = 1.97; other men, exp[.78] = 2.18, relative to mothers of dependent children). Moreover, results show that men, especially those without children, were also more likely to stay put with their entire family. These patterns suggest that, all else being equal, gender influences evacuation response more than parenthood and that this influence generally encourages men to stay in harm's way as women evacuate, particularly if dependent children are involved. This gendered difference is evident even after taking employment into account, which shows that those who were employed before the hurricane were significantly more likely to stay behind as other family members evacuated. Specifically, results show that employed odds of "staying by division" were exp[.45] = 1.56 times greater than those of the nonemployed, all else being equal. Elliott and Pais's (2006) finding that many evacuees lost their jobs after Hurricane Katrina suggests that this strategy was not entirely irrational or unfounded.

As for indicators of physical and material resources, our findings show no significant variation in evacuation response by age. However, financial resources do appear to have played a key role in such response. As popular accounts have suggested, we find that respondents from lower-income households were significantly more likely to stay behind to face the storm than respondents from higher-income households. Moreover, among those who did stay, lower-income respondents were more likely than higher-income respondents to become separated from family members. So not only were wealthier residents more likely to evacuate in unison, but they were also more likely to be able to keep their families together if they stayed.

These patterns are consistent with our hypothesis and suggest that although respondents do not typically cite a lack of money or transportation for failure to evacuate, financial resources do play an important role in determining who leaves and who does not and who becomes separated and who does not after staying to face the threat. In the case of Hurricane Katrina, anecdotal evidence suggests that income and wages may have played a particularly salient role in family-evacuation decisions because the storm hit at the end of the month, when many low-income families had depleted their monthly earnings and were waiting for new funds to arrive. The opportunity costs in lost wages from evacuation also distinguish those of working age from those beyond retirement age. Supplemental analyses (not shown) indicate that when employment status is excluded from the regression model, our indicator of age becomes statistically significant (at the .05 level) and negatively correlates with evacuation by division. This statistical shift implies that elderly residents were more likely to evacuate because they were less likely to be employed, freeing them from the worries and responsibilities of lost wages and employment.

Turning to the role of race, we find that after statistically controlling for the fact that blacks were more likely than whites to live in the city of New Orleans and to have lower incomes, evacuation responses still differed significantly between the two racial groups. To help illustrate these differences, Figure 4.2 presents the predicted probabilities of each type of evacuation response by racial/ethnic group, all else being equal (i.e., it statistically converts the coefficients in Table A1 in the appendices from log odds to percentages and displays them graphically). This graph shows that after controlling for all other variables in the model, whites were 27 percent more likely to evacuate in unison

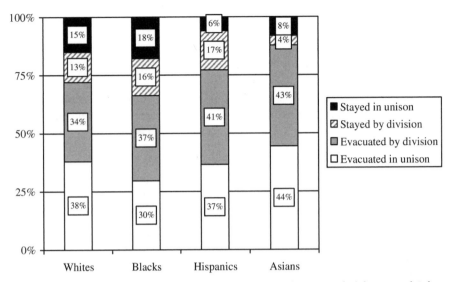

Figure 4.2. Predicted Probability of Evacuation Strategy by Race/Ethnicity, Net of Other Factors

Note: Regression estimation reported in Table A2; all variables are held at their sample means, except for those included in the graph.

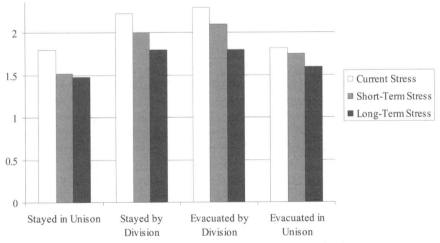

Figure 4.3. Predicted Stress Levels by Evacuation Strategy, Net of Other Factors

Note: Regression estimation reported in Table A2; all variables are held at their sample means, except for those included in the graph.

than blacks (0.38/0.30 = 1.27). By contrast, blacks were more likely than whites to engage in strategies involving family division and/or staying behind with all household members.

While we have no direct measures of social networks, we infer from prior research (Hurlbert, Haines, and Beggs 2000) that the race and class homogeneity of individuals' core social networks help to explain why blacks were less likely to evacuate in unison than whites and more likely to engage in one of the other evacuation strategies. Because blacks' networks were more likely to become strained by simultaneous demands placed on all core network members at once, we suspect that they were less able to gather the resources necessary to follow the safest strategy of evacuation in unison. In this way, we interpret race as a measure of the resources in the networks in which respondents were embedded as well as a measure of the groups' historical experience of discrimination and marginalization in the region.

Turning finally to religious faith, the Gallup survey asked respondents to name up to three things that helped them get through the difficult emotional time posed by Hurricane Katrina. Many respondents spoke about religious faith, social networks, and organizations. We find that those who listed prayer and faith in God among their primary sources of emotional support were also more likely to have stayed behind as other family members evacuated, even after controlling for other factors in our analytical framework, such as age, race, and residence. This finding suggests that faith was a critical influence in the decision to remain behind. Elliott and Pais (2006) use the same Gallup survey to show that such religious faith was particularly important in the interpretive schema of black residents in the region, a finding that contradicts Kroll-Smith and Couch's (1987) conclusion that disaster victims rarely frame disasters as acts of God.

To summarize, individuals least likely to follow the prescribed strategy of "evacuation in unison" before Hurricane Katrina's landfall were men, the employed, the low income, African Americans, and those expressing religious faith. An additive accounting of these factors presents a portrait not of welfare mothers or unemployed thugs, as popularly imagined, but rather of hardworking and religious black men who stayed behind to look after property and maintain employment in the face of a recurrent hurricane threat. In other words, those most likely to stay behind were those who formed the social core of the Gulf Coast region, not its margins, as popular media accounts often suggested.

Evacuation Response and Emotional Stress

Next we examine correlates of postdisaster stress using three indicators that tap respondents' current stress levels (at the time of the survey) as well as their self-reported prognoses for short- and long-term stress. Our indicator of current stress is a composite score derived from the following three-part question: "As a result of Hurricane Katrina, to what extent are you *currently* experiencing each of the following: (a) trouble sleeping, (b) feelings of anxiety, and (c) feelings of depression?" Answers to each part are scaled from 0 (none) to 4 (a great deal), summed, and divided by 3 to preserve the original range of 0 to 4, producing a multi-item indicator with a Cronbach's alpha of .79. Our indicator of "short-term stress" derives from the closed-ended question, "Now, looking ahead, how worried are you about what will happen to you in the next *few months*?" Similarly, our indicator of "long-term stress" derives from the question, "How worried are you about what will happen to you in the *next five years*?" Each of these two indicators is coded from 0 (not worried at all) to 3 (very worried) and analyzed separately to gain insight in the temporal nature of stress experienced by those affected by Hurricane Katrina. For the present study, we are particularly interested in whether the type of evacuation response employed by an individual correlates with feelings of personal stress following Hurricane Katrina. To examine this issue empirically, we estimated an ordinary least squares regression model for each of our three indicators of stress. Significant results appear in Table 4.3.

Table 4.3. Statistically Significant Predictors of Stress (p < .05)

Current Stress	Short-Term Stress	Long-Term Stress
Evacuated by division (increases odds by 1.57)	Asian (increases odds by 1.92)	Asian (increases odds by 1.58)
Childless male (decreases odds by 1.49)	Evacuated by division (increases odds by 1.71)	Stayed by division (increases odds by 1.43)
Stayed by division (increases odds by 1.48)	Stayed by division (increases odds by 1.57)	Evacuated by division (increases odds by 1.39)
New Orleans resident (increases odds by 1.43)	*Childless male (decreases odds by 1.37)*	*Childless male (decreases odds by 1.28)*
Father (decreases odds by 1.43)	Hispanic (increases odds by 1.37)	Black (increases odds by 1.25)
Black (increases odds by 1.17)	New Orleans resident (increases odds by 1.36)	*Father (decreases odds by 1.21)*
	Stayed in unison (increases odds by 1.27)	*Religious faith (decreases odds by 1.16)*
	Father (decreases odds by 1.24)	*Employed before hurricane (decreases odds by 1.14)*
	Black (increases odds by 1.24)	*Religious faith (decreases odds by 1.20)*

Note: Significant predictors are ranked in descending order of relative effect. Nonitalicized font references positive effects; italicized font references negative effects. See Table A2 in the appendices for full results, including nonsignificant findings.

At the time of the survey, a month after Hurricane Katrina made landfall, stress levels were high for everyone in the affected region, but there were important differences between New Orleanians and those from other parts of the Gulf Coast. At this time, all New Orleanians had been forcibly evacuated from their city, even if they had initially stayed and weathered the storm. Elsewhere in the affected region, many residents had returned home to live and/or to survey the damage and were already making plans for their future. Consequently, New Orleanians reported stress levels about a third of a point higher on the four point scale than those who lived outside the city (see Table A2 in the appendices). Furthermore, New Orleanians anticipated feeling significantly more stress in the coming months than those who had resided elsewhere in the region before the storm.

Whether this measure of anticipated stress is simply another indicator of current stress or an accurate predictor of future stress remains to be seen (see Kreps 1984). In the meantime, our findings are consistent with others who have pinpointed a need for long-term as well as immediate mental health assistance for New Orleanians and other Gulf Coast residents. Research is beginning to uncover the pervasive and protracted presence of depression, posttraumatic stress disorder, suicidal thoughts, and a number of other serious mental health concerns in the region (for a brief review, see Weisler, Barbee, and Townsend 2006). This development, coupled with a dearth of local mental health professionals after the disaster, undoubtedly constitutes one of the biggest problems currently facing the Gulf Coast and, in particular, New Orleans.

Remarkably, even after controlling statistically for geographic residence and other factors, individuals' evacuation response correlates significantly with expressed levels of stress one month after Hurricane Katrina hit. This relationship is evident in Figure 4.3, which shows the net effect of evacuation strategies on current stress levels after holding all other factors constant at their sample means. Those who became separated from family members, regardless of the circumstances, reported higher levels of stress than those who either stayed in unison or evacuated in unison. This pattern holds for both current stress levels and anticipated stress levels in the coming months and years. This result supports the work of Gill and Picou (1991), who find that after a 1982 train derailment in Louisiana, residents who experienced family separation harbored the greatest anxieties regarding the future prospects of their community and greater perception of future risks and in general were more negatively impacted by the event than those who maintained family unity.

One explanation for this long-term effect is that keeping the family together provides a sense of continuity and normalcy for individuals during traumatic events (Weine et al. 2004). However, this explanation contradicts respondent reports in the Gallup survey (not shown) that indicate that family separation was not one of the top three most stressful aspects of the storm. We reconcile this apparent contradiction by arguing that it was not family separation itself that caused higher reported stress but rather particular circumstances that may have led to the decision to separate or the circumstances that forced separation (e.g., needing to care for an elderly relative, dealing with special needs of family and friends, deciding whether to leave a flooding neighborhood, etc.).

Other factors in the R-5 framework also influenced levels of expressed stress following the storm. For example, racial minorities, including Asians and Hispanics, consistently expressed higher levels of stress about their short- and long-term prospects following the disaster than whites, even after controlling for residence in the city, household income, and other variables in the model. No doubt the history of discrimination in the South contributed to blacks' greater discomfort about being away from their homes and communities. In the case of Asians, many are Vietnamese refugees who settled in the region during the 1980s. Displacement caused by the storm may have rekindled concerns and emotions experienced in their initial dislocation from Vietnam and resettlement in the United States. Stress could also be particularly acute for members of this group because so many Vietnamese in the region lived in an ethnic enclave located on low-lying land in the eastern portion of metropolitan New Orleans, where flooding was severe and damage great (see Zhou and Bankston 1998). However, additional analysis (not shown) indicates that even after statistically controlling for whether respondents' housing was rendered unlivable by the disaster, Asians' anticipated stress remained consistently higher than other groups.

As expected, men reported less stress at the time of the survey and anticipated feeling less stress in the coming months and years than women. This pattern is consistent with prior research showing that men and women experience, manage, and report stress in very distinct ways. However, other roles and responsibilities—parenthood and employment—were not significantly related to differences in reported stress. Likewise, resources such as age and household income revealed no systematic variation in stress. Of the remaining factors, only religious faith influenced expressed levels of anticipated stress. Specifically, findings show that those who depended on religious faith to get them through the crisis anticipated lower levels of stress in the future, although their levels of stress at the time of the survey were no different than those who made no mention of faith as a key source of emotional support.

Together, these patterns indicate that although Gulf Coast residents confronted the same general threat, their experience of it differed substantially not only by race, residence, and religious faith but also by the type of evacuation strategy they employed. In the midst of the current mental health epidemic documented in New Orleans (Saulney 2006a), psychiatric professionals and caregivers may be wise to explore these issues with patients as they seek to provide them with a greater sense of control and improved ability to recover emotionally from the disaster.

CONCLUSION

This chapter has highlighted what Gulf Coast residents knew well before Hurricane Katrina became the costliest and arguably most shameful disaster in U.S. history: in the face of a "normal" hurricane threat, evacuation decisions are made with an exacting calculus that incorporates multiple concerns as well as the distinct possibility that no harm will come and that time, effort, and resources will be "wasted" in evacuation. As the path and strength of such a threat becomes clearer, residents adjust their decision making accordingly, but our analyses show that the outcome of the decision-making process varies systematically by risk, roles and responsibilities, resources, race, and religion. In the case of Hurricane Katrina, these sources of variation tended to leave working-class, black families most at risk for separation, with gender roles encouraging men to stay behind while others evacuated to safety.

We contribute to the study of disaster response by showing how evacuation strategies can and often do involve family separation and that such separation can itself become an important determinant of postdisaster stress. Our finding that widespread family separation occurred before as well as after Hurricane Katrina is surprising, especially given the literature's general assumption that family unity is prioritized during such events. This apparent contradiction opens fertile ground for future study. Specifically, more research is required to understand how families in natural disaster-prone areas plan for recurrent threats of disaster and how contextual factors influence these plans and subsequent coping strategies. On the basis of our results, we encourage future data collection efforts to include better measures of family and household membership and decision-making strategies as well as information on the timing and voluntary and involuntary nature of family separation. Our results may also assist officials responsible for preparing Gulf Coast residents for future weather-related disasters in targeting the populations most at risk of remaining behind. This effort might seek to alter these populations' decision-making processes in order to improve the chances of widespread, early, and orderly evacuation.

NOTE

Portions of this research received financial support from the National Science Foundation (award no. 0554818).

5

Race, Class, and Capital amidst the Hurricane Katrina Diaspora

John Barnshaw and Joseph Trainor

In the aftermath of Hurricane Katrina, the persistent inequities of urban life in New Orleans were laid bare for millions of Americans. As the levees were breached and the floodwaters rose in New Orleans, television images of thousands of citizens trapped outside the Louisiana Superdome and New Orleans Convention Center, without adequate food and water, caused many Americans to "rediscover" the urban underclass. Although the urban underclass is by no means a new phenomenon to social scientists, it has long been understudied, particularly within the disaster context. This project extends the insights of earlier works that locate the experiences of Hurricane Katrina evacuees within the larger context of sociostructural limitations and builds on previous research by Barnshaw (2006b) and Trainor, Donner, and Torres (2006), both of which demonstrated how the "choice" to evacuate was constrained by structured inequality and a lack of social resources. This work draws on Bourdieu's (1986) conception of social capital and focuses on how social capital, in the form of social networks, may or may not be converted into tangible resources for survivors in the aftermath of Hurricane Katrina.

LITERATURE REVIEW

Inequality and Disaster

Issues of structured inequality and stratification have long been understudied within the disaster context. This is largely due to the fact that beginning with the first studies conducted by the National Research Council and the National

Opinion Research Center in the early 1950s, inequality and stratification were not seen as particularly salient topics for disaster research (Quarantelli 2005). For many of the pioneers in disaster research, a disaster was seen as an event creating a disruption in the social structure (Endleman 1952; Fritz 1961). This conceptualization was heavily influenced by the need to understand civil defense and issues of population preparedness, particularly in relation to the threat of nuclear war. As a result, disaster was seen as a quasi-experimental context for understanding human behavior under extreme social disrupting events (Barton 1969; Dynes 1993; Hewitt 1983; Kreps 1984; Mileti 1999; Quarantelli 1982a, 1982b, 1985, 1987, 1995). This approach was informed by the functionalist perspective and sensitized researchers to focus on issues such as community organization, response, disruption, and resumption of services (Tierney, Lindell, and Perry 2001). Thus, for the majority of the past half century, disaster research has understood "disaster" as an aberrant event generating significant disruption for agents, organizations, and social structures. This model assumes that the "nature of disaster" is an event that surpasses an entity's capability to respond for a period of time that results in systemic disruption followed by a return to routine or "normalcy" (Stallings 1998) (see Figure 5.1).

A significant limitation with conceptualizing disaster in terms of disruption and return to normalcy is that it does not recognize the stratified nature of social structures and society, which leads to false perceptions regarding the manner in which divergent groups (both between and within any selected community) differentially experience the same environmental hazards. In the following section, we briefly discuss several of the corrective perspectives that have attempted to recontextualize disaster in terms of social stratification and inequality.

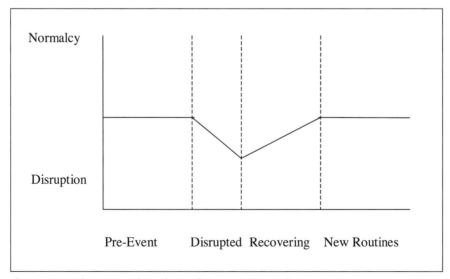

Figure 5.1.   Disaster as Disruption and Return to Normalcy

Most of the disaster research on inequality and stratification has focused on issues of vulnerability, or "the characteristics of a person or group and their situation that influence their capacity to anticipate, cope with, resist and recover from the impact of an extreme event or process" (Wisner et al. 2004, 11). In perhaps the first identification of vulnerability by stratification, Bates and colleagues (1963) found that working-class individuals in Hurricane Audrey suffered disproportionately greater loss than those of the middle or upper class in disasters. These findings were supported in subsequent disasters and extended to include stratification along racial, ethnic, political power, and gender lines and to illustrate how disaster exacerbates preexisting inequality (Barnshaw 2005; Bolin and Bolton 1986; Cochrane 1975; Killian, Peacock, and Bates 1983; Oliver-Smith 1986, 1989; Peacock and Bates 1982).

In reviewing the disaster inequality literature, it is important to recognize that although issues of stratification and inequality have been raised within the disaster context, it has been only within the past decade that these issues have been treated more systematically with a greater focus on understanding the impact of disaster events on the larger ecological and social structures (Peacock, Morrow, and Gladwin 1997). Similarly, Wisner and colleagues (2004) have argued that disaster is a product of social, political, and economic environments that are distinct from the natural environment. More recently, Klinenberg (2002) used a social autopsy approach in order to illustrate how a disproportionate number of heat wave victims were elderly working-class African Americans. In essence, demonstrating how Chicago's social structure created a stratified distribution of victims along race, class, gender, and age lines.

These many insights developed by the inequality and disaster approach are particularly noteworthy for the implications they have on how disparate groups experience disaster. Although all the elements of the construct have not been sufficiently tested to make claims as to their generalizability, the figure provides a useful heuristic for understanding how inequality may be exacerbated or ameliorated throughout the disaster cycle. For example, Figure 5.2 illustrates the potential variability of inequality within the disaster context. Previous inequality is illustrated as the relative change from baselines (line a) to the disruption brought about by disaster (line c), which becomes increasingly varied across time in recovery and the long-term period following the disaster. Throughout the model, variation in equality is exacerbated through access to differential resources, which is illustrated by the breaks in both horizontal length and vertical distance between the initiation of disruption (line b) and the start of recovery (line d). Finally, we also see the existence of a disparity in the net inequality or a permanent change in the relative position of the two groups (distance from line a to line a relative to the new distance from line e to line e).

Central to this model is the notion that at each stage there is the potential for inequality along financial, social, cultural, and educational lines that must be explored and understood. Although prior research has highlighted aspects of financial, social, cultural, and educational disparity, this work offers a model for explaining how each of these ameliorate or exacerbate social inequity for

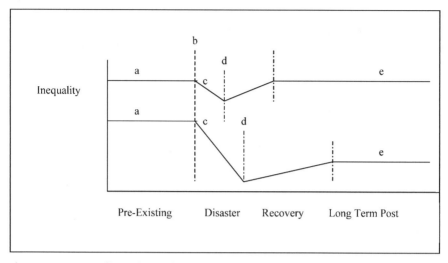

Figure 5.2.   Inequality and Disaster

individuals, social structures, and society following disaster (Bourdieu 1986). Although several previous scholars have attempted to link stratification with issues related to the forms of social capital and their social network expressions, few have attempted to contextualize this within an inequality framework (compare Barnshaw 2006a; Klinenburg 2002; Peacock, Morrow, and Gladwin 1997; Pelling 2003).

Social Capital as an Expression of Inequality

Social Capital

Social capital was initially conceptualized by Hanifan (1920) to describe tangible assets among individuals and families that make up a social unit. In the many studies since, however, the concept has come to mean a number of things, ranging from trust in individuals to structured relationships (Aldridge, Halpern, and Fitzpatrick 2002). Despite various applications, the concept did not matriculate into popular usage until Coleman, Kate, and Menzel (1966) used it to describe the types of relations that exist between individuals within both families and communities and demonstrated how these relations exert influence on life course outcomes. Following Coleman, Granovetter (1973, 1974) extended the idea that social connectivity could be influential by empirically demonstrating how social relations, or social capital, resulted in individuals receiving jobs.

Bourdieu (1986) expanded previous conceptualizations of social capital to include both collective resources and the networks that facilitate their shared use by arguing that the convertibility of social capital provides a mechanism for asset allocation for those in advanced social positions that frequently reproduces agents' positions in society as well as social structures. Thus, it is in this tradition that we adopt his definition of social capital as "the aggregate of actual or potential resources which are linked to possession of a durable network of more or less institutionalized relationships of mutual acquaintance and recognition" (248). This conceptualization is central to our approach as we explore how the amount of social capital a person can potentially possess is determined not only by the total economic capital but also through other forms of capital linked to a person through networks of association. Bourdieu's explicit recognition of the difference between using already owned (actual/personally possessed) capital (e.g., spending money from savings) and the analytically distinct process of converting social capital into other forms of capital (e.g., using relationships to get money from a friend) provides for the novelty of our approach. Through an examination of how social capital conversion/transformation into other forms of capital did and did not occur, we hope to gain a better understanding of how the social networks reinforce or reproduce power relations (Freedy et al. 1994; Hobfoll 1989).

Disaster and Social Capital

As social capital theorizing and research proliferated through the latter part of the twentieth century, its influence began to extend to disaster studies, as evidenced by Bolin's (1985) work, which used a quasi-social capital framework to identify the importance of social support in disasters, and Dynes (2002), who highlighted the importance of social capital in disaster response organizations. Similarly, Hurlbert, Beggs, and Haines (2001) demonstrated how social capital functioned in the aftermath of Hurricane Andrew. At the same time, a social-psychological line of research also emerged emphasizing the influence of social capital as a tool for resource acquisition in a manner similar to that posited by Bourdieu (1986). This approach labeled the conservation of resources model (Hobfoll 1989) and focused on material and nonmaterial resources as a source of distress and/or tool for coping during stress situations such as disasters. Although subsequent applications have focused more intently on resource loss (Freedy et al. 1994), the original articulation also made strong suggestions regarding the importance of family connections or "social support" as conduits for coping during disasters.

Disaster and a Lack of Capital Conversion

While each of the previously mentioned approaches has served to better conceptualize our understanding of social capital in disasters, these works have often focused more on individual and community resources as social objects rather than discuss their importance during disasters. In contrast, we focus on the process of social capital conversion/transformation into resources. This does not diminish the importance of previous scholarship but highlights the form and operation of the networks within which resources are embedded.

By focusing on social capital from a network and inequality perspective, as we follow the work of Ritchie (2004), who investigated the Cordova community following the *Exxon Valdez* oil spill. Ritchie examined actors' abilities to utilize resources within their social network and the manner in which agents were restricted access to social capital. By focusing on this analytical element, we see the practical utility of social networks in a given context and whether agents are able to utilize their social networks for garnering resources necessary before, during, and after a disaster. The major contribution of integrating an inequality approach into this line of research is that rather than looking at the presence or absence of resources, we attempt to better understand how different types of networks are amenable or resistant to transformation into tangible benefits during a disaster. Thus, our focus is on an agents' ability to "cash in" or transform resting potential, or social network of loose associations, into beneficial resource allocation following a disaster. Therefore, we aim to better understand how preexisting networks in the Katrina catastrophe created situations that inhibited the transformation of social capital into tangible resources, thus rendering their accumulated social capital either situationally useless or detrimental.

As suggested previously, social capital offers a powerful theoretical lens for understanding the social processes of stratification at work for individuals in disaster. Specifically, this research contributes to the developing literature on inequality by reconceptualizing disaster within a structured inequality framework and in so doing seeks to incorporate the larger sociological literature of network and social capital theories in order to better understand the manner in which the networks that link individual agents prevented or facilitated the activation of social capital in evacuation from Katrina. We suggest that the characteristics of these structures of association, as discussed by respondents in interviews, provide evidence to the manner in which networks provide an additional socially relevant location where disaster exacerbates preexisting inequality structures. We now turn to whether the transformation of social capital into other forms of capital was facilitated or prevented by the evacuees' networks.

METHODS

This exploratory research focuses on the transformation of social capital found in networks of association into other forms of capital for use during evacuation from New Orleans before, during, and after the hurricane. Despite a history of fruitful use of case studies in the disaster field, it is important to recognize the methodological benefits and limitations. Previous research by Yin (2003) has highlighted three major limitations of case study methods: a tendency to focus only on findings that support hypotheses, a lack of generalizability, and a potential for idiosyncratic findings. However, many of these issues can be overcome through proper design and analytic rigor. Proponents often suggest that most critiques of case study work in fact are due to failures of the analyst rather than the method (Yin 2003). Despite the contention that critics have overstated the limits of case studies, we attempt to mitigate the potential impacts.

DATA

In order to increase construct validity, we triangulate sources of evidence including quantitative data collected by the Kaiser Family Foundation (2005; Brodie et al. 2006) and qualitative evidence collected at multiple sites along the Gulf Coast region. While our data collection protocol was not specifically designed for network attributes, the exploratory nature of quick-response work allowed us to capture many instances where respondents discuss social networks in action. Most of these instances emerged where participants responded to questions of impediments, facilitators, and processes involved in the decision to evacuate or not to evacuate from Katrina. In addition, we have attempted to supplement wherever possible with official documents and reports, as well as media reports, to reflect additional challenges faced by Katrina survivors.

Qualitative Data

The authors were part of a team of eight researchers who, with funds provided through the Quick Response Grant from the Natural Hazards Research and Applications Information Center at the University of Colorado and the University of Delaware Disaster Research Center, conducted 79 recorded interviews and a number of informal interviews with evacuees in Texas, Louisiana, and Mississippi from September 15, 2005, to September 30, 2005. These interviews were conducted in a variety of locations, including Reliant Park in Houston, a number of smaller shelters in Louisiana and Mississippi, "on location" at the site of damaged homes, and at a hotel operating as a shelter. The focus of these interviews was broad, ranging from explorations of pro- and antisocial behavior, organizational responses, evacuation decision making, return decision making, and a number of other substantive concerns. Because of the preliminary nature of this research, analyses of these data also utilize many of the qualitative methodological techniques found in previous disaster research for assessing the influence of network characteristics (Phillips 2002; Stallings 2002; Wasserman and Faust 1994). Our total sample is disproportionately biased toward low-income African Americans. As such, this demographic breakdown limits but does not fully constrain the degree to which we are able to meaningfully discuss other groups. However, we recognize that this effort should most appropriately be interpreted as a study of the experiences of the working and underclass. Wherever possible, we use the interviews with middle- and upper-class respondents as illustrative of potential sources of patterns and variation; because of the limited number of respondents, these should not be interpreted as generalizable but rather as starting points for future, more systematic work.

Quantitative Data

As a supplement to the qualitative research conducted in the Gulf Coast area, this chapter also draws on additional quantitative research conducted among Hurricane Katrina evacuees under the direction of Robert Blendon at the Harvard University School of Public Health during September 10–12, 2005 (Brodie et al. 2006; Kaiser Family Foundation 2005). The quantitative research component involved a survey conducted by 28 research professionals and consisted of a random sample of 680 Hurricane Katrina evacuees. Detailed methodology from these data may be found in previous research and need not be explored further in this research (Barnshaw 2006b; Brodie et al. 2006).

ANALYTIC APPROACH

Our analytic approach to these data was designed in a manner to strengthen our validity and, where appropriate, to draw conclusions in instances where our findings replicate or vary from those of previous works. Content analysis of notes and interviews was carried out using ATLAS Ti, a computer software program for textual analysis. This program was used in order to identify discussion of respondents' evacuation activities where preexisting networks were mentioned. Special attention was paid to constant comparison both between and within respondents' discussions in search of patterns and variations. Specifically, we focused on the verification or rejection of theoretical suggestions, particularly in ways that could be compared across and between survivors' responses and the quantitative data. Most important, our focus was on explanation building and the identification of alternative explanations for posited phenomena.

ANALYSIS

Case Study Background

On Saturday, August 27, 2005, Max Mayfield, director of the National Hurricane Center, contacted Louisiana Governor Kathleen Blanco and New Orleans Mayor Ray Nagin to express his extreme concern about the imminent threat posed by the rapidly intensifying category 3 Hurricane Katrina (Lush 2005). In response, Mayor Nagin called for a voluntary evacuation of New Orleans and later, on August 28, ordered the first mandatory evacuation in the history of the city of New Orleans (Dunne 2005; Russell 2005; Schleifstein 2005). Subsequently, many of the presidents of the surrounding Plauqemines, Saint Bernard, Saint Charles, Lafourche, Terrebonne, and Jefferson parishes urged residents to evacuate (Nolan 2005). Of the more than 460,000 residents of New Orleans, it was estimated that between 100,000 and 120,000 residents were unable to evacuate before Hurricane Katrina because they did not have access to personal transportation (Laska 2004; Renne 2005; U.S. Bureau of the Census 2005b).

Demographically, New Orleans is a city that is approximately 67 percent African American, 28 percent white, 3 percent Latino, and 2 percent Asian (U.S. Bureau of the Census 2000a). Although approximately 46 percent of citizens in New Orleans owned their own home at the time of Hurricane Katrina, there are considerable levels of concentrated poverty within the city (U.S. Bureau of the Census 2000a, 2005a). The median household income for New Orleans was $27,133, and over 27 percent of New Orleans lived below the poverty line (U.S. Bureau of the Census 2005a). In addition, since New Orleans is feminized (53 percent female), this poverty also tends to be among the elderly, as nearly 12 percent of the population of New Orleans is age 65 and older (U.S. Bureau of the Census 2005a).

As Hurricane Katrina escalated to a category 5 storm on August 28, authorities established the Louisiana Superdome as the "refuge of last resort" for residents unable to evacuate New Orleans (Nigg, Barnshaw, and Torres 2006; Russell 2005). According to the State of Louisiana Emergency Operations Plan, a last resort refuge is

> a place for persons to be protected from the high winds and heavy rains from the storm. Unlike a shelter, there may be little or no water or food and possibly no utilities. A last resort refuge is intended to provide best available survival protection for the duration of the hurricane only. (Office of Emergency Preparedness 2005, 29)

Although the Superdome was considered a refuge of last resort, the Louisiana National Guard delivered three truckloads of meals ready to eat, enough to supply 15,000 people for three days (Russell 2005). For several hours on August 28, New Orleans buses were deployed to assist in transporting residents to the Superdome. However, despite the Emergency Operations Plan calling for New Orleans to utilize several hundred school buses, they were not deployed because the city was unable to find drivers (DeBose 2005). By the time Hurricane Katrina made landfall on August 29, an estimated 9,000 residents sought refuge in the Superdome, while an additional 3,000 people were housed in 45 shelters opened by the American Red Cross (Russell 2005).

At the time, although conditions in the Superdome were less than optimal, it appeared that the Superdome served as an adequate shelter of refuge, as there were no injuries or fatalities directly resulting from Hurricane Katrina in the Superdome. However, on August 30, the Seventeenth Street Canal was breached, resulting in significant flooding and the relocation of approximately 18,000 residents to the Superdome and approximately 20,000 evacuees to the New Orleans Convention Center, which was not a refuge of last resort but served as a reception center for displaced residents (Nigg, Barnshaw, and Torres 2006; Russell 2005). As conditions deteriorated inside the Superdome and the New Orleans Convention Center and the numbers of evacuees conditioned to swell to 46,000 between the two sites, Governor Blanco ordered the entire city of New Orleans to be evacuated on August 31. Although there were widespread media reports of the deteriorating conditions at both the Convention Center and the Superdome, both Director Michael Brown of the Federal Emergency Management Agency (FEMA) and Secretary Michael Chertoff of the Department of Homeland Security claimed to have no knowledge of the center as being used as a shelter until September 1 (O'Brien 2005).

As the orders to evacuate the Superdome and Convention Center were being given, it was announced that the Reliant Astrodome in Houston, Texas, would serve as a site for evacuees from New Orleans (Harris County Joint Information Center 2005c). By September 1, this news prompted a convergence at the Superdome, where between 30,000 and 60,000 people gathered, believing this to be the best place for evacuation from New Orleans (O'Brien 2005). Later that day, the first busload of evacuees arrived at the Astrodome in a school bus commandeered by a private citizen (Bryant and Garza 2005). Although the complete evacuation of New Orleans was expected to last only two days, the evacuation took longer than anticipated because of damaged infrastructure and overwhelming throngs, all seeking exodus from the chaotic scene. By September 2, officials stated that the Reliant Astrodome was holding approximately 15,000 evacuees, while Reliant Arena was holding an additional 3,000, and the Reliant Center would be opened, which was capable of housing up to 11,000 evacuees (Harris County Joint Information Center 2005a). Reliant Park is a sprawling four site property located in downtown Houston consisting of Reliant Stadium, which was not used for evacuees; the Reliant Astrodome, Reliant Arena, and Reliant Center, each of which became large shelters; the George R. Brown Convention Center, located approximately six miles from Reliant Park. Although comprehensive statistics prior to this period are piecemeal, Table 5.1 indicates the frequency of Hurricane Katrina evacuees at the four mass shelters (Reliant Astrodome, Reliant Arena, Reliant Center, and George R. Brown Convention Center) from September 4, when official statistics were taken, to the close of the shelters at 7:00 P.M. local time on September 20 before Hurricane Rita (Harris County Joint Information Center 2005c). At its peak on September 4, 2005, the four sites (Astrodome, Reliant

Table 5.1. Frequency of Hurricane Katrina Evacuees at Houston Mass Shelters

8:00 A.M.	Number of Citizens				
	Dome	*Arena*	*Center*	*GRB*	*Total*
September 4	17,500	4,500	2,300	2,800	27,100
September 5	17,500	2,300	3,800	1,300	24,900
September 6	4,000	2,300	3,800	1,300	11,400
September 7	2,930	1,800	2,000	1,366	8,096
September 8	2,500	200	4,488	1,422	8,610
September 9	2,243	88	4,633	1,659	8,623
September 10	1,950	14	4,025	1,291	7,327
September 11	1,450	14	2,723	1,076	5,263
September 12	1,417	14	2,166	1,083	4,680
September 13	1,409	0	2,351	1,063	4,823
September 14	1,068	0	2,021	1,069	4,158
September 15	779	319	1,577	928	3,600
September 16	0	890	1,477	816	3,183
September 17	0	1,655	0	482	2,137
September 18	0	1,449	0	362	1,811
September 19	0	1,285	0	307	1,592
September 20	0	976	0	147	1,123
September 21 ·	0	0	0	0	0

Source: Houston Joint Information Center (2005).

Arena, Reliant Center, and George R. Brown Convention Center) sheltered approximately 27,100 Hurricane Katrina evacuees.

Although Houston took in many evacuees, it was by no means the only host community. Within two weeks after Hurricane Katrina, 25 states were involved in the provision of sheltering for evacuees, and by September 30, evacuees were registered in every state and almost half the ZIP codes in the United States. Three-quarters of evacuees were staying within 250 miles, but tens of thousands were more than 1,000 miles away from New Orleans. By the end of 2006, just over one year later, 46 of the 50 United States were declared federal emergency areas (Federal Emergency Management Agency 2006)

FINDINGS

Personal Economic Resources as Capital

In looking at the individual resources portion of social capital, it is important to note the contrast between the vast majority of informants in our qualitative and quantitative samples from the underclass and the limited number of more affluent informants we interviewed. While more affluent respondents were no doubt experiencing a great deal of personal loss, in some ways their surplus wealth provided a buffer to the long-term impacts of the storm. For example, one gentleman we interviewed on the site of his completely destroyed waterfront property less than a month after the storm's impact was in many ways moving along the road to normalcy. He had been able to use savings to secure a new apartment, was collecting new material possessions, and had begun the healing process. Several middle-class informants stayed in hotels, and although they had lost all or most of their possessions, they were housed in rooms and could cook their own meals, clean rooms, and create new routines (Stallings 1998). In sharp contrast, many evacuees in mass shelters had little more than the clothes on their back and little or no privacy and had severely disrupted lives and few prospects for reacquiring their near complete loss of material possessions.

The level of economic resources cannot be overstated as significantly influencing how evacuation from the impacted area was experienced. Frequently, individuals with greater resources in the from of economic capital were able to locate a place to stay and could move on to the other tasks that were competing for the time and attention of less affluent "underclass" evacuees who were most often found in the shelters. Locating a place to stay outside the impacted area is illustrative of transformation or convertible capital as having economic resource for transportation, having human capital in the form of prior knowledge of a place to stay outside the impacted area, or social capital in being able to stay with a friend or colleague and dramatically influenced the time required for attempts to recover or the establishment of new routines.

Network Capital

Many evacuees reported fragmented or spatially concentrated social networks. A fragmented social network is a series of loosely connected linkages that may not produce actual benefits (Burt 1992). Recall from the earlier discussion that this research is concerned only with active potential as it manifests itself as social capital rather than resting potential.

For instance, suppose a working-class resident of New Orleans rented five different properties over five years and was acquainted with five separate home owners. However, since none of the property owners had known the tenant for very long, it is unlikely that any of them would prove to be a source for the resident to evacuate with. It is somewhat more plausible that if the resident had rented from only one property owner for five years, this network, though smaller, might provide a greater likelihood for activation of social capital for contacting the person to assist the renter in evacuation from New Orleans. A related feature of social networks is spatial concentration within social networks. Spatial concentration, or network density, refers to the linkages between ties within a given space or time (McPherson 1982; Wasserman and Faust 1994). Spatial concentration may be significant in the transfer of social capital, particularly within a disaster context, as geography may influence access to resources.

A 53-year-old working-class white woman stated that despite her five children and extended family all living in the impacted area of Louisiana, she was not able to access her network of family to assist her in evacuating or procuring resources in Houston:

> I was at my sister Anna's house in Louisiana. Unfortunately, I was dropped off prior to that [Hurricane Katrina making landfall] at Salvation Army on South Claiborne right around Methodist Hospital, in that area. . . . I was really upset about that. My kids left me behind, my five kids, they left me behind . . . you know, I thought, you know, people were supposed to pull together when things of this nature and this tragedy and this catastrophe happen.

Many of the evacuees interviewed in Houston were working-class elderly with few friends and represented a fragmented social network. As a consequence, these agents could not rely on others for assistance in the evacuation process or in the securing of provisional resources. Where a family may be able to send one member to wait in line for federal assistance, another member to fill out a change-of-address form from the post office, and another member to the store for supplies, individuals were often forced to navigate a new and emerging social structure alone or make choices as to which resource was most important to secure that day.

One working-class African American evacuee, separated from his entire family in Houston after two weeks, discussed the challenges of navigating everyday life with nothing:

> I'm between a rock and a hard place. . . . I have nothing. Nothing but the few clothes they gave me and that's it. . . . At that time that's all we had 'cause we didn't have any place to wash our clothes. So I washed what I had in the shower. . . . Then I had to take care of all my business [obtaining an identification card, change-of-address forms, and FEMA and Red Cross debit cards] and I couldn't get nothing done. There was no way. And it feels like I don't even exist.

The notion of social fragmentation is supported by the survey that found that 92 percent of evacuees were attempting to find housing or a place to live rather than at the shelters in Houston (Kaiser Family Foundation 2005). In addition, evacuees were also attempting to find (in order of importance) other family or friends, a job, schooling for children, and medical care (Kaiser Family Foundation 2005).

Many also reported being a part of a spatially concentrated social network. Several interviewees were members of large families, sometimes of 20 or more, all of whom lived in New Orleans and Orleans Parish; as a result, all were affected by Hurricane Katrina.

For some, the evacuation of Katrina marked the first time they left the state of Louisiana because they did not have financial resources to travel and had no relatives outside the state. This spatial density of social networks for these evacuees is illustrative of the difficulty of activating social networks even among large social and family groups even if the networks are spatially concentrated in the impacted area. Additional support for this is found in the survey, as 79 percent of evacuees reported that they did not have a friend or family member they were able to move in with until they got back on their feet. Conversely, individuals with extended social networks were able to utilize extended friends, family, and colleagues to stay in hotels, homes, or apartments in areas not impacted by Hurricane Katrina or Hurricane Rita. Thus, through their social networks, agents were able to convert their social capital into providing resources during the inoperability or destruction of their residence in New Orleans.

CONCLUSIONS

This chapter has attempted to place the events surrounding Hurricane Katrina within a stratification context and illustrate the effects that context has on the availability of social capital. After careful review of the existing disaster literature, this chapter has argued that in contrast to most previous disaster studies, which treat disaster as an aberrant occasion resulting in the disruption of the social system, disaster may exacerbate preexisting inequalities and disparity. Indeed, in order to avoid theories of middle range, it may be more substantive to conceptualize disaster within a stratification context than to conceptualize disasters as nonroutine events (Kreps and Drabek 1996; Stallings 1998). This issue is one not of semantics but of substantive importance. Thus, by highlighting issues of stratification within the disaster context, one explores preexisting stratification; how disaster may ameliorate or, as this chapter has argued, exacerbate inequality; and then how the disaster event may compound inequality and social network disparities over time.

In contrast to previous disaster research, we have attempted to apply theoretical application to substantive findings. Specifically, this study utilized the broad sociological theoretical literature on social networks, a component of social capital. We suggest that social networks have both resting and active potential, but the potential to activate such a social resource may be the most beneficial form within the disaster context. Thus, although an agent may have a large but fragmented network or a large but spatially concentrated network, the transfer of social resources may not occur as a result of the disaster context. Future disaster research should take into account social resources as social capital, particularly within the stratification context, and attempt to explain variation attributable to fragmentation and variation attributable to spatial concentration (Hobfoll 1989).

In addition, this research utilized triangulation in an attempt to provide a fuller understanding of the processes of disaster within the stratification and inequality context. By locating in-depth interviews within the larger, more representative survey of interviews, this research has attempted to show how both methods used together can provide a fuller understanding of the complex social processes resulting from Hurricane Katrina. Triangulation is an underutilized research method in the social sciences, particularly in disaster research. Although some of this may be explained by the cost-prohibitive nature of this research, it is possible that perhaps fewer, more rigorous methodological studies may provide more substantive results than many small qualitative investigations or a few poorly executed quantitative investigations. Although broad in scope, this research has touched on many issues and attempted to break ground in new substantive areas in the hope that future research will continue to explore how capital is transformed following disaster and how inequality is exacerbated so that remedies may be sought to ameliorate compounding inequality brought about by disaster.

NOTE

Please direct all correspondence to John Barnshaw, Projects Coordinator, Disaster Research Center, University of Delaware (87 East Main Street, Newark, DE 19716). This research is supported by a Quick Response Grant from the Natural Hazards Research and Applications Information Center at the University of Colorado and Institutional Funding from the University of Delaware Disaster Research Center. The authors wish to thank Havidán Rodríguez, Joanne Nigg, and Tricia Wachtendorf for their helpful comments and Lauren Ross for her transcription and editing assistance.

6

Understanding Community-Based Disaster Response: Houston's Religious Congregations and Hurricane Katrina Relief Efforts

Emily Holcombe

In the days after Hurricane Katrina hit Louisiana, Mississippi, and Alabama in August 2005, evacuated residents of the Gulf Coast arrived in cities all over the country. In fact, over 1 million people were displaced by the storm (Harden and Vedantam 2005), turning a disaster that struck one region into a crisis that affected the entire country. Houston took in over 150,000 evacuees, more than any other U.S. city (Campo-Flores 2006), and became responsible for providing shelter, money, and other forms of assistance. Houston's response will help determine how the displaced communities recover in the months and years to come.

Hurricane Katrina tested the ability of agencies and individuals in Houston to respond to a major social crisis. Money, supplies, and manpower were strained as a host of different organizations worked to provide aid. Attention has focused mainly on the large-scale efforts; however, the grassroots efforts in Houston and the other cities absorbing evacuees garnered less publicity. While community organizations are not typically equipped to provide the same large-scale relief as the government and large charities, their relief efforts after Hurricane Katrina were essential to the overall response. I focus on the religious community in Houston because congregations throughout the area were important participants in the relief efforts. Relief workers have estimated that religious groups provided shelter to 500,000 people throughout the region, including those housed in 500 to 600 Houston churches (Cooperman and Williamson 2005).

This study looks specifically at the response of Houston's congregations to the evacuees of Hurricane Katrina. Through interviews with leaders in these religious institutions, I detail the experiences religious congregations had while working with the evacuees, volunteers, and outside relief agencies. This study focuses on one important research question: how did congregations respond to evacuees in the few months following the storm? I examine the types of relief activities and how efforts were organized in each congregation. I address this research question within a framework of new institutionalism and therefore examine the norms and means of legitimating that emerged within the congregations during disaster response efforts and their connections with the community that indicate their place within an open system.

Beyond the importance of relief efforts for those who individually benefited, this study is sociologically important because it addresses how organizations, specifically community-based religious organizations, respond in a crisis. It tests theories of disaster response and adds a new element to existing research on faith-based service provision. Many of these topics remain understudied despite their importance in planning for future disasters, and this research seeks to fill the gaps and connect these seemingly separate research areas.

BACKGROUND AND SIGNIFICANCE

Social Disaster

Social disaster theory focuses on both the event and the social consequences that follow a disaster. A disaster can have a devastating impact on a community by disrupting normal social functions and altering social relationships (Erikson 1994; Fischer 1998; Quarantelli 1978). While all disasters by definition destroy communities, Hurricane Katrina's destruction was especially terrible. Not only were people killed and houses destroyed, but the storm ruined entire neighborhoods and scattered members of these neighborhoods across the country; essentially, the storm wiped out communities and left their structures depleted and inhabitants dispersed across the country. This natural disaster became a catalyst for a much larger social disaster, one that separated and displaced communities; it also opened new avenues for the provision of material resources and social support.

In the context of a sudden break from normal social relationships, the organized response to disaster becomes an important way to re-create social integration. Kreps (1978) argues that we can look at organized response to disaster in one of two ways: either as a collection of isolated responses by separate organizations or as an entire community-wide response where groups form a network of coordinated response. The disaster literature addresses response to disaster in both ways, focusing on the individual organizations that respond to the needs of those affected by disaster as well as the community-wide coalescence that forms.

Organizations responding to disasters vary in the types of services they are able to and choose to provide. Religious congregations are examples of community-relevant organizations, as their purpose is not disaster response and they may not have large amounts of resources dedicated to emergency response but do have close ties with the local community (Dynes 1970). While there are advantages to responding to disaster through other types of organizations, community-relevant organizations are uniquely capable of providing disaster relief because they are flexible and are able to work with and within the local community in order to identify what the needs are and coordinate a response (Dynes 1970).

Although few studies have focused specifically on religious response to disaster, some have addressed the role of the religious community in aiding victims. These case studies show that religious groups can respond quickly to a disaster and can address the needs of victims who may be overlooked by other efforts, as in the case of Hurricane Andrew (Provenzo and Provenzo 2002). Religious organizations can also take advantage of their worldwide influence to send funds and volunteers to support local efforts following a disaster, as in the case of the 2005 tsunami in South Asia ("Catholic Agencies Mobilize for Relief" 2005). These examples suggest that religious organizations might be among the first to respond directly to the needs of victims and may benefit from their worldwide influence and reach. In fact, observers and researchers studying Hurricane Katrina have noted that religious organizations were among the first on the scene to respond to the needs of those affected by the hurricane (Koenig 2006; Lou and Robertson 2005).

Although one might be concerned about disorganization plaguing disaster relief efforts, (Tierney, Lindell, and Perry 2001), Dynes (1978) argues that an emergency consensus forms to unify a community. He argues that a diverse group of individuals and organizations come to an emergency consensus when certain fundamental values, such as altruism and providing care for victims, trump all others that usually separate the institutions (Dynes 1978). Not only do organizations choose to work together because they believe in a common cause, but they are faced with so great a need that they must cooperate to meet these needs. While such reorganization may appear chaotic, society is actually restructuring in a positive and functional way to cope with disaster. In the case of religious congregations in Houston following Hurricane Katrina, the emergence of an emergency consensus could encourage these organizations to work with others, including those they may never have worked with in the past. The congregations may be more likely to work with secular organizations, for example, or with religious organizations of different faiths than they would be while providing services to the community during other times.

Organizations

Since religious work is mainly done through organizations, such as churches, theories of social organization are well qualified to explain religious activity (DiMaggio 1998). New institutionalism is particularly relevant to understanding the ways that these organizations function and respond to change, and this theory serves as the framework through which I understand the ways religious congregations organize to help the evacuees of Hurricane Katrina in Houston. New institutionalism theorizes that in order to legitimate their work, organizations institutionalize a series of myths and rituals to give value to the actions they take to reach their goals (DiMaggio 1998; Meyer and Rowan 1977; Selznick 1996). Culture is central to organizations, and efficiency is no longer the foremost concern. Understanding an organization means knowing its institutionalized, unspoken rules and informal constructs. The connection of this theory to religious organizations is clear, as meaning is of utmost importance to the actions taken by religious organizations.

Another argument of new institutionalism is that organizations must work with or within society by responding to their environments (Selznick 1996). In addition, an organization's ability to accept society's values in legitimizing its own actions will help predict the success and survival of that organization (Meyer and Rowan 1977). It is thus important to study organizations within their environments since both are affected and judged by society. In the case of religious congregations providing disaster relief, these organizations must work among other organizations trying to provide the same types of services by responding to the needs that other organizations leave out or create, and they must do so while taking into account the interests of the surrounding community. An important consequence of the relationship that religious organizations have with the outside community, especially the government, is that these organizations may begin to resemble secular organizations delivering the same types of services. According to DiMaggio and Powell's (1983) theory on institutional isomorphism, organizations become more homogeneous as a consequence of their position within an open system since they rely on other organizations for resources; in particular, organizations that work with the state grow more similar over time.

Faith-Based Service Provision

Researchers have grown increasingly interested in the unique services that religious organizations are capable of providing. They suggest that there is a distinction between social services provided by religious congregations and secular organizations as well as a distinction among religious groups. Bartowski and Regis (2001), in an examination of the charitable efforts of Mississippi congregations, found that leaders in these congregations argue that services provided by faith-based organizations are holistic, unlike services provided by secular organizations. Koenig (2006) focused on the significance of the religious community's role in the victims' spiritual and emotional healing following recent national disasters and acts of terrorism and argues that the ability of religious organizations to provide this type of service makes them unique and essential to disaster relief efforts. While another study found little influence of religion on the types of services that international relief organizations provide, the authors did find that religion plays a major role in how these organizations legitimize their activities (Kniss and Campbell 1997). Past research on religious organizations reiterates the importance of examining message and legitimation that new institutionalism highlights. In the case of response to the evacuees of Katrina, religious congregations may address the same material needs as other organizations, but with an emphasis on message and on providing other forms of support. Besides their distinctive offering of spiritual support and their means of legitimizing activities, researchers find that compared with secular charitable organizations, religious organizations rely more heavily on volunteer support, fewer receive government funding, and they are more likely to advertise their religious ideas to solicit report (Ebaugh et al. 2003).

Social service provision also differs among religious organizations. Leventhal and Mears (2002) articulated the key characteristics that determine whether a congregation becomes involved in social service provision: leadership, race, organizational characteristics, and social and political networks. Results of their qualitative study indicate that leadership matters most for congregations that are hierarchically structured, while churches involved in large service organizations are more adept at developing effective leaders and implementing additional social service programs (Leventhal and Mears 2002). Other research has focused on the racial makeup of congregations and has consistently shown that black churches are more likely to hold a central place in a neighborhood and provide more aid to the underprivileged (Cavendish 2000; Chaves and Higgins 1992). Past research suggests that congregations in Houston will differ in the services they provide by the characteristics of their congregants and the social connections of their leaders.

After surveying previous research, it is clear that little information has been gathered on the response of religious communities to natural disasters despite studies that show that religious organizations often respond first in a disaster situation and that services provided by religious institutions tend to differ in important ways from those provided by secular organizations. This research, besides being motivated by the enormity of this particular natural disaster, aims to fill this gap.

METHODS

My data are drawn from interviews conducted with leaders at religious congregations in the Houston metropolitan area. The sampling frame consists of every congregation listed in the Houston yellow pages, almost 3,000 in total. I stratified the sampling frame by denomination and selected 17 congregations at random. I conducted nine semistructured interviews with leaders at these congregations in February and March 2006. The denominations represented include Methodist, Catholic, Episcopalian, nondenominational Christian, Jewish, evangelical Lutheran, and Baptist, and the members of the sampled congregations range in socioeconomic status and race, although no congregations with a primarily Hispanic membership were surveyed. The congregations are also located in various areas of the city.

I conducted semistructured interviews with leaders at the congregations selected. I interviewed the person or people identified by each congregation as the most knowledgeable about the relief efforts; in most cases, this person was the head pastor/reverend/priest/rabbi, while in others, the leader was a service coordinator or volunteer. Interviewing was the best possible method for answering my research question because it enabled me to explore each congregation in some depth and explain the differences between each congregation's experiences. The discussion centered around a few major topics. The first part of the interview was designed to acquire some details about the congregation and included questions about the size of the church, the denomination, and the social, educational, and community service activities that the congregation participated in before the hurricane. The second part of the interview involved questions about the hurricane relief efforts. Subjects answered questions about their impression of the relief efforts overall, what efforts they participated in, how these particular projects were organized, how the congregation publicized the events, how many people volunteered, and whether they felt these efforts were successful. They also discussed general impressions of the relief efforts and the leaders' advice for the future.

RESULTS

Community Service Pre- and Post-Katrina

Even before Hurricane Katrina brought opportunities for service to Houston's congregations, the leaders I spoke with had been providing services to their communities for many years. A few examples of regular programs at the congregations include the following: three congregations either organize a food pantry in their own building or regularly assist with a food pantry at a neighboring congregation, three organize a clothing distribution center, two churches provide drug counseling services and one marriage counseling, three churches provide rent or utility assistance, and two congregations provide meals to members of the community. Besides these programs, some congregations focused on their own unique efforts. For example, a large black Methodist church provides health care services to their poorer community members and offers a free health clinic and AIDS testing.

The congregations' efforts at community service involve other religious and secular organizations in the city. One congregation works with Interfaith Ministries, an organization in Houston boasting member congregations from all faiths dedicated to service, and three participate in small neighborhood coalitions made up of a variety of religious organizations in their area. The Catholic and Episcopalian churches participate in activities organized through their dioceses, and others work with secular organizations, such as Habitat for Humanity and the Houston Food Bank.

Once the evacuees landed in Houston, every congregation became involved in at least one effort to help. Some started their own small projects, while others joined larger efforts by working with organizations like the Red Cross or the Houston city government. Some of the most common activities the congregations were involved in included collecting goods, serving meals, volunteering at shelters, and providing rent or housing assistance. Collection was by far the most common relief activity among the congregations sampled (eight of the nine congregations organized this activity) and usually was the first activity to begin and ended soon after the evacuees arrived. Eight out of the nine congregations were involved in the collection of goods: clothing, hygiene products, food, and so on. Almost all the congregations performing this type of service received an overwhelming amount of donations and had to spend a lot of time sorting the donations. This was a relatively easy way for the most congregants to contribute, and those congregations that participated in this activity described the willingness of their members to donate. The interviewee at a small Baptist church commented, "We had to beg people. 'Please don't bring us any more clothes. Please don't bring us any more food.'" Another leader called collecting "stuff" a "natural response," a sentiment echoed at many of the congregations that implemented collection drives. In fact, many of the congregations have organized collection drives in the past following other disasters or collect food or clothing on a regular basis to give to those in their community. The leaders agreed that it was easy to convince their congregants to give away the things they no longer need, and it allowed everyone to contribute without investing a lot of time.

Other common activities included providing meals to evacuees at a shelter or in the congregation's building and volunteering or working at shelters. At a nondenominational Christian church, for example, after speaking with evacuees she met at a local grocery store about where they were staying, the volunteer coordinator began organizing church members to bring meals directly to the evacuees' hotel. Of the nine congregations sampled, one served as a shelter for the evacuees of Katrina. This church, a small black Baptist church, housed evacuees in classrooms of their building. For three weeks, the church housed 30 people, all part of an extended family and all but four of whom were children. Volunteers from the church stayed overnight during this time, while other members brought food, clothing, and other necessities to the evacuees. Volunteers also took the children on trips throughout Houston during the day and tried their best to keep them busy and entertained. While this was the only congregation in my sample that housed evacuees, many others sent volunteers to other shelters throughout the city.

The characteristics of each congregation influenced the types of services it chose to provide. Whether the members of each congregation were able to identify with the evacuees because of their own social characteristics, such as race and socioeconomic status, influenced the activities of many congregations. For example, the leader at a black Baptist church that served as a shelter noted that the congregants were able to identify with the evacuees since many personally understood needing material assistance. Leaders and members at a large black Methodist church have a lot of experience dealing with the homeless population, partly because a large proportion of their own congregants are homeless. Thus, in a position to understand the evacuees who were homeless even before the storm, the church focused its relief efforts on serving this hard-to-reach group of people. Some of the congregations that were most unlike the evacuees who migrated to Houston mentioned that this made it difficult and slightly irrational for them to provide certain types of services, such as counseling or assistance finding housing. These congregations were more likely to be involved in services that did not require as much personal contact with the evacuees and as great an understanding of the experiences of poverty or loss, such as collecting donations or providing meals.

Organizational Strategies

According to nearly all the respondents, the idea of getting involved in the relief efforts came mostly from the congregants themselves. All the religious leaders interviewed noted that their congregants went above and beyond in their volunteer efforts after the hurricane. In Houston, volunteering became the norm, and many Houston residents were willing to clean out their closets or donate money to participate in the efforts. Since many residents already had ties to religious congregations in their communities, congregations could provide an avenue for contributing.

The congregations sampled were able to expand service activities already in place as well as create new ones. All but two of the congregations sampled were able to expand at least one existing service program to aid the evacuees, and every congregation added an entirely new program to address the problems experienced by evacuees. Several congregations continued efforts they participate in all year and expanded them to deal with the hurricane crisis. For example, a small nondenominational Christian congregation serves meals to the homeless one day each week. After the hurricane, they began making meals on a larger scale and bringing them to a local hotel housing evacuees. In addition, the members of a large Methodist church also serve meals every day year-round at the church and provide social services to individuals in the community, so they worked through these programs already in place to aid those affected by the hurricane. For example, although this church employs social workers to serve community members, they added two more social workers to the staff to deal only with the survivors of Katrina. In addition, three congregations that provide rent or utility assistance on a regular basis expanded their services to address the needs of the evacuees.

The importance of a congregation's personal, social, or business connections became readily apparent during my research, confirming the importance of examining organizations in their broader community context. The congregations' connections with the local Houston community (members of the community as well as other religious and secular charitable organizations), their connections with influential people in government or large charitable organizations, and their connections with other religious leaders throughout the country all aided the congregations' efforts. As community-relevant organizations with close ties to members of their neighborhoods, a few congregations focused their relief efforts on the evacuees who settled in their area. Neighborhood connections benefited a midsized evangelical Christian church that was located some distance away from the major shelter sites. Between 50 and 100 evacuees from the Gulf Coast region settled in the area, many with friends or relatives who belonged to the church. The congregation connected with these people through members of the church and the surrounding neighborhoods. Through its contacts with apartment complex owners and large stores in the area, the congregation was even able to set up many evacuees with housing and furniture. Many congregations also utilized contacts they had with other members of the Houston religious community. Four of the congregations sampled are part of coalitions with other congregations. These coalitions typically consist of congregations from a variety of denominations located in the same neighborhood, established for the purpose of doing charitable work in their community. Through these coalitions, two congregations were able to provide substantial help to other congregations in their neighborhoods that were serving as shelters for evacuees. Another congregation worked with the religious groups in its coalition to organize a major collection of goods.

Congregations that had close connections with local leaders involved in city government, charitable organizations, and businesses were able to play a major role in the city's efforts and find a niche to fill within the other efforts. A large Methodist congregation had significant connections within the Houston political community that enabled it to participate in a major way in the relief efforts. Congregations also benefited from being connected with other congregations throughout the country. For example, after the storm, the leader of a large Houston synagogue called the rabbi of a New Orleans congregation and invited him to bring his staff to Houston and share his office space.

While many congregations connected with other secular and religious leaders following the storm, some participated in efforts run through their denomination. Two of the congregations, for example, belonged to highly organized denominations: Episcopalian and Catholic. Both congregations raised money and participated in programs run primarily through their dioceses. The Jewish community is also well organized through the Jewish Federation and by organizations representing each denomination (orthodox, conservative, and reform). Thus, instead of running its own donation drive in addition to its other efforts, the synagogue sampled encouraged members to donate funds to the larger national Jewish organizations and kept in contact with these organizations to find out what the Jewish evacuees needed at every moment.

The Development of an Emergency Consensus

While the subjects did not agree on the effectiveness of the federal government or local Gulf Coast response to the victims of Hurricane Katrina, every person interviewed was proud to be a Houstonian after the storm. Respondents used the words "exemplary," "more than adequate," "overwhelmingly impressive," and "extraordinary" to describe the response of the Houston city government, religious community, and individual residents of the city. The respondents agreed that Houston reacted well, given the dire needs of those hit by the hurricane, and many expressed that Houston should be a model for cities planning for the future.

Not only did the respondents approve of Houston's response to the evacuees of Katrina, but they also felt that providing assistance promoted a sense of cohesion throughout the city. Their sentiments provide evidence that an emergency consensus formed in Houston in the months following the storm. In particular, the leaders spoke about expanding working relationships with other religious and secular organizations and establishing new ones. According to the theory of emergency consensus, even very different organizations are able to unify to respond to the community's needs following a disaster, and in Houston, as one subject noted, "all the different congregations, and all the different faiths came together." Another agreed and remarked, "It's such a joy and a pleasure to see people come together." The subject agreed that responding to the hurricane unified the entire Houston community since so many people came out and worked together to provide aid.

DISCUSSION

Summary of Findings

In order to assess the immediate response to the evacuees of Hurricane Katrina in Houston, I interviewed leaders in randomly selected Houston congregations to find out what relief activities they engaged in immediately following the hurricane. I focused on one main research question: what did the congregations do in the few months immediately following Hurricane Katrina to aid the evacuees? By interviewing these leaders, I was able to gain insight into what service activities each congregation participated in, how these programs were organized, and their reflections on Houston's relief efforts. In addition, I examined the theories of community-relevant organizations, emergency consensus, and new institutionalism in the context of disaster relief efforts in Houston following Hurricane Katrina.

I found that every congregation sampled did something to help the evacuees in Houston. In addition, every congregation had community service programs in operation even before the hurricane. Almost all the congregations were able to take advantage of a program already in place to institute a more elaborate response to the evacuees. Furthermore, all the congregations created new service programs. This study demonstrates how the organizational structure of religious organizations influenced their efforts to aid the evacuees of Hurricane Katrina. The religious leaders interviewed demonstrated flexibility and the ability to provide aid by going out into their communities. Congregations that were well connected both within and outside Houston and both inside and outside the religious community were able to utilize these connections during their relief efforts. Thus, the highly organized and personally connected structure of the religious community inside and outside Houston transformed the congregations' efforts from a grassroots, community-based relief program to something more nationally constructed.

Implications for Theory

This study's findings support theories of disaster response. The theorized benefits of providing services through community-relevant organizations, including their ability to fill in the gaps created by larger response projects, to be flexible in providing new services, and to mobilize volunteers and provide another avenue for response, were found to be advantages in the response of the religious congregations sampled to the evacuees in Houston. Respondents' reflections support the theory of emergency consensus, and the congregations' experiences suggest that consensus formed in Houston and even within each congregation. The religious leaders surveyed described a remarkably unified effort involving both church members and leaders with the goal of aiding the victims of Katrina at the center.

The results of this study also add something unique to theories of social organization while at the same time supporting existing theory. Culturally validated norms in the religious congregations facilitated participation and leadership during the relief efforts in the months after the storm. As new institutionalism suggests, existing within a larger environment influenced the efforts of congregations with ties to outside organizations, and positive relationships with members of the community benefited the congregations' efforts. And while theorists of social organization worry that institutionalized organizations are unable to cope with change, this study addresses the topic directly. I found that the institutionalized values already in place in religious congregations, including values such as giving and a sense of community, were able to shift slightly to benefit the congregations' efforts.

Limitations and Directions for Future Research

This study has some significant limitations that affect the outcome and the ability to generalize from its findings. First, the small sample size prevents drawing conclusions about the response of religious congregations following a disaster. The sample size also does not allow for comparisons among size, denomination, or sociodemographic characteristics of congregations, factors that likely matter in the provision of services. Additionally, because I spoke only with the providers of aid, I cannot tell whether the services the congregations provided were successful from the view of the evacuees or even members of the congregation. Moreover, I examined only the immediate response of these congregations. While this is a critical time in disaster response, it is likely that I missed other forms of relief more likely to be provided in the long term. For example, while material needs were most exaggerated during the months following Katrina, it is likely that the evacuees' need for emotional and spiritual support continued to grow after these first months.

However, the advantages of this study outweigh its limitations. Although the sample size was small, qualitative methods allowed for a greater understanding of the experiences of each congregation. And while this study focused on a very specific aspect of disaster relief, provided by a specific group of organizations during just the months following Katrina, research on this topic is lacking, and this study can begin to expand our focus on disaster response. These limitations also point to a need for future research. Researchers must continue to study the response of various organizations and individuals to disaster; the results of this study show that people and organizations do not work alone. Response to a disaster the magnitude of Katrina involves many actors, and this study demonstrates the ability of coordination among different groups. This study narrowly focuses on only one type of organizational response to disaster: that done through religious organizations. Clearly, other levels of response deserve careful study as well. This research also indicates a need for a more complex look at disaster response. Future research should take into account all levels of involvement in disaster response efforts and examine how these organizations function or do not function together. Researchers interested in religious provision of social services could also benefit by a more close examination of the differences that exist by denomination, race, and socioeconomic status of religious organizations and their service activities.

CONCLUSIONS

The need for services following Hurricane Katrina was so great that countless individuals and organizations worked to help. The unity that Houston showed in coping with the disaster is reflected in the experiences of the religious congregations interviewed in this study. Their experiences also show that organizations are able to adapt to fill a particular role in disaster response, and by understanding the magnitude, diversity, and organization of the Houston religious community, the city was able to integrate these groups in disaster response efforts immediately after the arrival of evacuees. Even within a group of religious congregations, each organization specialized in aspects of service delivery that they felt they were best able to provide, perhaps because they provide similar services year-round or because members of the congregation could identify with needing a particular form of support.

In sum, this study addressed a topic previously ignored in the disaster response literature: the response of the religious community to disaster. We have learned that religious organizations respond quickly to disaster and provide a wide range of services. They also work with each other and with secular organizations to serve disaster victims. As policymakers begin to plan for future disasters, it is imperative that they take into account all organizations in their community and find ways to encourage response at every level. This study examined how the religious community can be involved, and future research should determine how other organizations can serve. By bringing together the disaster response literature and religious organizations literature, research can show us how to most effectively utilize the advantages of all organizations to effectively respond following future disasters.

NOTE

The author is grateful for support provided by the Rice Undergraduate Scholars Program. The author also thanks Holly E. Heard for her helpful suggestions during this research project.

III

ONGOING DISASTER:
REACTION AND RECOVERY

7

After the Levees Broke: Reactions of College Students to the Aftermath of Hurricane Katrina

Kris Macomber, Sarah E. Rusche, and Delmar Wright

There would never have been such a slow response if white people were packed into a stadium, starving and watching each other die.

—Black female, age 19

This could happen to any of us. It was not right to bring up racism. Hurricanes are not racist.

—White male, age 20

Turn back the clock to August 27, 2005, and you will likely remember watching the news days before Hurricane Katrina stormed ashore the Gulf Coast. It seemed that meteorologists, news anchors, and news watchers were all prepared for the hurricane to hit. "It's gonna be a big one" filled the daily chatter at dinner tables and office coffee stations. Most were unaware, however, of the significant social implications of this pending disaster as we watched it swirl in the ocean. As residents of vulnerable areas began to prepare for Katrina's arrival, those watching the news caught a first glimpse of future victims. It became clear, quite soon, that many of the victims had two things in common—they were poor and black.

As sociologists, we spend a lot of time in the classroom teaching about social inequalities and social problems in America—topics many Americans do not often discuss. A sense of optimism grew as we thought, "With all of this news coverage, people will see the race and class inequalities that plague poor minorities, and what a wake-up call this will be to the millions of Americans who think that racism and classism are irrelevant in modern America!" Many instructors set aside scheduled readings for the week and instead led impromptu discussions about Hurricane Katrina. As is typically the case in the sociological classroom, student opinions about current events and social problems are divided. While some students saw the events surrounding Hurricane Katrina as reflective of social inequalities, others were also fierce in their attempts to protect the government and blame the victims, viewing this disaster as yet another example of the inherent incapability of poor blacks to take care of themselves. Still other students were confused as to why some Americans, media pundits, and politicians viewed the hurricane through a racial lens at all; as one white student voiced, "I don't understand why they're making it a racial issue."

As we found in our own classrooms and heard from other sociologists, students' reactions to the hurricane not only varied but also followed sociological patterns. The most obvious pattern was that our white and black students were frequently divided in their interpretation of events surrounding the disaster. As sociologists, we began to think about the O. J. Simpson trial and how the nation was polarized. Most whites were angry that Simpson was found not guilty, while many African Americans cheered his acquittal, seeing it as payback for the long tradition of racism in the American criminal justice system (see Hacker 2003). Was a similar process operating in the reactions to the aftermath of Hurricane Katrina? Were people coming to understand this disaster in different ways? Most important, would people recognize, with 24-hour media coverage, the social underpinnings of this natural disaster? Inspired by our students, a sense of pedagogical responsibility, and our own sociological imaginations, we set out to explore our students' varied and often polarized reactions to Hurricane Katrina.

It is not surprising that our students invariably held opinions about the events surrounding the Hurricane Katrina disaster since, as Dynes and Rodríguez (2005) explain, "Katrina was the first hurricane to hit the United States to the accompaniment of continuous (24/7) TV coverage" (see chapter 1 in this volume) The extensive, often live coverage of Hurricane Katrina and its aftermath granted the American public access to see the private hell the victims of the hurricane were living. Even more relevant to sociologists, however, is the fact that the media coverage of Katrina exposed public reactions to this disaster—and, similar to Eric Klinenberg's (2002) analysis of the 1995 Chicago heat wave, made an analysis of this "perfect storm" possible.

As Gilman (2005) asserts, "Of the many sorry things about contemporary United States that the Katrina catastrophe has exposed, perhaps none is more depressing than what it showed about the abiding divide in American thinking about race and racism." In other words, black and white viewers reacted to the same media coverage and images of Hurricane Katrina with different perspectives that, when "exposed in living color, are staggeringly instructive" (Ford and Gamble 2006). The media's portrayal of working-class and poor blacks struggling for their lives brought to the surface underlying issues of race that have plagued the history of this nation.

Further exposed were the public's often uncomfortable reactions to the fact that issues of poverty, as well as race, were highlighted in the media. Immediately after the hurricane had hit and the levees had been breached, Americans watched as water began to flood the city of New Orleans. Residents climbed to rooftops, many of them swam in a sea of sewage, while others scattered to find some sort of dry land. All the while, viewers watched and read, many wondering how this disaster could happen in America.

While many articles were written by sociologists and other scholars immediately following the aftermath of Hurricane Katrina, few, if any, utilized empirical evidence to support their insights into this situation. Most authors used a broad array of sociological insight and knowledge to understand what was going on at the Gulf Coast's "ground zero." There were several articles published by the Social Science Research Council (http://understandingkatrina.ssrc.org/) in mid-September 2005 that offer instructive perspectives on the social implications of Katrina. We used these insights to inform our empirical investigation of this tragedy. These insights not only helped shape our research design but also facilitated our analysis in important ways.

METHODS AND DATA

Inspired by the prospect of exploring reactions to Hurricane Katrina, we developed a short questionnaire that probed students for descriptive reactions about the disaster. Although somewhat less in depth than face-to-face interviews, this "qualitative questionnaire" was efficient, especially because we were able to administer the questionnaires only six weeks after the hurricane hit. The open-ended nature of the questionnaire gave students the opportunity to provide nuanced responses to open-ended questions, providing us with richly descriptive qualitative data.

The qualitative questionnaire consisted of three different sections: (1) a timed five-minute free-writing exercise, (2) seven open-ended questions that were similar to essay questions on written exams (these questions were also similar to questions on an interview guide), and (3) a demographic information page. The authors transcribed the written answers verbatim and then analyzed the data, coded the transcripts, and developed analytical categories from patterns that emerged throughout respondents' answers. In this regard, the questionnaire provided data about respondents' reactions to Hurricane Katrina that were longer and more detailed than those of traditional survey responses while still remaining anonymous. Indeed, several students' written answers espoused some overtly racist remarks that we doubt would have been provided in face-to-face interviews—especially if one of the authors, who is African American, were to conduct these interviews.

We administered the questionnaire to a diverse group of students at a large research university in the southeastern United States. In order to obtain a sample of students that was more racially diverse than random sampling would provide, we contacted instructors of classes that draw higher percentages of minority students. We thus were able to draw a sample of 104 students: 52 whites, 37 African Americans, five Latinos, five Asians, and five multiracial/other. The sample consisted of 69 women and 35 men. Of the total 104 respondents, 60 came from three different undergraduate English classes. These three different classes included majors from many different academic departments, including computer engineering, business, agriculture and environmental technology, textiles, biological sciences, horticulture, and communications. Out of the remaining 44 students, 22 came from an undergraduate sociology class (mostly majors in sociology, criminology, psychology, and education), and 22 came from an undergraduate Africana studies class (majors in psychology, political science, business, chemistry, meteorology, and biology). We did not collect data on students' social class; however, we obtained data on the socioeconomic status of the university population. Sixty-seven percent of African Americans, 33.5 percent of whites, and 51.1 percent of students who identify as "other" receive aid because of financial need (2004 University Student Survey).

There are two limitations of this sample. First, women are overrepresented ($n = 69$) and men underrepresented ($n = 35$) because of sampling of women's studies classes. Second, although we did not inquire about political identity or affiliations, three out of the five classes we contacted (the sociology class, the Africana studies class, and the English class cross listed with women's studies) tend to attract politically liberal students. Therefore, the following findings may not be generalizable to the entire college population. At the same time, we are confident that these patterns represent a segment of this population. In the following sections, we present patterns of students' reactions to Hurricane Katrina and the aftermath.

REACTIONS TO HURRICANE KATRINA

Four patterns emerged from the free-writing exercise and the seven open-ended questions: (1) the media paradox—media is racist/media exposed inequality, (2) criticisms of the government, (3) blaming the victim/supporting the government, and (4) comparisons of the hurricane aftermath to the "Third World."

The Media Paradox

A paradox regarding students' reactions to the media emerged as a product of two different patterns. On the one hand, students identified the media as racist, but on the other hand, many also said that the media exposed race and class inequalities in America. Students who identified the media as racist also recognized the inequalities that the media exposed. Hence, the paradox is that there is more of a continuum than a dichotomy between the students' perceptions of the media's portrayal of the aftermath. While some students believed the media to be racist and others believed the media exposed existing inequalities, there were many students whose responses fell between the two categories.

The Media Is Racist

Overwhelmingly, students perceived the media as racist. Students claimed that the media portrayed African Americans as violent troublemakers while portraying whites as struggling victims. The "looting" versus "finding" controversy repeatedly came up in students' responses, with 40 percent of students referencing it either once or several times throughout the questionnaire. This controversy began soon after the Associated Press printed two pictures—one of a black man carrying grocery items while wading through chest-high water and one of a white man and woman carrying grocery items while wading through chest-high water. The caption accompanying the white couple read, "Two residents wade through chest high water after *finding* bread and soda at a local grocery store after Hurricane Katrina came through the area in New Orleans, Louisiana" (Associated Press; emphasis added). The caption describing the picture of the black man read quite differently: "A young man walks through chest deep flood water after *looting* a grocery store in New Orleans on Tuesday, August 30th, 2005" (Associated Press; emphasis added). This controversy was circulated widely in the media, which ironically affirms this paradox in that the media itself pointed to both its own racism while also pointing out its duty to expose inequality.

To many students, the media was racist because they portrayed whites as "trying to survive" while portraying blacks as "criminals." The following responses express students' reactions to the media:

> The most racist entity of all was the news media. They only used terms such as looting and thug for African Americans. That is not right. (white male)

> The image that stands out most in my mind is the image of the people who found food. The images are of an African American boy and a white couple. The picture describes the African American boy as "looting," while the white couple "found food." This just proves that racism exists especially in the media. (black male)

This student denies that governmental racism exists and instead blames the media:

> Most of the poorest people left in New Orleans were black so of course the media is going to call that looting but if a white family was doing it, it would be helping its family. The media racially discriminates, not the government. (white female)

It was clear to these students that the media portrayed black and white victims differently. However, we are unsure whether these students would have developed such conclusions without the widespread coverage of the "looting" versus "finding" controversy. That is, there were also many news stories that pointed out racism in the media, so we expect that the media framed such responses.

The Media Unveiled Inequality

The second part of the media paradox was students' claims that the media exposed American race and class inequalities, of which they were previously unaware. An element of surprise was expressed in responses regarding how many people lived in such economic deprivation. In addition, some students commented that they felt like they had been left in the dark; they wondered why they hadn't been aware of these inequalities in the first place. Many felt as if the wool had been pulled over their eyes, and they blamed the government for hiding these inequalities. One white woman suggests that people might be reluctant to see that race has anything to do with this tragedy:

> People would like to believe that racism, especially racism in the government, is nonexistent, but Hurricane Katrina made it obvious that racism is still very much alive. . . . I think everyone knows deep down that it was a racial issue, whether they admit it to themselves or not.

Some students, like this black female, argued that the media seem to be preoccupied with disasters that victimized middle-class whites:

> Hurricane Katrina brought to mind the unfairness and inequalities that exist in America. I can't imagine in a million years that the government would allow a town of white suburban soccer moms to get killed in a storm. . . . September 11th is still an American obsession. People still cry about it, they are not over it. People still want to light candles about it. Of course, it was a horrific event and one that deserves respect but it still gets more talk and airtime than Hurricane Katrina and that was recent. This is America for you. God forbid white yuppies.

According to many students, the media brought awareness to race and class inequalities that were "hidden" to them. Much of what students cited as this newfound awareness were images of low-income housing. In addition, students claimed that they didn't realize the government could be so racist and expressed anger at the inadequate relief efforts, which they saw as consequences of a racist and classist government.

The media operated in two ways that influenced perceptions of the aftermath of Hurricane Katrina. On the one hand, students claimed that the media was racist because of the negative portrayal of African Americans as violent thugs. On the other hand, the media was a powerful tool in exposing that racism and classism still persist in America. According to Dynes and Rodríguez (2005), the media frames not only how people perceive disasters but also what people come to think of as important.

Criticism of Government

Criticisms of the government for the inadequate relief efforts during the aftermath of the hurricane were prevalent in students' reactions. Reactions to the relief efforts reflected mistrust and skepticism of the government. Specifically, these criticisms were expressed in three different ways: (1) students questioned how the government would have responded if the race and socioeconomic status of the victims were different; (2) students claimed that foreign preoccupation, specifically the war in Iraq, distracted the government from this domestic problem; and (3) students single-handedly blamed President Bush for inadequate relief efforts.

When criticizing the government's role in relief efforts, students questioned what would have happened if the majority of the victims were not poor African Americans. According to their responses, in the eyes of the government, poor people of color are not as valuable as rich whites—both in personal worth and how they were treated. The following responses express these comparisons:

> I would have to say that if the city were filled with rich whites, something different would have happened. (white male)

> If it had affected as many whites I think the government would have busted their tails to save as many lives as they could, but knowing that it wasn't, the attitude was more like, we'll get to them when we can. (black female)

> When homes and work and lives are washed away only anger is left. I wonder if that region was predominately white what the circumstances would be. If rich people are worth saving with all their pompous, snobby assets, then poor people damn sure are too. (black female)

Students were well aware of the socioeconomic status and race of the many of the victims and used these social markers to criticize the relief efforts. Resonating throughout their reactions was skepticism over not only how the government treats African Americans but also how the government values and treats poor people.

A second criticism of the government regarding the relief efforts pointed to American preoccupation overseas—specifically the war in Iraq. According to these reactions, the government was too distracted fighting a war in another country to properly prepare for or handle the aftermath of Hurricane Katrina. A recurrent theme in these responses was that relief efforts took too long because the government's money, time, and energy was tied up in the war. These students ascribed blame for the paltry relief efforts directly at the war in Iraq, suggesting that funds could be better spent:

> It seems to me that if you can have soldiers in another country fighting for the US and Iraqis, spending billions a day then you can take better care of the needs of people at home. (multiracial female)

> The leaders of this country did not treat this event as the major problem it was. They were also far too slow in response than I expected from them. Money being spent on (an arguably unjust) war should be used to help people here who rightly need it. (white male)

According to these students, the government's involvement overseas was a major barrier in handling this domestic disaster. These responses reflect feelings of domestic entitlement—American concerns should be top priority, not foreign affairs.

The third expression of government criticism of relief efforts was directed specifically at President Bush. Many students single-handedly blamed President Bush for the poor response to the aftermath. Since we did not ask students their political affiliation, we are uncertain whether these students formerly supported President Bush or if this disaster offers nonsupporters another reason to criticize him. Nevertheless, these reactions reflect students' readiness to attribute a large-scale problem to one person. Some of them unleash a bit of humor in their anger:

> President Bush can see weapons of mass destruction all the way in Iraq, but can't see a hurricane heading towards his own country. (black female)

This black female suggests not only that President Bush failed at effectively dealing with this situation but also that he, personally, is a detriment to our nation:

> Black people looked like scum, seemed like they did not matter. I never knew New Orleans had it like this—you never see that part on TV. GW Bush is such a selfish, incompetent fool, he is single-handedly ruining America. It's unbelievable . . . I just can't take it.

While both white and nonwhite students criticized the government in all three ways, African American students were more likely to fall into this category of specifically blaming the president. These responses of criticism not only illustrate disapproval for the president but, more substantively, also speak to how students ascribed blame. Rather than perceiving the aftermath as the outcome of collective deficiencies operating in the American government, these students put responsibility on the shoulders of one person—a person they feel should have taken better care of this country during a time of tragedy.

Blaming the Victims

In contrast to the previous responses that criticize the government for the relief efforts, some students, though fewer, maintained that the victims themselves were to blame for the issues surrounding the aftermath. Much of this blame was expressed by references to the violence and looting that ensued. Here, students voiced anger and frustration at the victims' behavior and blamed this behavior for the slow and/or inadequate relief efforts. It is important to note that racist sentiments were also a part of these reactions. One white male was so angry at the victims that he identified people who do not deserve to live:

> For those who were looting and raping, shooting at National Guard helicopters and police, those are the ones who should be left to die. For these low-life individuals to take advantage of a terrible situation to take it upon themselves to act like fools and not help their fellow men just need to be shot in the street. It's because of these people that the food and supplies got in late. It was unsafe to send troops into certain parts of the cities because the Blacks were running around like a bunch of monkeys tearing shit up. If it was up to me, I would have sent special teams into areas to take care of looters and thugs to kill them on the spot. . . . I understand looting to get water, food, but a fucking TV! We don't need people like this in our world and they don't deserve to live in it!

This same student later explained,

> It was the Black poor people that acted like fools when no one was watching them, such as the police etc. It just shows that they should not and will not ever be as civilized as everyone else which is why they'll always remain poor and on the bottom.

Another white male expressed some compassion for a select few but ultimately implied that individuals should not count on the government to help them:

> The victims of Hurricane Katrina were unfortunate to be caught in this situation but I feel the people themselves could have done more to make the situation less crazy. . . . Yes, I understand not everyone has a car to get out of town but there were a lot of knuckleheads that did not listen to the warnings to leave town so for those people who could've left but didn't well they got what they deserved . . . it was not our government that failed but the idiots who wanted free help from the government.

A focus on violence led these students to place responsibility for the aftermath of the storm directly on the victims. According to these reactions, had these poor African Americans refrained from "looting" and "shooting at helicopters," the government could have and *would* have helped them more efficiently. These comments were mainly from white males and appeared much less frequently than criticisms of the government. Although these responses were less common, we include them in this analysis because we suspect they may shed light on the reactions of the wider population.

Comparison to a Third World Country

Paralleling the criticism of the government was the shock expressed at how presumably uncharacteristic of America this disaster was. A recurring reaction throughout the transcripts was that the destruction and delayed relief efforts reflected a Third World country, not the "superpower" nation that America is generally thought to be. Many of these responses focus on the poverty and the race of the people they saw in the media images. One white woman admitted that the images evoked strong emotions:

> The images that came to mind when I saw images of Hurricane Katrina was absolute shock. The first time I saw pictures of Katrina I almost started crying—it was awful to see people in America in such a state. It looked like a third world country with absolutely no resources.

Like the television commercials we see asking us to adopt a child for "just 25 cents a day," the image of hungry black children is what stuck with this black woman:

> When I look at the television all I can see is little black children starving like this is some third world country or something.

Making comparisons of the aftermath of Katrina to a Third World country is not unique to our study. In fact, in September, only two weeks after Katrina hit, Dominguez (2005) wrote about these "Third World" comparisons, suggesting that they reveal a lot about what Americans *don't know* about their country. As sociologists, we know about these inequalities—but part of our goal in this research was to explore how people digested the images of thousands of poor African Americans in desperation, waiting for help. Would the larger public be shocked by the realities of segregation, poverty, and racism in a major American city once it is thrust in front of their faces? The fact that these students made Third World comparisons represents the common myth that America is a middle-class nation. The poor and needy in New Orleans were "real," and what many had thought of as "Third World" was suddenly a shocking American reality.

PERCEPTIONS OF RACE AND CLASS
THROUGH THE LENS OF HURRICANE KATRINA

Although the four emerging patterns discussed previously were developed from the entire qualitative questionnaire, one question was specifically designed to explore perceptions of race and class during the aftermath of Hurricane Katrina. To explore this, respondents were asked to answer the following question: "Many people have suggested that the effects of Hurricane Katrina were a 'racial issue.' What are your thoughts about this claim? Do you agree? Why or why not?"

In response to whether they thought the effects of the hurricane was a "racial issue," responses varied considerably. Because the question was open ended, we were able to derive six different response categories from students' written answers: (1) "Yes, this was a racial issue"; (2) "Yes, this was a racial issue, but this was also about social class"; (3) "No, this was not about race—it was about social class, the victims just happen to be black"; (4) "No, this was not about anything social—hurricanes are not racist"; (5) "No, but the media tried to make it a racial issue"; and (6) "I don't know." Table 7.1 presents the basic descriptive results of their responses, while Tables 7.2 and 7.3 analyze these responses by race and gender, respectively.

As evidenced in Table 7.1, the majority of students (36.5 percent) responded, "Yes, this was a racial issue." Many of the responses here pointed to the fact that most of the victims they saw were African American and that this was no coincidence. In terms of race, 22 percent of these responses were from white students, and 12 percent were from blacks. Attesting that the aftermath of Katrina *was* a racial issue, one white woman wrote,

> It was most certainly a racial issue. Even the way things were headlined displayed racism—there was one picture of a black man "looting a store" and a white man "collecting supplies" for his family. Same act but when race is included—African Americans are thought to be deviant. Again, if Katrina had hit an area of predominately middle class white families—I believe the media coverage and aid would have been a great more helpful to victims and responsive overall.

To the next student, it was obvious that this issue had everything to do with race, although she alludes to class issues:

> Yes. What color were the people you saw on TV dying? What color were the majority of the people in the superdome? Look at the big picture! Open your eyes!

Table 7.1.   Were the Effects of Hurricane Katrina a Racial Issue?

Responses	Total	Percent
"Yes."	38	36.5
"Yes, but also class."	14	13.4
"No, it was about class."	14	13.4
"No, nothing social."	18	17.4
"No, media made it."	5	5.0
"I don't know/unsure."	15	14.3
Total	104	100

The people who were left to die were lower class minorities who could not afford
to fly out on their golden chariots. (black female)

To these students, the victims did not receive adequate aid *because they were
black*. There was also an interesting gender finding here (see Table 7.3)—out
of the 38 students who thought this was a racial issue, 31 were women (31 percent), and only seven were men (7 percent). So, while images of poverty were
also prominent, most students (especially women) focused on the *race* of the
victims, not the socioeconomic status of the victims, to explain the aftermath.

While the majority of respondents believe that race mattered in this aftermath, 13.4 percent of respondents believed that the inadequate relief efforts
were outcomes of social class in addition to race. Black students were much
more likely to express this reaction than whites. Three times as many blacks as
whites thought that the inadequate relief efforts were outcomes of both race
and class. In terms of race, 10.6 percent of blacks, compared to 2.8 percent of
whites, connected race and class (see Table 7.2). Following are two comments
from black students that reflect the notion that the aftermath was the outcome
of both race and class inequality:

> I do believe it was a racial issue, but only on part with classism as well. These peo-
> ple were poverty stricken and didn't have resources to leave even if they did be-
> lieve that it was not going to be as bad as it was (which most didn't). I truly be-
> lieve if these people had chosen to stay in their homes, but were above the poverty
> line and white, that the response would have been quicker and more structured.
> (black female)

> Clearly, the issue of race comes up when a predominately Black town is left to suf-
> fer without food, shelter and supplies for a week. We cannot however let the issue
> of race overshadow the fact that poor is poor, and the ones in power oppress the
> poor regardless of race. (black male)

The second-largest group of responses to this question believed that both race
and class were connected to the aftermath of Hurricane Katrina. African American students were more likely to see race and class operating together than
whites. Only 2.8 percent of whites saw this as an outcome of both race and
class, compared to 22 percent of whites who believed this was just about race.
One explanation of this racial difference could be that as members of the
dominant racial group, white students saw the images on television of the hurricane victims and were more diverted by the color of the racialized others
than their black classmates who may have thought, "They are like me, but
poorer." White students may have halted their analysis at the color or race of
these victims, whereas black students perhaps continued their analysis by rec-
ognizing that these African Americans were, above all else, poor.

About 13 percent of students thought that social class was the primary force
operating in the aftermath, not race. It is important to note that a smaller yet

Table 7.2. Were the Effects of Hurricane Katrina a Racial Issue by Race?

Responses	Whites	Blacks	Other	Total
"Yes."	23 (22%)	12 (12%)	3 (3%)	38 (36.5%)
"Yes, but also class."	3 (2.8%)	11 (10.6%)	—	14 (13.4%)
"No, it was about class."	4 (3.8%)	9 (8.6%)	1 (1%)	14 (13.4%)
"No, nothing social."	17 (16.4%)	1 (1%)	—	18 (17.4%)
"No, media made it."	3 (2.9%)	1 (1%)	1 (1%)	5 (5%)
"I don't know/unsure."	2 (2%)	3 (3%)	10 (10%)	15 (14.3%)
Total	52 (50%)	37 (36%)	15 (14%)	104 (100%)

significant pattern emerged within these types of student responses. Students not only saw class as the major force operating in the aftermath but also expressed this concurrently with a "they just happen to be black" notion. That is, this disaster and the resulting problems affected poor people most directly, but these poor people *just happen to be black*. These students did not see race and class as connected but rather believe the victims' race was *merely coincidental*:

> I don't think it was a racial issue because it's a class issue. It just so happens that a big majority of minorities live there so it looks on the outside like it's racial. (black male)

> This was not a racial issue but an issue with low income [illegible] and it just happened that this group is mostly of a certain race. (white female)

> I believe it was more of a class issue. It just so happens that mostly African Americans were the ones that were in poverty. (black male)

Research on American color-blind ideology may help explain why the race and class of the victims are believed to be coincidental (see Bonilla-Silva 2001; Gallagher 2003). According to the color-blind ideology, race is not a factor in determining economic social location. What results is refusal to believe that race is a hindrance to success and social mobility. If skin color and race do not matter in U.S. society, why would they suddenly matter now?

Some students believed that this was a *natural* disaster and were almost confused as to why the aftermath *could* be attributed to anything but fierce weather. To these students, "hurricanes are not racist" or classist for that matter. Out of the total 17.4 percent of these responses, the majority were white students (16.4 percent) compared to only 1 percent of African American students. In fact, this is the second-largest reaction from white students; the largest response was, "Yes, this was about race." However, most of the whites who said it was about race were white *women*, whereas most in this category who said there were no social underpinnings operating are mostly white *men*. The following comments represent these beliefs that there was nothing social

Table 7.3. Were the Effects of Hurricane Katrina a Racial Issue by Gender?

Responses	Men	Women	Total
"Yes."	7 (7%)	31 (31%)	38 (36.5%)
"Yes, but also class."	5 (5%)	9 (8.65%)	14 (13.4%)
"No, it was about class."	6 (6%)	8 (7.7%)	14 (13.4%)
"No, nothing social."	10 (9.75%)	8 (7.7%)	18 (17.4%)
"No, media made it."	1 (1%)	4 (4%)	5 (5%)
"I don't know/unsure."	6 (6%)	9 (8.6%)	15 (14.3%)
Total	35 (34%)	69 (66%)	104 (100%)

about this disaster. One woman acknowledged class differences in vulnerability but simultaneously denied that class had anything to do with it:

> I can't say for sure but I don't think you can change the weather. Maybe the rich won't be affected as much because they're on the hill, but weather caused this, not anything else. (multiracial female)

A white male expressed that not only was this *not* a racial issue but that it was wrong to even suggest that racism was a factor:

> This could happen to any of us. It was not right to bring up racism. Hurricanes are not racist.

When this project was in the development stage, one of the driving questions was whether the public would recognize, with 24-hour media coverage, the social underpinnings of this natural disaster. The findings show a noteworthy racial difference—16.4 percent of whites saw no social underpinnings of this disaster compared to only 1 percent of blacks. Furthermore, the white *men* in our sample were most likely to express this reaction than any other reaction. White men were most likely to believe that there was *nothing social* operating before, during, or after the hurricane. This view is consistent with scholarship on privilege that suggests that privileged groups (in this case white men) maintain their privilege most easily by not acknowledging that inequality exists (e.g., Gallagher 2003; McIntosh 1989). While most students responded that this was a "racial issue" (36.5 percent, the second-largest reaction category (17.4 percent) was that there was nothing social about Hurricane Katrina and that the aftermath could be explained by none other than powerful weather.

A small percentage (5 percent) of respondents thought that the aftermath was not a racial issue but that the media made it a racial issue. It seems that these reactions reflect the idea that this was ultimately a natural disaster, but once the media got involved, it turned into a social and racial issue. Following are two reactions that represent the reaction that the media made this disaster a racial issue:

I'm pretty sure the hurricane isn't racist. As for the dealings of the aftermath—I don't think it was a racial issue until the media was involved. (white female)

I don't think so even though the media portrayed it that way. Most of the people in New Orleans are blacks so its is going to look like they were the only ones left in there but in reality they are the majority of people in the city. (white female)

It is difficult to determine what issues specifically these students were referring to, but it is possible they were referring to the accusations of inadequacy on the part of the government's dealing with the aftermath that came directly from news journalists. These reactions may also reflect the "looting" versus "finding" controversy, which was well publicized.

A significant percentage of students (14 percent) responded that they did not know if Hurricane Katrina was a racial issue. Some of these responses reflected an admitted lack of knowledge about what was happening; some admitted that they hadn't kept up with any coverage of the disaster and were therefore unqualified to answer the question. As one student responded, "Ever since I've lived on campus, I've been in my own little world. I am absolutely clueless about what's going on." Such responses may be indicative of American individualism and the lack of interest and concern over anything that does not personally affect an individual—regardless of the magnitude of it for so many other people.

DISCUSSION

This research provides insight into students' reactions of the aftermath of Hurricane Katrina. Many of the findings in this study speak to broader sociological issues that extend outside the scope of Hurricane Katrina as an isolated disaster. First, our findings illustrate that the media remains a powerful tool for shaping reactions. The focus on the "looting" versus "finding" controversy led many students to perceive the media as racist. Perceptions and reactions did not form in the minds of these students independent from the media's framing of this disaster. These findings support Dynes and Rodríguez's (2005) claim that the media framed what people considered important in this disaster. Without the media's focus on the racial discrimination, we doubt that many—specifically, whites—would have alluded to racism.

The media paradox leads us to deduce that the media not only is a powerful source of information transmission but may also have ideological power. For example, it is possible that white students' racial stereotypes about African Americans were confirmed by the media coverage. Alternatively, African Americans may have interpreted the media images as confirmation of enduring racial oppression in the United States. These differences matter because of the policy implications that may follow. It is not just the public who is influenced by the media and the framing of the disaster, but those in powerful political positions can be heavily influenced by these framings as well. As Dynes and Rodríguez (2005) suggest, "Television constructed the frame of meaning to which audiences and decision-makers came to understand Katrina" (2). If the media frames the aftermath as a result of victims' "bad behavior," then decision makers may address the matter within this framework. Our findings indicate that white male students were most likely to say that "nothing social" was underlying the aftermath of Katrina. This is problematic because the majority of political leaders who design and implement such policies are also mainly white men. If the white men in our sample were the most reluctant to see the social underpinnings of the aftermath, then it is possible that other white men (those in power) may also be reluctant to see these inequalities.

Criticisms of the government and their role in the relief efforts were widespread. An important pattern in these criticisms was the race and class comparisons that were made. The lingering question on the minds of many students is what would have happened if many of the victims were not poor and black. The second criticism of the government was expressed through claims that the U.S. government is too distracted by foreign preoccupation to adequately handle domestic needs. We did not ask students for their political affiliation, so we cannot be sure if these reactions were reflecting prior dissatisfaction with the war and with the government's role in the war. Regardless, these reactions speak to a sense of American entitlement. That is, many Americans believe that domestic needs should take priority over foreign involvement. When criticizing the government, black students were more likely than whites to specifically blame President Bush for the inadequate relief efforts. Criticisms here attacked the president's ability and character. According to these students, the president is incompetent and uncaring of poor minorities. These attitudes mirror a well-publicized comment by popular rap artist Kanye West that "George Bush doesn't care about black people." West's statement aired live on a music special hosted by NBC to raise money for the American Red Cross and was replayed often. Although West was scolded by many other celebrities and citizens alike for his comment, it is likely that many others nodded along in agreement with his assertion.

While most of the students in this sample placed blame for the aftermath on the government, there were students who attributed blame to the victims themselves. These reactions were most often accompanied with mentions of violence, looting, and other criminal behavior in which the victims engaged. To understand these claims, we must take into account the role of the media in framing such reactions. As explained here, media coverage conveyed the "important" issues to viewers so that the issues the media focused on in turn became what the viewers deemed important (Dynes and Rodríguez 2005). With much media coverage focusing on the "violent outbreaks" and "civil unrest," we can see how some students came to approach this disaster through the lens of violence.

The comparisons of the aftermath of Hurricane Katrina to the "Third World" may be indicative of American ethnocentrism, privilege, and the denial of poverty, especially as it is linked with race, in the United States. Dominguez (2005) suggests that we must take a closer look at these "Third World" comparisons, examining a very important question: What was "un-American" about the aftermath of Hurricane Katrina? Was it the lack of resources? Was it the images of *poor* people in distress waiting for help? If so, does this mean poverty is perceived as "un-American"? Or is it that many of these people were African American? If so, are African Americans in distress "un-American"? Or perhaps it was all of these combined—poor African Americans in despair waiting to be rescued. Certainly, these images are not images the public is accustomed to seeing despite the fact that large groups of poor minorities living in segregated communities has been a fundamental feature of American society since the beginning (Massey and Denton 1993).

Furthermore, this comparison of the aftermath of Hurricane Katrina to the "Third World" is problematic because New Orleans is an *American* city with a rich and lively history and a personality and culture that attracts millions of tourists each year. How can a child of such a wealthy and powerful nation come to be compared to an "underdeveloped," poverty-stricken nation? To see images reminiscent of this on our own soil was confusing and disturbing, but the students, while in part able to make the connection to black poverty in the United States, also reinforced our ideologies that steer us from this understanding by saying that this is uncharacteristic of our superpower nation.

The findings in our analysis also indicated that students came to understand the role of race and class differently in regard to Hurricane Katrina and its aftermath. There were some important differences between white and black students' reactions to the aftermath. While the majority of the sample branded the aftermath a "racial issue," black students were more likely to suggest that social class *and* race were linked in this disaster. As racial minorities, perhaps these black students are more likely to see social inequalities operating in their everyday lives and are more likely to also see the effects of class inequality as well. Meanwhile, for the white students, a fundamental function of the maintenance of their white privilege is believing in meritocracy (Gallagher 2003) and denying privilege based on skin color (McIntosh 1989) and social class status. As members of the dominant racial group, whites do not see discriminatory practices being carried out toward nonwhites and therefore believe that they do not exist. According to these white students, specifically the white men, all people are treated equally, so why would this hurricane be any different—this was, after all, a "natural" disaster.

CONCLUSION

We are hopeful that this research offers valuable insight into students' reactions to Hurricane Katrina and its aftermath. The media's coverage of the aftermath of Hurricane Katrina influenced important reactions: skepticism of the media's fairness in its coverage, distrust in the government response to the tragedy, perceptions of the victims' behavior, and finally the country in which we live. Clarke (2005) argues that it is important to examine disasters because "looking at disasters is a way to look at the social organization of society." The media's coverage of poor blacks struggling to survive brought to light a reality that many middle- and upper-class citizens in America wanted to ignore or, even worse, never knew existed.

Despite durable race and class inequalities, the aftermath of the hurricane tapped into how unaware many students are of the fact that these inequalities are "American" as apple pie. As the hurricane coverage of the aftermath left imprints on Americans' perceptions about race, class, the government, and the media, it also forced some to think about their country in a new way. The comparisons of New Orleans to the Third World says a lot about the invisibility of the American underclass. The assumption that "all" Americans are somehow middle class or above was debunked by the media's images of poor blacks desperately looking for help. These images shed light on a problem that has long been swept under America's rug—social inequality rooted in American race and class disparities. As with the terrorist attacks of September 11, Hurricane Katrina showed the American people that even the world's "greatest nation" is vulnerable to the unimaginable. Years from now, when Hurricane Katrina recedes back into Americans' consciousness, becoming just another historical event, we hope that this research helps keep the story alive.

8

Landscapes of Disaster and Place Orientation in the Aftermath of Hurricane Katrina

DeMond Shondell Miller and Jason David Rivera

Natural disasters that destroy the physical landscape of an area also weaken local residents' and outsiders' perceptions of place. As a landscape is shaped by human intervention, the perceptions about that place are also shaped. With an abrupt change in the topography, a forced change in the perception of the landscape takes place, causing a new and almost foreign outlook on the once familiar land (Basso 1996). According to Day (2002), communities understand places, and the understanding of a place is built on memories of the past. Communities resist abrupt change because such change threatens memories of the past linked to specific places. In the case of a natural disaster, a community has no control over the pace of change for the built environment. A disaster-stricken community can simply hope that the devastation does not significantly change the topographic sense of place among survivors. "After all, if the physical infrastructure of [a place] cannot withstand such catastrophes, how can the social infrastructure that also gives them shape?" (Elliott and Pais 2006, 295).

The physical existence of a place and its landscape allows the residents to form attachments with the land and project their values and culture into the future so that following generations may adhere to similar values (Foote 1988, 1997; Lowenthal 1985). Significant changes to the landscape impede the future generations' development of place attachment that is similar to past generations. Place attachment development is impossible to duplicate in future generations because specific features of the landscape are missing that were there in the past (Milligan 1998). Just as important as a person's first impression of another is a person's first impression of a landscape; the impression affects the way he or she perceives a place, positively or negatively. This first impression is pivotal to the understanding and perception of a place (Day 2002).

When communities are devastated by natural disasters, people do not have the ability to decide what is destroyed, but they do have the ability to decide what is reconstructed. Aspects present before the onset of disaster that are not reconstructed afterward symbolize the pieces of the society that are not "wanted" or aspects of the society that are "wished to be forgotten" in the future. Therefore, elements that are reconstructed symbolize the cultural values that the society seeks to highlight (Foote 1997). The rebuilding of specific elements emphasizes the important social and political ideals a society values and wishes to transmit to the next generation (Baker 2003). Because the topological and aesthetic landscapes have such an effect on the resident community, there must be an understanding of what places and landscapes signify to communities and society as a whole.

THE IMPORTANCE OF PLACE AND LANDSCAPE

People are unconsciously linked to the places they continually come in contact with simply because of the relationships they associate with that place (Basso 1996). In Keith Basso's book *Wisdom Sits in Places*, he describes how wisdom—the knowledge needed to survive in a geographical location—is imparted via the natural environment. Basso asks, "What is wisdom?" and Dudley, his Apache informant, responds by saying that "wisdom sits in places. It's like water that never dries up. You need to drink water to stay alive, don't you? Well, you also need to drink from places" (127). In essence, the landscape is instructive and, in fact, sustains life.

Place, where wisdom[1] resides, is important to the understanding of a people and how they react to changes in the world. Attachment to a physical landscape leads to place identity. According to Williams and Vaske (2002; Bow and Buys 2003), place identity is a dimension of place attachment, while emotional attachment is concerned with the "symbolic importance of a place as a repository of emotions and relationships that give meaning and purpose to life" (4). Individual place identities are formed over time from place-related personal experiences (Relph 1976). When several people experience similar qualities, objects, and problems associated with a locality, those multiple individual place identities coalesce over time to form a common group place identity (Bow and Buys 2003; Relph 1976). These bonds to a place occur through interactions of affect—"emotions, knowledge, beliefs, behaviors and actions in relation to a particular place" (Proshansky, Fabian, and Kaminoff 1983, as cited in Altman and Low 1992; Bonnes and Secchiaroli 2003; Bow and Buys 2003). Subsequent attachment to a given place can be measured by the degree to which individuals and communities are able to substitute the place in question for another. If a person or a community is able to move from one place to another with relative psychological ease, their degree of place attachment to the former place is relatively low in comparison to someone or a community that has difficulty moving from place to place because "new" places do not offer the same satisfaction as the initial place (Milligan 1998; Williams, Patterson, and Roggenbuck 1992). Psychological and symbolic connections to the land are weakened, if not altogether rearranged, by the destruction caused by disasters.

DISASTER LANDSCAPE AND THE ECOLOGICAL-SYMBOLIC APPROACH

Interacting and processing visual cues in a terrain marked by disaster serves as stimulus for the social construction of a new place identity. The information used to maneuver in the former environment is replaced with new information, or new wisdom, that is used to survive in a terrain ravaged by disaster. Both the nature and the perception of the devastation are important because these components help those in the area respond to environmental insults and decide how to navigate the different landscapes that are superimposed on the physical landscape. The ecological-symbolic approach "joins environmental sociology's assumption that biospheres and social structures are interdependent with a key assumption of symbolic interaction that people act on the basis of meanings they attribute to events and conditions. From this perspective, social responses to hazards and disasters are affected both by the nature of the disruption in the human and environment relations and the appraisals people make of those disruptions" (Kroll-Smith and Couch 1994, 28).

More specifically, the ecological-symbolic perspective posits that a community's response to devastations such as Hurricane Katrina is shaped by both the nature of the environmental disruption and the interpretative frames through which those disruptions are apprehended. People receive environmental information through interpretive frames that can be received from a variety of sources. Based on those appraisals, the place identity of a destroyed community defines its inhabitants by conferring victimhood status. Twigger-Ross and Uzzell (1996) contend that, "Some people do seem to use a place [as a] self-referent in order to present themselves as distinct from others. . . . In this sense, place functions in a similar way to a social category and therefore place identifications can be thought of as comparable to social identifications" (207). Furthermore, they contend that "there is evidence for the establishment and use of place in the maintenance of continuity of self and the use of place to create, symbolize and establish new selves." In essence, "the environment becomes a salient part of identity as opposed to merely setting a context in which the identity can be established and developed" (218). However, when a disaster rearranges the sociocultural, socioeconomic, and political landscapes of a specific place identification, the social identification associated with the place is also changed.

SUPERIMPOSED DISASTER LANDSCAPES

In this section, we consider the symbolic side of the ecological-symbolic approach to provide cues about the actions of residents who return to find a "new" social structure amid the disaster landscape. The term *structure* refers to "the structuring properties [rules and resources] . . . which make it possible for discernibly similar social practices to exist across varying spans of time and space and which lend them systematic form" (Giddens 1984, 17) and results in resources needed to order social life. Structure is made possible as a result of rules and resources that "[exist] only in and through the activities of human agents" (Giddens 1989, 256). The disaster landscapes exist not only as a structure but also as a parallel to the "normal structure" (predisaster) as individuals constantly refer back to it as a reflexive notion of the way reality *ought* to be represented. Critical to the understanding of human agency in the aftermath of a disaster is the existence of the disaster social structures, such as the sociocultural, socioeconomic, and the political landscapes. In essence, the rules and regulations governing normative behavior are different in the new context. From the disaster experience emerges a new set of rules for conducting life in the natural and human-constructed landscapes; the rules are redefined and internalized as a new way of life that must be reflexively monitored and interpreted so that humans can navigate the physical and socially constructed landscapes simultaneously.

Sociocultural Landscape

Changes in the sociocultural landscape after a natural or technological disaster, such as the flooding of New Orleans, are just as dramatic as changes in the physical landscape. These changes tend to be twofold in that they magnify the social situations that existed before Hurricane Katrina (Cutter 2005; Cutter, Boruff, and Shirley 2003; Miller and Rivera, in press). and show a collapse of community norms immediately following the disaster. The exposure of disadvantaged ethnic communities in New Orleans was made apparent with the passage of the hurricane. Before the storm, the African American population stood at 68 percent within New Orleans compared to a 32 percent presence statewide (Zedlewski 2006). Overall, 45 percent of all New Orleans residents of 16 years of age or older were unemployed, enhancing the presence of poverty among the city's population, of which over one-third of blacks were considered poor, higher than the national average, and the poverty rate of "other" races (specifically Asian Americans and Native Americans) was also above the nation's average (Zedlewski 2006). With such high poverty levels, one in five families did not own an automobile, while 8 percent of families did not have access to a phone service (Zedlewski 2006). Such extreme levels of poverty increased the vulnerability of poor, of which many were unable to evacuate under their own means.

Although these social conditions present before the storm were dismal on paper when comparing Louisiana to the nation, social conditions present before the storm influenced the development of a culture admired around the world:

> Vibrant arts and cultures in New Orleans shined the one bright beacon on an otherwise depressed landscape for low-income families. Indeed, many of the cultural practices and traditions that made New Orleans famous can be traced back to the city's poorest citizens and their ancestors. Arts and culture were key to New Orleans' unique character. (Zedlewski 2006, 7)

But, after Katrina, the cultural landscape, arguably the city's greatest asset, was significantly altered—possibly indefinitely. Although there was limited damage to the French Quarter of the city, which contained the famous Bourbon Street and many of the city's museums and galleries, many of which have resumed business (Jackson 2006; Robinson 2005), the other areas of the city that significantly contributed to its cultural landscape have been destroyed or forced to move to other areas of the nation. Mardi Gras Indian tribes brass band members, independent musicians, native cooks, church congregations, and parishes have been scattered across the nation, contributing to a void in the presence of people that were significant parts of the unique culture of New Orleans before the storm (Jackson 2006). Moreover, whole neighborhoods that contributed to the city's music and culture through the presence of organizations, small clubs, music venues, and home to the artists themselves have been completely wiped away.

During Hurricane Katrina, the collapse of the social institutions (i.e., public safety, hospitals, transportation, and so on) led to a setting in which one's life and one's outlook on life were fostered by individual stress and collective trauma, creating feelings of uncertainty and distrust—and a loss of social capital. Ritchie (2004) contends that "social capital, both informal and formal, are depleted in a corrosive community and trust between individuals, as well as abstract trust, is affected by an atmosphere of uncertainty" (366). With the diminishing social infrastructure, neighbors no longer trusted that their possessions would be safe while they were gone from their homes, and evidence of their distrust blanketed the landscape. Signs at the entrance of neighborhoods and in front of individual homes read, "We Don't Dial 911 . . . Looters Will Be Shot" (see Figure 8.1), "Looters Will Be Killed," or "You Loot We Shoot." These signs are tangible evidence of the erosion of trust in New Orleans and the Gulf Coast, pitting survivors against outsiders and neighbors against neighbors. The magnification of social dynamics within the disaster-affected community creates a sociocultural landscape that can either be improved on or left to fester into a "corrosive community" (Freudenburg 1997; Miller 2006).[2] In some ways, the magnification of social dynamics is beneficial to the resident community because the

Figure 8.1. Courtesy of DeMond Shondell Miller (2005)

forced "spotlight" on negative social dynamics does not allow authorities to ignore them, politically forcing leaders into dealing with negative aspects, thereby creating more beneficial social dynamics.

The remaining sociocultural landscape is one of reestablishment. Katrina destroyed lives and neighborhoods by forcing a majority of the contributors to the city's culture into relative exile. Those citizens who remained throughout the ordeal developed a sense of distrust toward their neighbors. The culture once indicative of New Orleans has been replaced by a transient culture, developing from the presence of temporary migrant workers. The existence of this new sociocultural landscape has altered the cultural component of the city that made it famous. Although there are initiatives to redevelop the sociocultural characteristics of the old city into the *new* New Orleans, the question to be answered is, Have the changes to the socioeconomic and political landscapes been altered by the storm significantly enough that through the city's reconstruction there will be the ability for the past culture to reassert itself, or will the new city develop its own culture that is significantly independent enough of the past that a new culture develops?

Socioeconomic Landscape

The socioeconomic landscape that emerges after a disaster has the potential to redistribute wealth among the local population as well as change the entities that have controlled the economic structure in the past. In the aftermath of a disaster, government and private business entities come into and leave affected areas for a variety of reasons. During the *Exxon Valdez* oil spill cleanup phase, many commercial fishers experienced heavy economic losses, while others had lucrative cleanup contracts, thus earning them the name "spillionaires." So too do the residents of New Orleans stand to experience the same shifts in economic standing as huge federal grants and lucrative cleanup and rebuilding contracts become available.

As has been seen in the sociocultural landscape of New Orleans, the city experienced high levels of unemployment and poverty before the storm, contributing to large economic station gaps between the rich and poor. Now the economy in post-Katrina New Orleans is showing an even greater widening gap between the rich and poor. This trend is increasing more since some of the temporarily displaced population is returning to the city in an attempt to gain or regain employment,[3] but according to past trends of displaced persons, the ability of these people to find employment is variable:

> Typically, most workers return to employment after being involuntarily displaced from their jobs, but sometimes after long spells of joblessness and usually with a significant loss in wages. Average displaced workers lose 15 to 20 percent of prior earnings once reemployed—commonly more if they are older or less educated. (Holzer and Lerman 2006, 10; see also Jacobson, LaLonde, and Sullivan 1993, 2005; Kletzer 1998)

In addition to possible decreases in wages, fewer displaced residents are returning to New Orleans, which may be attributed to the availability of jobs and housing (Holzer and Lerman 2006). Although currently there is increasing employment available in service industries, after the hurricane the physical landscape initially allowed a socioeconomic landscape to develop that supported employment only in low-wage labor, which was filled mostly by the influx of immigrants into the city after the disaster (Holzer and Lerman 2006). The influx of migrant workers into New Orleans was a matter of coincidence in reference to time and place, as the immigrants did not gradually immigrate into the city but instead "appeared" almost immediately after the disaster. Their "appearance" was not a random occurrence or surprising because the immigrant population had already been there before the disaster. It was only the void caused by displacement that made their presence more noticeable in relation to other racial segments of society.

The lack of people able to work has caused normally low-paying employers to try to lure workers to their establishments with the promise of high wages and incentives (see Figure 8.2). The socioeconomic conditions are dismal for certain industries; large infusions of funds will be needed to invigorate the multisector economy to its pre-Katrina state. Some estimates of capital outlays reaching $10 billion over the next year for infrastructure investment will be needed over the next year for employment, which would supply 169,000 jobs paying $40,000 salaries and $20,000 in other costs for a full year to rebuild the city. Subsidizing employment in this way will, it is hoped, stimulate the economy into reestablishing itself and indirectly give rise to the creation of local jobs in other occupations and industries (Holzer and Lerman 2006).

Figure 8.2.   Courtesy of DeMond Shondell Miller (2005)

However, if there is not enough affordable housing constructed in the area, employment opportunities will be extremely difficult to fill.

Katrina caused nearly 228,000 homes and apartments to flood, which included 39 percent of all owner-occupied units and 56 percent of all rental units in New Orleans (Brookings Institution 2005; Popkin, Turner, and Burt 2006). Because the city was built on land that is prone to flooding, a significant portion of the city's neighborhoods were completely destroyed (see Figure 8.3). Of all the ethnic groups residing in the city before the disaster, African Americans bore the heaviest damages to their neighborhoods because 75 percent of all flooded areas in New Orleans were made up mostly of African American residents (Brookings Institution 2005; Popkin, Turner, and Burt

Figure 8.3.   Courtesy of DeMond Shondell Miller (2005)

2006). Although it is undisputed that there needs to be extensive housing redevelopment, there is great concern in reference to avoiding old patterns of concentrating assisted housing and poor families into a few isolated neighborhoods (Popkin, Turner, and Burt 2006). In addition to creating less segregated housing patterns, the services available to rebuilt communities should have more equitable characteristics:

> Creating communities of opportunity and choice means not only constructing new housing, but also investing in good schools, health care, transportation, and other services. Further, it means ensuring access to sustainable employment" (Popkin, Turner, and Burt 2006, 11)

By investing in better services as well as constructing new homes, the socioeconomic landscape of New Orleans can be more equitable, prosperous, and sustainable than it was in the past. The socioeconomic landscape left in wake of Katrina is one of almost "Genesis." The storm has wiped away most remnants of the prior socioeconomic constraints of segregated housing and poverty and has left the possibility for a fresh start in the pursuance of a more equitable socioeconomic landscape that impacts the political landscape of New Orleans. After a highly contested mayoral election in the spring of 2006, incumbent Mayor Ray C. Nagin (D) won reelection against challenger Lieutenant Governor Mitch Landrieu (D), both of whom espoused rebuilding platforms that would initiate broad-based coalitions. An example of Nagin's promise to rebuild a more inclusive New Orleans is occurring with the development of a citywide plan. Fourteen months after Hurricane Katrina, the Unified New Orleans Plan (UNOP) held its first group meetings on October 14, 2006. UNOP was created to give a voice to all the citizens and communities to capitalize on federal and state recovery funds in a systematic coordinated effort for rebuilding and to allow individual neighborhoods to participate in their own recovery at the neighborhood and district planning levels to formulate one citywide plan.

Political Landscape

The political landscape that emerges in the aftermath of disasters fosters a sense of distrust in authority, especially when people feel that relief efforts and mitigation were not handled properly (Miller and Rivera 2006). Katrina's legacy has marred the political landscape and created a liability for policymakers who failed to craft sound environmental policies, support critical infrastructure (i.e., levees), and correct the dysfunctional aspects of local state and federal response systems by the close of the 2006 hurricane season—over 15 months after the disaster. In the aftermath of a disaster, political trust in authority must be reestablished or in some circumstances recreated to cope with the new sociocultural and socioeconomic situations.

Figure 8.4. © S. Kelley (*Times-Picayune*)

Although government units should attempt to establish as much trust as possible with the recovering population, the government must establish a minimal sense of "good faith" so that the local people feel the authorities are legitimate and have their best interests at heart (Aberbach and Walker 1970; Miller and Rivera 2006; Sabine 1952). Issues of trust arise as culpability and blame are assessed amid cover-ups, denials, and litigations (Edelstein 1988) (see Figures 8.4, 8.5, and 8.6). In the political landscape that developed in the aftermath of Katrina, the local and federal governments have had to attempt to make up for their participation in institutional hypocrisy (Thompson 2004), whether it was intentional or not.[4]

The political landscape of any given place is a response to both the sociocultural and the socioeconomic landscapes indicative to that specific place. The social dynamics of the place, theoretically in a democratic environment, mold the political landscape because the politics of the place develop to cope with indicative social conditions. Therefore, political landscapes vary from place to place just as topography and social conditions vary from place to place. However, an element that all political landscapes have attributed to them, if they are truly efficiently effective democracies, is their relative legitimacy in the minds of their resident population, which strengthens constituent trust in political leaders and decisions:

Republics and democracies attempt to decrease the overall distrust of the government by allowing the citizenry to participate and nominate individuals that will progress their interests; thus trust on the behalf of citizens toward a representative depends on the constituent's perception that the representative shares his or her interests. (Ruscio 1996, as cited in Miller and Rivera 2006, 40)

Securing constituents' trust within the political landscape of New Orleans will be difficult because of the lack of historical civic trust on the behalf of the largest segment of the city's population—African Americans (Miller and Rivera, in press).

Within the confines of the old sociocultural and socioeconomic landscapes that developed before Katrina, the political landscape developed to exclude the largely African American population from politics up until the second half of the twentieth century (Miller and Rivera, in press). The exclusion of this overrepresented portion of the population from politics has led to the alienation of this segment of the population from social services and past disaster relief, stimulating an ever-growing distrust in government authorities. The lack of attention given to this segment of the population is reinforced by

Figure 8.5.   © S. Kelley (*Times-Picayune*)

Figure 8.6. © John Sherffius (The Professional Cartoonist Index)

elected officials' comments about the situation African American residents found themselves in after Katrina passed: "We finally cleaned up public housing in New Orleans. We couldn't do it, but God did" (Baker 2005, as cited in Reagan et al. 2005, 29). Statements such as this significantly contribute to the concept that government authorities are lacking in their elected duty to keep the best interests of their constituents at heart in crafting legislation or making political decisions.

Katrina, however, has altered the preexisting sociocultural and socioeconomic landscapes significantly enough to create a totally new political landscape categorized by civic distrust and the establishment of more equitable social situations. The political landscape of the past, in which historically disadvantaged groups were continually neglected as a result of their lack of political clout, has been destroyed along with local communities. Currently, the political landscape is such that it is impossible to ignore the interests of the poor and disadvantaged portions of the city's population because of the amount of media coverage given to political and social neglect that plagued the old political landscape (Dyson 2006). The landscape has been forced into acknowledging the needs of the entire population and not just the historically more advantaged segments of the population. Just as the sociocultural and socioeconomic landscapes have a direct effect on the political landscape, so too does the political landscape have an effect on the other landscapes. Through the development of the political landscape, the other landscapes either will be stunted or will progress. It is with the help of individual leaders within the political landscape of New Orleans that the development of the sociocultural and socioeconomic landscapes can be molded to be more sustaining, equitable, and beneficial to the population that lives within all three coexisting and interdependent landscapes.

IMPLICATIONS OF DISASTER LANDSCAPE AND COMMUNITY RECOVERY

According to Ehrenreich and McQuaide (2001), following the first weeks after a disaster, victims may go through a "honeymoon" phase, characterized by feelings of satisfaction and general optimism about the future. But in the weeks that follow, victims make realistic appraisals of the lasting consequences of the disaster. This is when the landscape devastation and its psychological and emotional consequences of loss become apparent. Victims realize the direct and indirect impacts on patterns of landownership and use, wage labor, migration (uprooting and resettlement), and the general change in community dynamics. All the traditional community processes to which victims connect with the place may no longer exist (Ehrenreich and McQuaide 2001). A recognizable physical landscape sends a message of hope, rebuilding, and community renewal.

Both the landscape and "human culture are important factors that influence the way human communities comprehend their environments: people receive sensory input from their environment, but they interpret these from factors received from their families, friends, the mass media and other social organizations" (Gunter, Aronoff, and Joel 1999, 636). For New Orleans, a city with a long history of political corruption, economic disparity, and social inequality (Miller and Rivera, in press), the physical landscape serves as symbol of a social system awash in its own corruption before Hurricane Katrina. Environmental and long-term social recovery from a disaster such as Katrina is unprecedented; the situation is a "new species" of recovery in that the old approaches of coping with landscapes of uncertainty are not sufficient to address the overwhelming challenges brought on by the initial disaster and the continued trauma of a slow cleanup process, government uncertainty, and protracted legal processes. The restoration of landscapes—where the physical landscape, community corrosion, political mistrust, and local economy serve as a catalyst for the psychosocial healing—repairs community norms of reciprocity and restores a sense of place after Hurricane Katrina. By initiating the cleanup phase early and reestablishing normality in an area, the aesthetic appeal of the immediate landscape will serve as a catalyst for reinvigorating the present economy and restoring the long-term confidence in public officials. Finally, by reestablishing the symbolic connection to the larger ecological setting, citizens can reestablish their sense of place. The ecological-symbolic approach offers key insights into the socially constructed meaning of the physical environment and its profound impacts on the social, political, and economic dimensions of the city, state, and region. Ultimately, citizens who are connected to the land and place are stakeholders in the place and are more likely to play a key role in rebuilding a more environmentally secure, economically sustainable, and socially equitable region.

NOTES

1. Wisdom refers to the local knowledge needed to survive in a particular environment.

2. Picou, Marshall, and Gill (2004) assert that "although many factors have been identified as contributing to the emergence and persistence of corrosive communities, we contend that none are as debilitating as litigation processes that typically ensue to redress environmental, economic, social, and psychological damages" (1494).

3. According to Elliott and Pais (2006, 310), of the New Orleanians who were employed at the time of Katrina, only a quarter reported having the same job one month later in comparison to over two-thirds of respondents from outside the city.

4. Thompson (2004) explains that "institutional hypocrisy involves a disparity between the publicly avowed purposes of an institution and its actual performance or function. This disparity often develops over time as an institution comes to serve purposes other than those for which it was established" (212). In the case of the political landscape of Katrina, years of the government avowing social equity was contended when the hurricane exposed the social inequities of social circumstances and relief efforts.

9

A Community Study of Disaster Impacts and Redevelopment Issues Facing East Biloxi, Mississippi

Anna M. Kleiner, John J. Green, and Albert B. Nylander III

In the aftermath of an economic, natural, and/or technological disaster the challenges of community development are exacerbated multifold. An important element to providing effective relief, recovery, and development assistance is access to timely information *and* analysis. This is key to taking informed action in response to needs in the community. However, faced with the immediate problems and scarcity of resources at the local level to meet these issues, individuals and organizations must often forgo data collection and analysis in favor of providing food, water, shelter, and medicine. One way to help bridge the gap between providing services and information needs is through community-based research designed to connect community partners with researchers in the enterprise of information gathering, analysis, and sense making.

In this chapter, we draw from a wide variety of participatory and action-oriented conceptual frameworks (e.g., Reason and Bradbury 2001; Selener 1997; Stoecker 2005; Stringer 1999; Voth 1979) to support our position that community-based research is an effective strategy for building university/community partnerships while responding to disasters in terms of relief, recovery, and redevelopment. Our analysis is based on research conducted in and around East Biloxi, Mississippi, a community heavily damaged by Hurricane Katrina. We review primary and secondary data gathered through surveys, interviews, and field observation focusing on local efforts. We review several redevelopment planning efforts advocating goals and recommendations for Biloxi neighborhoods crafted by both local and external organizations. We then evaluate the appropriateness and effectiveness of community-based research as a strategy for university researchers to assist communities suffering from the aftermath of disasters.

DISASTERS, RESPONSE, AND REDEVELOPMENT

Oliver-Smith (1996) describes disasters as occurring at the intersection of society, technology, and environment, demonstrating society's weakness in achieving sustainable adaptation to critical features of the natural and social environment. Most disasters are linked to models and patterns of built development as they intersect with the environment. Although prevailing weather systems cause hurricanes, damage in a community results, at least partially, from concentration of populations, inadequate building regulations, and unprotected infrastructure (see Clarke and Short 1993, 378).

When disaster strikes, it tends to be a "totalizing" experience, impacting almost all of community life (Oliver-Smith 1996). Disruption to major social organizational elements and to physical facilities in a community results in individual and group stress and social disorganization of varying severity. People and communities face numerous challenges, in both material and nonmaterial terms, that vary with the scope and timing of the disaster (Oliver-Smith 1996). Unmet needs after disasters are often the result of the depth of existing social inequalities (e.g., class, race, ethnicity, gender) that create vulnerable populations, compounded by the inadequacies of institutional disaster assistance programs and regimes (Blaikie et al. 1994; Bolin and Stanford 1998; Morrow and Enarson 1996; Oliver-Smith 1996; Watts 1992). In sum, a disaster generally compounds the daily needs and troubles that people struggle with in their lives.

When evaluating disaster relief and recovery endeavors, it is necessary to determine what assistance is available and accessible and what assistance people need to reduce their vulnerability to disasters. Issues that quickly emerged after the 1994 Northridge earthquake in California were the repair or replacement of damaged housing and business districts, reflecting the overall vulnerability of people relying on the built environment for support of their daily activities (Bolin and Stanford 1998). Oliver-Smith (1996) notes that relocation or resettlement of affected populations is a common strategy of reconstruction efforts. The importance of place in the construction of individual and community identities and in the politics of interpersonal, community, and intercultural relations means that the loss or removal of a community by disaster can be profoundly traumatic (Erikson 1994).

The need to grieve and mourn is a major theme in research on disasters, especially from the perspectives of cultural anthropology and social psychology. Individual losses can be compounded by the destruction of communities, which results in grief for lost homes, social spaces and situations, and culturally important places and structures (Erikson 1994; Oliver-Smith 1996). In the case of the 1997 Red River Valley flood in Minnesota and North Dakota, fundamental patterns of community, work, family, and place were disrupted. Evacuated residents faced an experience that was completely unanticipated and beyond their previous experiences. Their sense-making abilities were severely limited in the days following the evacuation, and their sense of hopelessness was due, at least in part, to an inability to reconcile the devastating effects of the flood. For months, residents faced an unprecedented cleanup task for which they were unprepared (see Sellnow, Seeger, and Ulmer 2002). Core beliefs and assumptions about security, essential convictions about the stability of institutions, and the very viability of the community were literally washed away (Sellnow, Seeger, and Ulmer 2002).

Reviewing the literature, Oliver-Smith (1996) contends that interaction between disaster victims and aid workers is sometimes problematic, such as when there appears a contentious we–they dichotomy. Postdisaster aid may also alter the fabric and quality of local social relations. Multiple meanings are generated from the diverse voices in the rapid sequence of events following a disaster event. Interpretation becomes a contested field, and the power of representation is crucial in the politics of defining the occurrence and extent of disaster and aid distribution. Natural disasters "present an extraordinarily difficult context for inter-organizational and inter-jurisdictional coordination. When disaster threatens a community, it requires different responses from different organizations at different locations to set aside prior activities and focus time, effort, and attention on a common goal" (Comfort et al. 2001, 145; see also Sellnow, Seeger, and Ulmer 2002). The conditions of crisis in combination with informational needs may enhance the relative levels of uncertainty, and the sense-making capacity of individuals seeking to manage and contain a crisis may be overwhelmed, thus enhancing crisis-related damage (Sellnow, Seeger, and Ulmer 2002).

Bolin and Stanford (1998) emphasize the importance of identifying and addressing socioeconomic conditions that give rise to vulnerability. They maintain that this should be a major component of local recovery and development programs. Participatory and collaborative efforts between a variety of stakeholders, including government agencies, local nonprofit organizations, and residents may result in innovative and context-sensitive responses that more directly address people's needs. In large-scale disaster, the reconstruction process may last indefinitely, often evolving into development programs with the experts and their work becoming permanent fixtures in the social landscape (Oliver-Smith 1996).

When creating plans to mitigate and/or respond to disasters, two common problems arise. The first difficulty is emphasizing the presence of a plan as a document rather than emphasizing a planning process. The second challenge is that government officials, policymakers, and law enforcement officials may lack an awareness of the literature on planning for natural and technological disasters that could be useful for the development of their own disaster plans (Perry and Lindell 2003). There is a tendency to equate emergency planning with the presence of a written plan, with the plan as evidence of jurisdictional preparedness; however, planning is a never-ending jurisdictional process. Emergency planning should be conceived and implemented as a process and should address the logistics of both threat assessment and response (see Perry and Lindell 2003). Successful postdisaster plans encompass development writ large, with an eye toward the most vulnerable and long-term issues.

A PARTICIPATORY FRAMEWORK FOR DISASTER RESPONSE

Participatory action research has been used as a comprehensive theoretical framework to describe how and why researchers embrace local knowledge when responding to the needs expressed by people in communities and organizations and empowering them to pursue and achieve social change. Participatory action research aims to develop an alternative system of knowledge production based on the people's role of setting the agendas, participating in data gathering and analysis, and controlling the use of outcomes. The terms frequently used in the literature to describe broader participation in the research process have included participatory research, action research, praxis research, participatory inquiry, collaborative inquiry, action inquiry, and cooperative inquiry (Deshler and Ewert 1996).

In our analysis of disaster impacts and relief, recovery, and redevelopment issues, we use community-based research as a synthesizing research framework that includes several traditions of theory and practice of participatory action research derived from the following major assumptions and values: "(1) democratization of knowledge production and use; (2) ethical fairness in the benefits of the knowledge generation process; (3) an ecological stance toward society and nature; (4) appreciation of the capacity of humans to reflect, learn, and change; and (5) a commitment to nonviolent social change" (House et al. 1996, 6). Community-based research (CBR) emphasizes dialogue, joint research, empowering people to take action, allowing the poor to be creative and capable, and having outsiders (e.g., university researchers) serve as catalysts and facilitators as communities and their organizations respond to the social, economic, and political pressures of disasters.

Two noteworthy models of community-based research work are presented by Stoecker (2005) and Stringer (1999). Stoecker utilizes a project model moving through the four stages of diagnosis, prescription, implementation, and evaluation. Stringer presents the three steps to community-based research as look, think, and act. Borrowing from and augmenting these and other perspectives, we take a pragmatic approach, viewing community-based research as a "tool box" of strategies for engaging people—from community residents to professional researchers—in participatory processes of knowledge development and utilization. Multiple research methods are used within community-based research. These may include analysis of secondary data, surveys, focus groups, interviews, and field observation as well as alternative approaches, such as facilitated group dialogue and consensus building.

In East Biloxi, Mississippi, we applied a community-based research framework to our collaborative work with several individuals and nonprofit organizations in order to develop research questions in association with the aftermath of the hurricane, explore secondary data from the U.S. Census, engage in field observation, conduct a needs assessment survey, and provide input through qualitative interviews. We facilitated participatory needs assessment strategies to help identify immediate and longer-term problems faced by the community and to address the needs of the residents in their struggle to cope with the disaster of Hurricane Katrina.

PROJECT CONTEXT AND RESEARCH METHODS

This project resulted from multiple organizational networks of people assessing and responding to the disaster. Central to this was the role of Oxfam America, which was assisting in disaster relief and recovery. We had previously worked on projects in collaboration with Oxfam and its partners, including the Rural Coalition and the Mississippi Association of Cooperatives. In the aftermath of the hurricane, Oxfam requested assistance in relation to some of its local partner organizations, especially the East Biloxi Coordination and Relief Center (hereafter EBCRC or the Center). A trip was made to the area and the Center to meet with representatives from several organizations and discuss the need, if any, for research assistance. A Biloxi city councilman and representatives from several of the nonprofit and faith-based organizations working with the Center identified a desire to conduct a needs assessment survey and utilize the data to inform and coordinate services and engage in advocacy.[1]

Additional researchers made a follow-up visit to East Biloxi with the intention of working with other volunteers to canvass the neighborhood and complete questionnaires.[2] Despite great initiative, this met with minimal success. Given the level of activity at food distribution sites and places providing other essential goods and services, the researchers and Center volunteers decided to complete questionnaires where people were congregating for these services. Treating the questionnaire as a combination intake form and needs assessment instrument, data were collected at these sites and at the EBCRC office. After completion of this visit, the Center and its partner organizations continued to complete questionnaires and use them as immediate tools for preparing work orders for volunteers. Photocopies of the questionnaires were sent to the university-based researchers who collaborated with a group of volunteers to enter the data for storage and analysis.[3] Periodically, the researchers would send updates of the data set back to the Center. These data were collected from September through November 2005. In December 2005, a local computer technician partnering with the Center agreed to take responsibility for structuring a version of the database for case management in a user-friendly form. Additional data could then be collected and managed through the Center office, eliminating the need to send this material elsewhere.

Established immediately after Hurricane Katrina, the EBCRC provided multiple services, including (1) information sharing and collaboration among several organizations; (2) serving as a clearinghouse of information for local residents and volunteers, (3) advocacy for the needs and interests of local residents and others impacted by the storm, and (4) facilitation of partner groups to provide direct services (e.g., tree cutting, house gutting, access to food and supplies).

In tandem with the needs assessment survey, 13 informal qualitative interviews were conducted with people in the area who were in need of assistance and/or were providing help. Additionally, observation was documented in the form of field notes. Over the course of four visits, informal interviews were conducted, meetings were attended, and services were observed. This part of the project was formalized and expanded after the needs assessment survey data set was finished and the database began to be utilized more as a case management tool.

On the recommendation of partners affiliated with several organizations, including the EBCRC, a semistructured questionnaire with open-ended items was designed and pretested with service providers working in East Biloxi, along the Mississippi Gulf Coast, in southeastern Louisiana, and on the Mississippi Delta. The partnership expanded to include two faculty members and five graduate students from the University of Michigan School of Public Health. By April 2006, over 150 qualitative interviews had been conducted (Green et al. 2006).

To summarize, this study involved the use of multiple research methods, including qualitative and quantitative approaches. The researchers engaged in (1) observation of several activities (direct service, disaster response training, planning activities); (2) field interviews conducted with residents, relief workers, and others in impacted communities; and (3) intake/needs assessment survey with community residents and others in the area seeking assistance. For this study, we rely primarily on data collected in and around East Biloxi.

RESULTS

Assessing Vulnerability and Needs before and after the Disaster

Before Hurricane Katrina, the coastal area of Biloxi appeared to be thriving economically; however, segments of the city's population, such as in the East Biloxi neighborhoods, were particularly vulnerable. Data from the U.S. Census demonstrate that residents of East Biloxi neighborhoods, identified by the 39530 ZIP code, faced socioeconomic challenges before the disaster (Table 9.1). Compared to the city of Biloxi as a whole, East Biloxi had lower levels of educational attainment and incomes, higher poverty rates, and a higher proportion of Biloxi's minority racial/ethnic groups, especially African American and Asian, primarily Vietnamese. Residents of East Biloxi

Table 9.1.   Socioeconomic Characteristics of East Biloxi/Biloxi, Mississippi

Socioeconomic Characteristics	Biloxi	39530 ZIP Code, Biloxi	Survey[1] (total n)
Total population/sample	50,644	17,214	879
Age			
Median age	32.5	30.3	51.0
Population 65 years and over	12.0%	14.2%	18.0% (879)
Race/ethnicity			
White	71.1%	58.3%	—
Black/African American	19.0%	27.8%	—
Asian	5.1%	9.2%	—
Other (American Indian, Pacific Islander)	1.4%	2.4%	—
Two or more races reported	2.4%	2.3%	—
Hispanic or Latino (any race)	3.6%	3.8%	—
High school graduate (for adults >25 years)	81.9%	72.8%	73.5% (795)
Income and poverty			
Per capita income (1999)	$17,809	$15,791	—
Median household income (1999)	$34,106	$26,187	—
Individuals below poverty line	14.6%	22.6%	—
Household income			
<$10,000	—	—	34.3
$10,000–$19,999	—	—	30.4
$20,000–$29,999	—	—	15.3
$30,000–$39,999	—	—	11.4
$40,000–$49,999	—	—	5.1
>$50,000	—	—	3.5 (805)
Housing			
Renter-occupied housing	51.1%	56.0%	37.4%
Owner-occupied housing	48.9%	44.0%	62.6%
Median value of owner-occupied housing	$92,600	$65,300	— (873)

[1] Needs assessment survey, conducted September–November 2005.

Sources: U.S. Bureau of the Census, American FactFinder. Table constructed by John Green, with input from Anna Kleiner and Duane Gill.

were more likely to rent their homes, and the value of owner-occupied units was lower than the city as a whole.[4]

Examination of needs assessment data collected in the months following the hurricane revealed that respondents tended to be older and less educated than the overall population of the city, and they had low household incomes. Jobs previously held by the respondents included fishing, construction, casino services, cooking, and a wide array of general labor activities. Some respondents reported being disabled. Assessing these characteristics, it is clear that in addition to having their lives altered by Katrina, many community residents were vulnerable as a result of their socioeconomic status, and these situations made them more susceptible to the myriad of economic, psychosocial, and physical impacts of the disaster.

Asked to identify their immediate needs, residents identified lack of clean water, food, clothing, housing, and health care. While the first three needs were quickly provided by relief organizations, the latter two were more problematic. Housing is critical in terms of both providing actual shelter and as a primary place where lives are led. Homes represent a major segment of a community's physical infrastructure, especially for those in the lower and middle classes where housing is often the primary economic asset.

The sample of people surveyed in this needs assessment reported a higher rate of home ownership at nearly 63 percent when compared to the ZIP code's 44 percent (see Table 9.1). This discrepancy was likely due to home owners having a greater tendency to remain in or return to the area after a hurricane to assess and deal with property damage. Respondents reported extensive damage to their homes (Figure 9.1). Nearly one-quarter said their home was

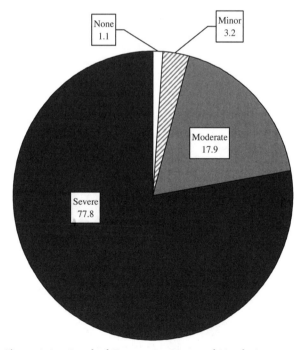

Figure 9.1.   Level of Damage to Home of Needs Assessment Respondents in East Biloxi, Mississippi (*n* = 849)

Table 9.2.   Housing Characteristics of Needs Assessment Survey Respondents in East Biloxi, Mississippi

Housing Characteristics	Percent
Home-owner's/rental insurance (% no)	52.4
	(450/858)
Flood insurance (% no)	83.8
	(724/864)
Home still standing/still on foundation (% no)	24.7
	(215/872)

Source: Needs assessment survey, conducted September–November 2005.

either off its foundation or no longer standing. Asked to rate the level of damage, almost 78 percent reported it as severe (Figure 9.1). Our observations showed people living in damaged houses, area shelters, tents, and trailers. Not only did this present challenges for assessing needs, but it was also problematic for the delivery of services.

Housing damage was especially problematic for those without insurance. More than one-half of the respondents to the needs assessment survey did not have home owner's/renter's insurance, and the percentage of flood insurance coverage was even more troubling with 84 percent reporting no coverage (Table 9.2). There was a debate between home owners, insurance companies, and the government regarding whether damage to homes caused by "wind-driven rain" should be covered under particular insurance policies. This has resulted in uncertainty for residents in terms of what they can do to rebuild their lives economically, socially, and emotionally.

Health is another critical concern in the wake of disaster. Typically, a large portion of the population will be in need of health services following a disaster, but health status and access to health care via insurance coverage before the event are important for addressing vulnerability. Approximately 45 percent of the needs assessment survey respondents reported not having any form of health insurance coverage, while close to one-quarter of them relied on a government-funded program (Table 9.3). Furthermore, the self-rated health of community residents was low (Figure 9.2). Nearly 54 percent of respondents ranked their health as poor or fair. Approximately 44 percent indicated some type of existing health issue within their household, with many reporting respiratory problems and skin irritations associated with the hurricane's effects. Additionally, there were challenges associated with prestorm health conditions exacerbated by the storm, such as high blood pressure, hypertension, disabilities, and the need for diabetic and dialysis treatments. A concern identified by several service providers was mental health. They observed that people were in shock, grieving, and in need of professional assistance.

Table 9.3.   Health Insurance Status of Needs Assessment
Survey Respondents in East Biloxi, Mississippi

Health Insurance	Percent
None	45.0
Government program	24.3
Private insurance/job-provided benefits	27.7
Other	3.0
	(n = 846)

Source: Needs assessment survey, conducted September–November 2005.

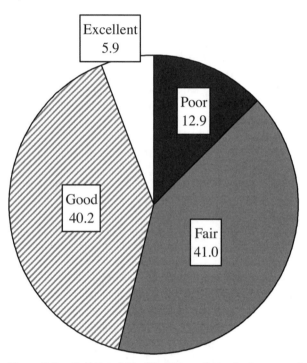

Figure 9.2.   Self-Rated Health Status of Needs Assessment
Respondents in East Biloxi, Mississippi (*n* = 846)

PERSPECTIVES FROM THE FIELD: INTERVIEWS WITH
DISASTER SURVIVORS AND SERVICE PROVIDERS

Field interviews with disaster survivors, volunteers, and relief workers revealed perceptions of several major impacts of the storm on individuals,
families, and the community. Their interpretation was that many people not
only remained homeless long after the hurricane but also were deeply traumatized. They anticipated it would be a long time before substantial assis-

tance would be realized. Short-term housing continued to be a major concern, with too few Federal Emergency Management Agency (FEMA) trailers, hotels at capacity, and skyrocketing rents for the permanent housing that remained intact. Long-term replacement housing was not expected to be widely available anytime soon. People needed to know how to rebuild and how to obtain the financing to do this.

Survivors, the interviewees surmised, needed a great deal of health care and social support as well. General practitioners, specialists, and medicines were in short supply. There were perceptions of serious mental health needs in the community. Full-time mental health experts were desired, along with teams of skilled mental health volunteers. Many East Biloxi residents are elderly, and respondents argued that this compounded problems associated with coping with disaster.

As with other communities along the Gulf Coast, numerous organizations were involved in providing relief and recovery assistance following the hurricane. When asked to assess the disaster responses provided by the different organizations, the interview participants noted that churches, faith-based groups, and other nonprofit organizations appeared to have provided the bulk of the services in a consistent manner. Local churches quickly mobilized to serve food. A large multidenominational faith-based network from outside East Biloxi was established at a local park to provide essential services, such as water, food, and clothing. Observation across the community also showed a wide variety of local, regional, national and international organizations providing services. Among these were Hands on USA, International Relief and Development, Islamic Relief, Save the Children, Urban Life Ministries, and Oxfam America.

As expected, the two largest relief-oriented nongovernmental organizations providing services in the area were the Red Cross and the Salvation Army. There was an expectation that these organizations would serve community residents impacted by the hurricane. The Salvation Army had a clear presence in East Biloxi through its relief distribution center on the grounds of an old sports stadium where water, food, clothing, money/gift cards, and limited medical assistance were provided. It also served as one of the places where volunteers, primarily those associated with churches, stayed in tents and campers.

A major challenge faced by disaster survivors seeking services was the dramatic level of need and the limited access points. This resulted in long lines and timely waits, with people sometimes receiving a ticket to come back at another time or on a different day to obtain assistance. Interestingly, a disproportionate amount of attention was directed toward security at these sites, often to the detriment of the delivery of services. Although providing some level of security, many of the faith-based centers avoided the need for such heavy-handed "lockdown" actions.

As for the responses from government agencies, one respondent maintained that FEMA was "shamefully absent" and arrived only in response to community leaders lobbying in Washington, D.C. The perception was that FEMA had not understood portions of the city and their needs. Communication had broken down as to what people needed, where the needs were located, and what was available through FEMA and other organizations. Hundreds of people requested tents while waiting for FEMA trailers to arrive. Respondents indicated there had been problems when the trailers arrived, such as multiple trailers being delivered to the same address and utility hookups and trailer keys not being available, thereby restricting access.

Our field observations during December 2005 and February/March 2006 indicated a reduction in the presence of relief operations that were initially established by numerous nonprofit and faith-based organizations throughout the community. Many (but certainly not all) of the relief "tent" sites and the volunteers were increasingly absent as time passed. The Salvation Army continued to distribute bulk food items, but organizations serving hot meals were scarce. One person indicated that too many contractors were taking advantage of the free meals, with fewer residents using the services; hence, hot meals were no longer being served in some places. Another individual indicated that it is time for people to "get a job." Still, there were several committed individuals and local organizations operating meal sites, often with support from larger extralocal networks. Unfortunately, they lacked access to the level of resources found among large-scale organizations with major fund-raising capabilities. Thankfully, many more residents had received FEMA trailers. Several homesites had also been cleared of their damaged structures. Many of the large debris piles disappeared. Several of the casinos and accompanying resort hotels were repaired and were open and hiring workers.

Despite the exodus of many relief operations from the community, grassroots mobilizing has continued to evolve in East Biloxi and throughout the Gulf Coast region. Oxfam America, one of the largest relief organizations to have field representatives on the ground in the region one year after Hurricane Katrina, was proactive in creating the Steps Alliance for South Mississippi (STEPS), a coalition of 34 organizations collaborating on numerous recovery efforts (A. Edwards, personal communication, October 13, 2006). Comprised of church leaders, attorneys, and a wide variety of community activists, STEPS is a unified voice for low- and moderate-income hurricane victims (STEPS 2006).

Another successful outcome of grassroots mobilizing has been the creation of Coastal Women for Change, a nonprofit organization comprised of women from East Biloxi and other Gulf Coast communities dedicated to empowering women to become active participants in the reconstruction of coastal communities. Coastal Women for Change provides advocacy for neighborhoods seeking security and the opportunity to rebuild and is represented on a variety of nonprofit and government committees involved in recovery efforts (Coastal Women for Change 2006; STEPS 2006).

DISCUSSION: ROLLING THE DICE ON REDEVELOPMENT?

As our field interviews and survey were first being conducted, Governor Haley Barbour was coordinating a series of "Mississippi Renewal Forum" redevelopment planning meetings and design charettes for professionals in architecture, regional and community planning, civil and transportation engineering, environmental advocacy, codes and laws, retail, economics, public process, and communications along the Gulf Coast (see Mississippi Renewal Forum 2006). After visiting with architects and community leaders and touring the community, a 30-member design team identified East Biloxi as the worst-hit area in the city of Biloxi and then commenced "a frantic three day process of designing a reconstruction plan" (Mississippi Renewal Forum 2006, 6). Proposed strategic actions for East Biloxi included restoring the smaller-scale grid of streets and blocks to accommodate higher-density condominium housing, introducing a new development code into East Biloxi immediately, and creating a casino corridor in distinct areas near the bay and downtown, enhanced by retail development and an entertainment district. However, the plan also recognized East Biloxi as the traditional, mixed-income center of the African American and Vietnamese communities and proposed that part of the neighborhood be reconstructed (according to building and flood-elevation codes) for low- and middle-income families and workers who wish to live in close proximity to casino and shrimping operations.

During the time of our field research, many local residents and relief workers in East Biloxi reported having no prior knowledge about the governor's meetings, such as one held at a casino in Biloxi. Although a few volunteers heard about it, there was a shared perception that invitations to participate were not extended to the general public. One respondent mentioned that two "planners" were "touring" the community and came to visit the EBCRC. These planners appeared to be confused about why community people were not invited to the governor's meeting.

Deeper questions in regard to redevelopment lingered in people's minds: Who is going to protect the neighborhoods in East Biloxi? What needs to be rebuilt? Because redevelopment planning meetings were being held and policies were being changed, we asked respondents at the end of our needs assessment survey what recommendations they had to offer for redevelopment. It is telling that only one-third of all respondents shared opinions as to what should happen in East Biloxi, which may reflect the fact that most respondents were focusing on immediate needs associated with daily survival. Many of them made this exact point in explicit terms. Those providing responses noted that as the community redevelops, some would like to see more homes for "regular people," not just casinos with resorts for "rich" people. Some of the common recommendations were to improve the overall infrastructure of Biloxi, such as through better transportation, public facilities, youth activities and schools, and downtown shopping establishments. Other suggestions included building a "safer" community by building at higher elevations, cleaning up and beautifying the community, acquiring more government assistance, and bringing in more employment opportunities including those offered by the casinos. There were respondents who expressed a desire for cooperation and inclusiveness during the redevelopment process. There was also a local interest in preserving history. Respondents believed there needs to be a team that knows how to do this. This team could include "experts" from both within the community and outside the community. People know what the architects want, but they feel that the architects do not know what the "community" wants. In all, it seemed as though the community needed organizers to translate the needs of Biloxi to broader audiences. An effort to do this commenced in January 2006.

The EBCRC was renamed the Biloxi Relief, Recovery, and Revitalization Center (BRRRC) in January 2006 as it launched the "East Biloxi Community Restoration Initiative," an effort to implement more participatory community planning and rehabilitation. As a community-based organization, the BRRRC recognized a critical need for revitalization by engaging in a grassroots needs assessment process, participatory planning, and empowerment evaluation for the recovery and preservation of East Biloxi (see BRRRC 2006). With the assistance of an outside consulting firm, the community data collection phase was initiated as a strategy for identifying neighborhood priorities with recommended actions. Data were derived from land use and building condition surveys, 511 completed resident surveys, six community meetings, and interviews with community leaders. Surveyors, primarily representatives of several community-based organizations providing relief in East Biloxi, collected demographic information and explored people's likes and dislikes of the area and what they viewed as the most important concerns for the future (BRRRC 2006).

The BRRRC plan identified East Biloxi's most pressing concerns since Hurricane Katrina as affordable housing, employment opportunities, and loans to improve or purchase homes (BRRRC 2006). While neighborhood residents recognized the gaming industry as a source of employment and revenue for public infrastructure, they perceived an expansion of this industry potentially increasing crime, pollution, and housing costs; decreasing housing availability; and negatively influencing children. According to the report's authors, respondents also expressed a strong desire for small independent retail development, a more diversified economic base, a diversified housing stock ranging from owner-occupied to public housing, a renewed sense of community through the establishment of community facilities, and recognizable linkages between the community's past and future opportunities. Their recommendations included to continue public forums, to work with community-based financial groups to educate home owners and other residents, to establish a loan fund for rehabilitation and construction of homes, to explore creating a community land trust or similar program to pool resources, to mandate that luxury condominium developers include a percentage of affordable housing units, to create an East Biloxi police precinct, and to create job training programs, especially in industries engaged in redevelopment (BRRRC 2006).

At least two other redevelopment plans have been proposed for the city of Biloxi. Utilizing several committees of Biloxi residents and business representatives, Mayor A. J. Holloway developed a citywide plan, "Reviving the Renaissance," proposing to expand the gaming and entertainment industries and the area's shrimping industry while also recommending housing redevelopment using Biloxi Housing Authority resources and federal tax incentives for affordable housing (see Reviving the Renaissance 2006). A second plan building on the redevelopment efforts and recommendations of the Mississippi Renewal Forum, "Reviving the Renaissance," and the BRRRC planning process was developed through Living Cities, a national organization that invests in the rejuvenation of urban areas (see Living Cities 2006). Although the city of Biloxi has recently adopted the Living Cities plan to guide rebuilding efforts, the city continues to negotiate building plans and variance requests with private developers on a piecemeal basis as proposals are submitted. The city has determined that coastal areas closest to the Gulf and Biloxi Bay are too vulnerable for dwellings and are more appropriate for casino development. Residents of East Biloxi continue to work to control their individual and collective destiny by promoting a viable mix of residential and small commercial land uses in the center of its neighborhood (A. Edwards, personal communication, October 13, 2006).

There is both promise and peril inherent in redevelopment planning efforts. We recognize the potential collaborative power of the community planning processes as well as potential conflicts between plans that vary in their forms of participation, goals, and recommendations for Biloxi neighborhoods. While it is critical for intentional plans to be developed and for partnerships to be forged between local and outside groups, the fundamental question remains as to which redevelopment recommendations will have the most currency and feasibility within this community. In the wake of disaster, many people are not able to participate in planning activities, as they must devote so much physical and emotional energy toward getting their lives back together. Access to affordable housing for home owners and renters, the persistent lack of insurance to cover storm damage, and the potential inability to meet new building elevation requirements remain critical issues for East Biloxi residents. Many residents are trying to move forward with renovations and rebuilding of their homes and businesses, though locating reputable contractors to successfully complete projects and acquiring financing remain key challenges. New height restrictions governing rebuilding were scheduled to commence in January 2007. Adhering to these height restrictions is estimated to add $30,000 to the overall cost of rebuilding a single-family home (A. Edwards, personal communication, October 13, 2006).

Drawing from this case study and literature from research on disasters and greater community involvement in planning and response (e.g., Bolin and Stanford 1998; Morrow 1999; Sellnow, seeger, and Ulmer 2002), we contend that our community-based research strategy in East Biloxi was a useful tool providing valuable information that guided the Center's response efforts and facilitated its development of additional partnerships within that community. The collaboration was an organic process developed through interaction with people and organizations working at the grassroots level of a struggling community and evolving to other levels of organizational and government structures. Meeting critical informational needs in the community increased the effectiveness of organizational response to disaster and the ability of storm victims to navigate a variety of assistance offered to them while supporting their sense of dignity and self-worth.

Through several conversations with people in the area, it was later determined that an effort was needed to comprehensively document the insights of on-the-ground service providers, with particular attention to their successes, challenges they have faced, and recommendations for the future. Local organizations, including nonprofit and faith-based groups, have an important role to play in planning for disasters, responding to them, and redeveloping a community's social and physical infrastructure. As a way to amplify their voices, a group of community-based researchers documented the experiences, needs, and recommendations of those who are working on the front lines in response to disasters (Green et al. 2006). Using a standardized interview schedule, the qualitative interview portion of the project was expanded to include anyone interested in participating along the Mississippi Gulf Coast from Biloxi to Long Beach, southeastern Louisiana in the vicinity of Hammond,[5] and the Mississippi Delta.[6] The partnerships also expanded to include faculty and graduate students from the University of Michigan School of Public Health.[7]

As this case study of East Biloxi illustrates, community-based participation in recovery and redevelopment activities, built on university/community partnerships, is an effective grassroots empowerment strategy for helping to address a community's short- and long-term needs. Participatory research activities, such as conducting needs assessments, mapping assets, and evaluating responses using tools that incorporate community residents, relief workers, and diverse organizations in the process allow for the generation of data and analysis applicable to providing direct services, advocating for the needs of the most vulnerable, and planning for future crisis events.

NOTES

1. Councilman Bill Stallworth, volunteer Megan Allchin, and Center coordinator Lucille Bennett provided much needed guidance, assistance, and leadership at the Center.

2. Researchers included Dr. Anna Kleiner of Southeastern Louisiana University and John and Eleanor Green and graduate students Sharon Williams and Justina Garcia of Delta State University.

3. Additional volunteers included coauthor Dr. Albert Nylander and Sarah Leonard of Delta State University.

4. The 39530 ZIP code is that part of the city where most of the needs assessment respondents lived before the storm. It is used here as a general proxy for East Biloxi, although it actually incorporates a broader area than just that part of town.

5. Graduate students from Southeastern Louisiana University who worked with Dr. Anna Kleiner include Wilicia Blount, Denise Donlan, Lakisha Hills, Ayanna Jackson, and Earnestine Lee.

6. Graduate students from Delta State University, including Monica Rosas and Sarah Leonard, worked with Drs. John Green and Albert Nylander as well as with Eleanor Green.

7. Numerous participants from the University of Michigan School of Public Health worked with Drs. JoLynn P. Montgomery and Irene S. Bayer, including graduate students (see University of Michigan School of Public Health 2005).

10

Rebuilding New Orleans Neighborhoods after Hurricane Katrina: Toward a Theory of Social Structure and Cultural Creativity

George E. Capowich and Marcus M. Kondkar

One of the main concerns for rebuilding New Orleans after Hurricane Katrina is to rehabilitate the city's neighborhoods and economy in ways that nurture the cultural creativity that has long been part of the city. Historically, New Orleans has been known for its unique mixture of traditions, values, social structures, and ethnicities. Many observers have characterized New Orleans as more similar to European and Latin American cities than to other U.S. cities. The city's distinctiveness is seen in many aspects that range from daily interactions among residents to innovations in the city's architecture, food, visual arts, and music. Sociological theory has a vital role to play in the recovery. Analytical frameworks and related research in the discipline can enlighten our understanding of how social structure influences cultural creativity, thereby advancing theoretical knowledge as well informing the planning and implementation of recovery policies.

This chapter's objective is to develop an axiomatic theory of the relationship between social structure and cultural creativity. Cultural creativity is viewed as an emergent property emanating from social structure generally and more specifically from neighborhood social structures and patterns of interaction that provide the contexts for cultural creativity. While axiomatic theory is commonly used in geometry, it is less prevalent in sociology. Axiomatic theory, briefly put, is a framework that begins with a set of abstract definitions that leads to scope statements that in turn lead to a series of relational statements consisting of axioms and propositions. In order to create such a framework, this chapter integrates classical sociological theory (e.g., Durkheim 1960; Simmel 1971, 1978), Collins's (1998, 2004) theory of interaction rituals, and modern social structural network theory (e.g., Burt 2004; Coser 1975; Granovetter 1983;

Hunter 1985). Although axiomatic theory is not directly testable, there are neighborhood-level data available in New Orleans that can assess the validity of axioms and propositions that can serve as a foundation for the future creation of an empirically verifiable causal theory.

CULTURAL CREATIVITY

We begin by defining creativity as the capacity for producing diverse cultural products. Cultural products include ideas, art, music, science, religion, ideals, and recreation. By this definition, creativity involves innovation rather than replication, deviance rather than conformity. Furthermore, rather than regarding cultural production as some autonomous property of individuals or groups per se, we begin with the assumption that cultural creativity is an emergent property of interaction patterns in social networks. It is an intrinsically social phenomenon. We argue that cultural creativity has a life of its own that varies from one setting to another. It varies in terms of pace and quantity and also in terms of the diversity of creations.

What explains the vast differences in creativity across communities? What does the social structure of interaction that leads to innovation and creativity look like? The ideas of the classical sociologists Simmel and Durkheim in particular form an instructive starting place to address these questions.

CLASSICAL THEORETICAL FOUNDATIONS

Both Simmel and Durkheim devote considerable attention to the complex relationship between creativity, or individuality, and social structure. Simmel argues that creativity, the ability of actors to produce culture, is a product of *interaction* among individuals and groups. One of Simmel's central concerns is the effect of population growth on individuality. He explains that as the social circle expands around an individual, a number of things change. First, the strength of the bonds that tie individuals to one another weaken as the number of individuals increases in any given group. Second, as the number of individuals increases, so too does competition and the division of labor. Third, individuals become more distinct from one another because "individuality in being and action generally increases to the degree that the social circle encompassing the individual expands" (Simmel 1971, 252).

As a community grows, there is more room available to develop individuality and uniqueness, but conversely, as that community grows, it also becomes less distinct, that is, less differentiated as a group from the wider society in which it exists. Simmel also suggests paradoxically that the expansion of a group's size can reach a point where the individuality it makes possible is ultimately threatened. There is a point of critical mass where a group becomes so large that its members are likely to espouse one simplistic idea rather than many distinct, more complex ones. He describes a dialectical relationship between the creative forces of individuals and groups ("subjective culture") and the expanding mass of cultural objects already in place ("objective culture"). Each is shaped by the other. Simmel argues that as objective culture expands, it hampers the creative forces of individuals and groups that produced it in the first place. Objective culture grows at the expense of individual culture:

> This discrepancy seems to widen steadily. Every day and from all sides, the wealth of objective culture increases, but the individual mind can enrich the forms and contents of its own development only by distancing itself still further from that culture and developing its own at a much slower pace. (Simmel 1978, 449)

Simmel's objective culture, like Max Weber's iron cage of rationality, may threaten and constrain individuality and the diversity of cultural expression. This suggests that sustained creativity and individuality require a balance of sorts: the individual can enrich the forms and contents of its own development by simultaneously remaining separate from and interacting with mass culture. Indeed, Simmel argues that individuals can cope with the threat to individuality imposed by the hegemonic mass of objective culture by retreating into a number of smaller groups. It is a balancing act of having one foot in a large circle and the other in a small circle.

Émile Durkheim (1960) also argues that the rapid pace of dynamic density, an increase in the population, and the interactions between people have freed individuals from the constraints of parochial life where conformity to group norms and functional unity are paramount. The modern individual is elevated to sacred status demanding recognition of individual tastes and preferences, distinctive cognitive opinions, and ethics. It follows that creativity flourishes where individuals are free to be different.

But for Durkheim, too much freedom can be a bad thing. The excessive weakening of norms can also make people feel lost and incapable of establishing reachable goals when the sky is the limit. Once again, the notion of balance emerges. Durkheim contends that individuals can harness the benefits of individuality when there is equilibrium between the individual and society with respect to the degree to which the individual is integrated into and regulated by a group.

Creativity and Interaction Rituals

Durkheim also emphasizes the significance of shared ritual practice as a method of affirming the moral order or the solidarity of a group. While Durkheim stresses the importance of religious rituals as highlighting the distinction between the sacred and profane, Goffman (1959, 1967) extends this analysis by noting that all interactions in everyday life are ritualized so as to highlight agreed-on norms. Interaction rituals are characterized by copresence, a common focus of attention, and a shared emotion or mood. In his analysis of the social history of philosophy, Collins (1998) uses insights from Durkheim and Goffman to develop a theory of interaction rituals that he then uses to explain networks of creativity in global intellectual life. He explains that interaction rituals

> connect symbols to social membership, and hence both to emotions of solidarity and to the structure of social groups. . . . [The theory of interaction rituals] accounts for variations in solidarity and belief found across different social structures, and for the dynamics of individual lives. A specific form of this emotional energy is what we call creativity. (20)

The "ritualism of social encounters" (Collins 1998, 22) varies along a continuum resulting in differing intensities of social solidarity, emotional energy, and cultural capital. Social structure is composed of repetitive encounters and interaction rituals that range from highly charged interactions related to the sacred to the unremarkable fleeting rituals of everyday life (e.g., greetings among strangers and acquaintances in public places) that may hold no immediate significance for individuals. As individuals move through encounters, they develop what Collins refers to as a particular "interaction ritual chain," a symbolic repertoire that "constitutes their *cultural capital*" (29).

Collins acknowledges that patterns of interaction are shaped by network configurations. Structural opportunities for interaction vary with one's position in a particular network. One needs to understand the geometry of networks to see the types of possible interactions. In the context of intellectual life, ideas deemed creative, new, and important emerge from ritual interactions in favorable locations in networks of intellectuals. Furthermore, Collins notes that "intellectual creativity comes from combining elements from previous products in the field" (1998, 32).

These observations form the starting point for a more systematic analysis of the social structure of creativity that is informed by network theory.

Modern Social Network Theory

The balancing act identified by Simmel and Durkheim and the patterns of interaction rituals discussed by Collins occur within and among the contexts of neighborhood networks. Network analysis requires us to examine the geometry of social interactions by focusing on the links among actors in a social system in order to identify the types of networks that are conducive to innovation and creativity.

Let us start by comparing ideal types of social networks: in one ideal type (see Figure 10.1), members are tightly knit, have strong ties to one another, but have very little contact, if any, with outsiders. There are very few, if any,

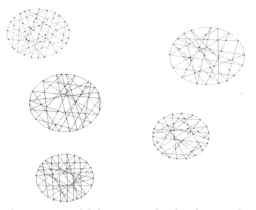

Figure 10.1.   Tightly Structured Isolated Networks

structural holes or absent links among members. This could be a network of academics, research scientists, members of a hippie commune, religious cult members, inner-city gang members, or a small, isolated neighborhood.

While the individuals within one of these networks are likely to be quite different from individuals in any of the others, the structural configuration of these groups is the same, and as such they share a number of characteristics. Group norms and expectations are well defined and clear. Within each group there is a tendency toward conformity as the group is able to exert control over its members. Members experience a strong sense of belonging and can expect a relatively high degree of cooperation and support from one another in times of need. Information, ideas, and resources are likely to be shared relatively equally. These networks tend to resist change. Members are exposed only to each other. Nothing new comes in or out of the group. Paradigm shifts are unlikely.

In another ideal type, network members are fragmented and very loosely, if at all, tied together (see Figure 10.2). This network is full of structural holes. Examples might include commuters in an airport terminal, shapeless housing developments characteristic of urban sprawl, or scattered dwellings in a suburban neighborhood.

It is difficult to define a boundary around this type of network, and it is hard to identify shared norms. These groups have a relatively high degree of diversity and high division of labor within them, and members have no sense of common belonging. Members are atomized and are unlikely to become involved in one another's lives. Relationships are fragmented and fleeting. There is very little cooperation or meaningful interaction. Things are constantly changing. There is very little collaboration, creative or otherwise.

While both of these network structures are found in modern American neighborhoods, neither is conducive to interaction patterns that promote

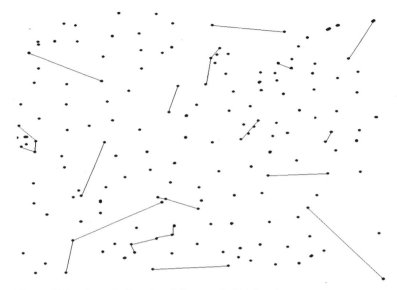

Figure 10.2.   Loosely Structured Fragmented Network

innovation and creativity. Different types of interaction patterns bring with them various advantages and disadvantages for their residents. For example, one researcher has argued that neighborhoods, such as those in Figure 10.1, that are isolated from wider society with respect to interaction patterns and opportunity structures become susceptible to various "ghetto-related behaviors," as residents are increasingly cut off from networks of information and assistance (Wilson 1996). Nothing new comes in or out. Residents in neighborhoods such as these experience relatively low levels of mobility and, given the lack of outside contacts, are more likely to be dependent on other residents in their daily lives.

In her study of conflict and social control in suburbia, an environment that may be more akin to the network structure in Figure 10.2, M. P. Baumgartner (1988) finds that while suburbanites enjoy freedom of mobility and functional independence from one another, levels of interaction are so minimal that conflicts are generally handled through avoidance. Relationships are fragmented and fleeting, and residents are unlikely to engage in cooperative or collaborative patterns of behavior. Thus, while they do not get into violent confrontations with each other, they are also unlikely to help each other in times of need. Baumgartner characterizes this as "moral minimalism."

So what network is conducive to interaction patterns that promote innovation and creativity? Such a network combines components of the previous two examples (see Figure 10.3). The theoretical literature discussed previously suggests that links, or bridges, among diverse networks are the catalysts for creativity because they are the meeting places where differences merge. They are

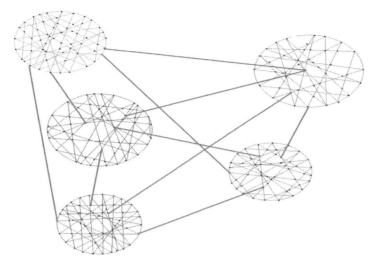

Figure 10.3.   Tightly Structured Linked Networks

the contexts for a dialectical exchange where cultural production is informed by diversity. Creativity is nurtured through brokering links among closely knit groups because these linkages fill what otherwise would be structural holes among isolated groups. It is from these structurally bounded interactions that cultural creativity emerges.

COMMUNITY AND HUMAN NETWORKS

Since the 1980s, community scholars and network analysts have conceptualized community, a sometimes nebulous term, in a systemic way in terms of human and institutional networks at the neighborhood level (e.g., Taub, Taylor, and Dunham 1984; Wellman and Leighton 1979). Using networks to specify community operationalizes the concept of community. Moreover, focusing on the neighborhood level is an outgrowth of research that highlights the fact that the immediate proximity of a geographic neighborhood (e.g., face blocks[1]) heavily influences people's perceptions of their neighborhood and affects the general functioning of the community (Taylor, Gottfredson, and Brower 1984).

Hunter (1985) extends the systemic view of neighborhood communities by specifying three dimensions of social order that he conceptualizes as networks. The first is the private social order, which consists of primary groups, including family and close friends, bound by love. This order is characterized by close personal ties among its members. The emergent bonds that link individuals within this social sphere result from interactions and emotional commitments among members (Strauss 1978).

The parochial social order is the second dimension of neighborhood social order. It is characterized by the personal and civic acquaintances that arise from routine activities and interpersonal interactions that occur in and around a neighborhood through work, recreation, leisure, volunteering, and shopping. While parochial relationships lack the affect associated with the private order, they involve interpersonal obligations that correspond with several of Warren's (1984) functions of community, including social control, mutual aid, and socialization. In addition, parochial networks provide the mechanisms for realizing social capital, which is defined as the capacity to make "possible the achievements of certain ends [solve local problems, realize common objectives] that in its absence would not be possible" (Coleman 1988, as quoted by Sampson,1995).

This second dimension of social order is one of the key components for specifying the relationship between neighborhood social structure and cultural creativity because it provides the context for understanding how members of otherwise homogeneous groups come into contact with people external to their immediate social group. Ronald Burt (2004) uses network analysis to examine where good ideas come from in a network. He argues that opinions and behavior are more homogeneous within than between groups and that individuals who are connected across groups are exposed to more diverse ways of thinking and behaving. Similarly, Mark Granovetter (1983) argues that weak ties are more beneficial than strong ties in exposing actors to new information and resources. Rose Coser's (1975) work complements Granovetter and the work of others by showing that weak ties among diverse groups form an opportunity for reflection because individuals from homogeneous groups witness and react to other behaviors, values, and customs. People within the homogeneous groups are able to see their own views in light of the reactions of others. As philosophers of creativity and artists have indicated, insights into the human condition contained in artistic creations result from a reflection that emerges from diverse interactions that characterize daily life and give rise to innovation. A creative spark may dwell within an individual and be nurtured by like-minded people, but diverse social interactions provide a context necessary for that spark to grow into a flame of activity that produces cultural innovation.

The public sphere is Hunter's third dimension of social order and consists of public agencies and private companies that provide the goods and services necessary for daily life. Rather than a network of people, this dimension is an institutional network that provides public services (e.g., public safety, utilities, education, recreation) and private necessities (e.g., jobs, consumable items).

This dimension of social order is the other key component for our consideration of social structure and creativity because the geographical distribution of stores, places of employment, and recreation areas furnish the bridges (links) among human networks from diverse neighborhoods. Along with the parochial social order, this dimension specifies the geographic ecology of areas that present an opportunity for interactions among diverse neighborhood residents. This geographic area can be thought of as the context for the friction of space (i.e., bridges) among various people.

Two general comments provide a context for understanding how these dimensions of social order coexist. One is that people have multiple role demands (family, work, civic) that operate simultaneously to structure daily life. Furthermore, these dimensions are characterized by overlapping, interwoven sustenance-related activities that make up daily routines. Different neighborhoods, depending on the nature of the social orders and the characteristics of surrounding areas, will manifest different types of activities representing different ecological dynamics (Berry and Kasarda 1977). The timing and tempo (pace) of activities also will vary. For example, neighborhoods that contain or are close to bars and restaurants will have more foot traffic in the evening compared to neighborhoods that are close to office buildings.

NETWORK ANALYSIS

Network theory and network analysis have a long history of application in sociology by applying the major concepts of graphs in mathematics. The basic definition of graph is "a mathematical object consisting of points, also called vertices or nodes, and lines, also called edges or links" (Newman, Barabási, and Watts 2006, 1–2). Using these concepts within sociology, a network can be represented as a set of identifiable links that connect social actors (nodes) in patterns of interactions. In a broad array of social science applications, the mathematical terminology of graphs and network characteristics has been adapted to sociological interactions among people (e.g., centrality, connectivity, path distances) in order to analyze human networks,[2] behavioral characteristics, and key sociological variables, such as social influence, social cohesion, and identity development.

Human networks develop and change over time as nodes and links disappear and new ones are added. Consider, for example, friendship networks that over time contract and expand as people change jobs, divorce, and become engaged in either conflictual or cooperative endeavors. On a less intimate level, people's interactions at a business or playground will change in similar fashion as people migrate in and out of the neighborhood, businesses close and new ones open, and recreation experiences take on either a positive or a negative character.[3] "The [social] ties people make affect the form of the network, and the form of the network affects the ties people make" (Newman, Barabási, and Watts 2006, 7).

There are three points to emphasize here. First, this conceptual understanding of networks approach focuses on the reciprocal relationship between the social structure that is the context for human networks and the dynamic character of the behavior within them. Network interactions are temporally and structurally dependent. Second, networks are viewed as stochastic systems, making the study of networks amenable to statistical analysis because the human interactions within defined networks can be thought of as probability distributions. Third, it is well known that individuals within one network provide linkages to other networks and that this affects the shape and character of multiple networks. For example, two members of an informal basketball team might work together and involve a coworker in the games. In turn, another person on a second ball team might live in a different neighborhood and bring in a friend/neighbor from a different part of town. Both of these examples illustrate the dynamic nature of neighborhood networks that change the nodes and links of all the networks involved.

This approach is based on a long history of network analyses. Solomonoff and Rappoport (1951) demonstrated mathematically that as the ratio of network links to nodes increases, the network changes from a collection of disconnected nodes to a set of connected nodes. Moreover, the set of network nodes can display a range of connectivity (i.e., from weak to strong) as the expected number of nodes that can be reached from a randomly chosen node either increases or decreases (Pool and Kochen 1978). Sociometric studies have used this basic idea to show how the number of links that connect a randomly selected pair of individuals increases as the networks' interconnectivity increases. Milgram (1967) discussed this conceptually in his well-known essay on the small world phenomenon, and Travers and Milgram (1969) demonstrated this empirically. They report that assuming 1,000 acquaintances for each person, most pairs of people can be connected through two intermediate contacts.

This does not address issues of which cultural creations will take hold in society aesthetically, gain popular success, achieve commercial success, or represent advances in their respective fields (e.g., music, architecture, visual arts, cuisine). Rather, the axiomatic framework represents a theoretical representation of the social milieu that can give rise to cultural innovation. In general, as the density of networks increases and bridges across different networks develop, then the growth of weak social ties (see Coser 1975; Granovetter 1983) as a milieu for creativity and reflection has the chance to develop and the likelihood of cultural creativity emerging increases stochastically. The opportunity for cultural innovation increases because increased density of network ties increases the connectivity among diverse homogeneous groups, thereby reducing the distances among actors across otherwise homogeneous networks.

CONCEPTUAL DEFINITIONS

Based on the literature reviewed here, we begin the theory-building process by proffering the following basic definitions for key concepts that guide the study of social structure and cultural creativity conceptually and empirically:

Cultural creativity. The capacity for cultural innovation in diverse disciplines (i.e., visual art, music, ideas, architecture, cuisine).[4] This definition also includes the scope of the theoretical propositions set forth later in this chapter.

Nodes. The units of a network (people, positions, collectivities) that can be connected to others.

Links (bridges). Ties that connect nodes within a network and reveal a geometric configuration.

Interactions. Routine human encounters in public places.

Neighborhood characteristics. These include demographics, population density, and physical traits, such as housing conditions.

RELATIONAL STATEMENTS

These represent theoretically derived if–then statements that express relationships among the major concepts. They take two forms: axioms (derivative statements for other theoretical statements) and propositions (combinations of axioms). See Reynolds (1971) for a full discussion of these definitions.

Axiom 1. If links provide bridges across diverse nodes, then diverse interactions occur.

Axiom 2. If diverse interactions occur, then weak ties develop across diverse nodes.

Axiom 3. If weak ties develop across diverse nodes, then diverse interactions continue.

Axiom 4. If diverse interactions continue, then diverse links persist.

Proposition 1. If Axioms 1 to 4 are combined, then opportunity for cultural creativity increases stochastically.

Empirical Plausibility of Axioms and Proposition

New Orleans is a valuable setting for such theorizing because extensive social histories of the city's neighborhoods show that neighborhoods with distinct cultural and ethnic identities developed in a layer-cake fashion. It is common throughout the city to find clusters of both high- and low-income housing within the same few blocks within an individual neighborhood. It is quite typical, for example, to pass through affluence, poverty, and working-class areas within several blocks. The geography of New Orleans makes it conducive to walking, creating a dense context for diverse interactions among very different people on a routine basis. Moreover, the locations of commercial and recreational areas provide the structural bridges and linkages among diverse residential groups.

There are two additional points related to applying the theoretical propositions to the city of New Orleans. The layer-cake nature of the city's neighborhoods means that even within neighborhoods that are relatively homogeneous ethnically or by social class, there is still a mix of people from various backgrounds. For example, the neighborhood known as the Garden District is fairly wealthy and largely white. However, there are blocks and street segments within this neighborhood that are populated by poor minorities. Furthermore—and perhaps more important—diverse neighborhoods with very different demographics are contiguous. Data from the 2000 census illustrate how three neighborhoods exemplify the diverse contiguousness of residential areas (see Figure 10.4). The Garden District, which is 89.2 percent white, is bounded on one side

Figure 10.4.　Neighborhood Map 1: Orleans Parish (Map created by the Greater New Orleans Community Data Center [http://www.gnocdc.org] based on boundaries provided by the City Planning Commission of New Orleans and used with permission.)

by the Irish Channel, which is 26 percent white, and on the other side by Central City, which is 9.9 percent white. The dividing line between the Garden District and the Irish Channel is Magazine Street, a major commercial area and major bus line. On the other side, the Garden District abuts Central City at St. Charles Avenue, a major thoroughfare with a streetcar line and businesses. There are many examples of this throughout the city.

This configuration means that residents from these neighborhoods interact on a regular basis at points along Magazine Street and St. Charles Avenue and that people's travel routes to and from these nodes for work, shopping, and recreation also bring people into contact. The interactions that arise from routine behavior within this type of neighborhood structure and its dimensions of social order (Hunter 1985) represent a context that presents the opportunity for loose ties among diverse people to develop (Granovetter 1983) and for individual and collective reflection (Coser 1975) to take place.

The axioms and proposition that we have presented suggest that this is the kind of social environment that provides fertile ground for cultural creativity and innovation to occur.

THE PLANNING AND REBUILDING PROCESS

The planning process for rebuilding New Orleans neighborhoods is underway at the time of this writing, and neighborhood planning meetings have been taking place since November 2005. Districts are now beginning the process of combining these plans into district-level project proposals. The overall strategy is for neighborhood associations to plan specific rebuilding projects and pass them on to the district level, where the individual neighborhood plans can be combined and coordinated into one plan for each district. These plans are then forwarded to the parish or city level, where a master plan can be developed.

Some neighborhood associations have invited other contiguous neighborhood associations to attend and participate in their meetings, while others have forged ahead autonomously. Some neighborhood associations, consciously or not, have developed plans that are particularly conducive to interaction patterns that link diverse groups in ways that foster cultural creativity, while others have not. The Milan neighborhood association plan serves as a particularly good example of a planning process informed (again, consciously or not) by the sociological insights discussed in this chapter. Milan's project proposals (see Figure 10.5), if adopted, will create and sustain links between diverse face blocks and the contiguous neighborhoods around it. For example, Project A, the development of Louisiana and Claiborne avenues as major commercial corridors (similar to Magazine Street discussed earlier), will foster routine interaction among residents of at least three other

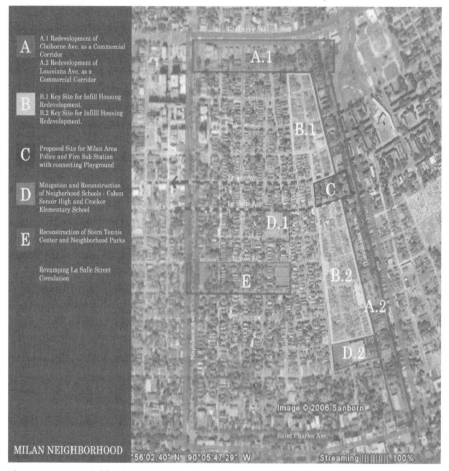

Figure 10.5. Neighborhood Map 2: Milan (Map created by Citizens of Milan in association with Byron J. Stewart & Associates and used with permission.)

contiguous neighborhoods, each with its own unique characteristics. Similarly, Project C, the building of a police and fire substation and a connecting playground on the eastern periphery of the neighborhood, will serve as an important bridge between Milan and Central City neighborhoods. With respect to recreational resources, Project E, the development and expansion of a public recreational tennis center and park spaces across various face blocks up to the western edge of the neighborhood, connects those face blocks with the adjacent neighborhood (Uptown) in significant ways.

From a planning policy standpoint, we strongly recommend that the planning process at the district and parish levels consider the importance of rebuilding in ways that maintain and promote cultural creativity with the sociological insights discussed in this chapter. Transportation routes, commercial centers, child care facilities, schools, churches, recreational resources (parks, playgrounds, basketball courts) should be developed and located in ways that link neighborhoods, promote interaction across diverse face blocks, and capitalize on the cultural diversity of the city.

SUMMARY AND CONCLUSIONS

The preliminary steps we have outlined to build a theory of social structure and cultural creativity combine several lines of thought. Classical sociological theory emphasizes that the production of culture is a result of human interactions among individuals and groups and suggests that creativity flourishes where individuals are influenced by their groups but not overregulated by or overintegrated into them. Sustained creativity requires a balancing act where individuals are exposed to influences from both within and outside of their homogeneous networks.

Network theory and analysis operationalize these ideas by focusing on how neighborhood social orders and configurations form the social structural context for this balancing act to become realized. This structure enables social ties, sometimes fleeting and other times persistent, to develop and change over time. In particular, the weak social ties that result from human interactions link individuals and prompt reflection about one's homogeneous group as well as the other groups, thereby giving rise to an opportunity for creativity. It is necessary to point out also that the opportunity for reflection is open to individuals who witness these diverse interactions, not only those who participate. In this way, the chances for creativity spread because these interactions become part of the city's social environment.

The axioms and proposition set forth in this chapter represent a modest starting point for building this kind of theory. Much work remains before a bona fide, testable theory can be created. The empirical plausibility of the axioms needs to be expanded by compiling demographic and structural data for all neighborhoods and the areas of the city that link residents. These data are readily available. In addition, data will need to be collected on interactional zones: those areas where people from various neighborhoods and the diverse sets of people within neighborhoods meet to interact. This will allow a refinement and expansion of the axioms. An expansion of the theoretical precepts contained in this chapter will form a broader foundation for future theory building that can focus on deriving testable hypotheses pertaining to the relationship between social structure and cultural production. In addition, these same concepts and propositions form a foundation that can guide the rebuilding of New Orleans neighborhoods.

NOTES

1. Face block refers to the line of sight one has from a residence/business along a neighborhood block.

2. For example, the General Social Survey has a section that asks respondents to name people with whom they discuss personal matters.

3. Consider interactions at an outdoor basketball court. Teams form spontaneously and compete informally. Games that result in conflict or are lopsided with one team dominating consistently might lead to change, whereas competitive, friendly games might result in continuous contact among the same groups.

4. At this early stage of theoretical development, there is no need to specify the kind of cultural innovation, as axiomatic theory is intended to point the way for further research and application.

IV

POSTDISASTER
INSTITUTIONAL CHANGE

11

Hurricane Katrina and Its Impact on Education

Ashraf M. Esmail, Lisa A. Eargle, and Shyamal K. Das

Many studies have looked at important issues about psychological and social impacts of technological disasters. With stress associated with social structure, it is reasonable to conclude that social capital is affected by collective and individual stress. Stress reactions after disasters result in changes in social dynamics, the way groups and people relate (Erikson 1976). What may be referred to as negative changes in associations may represent changes in social capital. As social interaction decreases, trust is not developed in the same way it is before the disaster, which may add additional stress.

Research has been unable to reach a consensus or a collective definition of social capital. Kawachi et al. (1997) suggest that despite important advances, the definition and measurement of social capital remains at nascent stages. There seems to be a huge gap between the poor and rich affecting the social organizations of communities, and this has significant implications for the public's health. Paxton (1999) finds some decline in social capital, showing instead some decline in a general measure of social capital, a decline in trust in individuals, no decline in associations, and no general decline in trust in institutions.

Social capital is inherent when discussing technological disasters and its impact on the community. Research indicates that following a technological disaster, communities are characterized by a lack of consensus about environmental change, general uncertainty, and social disruption (Gill and Picou 1998). Further, people outside the community or area impacted by the technological disaster are not capable of fully understanding the stress and trauma connected to the event. Consequently, they are unable to offer support (Edelstein 2000). According to Arata et al. (2000), when analyzing postdisaster communities' experiences, one often finds that current symptoms of anxiety, depression, and posttraumatic stress disorder are associated with avoidant coping strategies and conditions of resource loss. Gill and Picou (1998) suggest that long-term disruption and stress characterize disasters based on sociological and psychological research. Their results indicate the presence of chronic community stress and a relationship between level of community stress and threat to health. Picou, Marshall, and Gill (2004) indicate that the status of litigation and litigant stress during disasters serve as prominent sources for event-related psychological stress and perceived community stress. The authors conclude that litigation is a critical characteristic of technological disasters that prevents timely community recovery and promotes chronic psychological and social impacts.

Kasperson and Pijawka (1985) analyzed societal responses to hazards. Some of their findings are that (1) hazard management increasingly focuses on technological, not natural hazards; (2) public evacuation compliance is greater for technological than natural hazards; (3) resources allocated to deal with technological hazards tend to be less than those allocated for natural resources; and (4) hazards unfold over time as a process, with distinct stages of human needs being followed by responses to those needs.

YOUNG ADULTS AND DISASTERS

Goenjian et al. (1994), in a study conducted a year and half after the earthquake in Armenia, looked at the severity and frequency of posttraumatic stress reactions among young adult and elderly victims. The study showed that greater rates of chronic severe posttraumatic stress reactions were found among the highly exposed disasters and that there was a positive correlation between loss of family members and severity of posttraumatic stress reaction. Finally, the findings indicated that after a major natural disaster with subsequent multiple adversities, a large portion of the adult population may experience chronic and severe posttraumatic stress reactions. Chung et al. (2005) studied the differences between posttraumatic stress responses of younger and elderly community residents who had been exposed to two technological disasters (a train collision and an aircraft crash). The study found that avoidance, intrusion, and the total impact of the disasters were significantly correlated with all general health subscales for both younger groups and the elderly groups.

Palacio (2004) explored the narrative accounts provided by a nonclinical sample of young adults and their parents concerning the September 11, 2001, attacks. Results showed anxiety, disbelief, nonmaterial loss, fear of recurrence, and the meaning-making of the events of September 11, 2001. The results showed that the coping method and the degree of that coping was completed in an active rather than a passive manner and largely determined the coherence, depth, and quality of their meaning-making structures. Bolton et al.

(2004), looking at 115 young adults who survived a shipping disaster in 1988, found that effects on psychosocial functioning following traumatic experience are mediated through psychopathology.

Recent research looking at the impact of Hurricane Katrina found young adult victims of Katrina are finding relief through writing (Anonymous 2005). Journals, written accounts, and letters of the Hurricane Katrina disaster have helped young adults deal with the tragedy. In response to recent hurricanes, the Young Adult Library Services Association created an informational resource called Serving Teen Evacuees in Libraries (Tabor 2005). Parslow, Jorm, and Christensen (2006), looking at the impact of a bushfire in Canberra, the national capital of Australia, identified the extent to which tobacco use was affected by an experience of a natural disaster and the resulting symptoms of posttraumatic stress disorder (PTSD). Results showed that trauma experiences can increase tobacco use in young adults in spite of whether these experiences result in PTSD symptoms. Parslow, Jorm, and Christensen. (2006), using the same data, found that demographics and pretrauma mental health increased the likelihood of exposure of trauma threat, reporting PTSD symptoms, and reaction to the trauma.

POVERTY AND ITS IMPACT ON RECEIVING A COLLEGE EDUCATION

The *Journal of Blacks in Higher Education* (1999) reports that African American college students are 20 percent less likely than their white counterparts to graduate from college. Sixty-nine percent of those students say they are leaving college because attending college is too expensive. In addition, many students do not enter college because their families need the income that the student can provide through employment (Nyhan 2005). Furthermore, many programs (such as tax deductions for tuition payment) benefit middle-class families instead of poor families. Finally, the diversion of funding from needs-based to merit-based scholarships has hurt lower-income students (*Journal of Blacks in Higher Education* 1999).

According to the Democratic Party (2006), more than 70 percent of Pell grants are awarded to students whose family incomes are less than $20,000 per year. Yet funding for these grants has been under attack (Miller 2006). Measuring Up 2000 reports that funding for remedial programs in colleges and universities continue to be underfunded. Yet, many minority and low-income students need these courses in order to successfully obtain a college degree (McCabe 2000).

DISASTERS AND THEIR IMPACT ON CHILDREN

Several studies have examined the impact of natural disasters on children. Kilic, Ozguven, and Sayil (2003) examined the effects of parental psychopathology and family functioning on children's psychological problems six months after the earthquake in Bolu, Turkey. The results showed that the severity of post-traumatic stress disorders in children was affected mainly by the presence of PTSD and the severity of depression in the father. State and trait anxiety scores of children were related to general family functioning. The constellation of PTSD symptomatology was different in fathers than in mothers: the most common type of symptoms was "externalizing" in fathers with PTSD. The study supported the notion that the mere presence of PTSD in parents may not be enough to explain the relational process in families experiencing trauma. Their findings suggest that when fathers become more irritable and detached because of PTSD symptoms, this may affect children more significantly. Durkin et al. (1993) examined children both before and after a flood disaster in Bangladesh and tested the hypothesis that stressful events play a causal role in the development of behavioral disorders in children. Results find that between the pre- and postflood assessments, the prevalence of aggressive behavior increased from zero to nearly 10 percent and that 45 of the 134 children who had bladder control before the flood (34 percent) developed enuresis.

Posttraumatic stress disorder is an illness that often happens after a traumatic event. Grinage (2003) discusses some things that you can do to help yourself: (1) take your medicine just the way you doctor tells you, (2) try to lie down to sleep at the same time every night, (3) have a place to sleep that is dark and quiet and that has a comfortable temperature, (4) try not to eat within two hours of lying down to sleep, and (5) get regular physical exercise and eat a balanced diet.

Studies have looked at children's responses to natural disasters and how to help children deal with such tragedy. Mercuri and Angelique (2004) indicate that it is important to ask children directly about their responses to disasters, regardless of disaster type, rather than relying on caregivers' assessments. Further, witnessing life-threatening situations and scenes of destruction elicits more stressful reactions than the type of disaster experienced. The perceived threat, rather than the disaster agent itself, is deemed the more important factor in children's postdisaster psychopathology. Hagan et al. (2005) suggest that pediatricians can assist community leaders and parents not only by accommodating the unique needs of children but also by being cognizant of the psychological responses of children to reduce the possibility of long-term psychological morbidity. The effects of disaster on children are mediated by many factors, including parental reaction, personal experience, stage of disaster response, developmental competency, and gender. According to Hagan et al. (2005), pediatricians can be effective advocates for the family and child, and the community level and can affect national policy in support of families.

Gately (2005) discusses 20 ways to help students deal with tragedy. Some of these are applying problem-solving strategies, maintaining a proper perspective, increasing involvement in the community, using opportunities in the classroom to discuss relevant social issues, and allowing students to express their feelings and share their experiences.

Prewitt Diaz (1999) discusses some techniques that helped Puerto Rican children deal with stress as a result of Hurricane Georges: (1) the talking approach, (2) the drawing approach, and (3) the writing approach. The talking approach allows the migrant child to talk about his or her feelings relating to the disaster. In the drawing approach, the teacher or counselor provides paints and crayons and asks the child several questions (e.g., "Can you make a drawing of what happened during the disaster?"). The writing approach may be used with adolescents and older migrant children. Utilizing pictures or paper clippings as a stimulus allows the student to write about his or her disaster experience.

POVERTY AND ITS IMPACT ON CHILDREN'S EDUCATION

Much research has looked at the impact of poverty on education. Roslyn (2005) demonstrates that we must give children who live in poverty an equal chance of learning. Acker-Hocevar and Touchton (2002) find that principals believe that poverty is intertwined with teaching and learning as well as with the way teachers view students and their parents. The children in these schools face a number of barriers, and their number one interest is not education but survival. Anonymous (1996), estimating the impact or children's poverty on the value of their paid work later in life (and thus the economy), suggests that every year of child poverty at current levels is costing tens if not hundreds of billions of dollars in future productivity. The midrange estimates vary from $86 billion to nearly $177 billion.

Stanton-Chapman et al. (2004), examining the effects of risk factors present at birth on language development in preschool utilizing the Preschool Language Scale—3, find that the accumulation of multiple risk factors appears to increase the negative effects of poverty. Haughey, Start, and Da Costa (2001), analyzing ways to reduce poverty's impact on education, find that a combination of three interventions—focus on literacy, continued professional development, and smaller classes—was successful in helping first-grade students in high-poverty, high-transiency environments make solid gains in social and academic abilities.

Many studies look at the impact of housing and neighborhoods on poverty and education. Martinez (2000) discusses the previously mentioned theories and gives a contemporary validation to "step forward in trying to understand the ways in which neighborhoods relate to children's development and the relations among neighborhood structure, family processes and children's outcomes" (109). Martinez also references decades of "worsening life conditions" of African American families and their children in urban environments (1). Nichols and Gault (2003) suggest that homelessness and housing instability will continue to be a major issue for families living in poverty, further increasing children's school instability. Ladd and Ludwig (1997) suggest that providing public residents with Section 8 vouchers will not necessarily improve the educational opportunities of children in these families. The main reason is that most of the families who participate are likely to move to other parts of the city, where the schools are not much better than in areas serving public housing projects. However, when families are given Section 8 vouchers that can be used in census tracts with low poverty rates, the educational opportunities for these children are likely to improve. The program restriction that families live in low-poverty areas encourages many families to move to the suburbs and apparently helps them avoid the less effective schools.

Many studies find that that poverty does not have a direct effect on children's education. Research indicates that other factors may have a direct effect. Hill and O'Neill (1994) find that increases in the mother's hours at work bear significant negative effects on child's achievement. The effect is only partially compensated for by higher income among these young children. They find that the mother's welfare dependence is associated with a reduction in the child's Peabody Picture Vocabulary Test score, an effect that is not explained by poverty persistence.

According to Mayer and Jenkins (1989), the racial and socioeconomic mix of a high school has little effect on white students' academic achievement and on students' chances of attending college. They find that the effect of the socioeconomic mix of neighborhoods and schools on achievement of elementary school students, on graduation rates of high school students, on teenage crime, and on early labor market experience is weak. However, growing up in poor neighborhoods seems to increase teenage pregnancy rates, and this may impact their education and their future.

Myers, Kim, and Mandala (2004), using data from 1996, 1998, and 1999 Minnesota comprehensive statewide testing of eighth graders, examined whether black students perform worse than white students because blacks are more likely to attend high-poverty schools. They find that school poverty or other characteristics of students, their programs, and schools in which they participate explain little of the test score gap. They concluded that much of the white–black test score gap can be attributed to racial differences in treatment.

From the discussion presented in the previous sections, disasters impact not only individuals but also institutions and communities in numerous ways. Adaptations or adjustments must occur at all levels, with some of these adjustments and impacts having long-term consequences. In the following sections, we examine the many ways that Hurricane Katrina affected students and the higher-education system, from the kind of educational experiences students have to changes in the way that the higher-education system operates.

DATA AND METHODS

This chapter provides a case study of Hurricane Katrina's impact on the education system. In particular, we discuss the changes that have occurred in the learning process for students in higher education as well as changes in the structure and functioning of the higher-education system. Our information is based primarily on articles in the *Chronicle of Higher Education* and its coverage of Katrina's impact on colleges and universities. The impacts that have occurred can be classified into eight categories: (1) changes in the location of educational activities, (2) changes in the types of courses and programs offered, (3) changes in teaching methods, (4) potential changes in learning outcomes, (5) changes in educational funding, (6) changes in government policies, (7) emerging controversies, and (8) emerging experiential learning and research opportunities. Examples of each of these impacts are discussed in the next section.

FINDINGS

Changes in the Location of Instruction

When Hurricane Katrina hit the Gulf Coast of the United States, severe damage to educational facilities occurred. The main type of damage experienced occurred from flooding rains, storm surge, and failed levees. Some institutions, such as Southern University at New Orleans (which was located in the Ninth Ward of New Orleans, the area most heavily damaged and longest to stay inundated by floodwaters), were totally destroyed by floodwaters and will have to be completely rebuilt. Even those educational institutions that experienced less devastating damage have lost instructional, office, and dorm space because of damage and subsequent repairs (Gravois, 2005).

Institutions have responded to these losses of space in a number of ways. Southern University at New Orleans leased the use of portable trailers that are positioned on or near the campus (Southern University at New Orleans 2006). Tulane University leased a cruise ship from an Israeli company for office, dorm, and student activity use. They are currently in the process of modifying the cruise ship to meet these and instructional needs (Fogg 2006c). Delgado Community College and Dillard University have relocated their classes to a limited number of undamaged facilities on campus (Delgado Community College 2006). During the fall semester, affected colleges and universities arranged for the enrollment of their students at other institutions of higher education across the nation, agreeing to give credit to courses taken at these other institutions (American Federation of Teachers 2005).

Changes in Programs Offered

Given the extent of damages received, the costs to be incurred from repairing or replacing these facilities and the costs associated with leasing facilities, Southern University and Tulane University fired faculty and staff and reduced the number of degree programs offered (*Chronicle of Higher Education* 2005; Selingo 2005). Tulane has also, as a means of repairing the campus and making it fully operational as quick as possible, instituted a new community service requirement. Students are required to take a course where they participate in the rebuilding and revitalization of the campus before they can graduate (NBC Nightly News 2005; Tulane University 2005). Delgado Community College has changed the mission of its institution to focus more on vocational training programs and less on liberal arts learning (Evelyn 2005).

Most other institutions have increased course enrollment size to reduce the number of classrooms and instructors needed for courses. In many cases (e.g., Delgado Community College), both students and instructors are uncertain about a course being offered on the basis of enrollments until the first day of class. In addition, the number of courses that an instructor teaches during the semester has been increased to reduce institutional operating costs (*Chronicle of Higher Education* 2005; Fogg 2006b). Moreover, many institutions have expanded the number of courses being offered online (Carnevale 2006a).

Changes in Teaching Method

As mentioned previously, more courses are being offered online. Teaching a course online is a different experience from teaching in a traditional classroom setting where faculty and students interact face-to-face. Lectures are posted under "Course Documents" or "Assignments" for students to access. Examinations are accessed via a website, and a specific time is set by the instructor for a student to access the exam and complete the questions. Papers are submitted in a "digital drop box," similar to an e-mail attachment. Results of the grading of examinations and papers are revealed to a student in the same format. In terms of office hours, specific days of the week and times of day are set aside for students to e-mail and chat directly with professors online.

The use of online teaching as a means of instruction at traditional "brick-and-mortar" universities and the emergence of "virtual universities" are trends that were already underway in many educational institutions. The impact of Hurricane Katrina has expedited the utilization of the Internet and online instruction as educational delivery tools. Many users cite the convenience of taking courses anytime and anywhere they want, the ability to take courses simultaneously at multiple institutions to accelerate the process of receiving their degrees, and the "straight-to-the-point" content of the courses as why online courses are attractive.

Teaching classes with larger enrollments also changes the type and number of assignments. In teaching classes with more than 50 students (the "mass class"), it is difficult to grade a number of written assignments, such as research papers or essay examinations. In lieu of such assignments, many instructors instead choose to use a multiple-choice, true/false, or fill-in-the-blank type of examination questions. It also becomes difficult to have class discussions on topics or have students participate in group activities. Moreover, as the number of courses that faculty members are required to teach increases, the less time they have to prepare for any one class meeting or course. These faculty members have less time to devote to any student's questions during and after class. While this type of instruction is common for introductory-level courses at large universities, many institutions have purposely tried to avoid having "mass classes" because of the lack of in-depth instruction that takes place.

With the relocation of classes into temporary facilities, often the architecture and telecommunications accessibility impedes instruction. Classes are offered in facilities not designed for instruction, so the lighting of the room may not be adequate. In addition, there may not be enough space or seating available, and Internet access may not be present. Therefore, instructors may rely on older methods of instruction, such as simply talking or writing notes on a portable blackboard. Writing notes on a board takes longer, with less material covered than can be covered in PowerPoint presentations. Lecturing without the use of audiovisual aides also means that instructors may have to repeat themselves for students to have all important items compiled in their notes. They may have to make copies or pass around figures and diagrams during class instead of projecting such information on a screen. Teaching classes with these techniques requires that a different set of skills be utilized more often than teaching classes with newer technologies. In the case of Southern University, laptops have been placed on portable carts for use around the North Campus (Southern University at New Orleans 2006).

In addition, given the amount of damage to other parts of the campus and the surrounding communities, many students and instructors lost their residences and their possessions. Hence, both may be desperately attempting to find a place to live and to replace lost educational materials. Computers were lost and, with that, the ability to type documents or send documents on the Internet. Projects stored on disk were damaged and/or lost. Books and lecture notes were destroyed (Fogg 2006a). For a lucky few, Southwestern University in Texas developed a program, financed by the Mellon Foundation, to bring guest scholars to their campus and assist them in the recovery of their course materials (Mangan 2005).

Furthermore, both faculty and students are dealing with the stress of losing what they owned, having to adjust their routines to traveling to different parts of campus, working in a different environment, and doing their work in a different manner (Hebel 2006). They are having to make adjustments for navigating through construction and teaching/learning in noisy and dirty environments. Hence, both faculty and students have to be more patient with each other and take more time to discuss issues that, under predisaster circumstances, would not have occurred.

Changes in Learning Outcomes

With a major disaster, one might automatically assume negative impacts on student learning outcomes. To be sure, at least for the short term, student learning was severely impaired. In the long term, it may be not as devastating. Materials and facilities can be replaced. Students are receiving a real-life educational experience in that they see that they cannot take people, things, and places for granted. Hence, a new appreciation for life may emerge (NBC Nightly News 2005).

Students will receive a hands-on experience by working together to rebuild their schools, communities, and organizations. It is hoped that they will see that each and every person can make a contribution to society and that no institution or community can exist with people and teamwork. Because of changes in facilities and methods of instruction used, students will learn the value of being flexible and how to do so in their lives. They will also learn how to use and take advantage of the resources that they do have (Mangan 2005).

With proper counseling, students can learn ways to cope with the stresses associated with living through a disaster (Mangan 2006c, 2006d). They can also learn how to use their experiences to help others in the future.

Changes in Educational Funding

Many institutions rely primarily on student fees and revenue from state and federal sources to finance their operations. With the advent of Katrina, the Gulf states' legislatures and Congress passed emergency funding provisions to aid with the cleanup and rebuilding of institutions (Field 2006). In addition, foreign nations (e.g., Qatar) are contributing millions of dollars in hurricane relief donations to colleges and universities in Louisiana and Mississippi (Mangan 2006a). Moreover, former U.S. presidents George H. W. Bush and Bill Clinton have teamed with the United Negro College Fund (UNCF) to raise funds to rebuild Katrina-impacted historically black colleges and restore their student scholarships (Mangan 2006b).

UNCF is one source of additional funds that are available to hurricane-impacted students. Delgado Community College has, for example, created the Katrina Victims Student Relief Fund to provide assistance in covering the costs of books, supplies, transportation, child care, and so forth for its students (Delgado Community College 2006). Louisiana's higher-education commissioner announced plans to offer needs-based grants of $1,000 to each student who plans to enroll or reenroll at a Louisiana college or university (Mangan 2006e).

Changes in Policies

As a result of hardships faced by institutions in the aftermath of Katrina, the Federal Emergency Management Agency (FEMA) rules have been changed to distribute disaster funds to private colleges and universities in the event of future disasters. Before the 2007 fiscal year, private institutions are required to seek loans from the Small Business Administration (Brainard 2006).

The Education and the Workforce Committee in Congress issued a report that seriously criticizes the Bush administration and FEMA's handling of disaster recovery funds to Katrina-affected colleges and universities. The report calls for the appointment of an education-recovery czar in the Department of Education to oversee the distribution of relief funds to educational institutions. This would require a transfer of responsibilities as well as funds from FEMA to the Department of Education (Mangan and Selingo 2006).

EMERGING CONTROVERSIES

One emerging controversy as the result of Katrina is that many institutions, like individuals, are finding that their insurance policies were inadequate or did not cover damages incurred from flooding. Xavier University of Louisiana is suing American Bankers Insurance Company of Florida and Travelers Property Casualty Company of America for failure to reimburse the university for its losses. Dillard University, Loyola University of New Orleans, and Tulane University are also pursuing cases against insurers (Mangan 2006j).

Another emerging controversy involves the firings and layoffs of faculty and program cuts at Katrina-impacted colleges and universities. The American Association of University Professors (AAUP) is investigating whether institutions followed their own policies and procedures and AAUP guidelines for such matters. As part of the investigation, AAUP sought to meet with college presidents as well as interview faculty and staff at the affected institutions. The presidents of Tulane and Loyola universities have declined the offer (Fogg 2006b).

A third controversy involves the proposed merger of Newcomb College and Tulane University as part of Tulane's restructuring plan. Newcomb College was initially founded as a women's college and maintains its own endowment. Alumni and the Newcomb heirs have filed suit to keep the merger from occurring, which would transform the college from a women-only to a coeducational institute within Tulane University. Tulane argues the merger would strengthen undergraduate education and streamline costs, but the plaintiffs argue it would do the opposite (Mangan 2006h). The Newcomb heirs also argue that Tulane would violate the terms of Josephine Louise Newcomb's 1886 donation to the institution. One of those terms is to have Newcomb College serve as a women-only college (Mangan 2006i).

EMERGING EXPERIENTIAL LEARNING
AND RESEARCH OPPORTUNITIES

Although Katrina caused major damage and loss of facilities, materials, and livelihoods, one positive outcome has been new opportunities for students to apply knowledge and skills learned in the classroom. The New York Times Student Journalism Institute, along with Dillard University, has a select group of minority journalism students interning in New Orleans. These interns are producing coverage on Katrina's aftermath as well as dealing with sensitive issues (such as racial images in the media) along the way (Mangan 2006f).

In addition, students from Millsaps College in Mississippi assisted the Red Cross by designing and implementing an online database to register and communicate with Red Cross volunteers. The students will present their work at the International Conference on Software Engineering Research and Practice (Carnevale 2006a). Public health students at Tulane University and Louisiana State University Health Sciences Center at New Orleans are filling vacancies in local health agencies, which have lost as much as 90 percent of their staff after Katrina hit (Mangan 2006g).

Within the American Sociological Association conference, the number of sessions and paper presentations devoted to disaster research have increased between 2005 and 2006, the pre- and post-Katrina years, respectively (American Sociological Association 2005, 2006). A group of social science scholars met at the Social Science Research Center at Mississippi State University in November 2005 to develop a set of guidelines for research on disasters. Some of their recommendations are to use research to prevent disasters, aid in disaster recovery, provide comparative analyses across disaster types, and further understand the social impacts of disasters on population subgroups (Social Science Research Center 2006).

Finally, demand for the specialized work of artisan students at the American College of the Building Arts has increased. Katrina destroyed many historical buildings in the Gulf region, and rebuilding efforts have focused on restoring the area to its former antebellum appearance. Students at the American College create ornamental ironworks, timber frames, special types of brick, and old-styled furniture (Biemiller 2006) that can be used to replace damaged historical items.

CONCLUSION

This chapter examined some of the short-term changes that have occurred in higher education as the result of Hurricane Katrina. Future research should examine the long-term consequences of these changes in terms of both student learning outcomes and the structure and functioning of the higher-education system. Perhaps the comparison of post-Katrina enrollment, matriculation time, and graduation rates of affected institutions would be one way to examine the long-term effects of the disaster on education. Another avenue of research could examine the previously mentioned changes that have taken place in higher education (such as funding practices, policy changes, and research opportunities) to see how many remain in place in the future.

12

Health Needs, Health Care, and Katrina

Nancy G. Kutner

Loss of life and damage to individuals' health, both physical and mental, are especially disturbing outcomes of a disaster. Health problems include both immediate and long-term concerns and include people who remain in the area and those displaced from the area. Mental health problems can persist for years after a disaster experience. Studies indicate commonalities in mental health outcomes for people impacted by disasters, but individual and community mental health responses also vary depending on the type and magnitude of the disaster and influences from social structure and cultural factors. Health policy professionals in the United States have viewed events surrounding Hurricane Katrina and its aftermath as providing strong evidence supporting the need for health care system changes which they view as essential for public health preparedness in the United States. The Katrina catastrophe must be viewed also from a sociological model of health and illness in which social conditions—especially the intersection of race, class, and poverty—serve as fundamental determinants of health.

IMMEDIATE IMPACTS OF KATRINA ON HEALTH AND HEALTH CARE SERVICES

Deaths and Injuries

Surveillance data for September 2005 reported by the Centers for Disease Control (CDC) indicated numerous illnesses and injuries among persons who remained in the New Orleans area (CDC 2005). As of July 2006, more than 1800 Katrina-related deaths had been reported in Louisiana and Mississippi (Weisler, Barbee, and Townsend 2006). More than 200 deaths occurred in hospitals and nursing homes during the storm (Weisler, Barbee, and Townsend 2006). A geriatrician in New Orleans estimated that about 75 percent of people who died in the hurricane were aged 75 or older—people who were also likely to be African American, to lack access to transportation, and to have limited access to medical care and social support (American Geriatrics Society 2006). Without the heroic emergency efforts of health care workers (Hansen 2006), first responders, volunteers, private citizens, and government and military personnel, a much higher rate of fatalities would have been likely in the region (Weisler, Barbee, and Townsend 2006). Although an estimated 1.2 million residents escaped the direct impact of Katrina by evacuating the Gulf Coast, displaced residents, as well as those who did not leave the area, experienced Katrina-related health consequences.

The full extent of mortality associated with Katrina will probably remain unknown. The CDC attempts to differentiate between deaths directly related to the physical force of a hurricane and indirectly related deaths caused by unsafe or unhealthy conditions existing during the evacuation phase, occurrence of the hurricane, or posthurricane/cleanup phase. Natural causes of death are considered storm related if physical or mental stress before, during, or after the storm exacerbated preexisting medical conditions. The majority of deaths directly and indirectly related to Katrina occurred in Louisiana and Mississippi; however, Katrina-related deaths also occurred in Florida when the storm rapidly strengthened to a hurricane and in Alabama, where people died from natural causes exacerbated by the hurricane (CDC 2006b).

Impact on Health Care Services

Many hospitals and nursing homes were damaged or destroyed by the hurricane and subsequent flooding. Charity Hospital in New Orleans, the only level I trauma center for the entire Gulf Coast region, struggled to continue operating for a "desperate week" (Berggren and Curiel 2006), but eventually it was flooded and closed. University Hospital, the other large state-run hospital in New Orleans, also closed. About 11 federally funded community health centers in Louisiana and Mississippi were destroyed, and 80 others were severely damaged (Nesmith 2006). Katrina destroyed or severely damaged 94 kidney dialysis clinics in the area most directly affected by the storm, and 27 clinics remained closed as of January 2006 (Clemons 2006). Medical and prescription records were destroyed, pharmacy and distribution networks were disrupted, and established patient care transportation networks were no longer operational.

HEALTH STATUS AND HEALTH CARE SERVICES
IN THE AFTERMATH OF KATRINA

The Following Months

Mortality and Morbidity

Although it is not a source of official mortality statistics, the *Times-Picayune* carried 25 percent more death notices in January 2006 than in January 2005. It is generally agreed that suicide rates increased, but exact figures are not known because it is difficult to accurately estimate the population size that serves as a denominator, and some self-inflicted deaths remain unclassified (Weisler, Barbee, and Townsend 2006). The deputy coroner of New Orleans reported that in the four months following Katrina, the suicide rate in Orleans Parish almost tripled, from 9 to 26 per 100,000 (Saulny 2006a).

In Orleans and Jefferson parishes, over half the housing units surveyed in mid-October 2005 had a member who had incurred an illness since Katrina (CDC 2006a). Health complications became increasingly evident in patients with chronic diseases that were irregularly or inadequately managed following Katrina, especially patients with cancer, cardiovascular diseases, human immunodeficiency virus, diabetes, substance abuse, and mental illness (Berggren and Curiel 2006; Weisler, Barbee, and Townsend 2006).

Mental Health Issues

About seven weeks post-Katrina, the CDC conducted a rapid needs assessment survey of returning New Orleans area residents in Orleans and Jefferson parishes. Responses by half the sample indicated *possible need* for mental health assistance, and one-third had *probable need* for mental health assistance. Initial estimates from the Substance Abuse and Mental Health Services Administration (SAMHSA) projected a need for mental health assistance for 500,000 residents. Deaths have been attributed to stress exacerbating underlying health problems (Berggren and Curiel 2006).

Mental health crisis counselors in Mississippi reported having had more than 1 million "brief encounters" (less than 15 minutes) and more than 150,000 "longer encounters" to answer questions and provide information. Most of these longer encounters were single visits, but some individuals were seen more than once. Of the longer encounters, 9,537 patients required mental health referral for more intensive treatment, and 2,264 required substance use disorder treatment. Project Helpline crisis calls in Mississippi from persons dealing with depression and anxiety increased 61 percent for the period from March 1 to May 31, 2006, compared with the period from October 1 to December 31, 2005. In Louisiana, more than 158,000 referrals were made from September

2005 to May 2006 by mental health crisis counselors who were supported by the Federal Emergency Management Agency (FEMA) and SAMHSA (Weisler, Barbee, and Townsend 2006). Additional persons may have independently sought treatment or received private referrals for mental health needs.

Surveys conducted from February to May 2006 of first responders in New Orleans (police, firefighters, and emergency medical technicians [EMTs]) indicated symptoms consistent with posttraumatic stress disorder (PTSD) in 10 to 20 percent and symptoms of depression in about 25 percent; 40 percent expressed a desire to receive counseling, which is a high proportion for first responders (Lamberg 2006; Weisler, Barbee, and Townsend 2006). In February 2006, a survey of trailer and hotel residents receiving FEMA subsidies indicated that 68 percent of the female caregivers who responded indicated symptoms of depression, anxiety, or other psychiatric disorders. In addition, these women were 2.5 times more likely to have children with mental health problems than women whose responses indicated low levels of psychiatric disorders (Weisler, Barbee, and Townsend. 2006).

Among approximately 1,600 Louisiana children in grades 4 to 12 who completed a needs assessment and screening survey from December 2005 to May 2006, 54 percent met criteria for consideration for mental health referral, with symptoms of PTSD or depression, while more than 14 percent requested counseling. Even among preschool and early elementary (grades 1 to 3) children for whom parents completed surveys, about 31 percent of the children appeared to meet criteria for mental health referral based on reported symptoms of irritability, headaches, and sleep problems, including nightmares, and about 40 percent of these parents were seeking services for their children (Lamberg 2006).

About 50,000 residents of New Orleans were evacuated to Dallas, where they were housed in the Convention Center and Reunion Arena. Volunteer mental health professionals, about 70 percent of whom were psychiatrists, set up a crisis clinic in the medical triage unit at the Convention Center. In the time period from September 1 to 15, 2005, these volunteers saw 419 persons one or more times. Most of those seen were African American adults from the New Orleans area, and slightly more than half were women. Clinicians gave a diagnosis of acute stress disorder or new depressive or anxiety disorder to about one-third of the persons they saw. A second Dallas study conducted a needs assessment between November 2005 and February 2006 for individuals who were evacuees of both Hurricane Katrina and Hurricane Rita, most of whom were housed in apartments paid for by FEMA. About 10 percent of the 500 respondents reported symptoms suggestive of PTSD, and a larger number reported individual symptoms of traumatic stress. For these persons, not only the distressing events of the actual hurricane experience but also the uncertainties surrounding continuation of FEMA support contributed to an ongoing sense of duress (Lamberg 2006).

Access to Health Care Services

As of mid-September 2005, half the displaced Katrina survivors who had gone to Houston lacked any form of health insurance, and 40 percent reported chronic health conditions, such as heart disease, hypertension, diabetes, or asthma. Many of these persons had depended on Charity Hospital in New Orleans for their ongoing care and needed to find facilities in their new location that could provide uncompensated care (Brodie et al. 2006). Relocated persons who relied on Medicaid to cover their health care experienced difficulties using their cards in another state or had to reenroll because Medicaid, being a state-based program, is not portable across state lines (Rosenbaum 2006).

Almost one-fourth of the New Orleans area respondents in the CDC survey conducted in October 2005 reported problems in obtaining medical care and prescription medications, including closure of usual provider site (CDC 2006a). Only 15 of 22 New Orleans hospitals were open as of April 2006, providing only 2,000 of the usual 4,400 beds. Patients were often not sure which hospitals were open and what services were available. Health care in New Orleans seven months after Katrina was described as "unacceptably primitive" (Berggren and Curiel 2006, 1551).

Limited hospital capacity also caused serious problems. Emergency department patients cannot move into hospitals when beds are not available. Because of limited availability of chronic care facilities, there was a lengthening of stays in acute care hospitals whose costs exceeded Centers for Medicare and Medicaid Services (CMS) reimbursement. These additional uncompensated expenses threatened recently reopened hospital beds to close again (Berggren and Curiel 2006).

Many physicians and other health care professionals left the region (Berggren and Curiel 2006; Connolly 2005; Voelker 2006b). In April 2006, it was estimated that only 140 of 617 primary care physicians and only 22 of 196 psychiatrists returned or continued to practice in New Orleans. Only about one-fourth of the physicians who were participating in the Medicaid program in the Gulf Coast area before Katrina were participating as of June 2006 (Weisler, Barbee, and Townsend 2006). As of September 2006, marked shortages of primary care physicians, psychiatrists, orthopedists, oncologists, ophthalmologists, dentists, and nursing personnel were reported. Most patients with nontraumatic acute health problems, such as skin conditions, could access health services, but preventive care and diagnostic tests were difficult or impossible for most patients to obtain (Voelker 2006a).

Of particular concern, there was a lack of mental health services at a time when these services were most needed. Although community mental health outreach activities started days after the hurricane, the number of mental health facilities and care providers was not adequate (Berggren and Curiel 2006; Voelker 2006b). SAMHSA funded the Katrina Assistance Project, under which more than 1,200 volunteer, licensed mental health and substance abuse professionals conducted more than 90,000 counseling sessions and made more than 13,700 referrals for mental health and substance abuse treatment and for social services through April 2006. Funding for this program ended on June 30, 2006, however, and many of the volunteers subsequently left the region. The Stafford Act of 1974 stipulates that funding for SAMHSA mental health treatment can be used only for crisis management, not for continuing treatment (Weisler, Barbee, and Townsend 2006).

Access to inpatient psychiatric services was greatly curtailed. In the New Orleans metropolitan area, including Orleans, Chalmette, Jefferson, and St. Bernard parishes, there was a 57 percent reduction in psychiatric beds from pre-Katrina to early July 2006 (Lamberg 2006). The closing of Charity Hospital, which before the storm had 96 psychiatry beds, had a critical negative impact. Police and EMTs picked up about 100 patients each month needing hospitalization for acute psychiatric illness, some of whom had to be transported 100 to 150 miles away for hospital admission. As of mid-June 2006, there were only two psychiatry beds available within 25 miles of New Orleans and no inpatient substance abuse detoxification beds closer than 75 miles away in Baton Rouge (Weisler, Barbee, and Townsend 2006).

Long-Term Concerns about Health Needs and Health Care

Toxic Exposure

The floodwaters that covered much of New Orleans for almost two months contained a mix of raw sewage, bacteria, oil, heavy metals, pesticides, and toxic chemicals. As the "Katrina cough" became prevalent and a large number of people developed allergy-like sinus and respiratory problems, a so-called Katrina Krud syndrome emerged, which is believed to be linked to the dust and mold in the air (Nesmith 2006). Piles of debris remaining in yards lined many streets, posing risks to mental as well as physical health because the debris was a continuing reminder of the disaster. As Saulny noted, these visual reminders are "a major part of the problem . . . the people of New Orleans are traumatized again every time they look around" (2006a, 1).

Mental Health Needs

Recurring and distressing thoughts of a disaster can sustain stress, and some individuals who appear to cope reasonably well during the acute crisis subsequently develop PTSD or depression (Voelker 2006b). Psychiatrists believe that longer-term adverse effects of Katrina can be expected to be substantial, requiring ongoing follow-up assessments to ascertain needs for mental health services. Stressful life events and chronic stress are known to be associated with an increased risk for psychiatric disorders, especially depression. Depression in turn may be associated with increased risk for chronic conditions such as hypertension, heart disease, and diabetes (e.g., Musselman and Nemeroff 2000).

Psychiatrists argue that federal assistance is needed to continue funding for the SAMHSA volunteer counseling programs until more resources are available. They believe that Congress should consider amending the Stafford Act to allow states the necessary financial flexibility to use future SAMHSA crisis counseling funds to continue treating people beyond the immediate crisis management phase. They also recommend that Medicaid patients 18 years and older who require psychiatric treatment should be admitted to freestanding psychiatric hospitals if no other beds are available in psychiatric hospitals that are attached to medical hospitals.

Viability of the Health Care Infrastructure and Implications for Community Rebuilding

Long-term funding is needed to rebuild the health care infrastructure of the Gulf Coast region and to attract physicians and other health care professionals to staff outreach and treatment programs. Medical education has suffered, and a pressing need for federal assistance to rebuild the area's teaching hospitals and training programs exists. Hospitals such as Charity in New Orleans are major graduate training facilities, and if these hospitals are closed, there is no support for young physicians, and a major pool of physicians likely to remain in the area will be lost. Medical residents are the care providers for most underinsured patients in major metropolitan areas such as New Orleans. Funds for medical residents' salaries were withheld when Charity closed, however, because CMS funding for these salaries is allocated to hospitals rather than to individuals.

Lack of housing for health care workers is also a very important issue. Provision of health care requires availability of health care workers, but health care workers must have places to live as well as jobs. A shortage of nurses and nursing assistants existed pre-Katrina and is much worse post-Katrina. Because they do not have enough staff, many clinics that provide kidney dialysis in New Orleans now operate at reduced capacity, providing treatments on three days rather than six days a week. Dialysis patients who evacuated and want to return to New Orleans often cannot be accommodated because the available dialysis chairs must be used for emergent new cases. This "domino effect" (lack of housing/lack of staff/reduced health care availability/inability of evacuees to return) affects opportunities to restore the city's population and economic vitality. Thus, "the shortage of health facilities and clinicians probably has altered the repopulation of affected areas" (Lambrew and Shalala 2006, 1395).

KATRINA HEALTH OUTCOMES IN COMPARATIVE PERSPECTIVE

Posttraumatic stress disorder and other mental health problems are reported by many survivors of disaster and conflict events (Horowitz 2001; Horowitz,

Stinson, and Field 1991; McFarlane and Papay 1992). The particular types of mental health problems identified and their reported prevalence vary, however. The nature and scope of the disaster and culturally conditioned coping responses contribute to this variation (Elliott and Pais 2006; van Griensven et al. 2006).

Findings from surveys of adult and child survivors of the 2004 tsunami in southern Thailand have recently been reported (Thienkrua et al. 2006; van Griensven et al. 2006). Although the tsunami disaster included more extensive loss of life than is known to have occurred during Katrina, both events were characterized by uncontrolled flooding and the threat of drowning, separation of family members, and places of residence being destroyed. Elevated rates of PTSD, anxiety, and depression were found among adult tsunami survivors eight weeks after the disaster, with higher rates for anxiety and depression than for PTSD symptoms. The greater prevalence of anxiety and depression compared to prevalence of PTSD symptoms was consistent with findings from other postdisaster studies (Cardozo et al. 2004; Lopes Cardozo et al. 2004).

When a follow-up survey was conducted among adult survivors nine months after the tsunami disaster, the rates for mental health disorders had decreased but still remained elevated. Symptom rates were higher for displaced persons than for nondisplaced persons, especially at the time of the eight-week survey. Mental health problems were more likely to be reported by those who incurred losses, especially loss of a family member, injury of self or family member, loss of home or property, and loss of livelihood. Persons with lower educational levels and those who did not have an income after the tsunami and those who used illicit drugs or had a prior diagnosis of mental illness were more likely to report mental health problems. From a multivariate analysis, loss of livelihood was independently associated with PTSD, anxiety, and depression (van Griensven et al. 2006).

Symptoms of PTSD and depression were also identified in two surveys of children aged 7 to 14 years who were tsunami survivors, conducted at two months and nine months after the event (Thienkrua et al. 2006). Prevalence rates of PTSD symptoms in children were similar to those found in adult survivors in the same geographic area. The prevalence of depressive symptoms was lower among children than among adults, but the risk of depressive symptoms increased significantly with the child's age. Older children may have been better able to recognize salient losses, especially loss of family and social networks. Unlike the adults surveyed, prevalence rates of PTSD and depression among child tsunami survivors did not decrease significantly over time in spite of the government's immediate provision of mobile mental health teams to offer psychological services to children in tsunami-affected provinces.

Several observations can be made about the mental health findings from Thailand compared to the evidence that has accumulated from surveys conducted among Katrina-affected persons over the year following the event. In both cases, there has been evidence of elevated rates of symptoms of PTSD, depression, and anxiety, especially among persons with physical health problems or chronic illness. For example, in our interviews with more than 400 dialysis patients in New Orleans who were Katrina survivors, an elevated rate of PTSD symptoms has been found. In the tsunami-affected respondents studied by van Griensven et al. (2006), mental health problems were more likely to be reported by displaced persons. Similarly, Elliott and Pais (2006) found that displaced residents of New Orleans reported more stress than nondisplaced residents approximately one month after the storm, and residents who evacuated expressed more concern about the future than those who did not evacuate. Symptoms of depression and anxiety among adult tsunami survivors had improved by nine months after the event (van Griensven et al. 2006), but depression and anxiety were more frequently reported in the spring months of 2006 than in the fall months of 2005 by Katrina survivors in the New Orleans area (Weisler, Barbee, and Townsend 2006).

Van Griensven et al. (2006) emphasize the importance of being able to return to a familiar livelihood as a normalizing influence for adult tsunami survivors. They report that multiple government and nongovernmental organizations in Thailand implemented programs to assist with restoration of livelihood as well as providing continued mental health support. At the same time, it is important to note that ongoing mental health support was not associated with a decrease in mental health problems of child survivors. Children need targeted therapy to help them deal with insecurities that are likely to accompany experiencing multiple losses. Long-term follow-up is especially important for children, which Katrina observers have recognized (Dewan 2006). Children do not have the ability to absorb months of stress and untreated medical problems without long-term consequences (Dewan 2006). Reports from surveys of children affected by Katrina document pervasive mental health concerns, and these needs of child survivors require special attention.

Katrina qualifies as a "complex disaster" based on its far-reaching community impact (Silove and Bryant 2006). The impact and aftermath of the Katrina disaster have been qualitatively different from other disasters that have occurred in the United States (see the introduction to this volume). While the aftermath of other hurricanes and even the terrorist attacks of September 11, 2001, can be described as demonstrating movement from acute crisis to active recovery within a few months, New Orleans has been described as moving only "from acute crisis to chronic crisis" (Howard Osofsky, quoted in Lamberg 2006). The challenge of "reassembling health care systems, jobs and homes" is "incredibly complicated" (Fred Cerise, quoted in Voelker, 2006a).

One year after the storm, attention was starting to focus on identifying ways in which a post-Katrina health care system could more adequately address the needs of New Orleans residents, especially poor and uninsured residents. Elements of these discussions included building a decentralized system of safety-net services, strengthening partnerships between academic institutions and a mix of public and private agencies, and—a high priority—establishing electronic medical records (Voelker 2006a). In the next section of this chapter, I discuss health policy observers' view that Katrina turned a spotlight on the crucial need in the United States for "public entitlements for the low-income population in the name of public health preparedness" (Rosenbaum 2006). In the final section, I turn to the sociological perspective that social conditions are fundamental causes of health and illness and the relevance of this perspective as a framework for Katrina analyses.

GOVERNMENT, HEALTH, AND KATRINA

Katrina was a modern catastrophe because the extensive damage associated with it reflected inadequate planning and inadequate response to a predictable natural event. Lack of timely government response to the needs of people crowded in the Superdome certainly contributed to deaths and increased morbidity in the acute phase of Katrina and very likely in the following months as well (Brodie et al. 2006). In addition, it is argued that "assistance for the chronic phase of the health care crisis has been excruciatingly slow to materialize" (Berggren and Curiel 2006, 1550). Community health centers need increased federal support (Nesmith 2006), and continued funding is needed for long-term mental health services (Weisler, Barbee, and Townsend 2006). Medical facilities such as Ochsner Clinic in New Orleans reported being severely strained by providing uncompensated care. As noted previously, protecting graduate medical education—despite its key importance to the health care infrastructure—appeared to be a low priority for government agencies (Berggren and Curiel 2006). Although the CMS announced that it was negotiating a waiver to help mitigate the deficit in the salaries of displaced residents, these bureaucratic changes have proceeded at an incredibly slow pace.

The federal government, as a major health care financing resource, is a crucial force in health care planning. As Light (2004) points out, however, a "good health care system" from the government's perspective is focused more on minimizing the cost of medical services than on providing accessible care to all. Responsibility for public health preparedness is delegated to the highly political CDC, and the goal of health care accessibility receives limited attention.

Even if the needed funding to restore and rebuild health care services in the Gulf Coast area is made available, there is concern that residents are so pervasively uninsured that they might not be able to sustain reclaimed facilities. Displaced workers were left without health insurance and represent one of the largest groups ever to lose coverage in a single event in U.S. history. As Rosenbaum (2006) observed,

> Katrina . . . served to reinforce an already exhaustive amount of evidence regarding the population and public health consequences that flow from the nation's approach to financing health care. Thousands lost their jobs, and already limited

prospects for employer coverage declined further. Exceedingly poor evacuated survivors, a large proportion of whom were in poor health, found themselves cut off from Medicaid. Community health systems in the shelter states showed the strain of struggling with the added burden of thousands of persons unable to pay for health care. Emergency medical personnel . . . could offer short-term assistance, but volunteer clinicians on emergency deployment clearly were in no position to address evacuees' long-term health care needs. (438)

Expanding the existing Medicare system to provide health care coverage for all citizens is one solution that has been proposed in discussions of national health reform. Because entitlement to treatment for individuals with permanent kidney failure is a Medicare program (the End Stage Renal Disease [ESRD] Program of Medicare), it is informative to consider the case of dialysis care in the context of Katrina. Both patients and dialysis care providers faced extraordinary challenges during Katrina. Individuals who had life-threatening chronic health conditions; individuals who were frail, disabled, and/or elderly; and individuals who lacked socioeconomic resources to help them evacuate in a timely way when Katrina struck were at high risk, and these characteristics are applicable to many dialysis patients. Assistance received from CMS, which manages the ESRD Program, was openly criticized at the November 2005 annual meeting of the American Society of Nephrology by physicians who were on the front lines during the crisis. For dialysis patients who survived and remained in the greater New Orleans area, loss of access to Charity Hospital was undoubtedly problematic; many low-income dialysis patients depend on a location such as Charity for emergency needs that arise on weekends and evenings when dialysis clinics are not open. Dialysis patients *do* have portable insured coverage of their health care, however. In addition, dialysis care teams' efforts to address multiple patient needs can benefit socially disadvantaged and isolated individuals, particularly in a time of emergency.

Although proposed in the bipartisan Grassley-Baucus Bill, providing Medicaid coverage on an emergency basis to all low-income and disabled individuals affected by Hurricane Katrina was not supported by the president and Congress. Lambrew and Shalala (2006) argue that

for future disaster preparedness, Congress should enact a permanent, Emergency Medicaid authority. Medicaid has the eligibility and payment systems in place to quickly extend coverage to broad or targeted groups. Fully funded, temporary expansions could be triggered by legislative criteria or an executive agency designation. This would create a health insurance safety net that would help not only low-income but all individuals whose system would be strengthened by the financing of care during crises. It could also protect the public's health by removing financial barriers to prevention and containment among individuals exposed to contagious diseases. (1396)

In addition to the need to be better prepared for natural disasters such as hurricanes, the possibility of a widespread influenza pandemic and concerns about terrorist events underscore the need for preparedness for public health emergencies. Regardless of the specific strategy adopted to accomplish this, acceptance and implementation of the concept of universal access to health care can be viewed as a basic tenet of preparedness for such events (Lambrew and Shalala 2006; Wynia and Gostin 2004). There is also the possibility that such preparedness could stimulate consideration of meaningful national health reform (Rosenbaum 2006).

SOCIAL CONDITIONS AS FUNDAMENTAL CAUSES OF HEALTH PROBLEMS

Hurricane Katrina impacted many people whose ability to access health care was already limited by underinsurance or lack of insurance. In the words of an African American physician who saw evacuees who came to Grady Hospital (Atlanta's counterpart to Charity Hospital in New Orleans), they represented "a bunch of people who have less than optimal health care to begin with, and they have a large number of these diseases that people who get less than optimal health care end up getting" (Payne 2005). Prominent among these diseases are diabetes, asthma, heart disease, and hypertension.

In addition to the role of disparities in health access, living environments and behavioral factors, including smoking and alcohol abuse, as well as race, may increase individuals' risk for serious chronic health conditions (Minkler, Fuller-Thompson, and Guralnik 2006). Data for 2004 from Louisiana indicated that about 12 percent of African Americans had diabetes, compared with 7 percent of whites. However, about 16 percent of persons in Louisiana living in households with an annual income less than $15,000 had diabetes, while less than 5 percent of those living in households with an annual income more than $50,000 had diabetes. Thus, the common denominator is lower socioeconomic status. Indeed, there is a "ubiquitous and often strong association between health and socioeconomic status" (Link and Phelan 1995, 81). Factors related to socioeconomic status "shape individuals' exposure to and experience of virtually all known psychosocial, as well as many biomedical, risk factors" (House 2002, 125).

The strong link between socioeconomic status and health status is important in any analysis of health outcomes following Katrina. Persons with preexisting chronic health conditions were at increased risk of adverse effects when they suffered dehydration or could not access their medications. Because injected insulin must be refrigerated, spoilage was a major concern even if individuals had their medication with them. Not being able to eat after taking insulin also posed a risk. Concern about accessing an unfamiliar medical facility may have prevented some people from resuming proper medical care.

The incidence of kidney failure is especially high in the Southeast. African Americans and lower-income persons have increased risk for kidney failure, largely because of their increased prevalence of hypertension and diabetes. The majority of kidney failure patients receive dialysis, and approximately 5,800 patients were known to be receiving dialysis in the region where Katrina struck. Because dialysis patients are disproportionately characterized by lower socioeconomic status and frequently are limited in physical functioning, many may have had difficulty reaching safety or leaving the area and reaching another destination in a timely way. It is essential that patients dependent on hemodialysis receive regular maintenance treatments, typically Monday/ Wednesday/Friday or Tuesday/Thursday/Saturday, but there were accounts of patients who went more than a week without hemodialysis (Molaison 2006). As of January 2006, the CMS had attributed an estimated 148 dialysis patient deaths in the affected region to the effects of Katrina, and another 300 patients remained unaccounted for (Clemons 2006).

Silove and Bryant (2006) postulate that the factor most conducive to recovery from trauma and resulting stress for survivors of any disaster may be individuals' perception that conditions of safety and predictability have been restored. Thus, rather than individual counseling or other psychological interventions, "stabilizing the social environment and creating opportunities for survivors to resume their livelihoods and take control of their lives may be the best 'therapy' for the community as a whole" (577). In the case of Katrina, however, individuals' prestorm social environment may have lacked stability, and many lower-socioeconomic persons may have lacked regular employment. Adults' ability to return to work appeared to be a very important part of the recovery process in tsunami-affected Thailand, and the government reportedly provided occupational training and "restoration of livelihood programs" (van Griensven et al. 2006). This illustrates an important way in which individuals' optimal health is linked to meaningful occupational opportunity.

People impacted by Katrina have been described as being "at risk before the storm struck" (Payne 2005), which implies a continued risk for physical and mental health problems. Silove and Bryant (2006) note that religion and spirituality are resources that can promote recovery because they offer a sense of faith, hope, and social reintegration. Religion and spirituality are important components of life in the southern United States, especially among African Americans. In their study of Katrina survivors, Elliott and Pais (2006) found that African Americans were more likely than whites to report "leaning on the Lord" as a source of emotional support in the immediate aftermath of the storm. A culture of "keeping on keeping on" has been described as characteristic of African Americans in New Orleans, indicating acceptance of externally imposed conditions that are viewed as beyond the individual's power to change. It will be important to consider the role of these sources of existential meaning in Katrina recovery. A constellation of factors—social, material, economic, cultural, and human rights—are implicated in health outcomes and are relevant for the ongoing response to the Katrina catastrophe.

13

Reconstructing New Orleans after Katrina: The Emergence of an Immigrant Labor Market

Katharine M. Donato, Nicole Trujillo-Pagán,
Carl L. Bankston III, and Audrey Singer

In August 2005, Hurricane Katrina hammered the coastal regions of Louisiana, Mississippi, and Alabama and became the most destructive and expensive natural disaster in U.S. history. The official death toll currently stands at 1,464 (Louisiana Department of Health and Hospitals 2006), and the approximately $109 billion of federal funds has been spent for emergency relief and longer-term recovery and rebuilding (Liu, Fellowes, and Mabanta 2006), topping the destruction caused by Hurricane Andrew in 1992.

While the immediate aftermath focused on the inadequacies of the relief efforts, a rising death toll, and the more than 1 million persons displaced by the storm (including legal and illegal immigrants), subsequent concern shifted to reconstruction in these areas. Across the period, newspapers reported that Spanish-speaking, foreign-born laborers were arriving in large numbers, many lured by the promise of better earnings in the construction industry, which was temporarily protected from sanctions if found to employ unauthorized workers.

In this chapter, we attempt to shed light on the immigration experience in New Orleans in the aftermath of Hurricane Katrina. We set the context by presenting a brief history of immigration to the three Gulf Coast states affected by the hurricane. As reported here, this section documents that the post-Katrina migration of Mexican and other Latin American migrants to the southern Gulf Coast states continues a new chapter of immigration to the region, one that began in the early 1990s. We follow this section with a description of the immigration situation immediately after the hurricane hit and over the longer term. We discuss the population estimates that emerged during this period and what they did not tell us about immigrants in the region and preliminary findings from fieldwork activities that began in October 2005 and ended in August 2006.[1] We end this chapter with a discussion of what our findings imply for immigrants in New Orleans as well as for studies addressing post-disaster immigrant labor.

HISTORY OF MIGRATION TO THE
GULF COAST: PRE-KATRINA PATTERNS

We begin by describing the extent to which immigration to Alabama, Louisiana, and Mississippi has ebbed and flowed throughout history. We also describe recent patterns and shifts in the characteristics of the foreign born, including the size, growth, and socioeconomic status of these populations since the 1990s. The data we use largely derive from the 1990 and 2000 Public Use Microdata files and the 2004 American Community Survey.

The earliest known inhabitants of the area that now constitutes Louisiana, Mississippi, and Alabama were the Mississippian Moundbuilders, a Native American nation that dates back to A.D. 900 (Stein 2006). Named after the Mississippi River valley they inhabited, this Native American culture flourished in the centuries leading up to the arrival of Europeans in the early 1500s. Once they arrived, diseases were introduced, and the once-unified Native American nation broke into smaller tribes, including the Cherokee, Chickasaw, Choctaw, Creek, and Seminole.

Although Spaniards were the first European explorers of the region, French fur traders colonized the area after traveling down the Mississippi River to expand their hunting territory. Subsequently, England also explored the area, and eventually all three nations claimed parts of this region. The first Acadian exiles arrived in Louisiana after British forces exiled them from Acadie, their homeland on the Atlantic Coast of Canada. Between 1764 and 1788, thousands of desperate Acadians sailed to New Orleans and settled in southern Louisiana, and their descendants (e.g., Cajuns) remain an important cultural influence today (Henry and Bankston 2002).

Generally, most immigrants who arrived in the New World settled in the northeastern part of the country rather than in the fertile areas of the South because of arbitrary colonial policies and the difficult conditions of southern cities, where overcrowding and illness were common. As a result, early development in southern coastal regions diverged from that in northern regions, and two geographically and socially distinct worlds emerged. Northern cities developed a strong capitalist system dominated by food production, but southern cities engaged in export production with slave-based plantations dominated by a landed aristocracy and an elite hierarchical social system. By 1860, census estimates suggest that 1.2 million slaves were concentrated in Louisiana, Mississippi, and Alabama (University of Virginia 2006).

Immigration to the southern colonies consisted of a disproportionate number of British, French, and Spanish aristocrats and poor indentured servants from Europe. In fact, 60 percent of the nation's wealthiest, but only 30 percent of its free population, lived in the South. Gradually, as southern labor markets' economic and social development stagnated and became increasingly isolated from western transportation routes, there were fewer jobs, and fierce competition emerged between immigrants and the U.S. born. With little economic pull for new immigrants, the region did not experience much of the large-scale U.S. immigration that occurred in the late 1800s and early 1900s.

The Gulf Coast states of Louisiana, Mississippi, and Alabama still represent the poorest stretch of major coastline in the United States. Census estimates suggest that, in 2005, at least 16 percent of households in these states' populations had incomes below the poverty level (U.S. Bureau of the Census 2005a). In 2002, half of the eight slowest-growing U.S. metropolitan areas were located in these states. Therefore, the three states reflect a region that is culturally, economically, and demographically distinct from the remainder of the nation but also, arguably, from cities like Atlanta and the rest of the South.

Louisiana deserves special attention given the role that its Port of New Orleans has played in the past 300 years. Located at the mouth of the Mississippi River, the Port of New Orleans has been a center for international trade since 1718, when it was founded by the French. Since then, the Port of New Orleans, known as the "Gateway to the Americas," has been a strong source of economic vitality. During the twentieth century, the port became a center for U.S. trade with many nations in Latin America and the Caribbean basin. By the early 1980s, it was the second busiest in the country, but its relative importance then declined, although it remains an important port for exporting raw grain from the Midwest and importing crude oil and petrochemicals.[2] Through the port's presence, New Orleans developed a history of strong contact with nations to its south, and this has indelibly shaped the state's economy and has contributed to immigration.

The Foreign-Born Population in Louisiana, Mississippi, and Alabama

Using the 1 and 5 percent Public Use Microdata from the census, our examination of the patterns and trends of the foreign-born population in Louisiana, Mississippi, and Alabama reveals several important findings.

First, throughout most of the twentieth century, patterns and trends in the foreign-born populations of the three states were highly particularistic and differed from elsewhere in the nation with respect to national origin and size (Donato and Hakimzadeh 2006). Early in the twentieth century, most immigrants to the three states were from Europe. In Louisiana, Italy was the top national origin of immigrants, while in Mississippi and Alabama, Germany was the top national origin. By the second half of the century, however, the foreign-born population in Louisiana began to differentiate itself from that in Mississippi and Alabama. Reflecting the trading relationship between the Standard Fruit Company, located in New Orleans, and banana growers in Honduras, many Hondurans began to settle in the city. In 1970, Hondurans were the largest national origin of immigrants in Louisiana, representing 12.8 percent of the state's foreign born. Although it dropped to 6.7 percent in 1980, it grew by 1990 and 2000 (to 9.2 and 9.7 percent, respectively). The earliest Honduran arrivals included wealthy young women sent for a U.S. education, clerks and managers for Standard Fruit, and poor immigrants who worked as mechanics and carpenters at the port. In the fall of 2006, estimates suggested that New Orleans was home to 140,000 to 150,000 Hondurans, the largest Honduran community in the nation.

The foreign-born population in Louisiana was also different than that in Mississippi and Alabama because it included many foreign-born refugees, including some Cubans and many from Vietnam, during the second half of the twentieth century.[3] By the end of the 1990s, estimates suggested that 25,000 Vietnamese lived in Louisiana, and many were concentrated in an ethnic enclave in eastern New Orleans. Although the first to arrive largely worked as unskilled laborers, the Vietnamese in Louisiana have opened small businesses, from restaurants and small groceries to commercial fishing operations. By the 1990s, approximately one of every 10 Vietnamese men worked as fishers and shrimpers, and they accounted for one of every 20 workers in the state's fishing industry.

In Mississippi and Alabama (and to a lesser extent in Louisiana), foreign-born Germans have been highly represented since early in the colonial period. Although many Germans lived in coastal villages along the Gulf, others were plantation owners. Eventually, their presence in the region led to intermarriage and the emergence of German Cajuns. Germany still remains among the top immigrant-sending nations for Mississippi and Alabama. In 1990, it represented 8.5 percent of the foreign born in the two states, but by 2000 it dropped back to 7.6 percent.

Therefore, the second major finding from our historical view of immigration to the three Gulf Coast states is that since the 1990s, immigration began to take on the attributes of the U.S. foreign-born population as a whole. By 2000, data suggested that the Mexican-born population had substantially grown, and so too had the concentration of the foreign born in metropolitan areas.

For example, although Mexico represented the largest source of immigration to the United States for many decades, it first appeared among the top-five sending nations to these Gulf Coast states in 2000. At that time, Mexico represented the national origin of 8 percent of the foreign-born population in Louisiana, 27 percent of Alabama's, and 24 percent of Mississippi's. Figure 13.1 illustrates the especially dramatic increases in the Mexican-born population in Mississippi and Alabama during the 1990s.

In the early 1990s, as employers met a strong labor demand, Mexican migrants came to Louisiana to work in shipbuilding and fabrication yards in southern coastal areas of the state (Donato and Bankston 2007; Donato, Stainback, and Bankston 2005), and many in Mississippi and Alabama were employed in casino construction or in forestry (Elliott and Ionescu 2003; Mc-

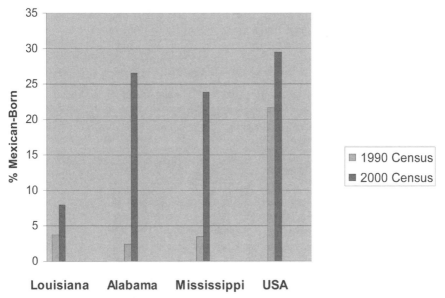

Figure 13.1. Mexican Foreign-Born as Percentage of Total Foreign-Born Populations in Louisiana, Alabama, and Mississippi, 1990 and 2000
Source: 1990 Census of Population and Housing and Census 2000, Summary File 3.

Daniel and Casanova 2003) Other Latinos also played a large role in Louisiana's foreign-born population in the 1990s. In addition to already settled Hondurans, thousands of new Hondurans and migrants from other Central American nations, including Nicaragua, arrived after Hurricane Mitch battered that region in 1998.

Figure 13.1 also reveals that, during the 1990s, the Mexican-born population grew more rapidly in Alabama and Mississippi than in Louisiana. Although small in absolute size and relative ranking, the foreign-born populations in Alabama and Mississippi approximately doubled and experienced a higher rate of growth than did the nation as a whole during the 1990s. Louisiana, on the other hand, experienced a slower pace of growth (32.6 percent increase), leading to a substantial drop in its foreign-born state ranking (from twenty-sixth place in 1990 to nineteenth place in 2000, out of 51).[4]

A final distinct feature of the foreign-born populations in the three Gulf Coast states is that most settled in metropolitan areas. Figure 13.2 describes the increase in foreign-born persons in the three Gulf Coast states and their concentration in metropolitan areas. In Louisiana, as the foreign-born population increased, so too did its concentration in the New Orleans metropolitan area. In Mississippi, although the population grew somewhat since 1990, foreign-born persons were especially concentrated in the Biloxi metropolitan area in 2000 and 2004. Only in Alabama was the trend toward metropolitan

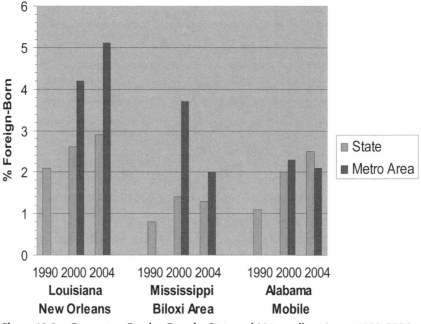

Figure 13.2.   Percentage Foreign-Born by State and Metropolitan Areas, 1990–2004

Note: In 2000 and 2004, New Orleans refers to New Orleans City; Biloxi area refers to the cities of Biloxi, Gulfport, and Pascagoula; Mobile refers to Mobile County. These definitions are consistent with the Census Bureau's 2005 hurricane data site [see http://www.census.gov/press-release/www/2005/katrina.htm].

Sources: U.S. Census Bureau [2000] and 2004 American Community Survey.

concentration somewhat attenuated. Although the foreign-born population increased in that state, the concentration of the foreign born in Mobile was not much higher than in the state as a whole.[5]

In summary, demographic shifts in immigration to the Gulf Coast states began in the 1990s. By the turn of the twenty-first century, Mexico was the leading sender of immigrants, and many now lived in large urban areas. These trends were in line with larger national trends, making immigration to this region far less particularistic than in the past. Unknown then but more clearly understood now is that this immigration context, especially in New Orleans, represented the calm before the literal storm.

IMMIGRATION TO GULF COAST STATES: EFFECTS OF HURRICANE KATRINA

Immediately after the Storm

In the weeks immediately following the storm, disaster restoration industries quickly became a magnet for Latino immigrants who were lured by the promise of high pay and an emergency federal decree temporarily suspending immigration enforcement sanctions. In the days after the hurricane, President Bush also temporarily suspended the Davis-Bacon Act (Edsall 2005). Under usual circumstances, the act requires federal contractors to pay the prevailing wage in the region. With its suspension, contractors were permitted to pay lower than the average or prevailing wage.

By early October, the media began to describe how employers were seeking Latino immigrants to help rebuild the affected areas. Articles with titles such as "Illegal Workers Eyeing the Gulf Coast," "Big Easy Uneasy about Migrant Wave," "La Nueva Orleans," and "A New Spice in the Gumbo" all signal the role that immigrants, many of them Latino laborers, began to play in the efforts to rebuild (Eaton 2005; Rodríguez 2005; Root and Davis 2005; Sanchez 2005). Although they quickly responded to the labor demand, Latino workers were not immediately welcome. An epitome of this sentiment originated from New Orleans Mayor Ray Nagin, who asked at a forum with business leaders, "How do I make sure New Orleans is not overrun with Mexican workers?" (Hispanic Business 2005). Although the remark provoked a joint statement about unity by civil rights and Latino organizations, it also mobilized many in the region who believed that contractors favored cheap, foreign labor over local and more expensive native workers. In the context of a racialized New Orleans, criticism from local Gulf Coast residents grew, and one consequence was that the prevailing wage rule went back into effect approximately two months after its suspension.

By December, newspaper reports suggested that undocumented immigrants from Mexico in New Orleans earned $10 an hour, working 10 hours a day, seven days a week (Amrhein 2005; Campo-Flores 2005; Fletcher and Pham 2006; Pickel 2005) One news article described work in the battered areas of the Gulf Coast as an extraordinary opportunity for immigrants looking for work as long as they were willing to work 70 to 80 hours a week (Martinez 2005). Others focused on the problems that undocumented immigrants faced—being abandoned by contractors, receiving less than or none of the pay promised, and experiencing other violations of workers' rights (Fletcher and Pham 2006; Plocek 2006; Roig-Franzia 2005). Although there were no official estimates, Andy Guerra, president of the Gulf Coast Latin American Association, told the Gannett News Service in November 2005 that about 30,000 Latino workers—both U.S. residents and new immigrants from Mexico and Central America—had flocked to the Gulf Coast since Katrina.

What also remained unclear was whether the temporary influx of Mexican and other Latino immigrant laborers would remain in the New Orleans area after the cleanup work was completed. Although most migrants may not have intended to stay, migration studies suggest that the longer those jobs last, the more likely they will settle permanently. Hurricane Andrew led to the settlement of many immigrants in southeastern Florida. The hurricane, combined with the displacement of thousands of residents, triggered a construction boom that attracted large numbers of Latino immigrants, many of whom then settled in the area. In towns hard hit by the storm, such as Homestead, the Latino population grew by as much as 50 percent during the 1990s (InfoPlease 2005).

The Numbers Story

The city of New Orleans (Orleans Parish) had an estimated population of approximately 455,000 in July 2005, just before Hurricane Katrina hit. Although the city had experienced population decline in the decades before the storm, it sustained enormous population loss after Katrina. By early 2006, anecdotal evidence documenting the presence of Latino immigrant workers grew. So too did the demand for population estimates. Many of the earliest studies based their estimates on small surveys or indirect assessments of the population living in hurricane-affected areas. Next we summarize these population figures and assess what they tell us about immigrants in these areas. In general, this wave of studies addressed how many persons were living in households in New Orleans after the hurricane. All faced similar limitations; there was urgent need for the information, yet at the same time, limited ways of assessing population counts and characteristics of the population, especially race and ethnicity, were in great demand but nearly impossible to estimate. The biggest limitation of studies estimating the population's size and composition was that most excluded persons living in group quarters and temporary housing such as hotels and dormitories.

The first population estimates were developed by the city's Emergency Operations Center (EOC). Based on a rapid population survey first conducted in November 2005 and repeated in December 2005 and January 2006, the estimates were the first from the field of the overnight and daytime populations in residential units. The estimate of 181,200 for Orleans Parish in December 2005 was based on a stratified random sample of single-family households and did not include group quarters. Moreover, no details about characteristics such as race, ethnicity, and nativity were collected.

The Louisiana Department of Health and Hospitals (DHH) produced parish-level population estimates beginning in October 2005 based on a trended ratio of public school enrollment to the total population. However, because public schools were closed in New Orleans through December 2005, the survey had to rely on alternative sources for areas that had no enrollment figures. For Orleans Parish, they relied on results from the December 2005 EOC rapid population estimate survey that did not assess foreign-born status.

By early 2006, using different techniques, Claritas and RAND released population estimates (Claritas 2006; McCarthy et al. 2006). Claritas's January 2006 estimate was 174,000, while RAND's March 2006 estimate was 155,000. Claritas updated their estimates in June 2006 when Orleans Parish was estimated to have a population of 214,486. RAND's estimated population for September 2006 was set at 198,000.

In June 2006, the U.S. Bureau of the Census released population data for 117 hurricane-impacted counties and parishes in the Gulf region. Two data products were released, and both used special methods to produce estimates for the "prestorm" and "poststorm" population. The first product was a set of estimates of the total population for July 1, 2005, and January 1, 2006, representing the population roughly two months before the storms and four months after hurricanes Katrina and Rita hit. Orleans Parish was estimated to have lost 278,883 persons in the poststorm period, resulting in a population of 158,353 in January 2006. These estimates referred to the population in housing units.

The second data product derived from the American Community Survey (ACS), which was in the field at the time the storm hit and therefore offered pre- and post-Katrina estimates of population and its characteristics. The release of these data brought an onslaught of news articles that reported ACS findings to be consistent with large numbers of immigrants in New Orleans. However, there was little in the ACS data release providing evidence of this idea. Using these data, Frey and Singer (2006) reported that the New Orleans metropolitan area was more white and less poor after the storm but that the share of Hispanics changed minimally over the period, remaining at about 6 percent. In addition, the foreign-born population was estimated to be roughly the same before and after the storm, approximately 6 percent. This finding was certainly related to ACS sample design, which did not include group or transitory quarters—a big limitation for understanding immigrants in storm-affected areas. Its coverage of the metropolitan area rather than parishes/counties also led to fewer insights about immigrants.

With funding and assistance from the Centers for Disease Control (CDC), the DHH expanded and replicated the EOC's rapid population estimate survey in several of the most-hurricane-affected parishes (Orleans, Jefferson, Plaquemines, and St. Bernard) during the summer of 2006. Orleans Parish was estimated to have reached 187,525 persons in August 2006, with a margin of error of ±11.5 percent. In addition, 8.8 percent were estimated to be Latino.

Therefore, despite the release of ACS pre- and post-Katrina data, no comprehensive source of data yet exists to measure the size and attributes of the immigrant population in the Gulf Coast states. With little quantitative data to describe the population, immigrants remain largely invisible in formal estimates. Yet they are visible to residents and visitors where Spanish-language signs now appear along main thoroughfares (e.g., Williams Boulevard and West Esplanade in Kenner) and advertise money orders that can be sent to Mexico. A clear sign of their presence was the recent front-page article of the *New Orleans Times-Picayune*. Not only did it describe new Latino migrant residents in the city, but the newspaper provided captions under the articles' photographs in both English and Spanish, and the entire article was reproduced in Spanish on inside pages of the paper (Waller 2006).

The Immigrant Population in New Orleans Post-Katrina

In this section, we rely on our own (and other) field observations to under-stand the early Latino immigrant experience in New Orleans in the aftermath of the hurricane. We approached our fieldwork with the expectation that the economic situation of New Orleans, especially the jobs that immigrants do and the industries in which they are found, would not change much in the post-Katrina period. In contrast, from our immigrant and employer conversa-tions, we learned that the local labor market was more volatile than we ex-pected. Consistent with this line of thinking were reports that suggested that reconstruction in New Orleans would be slow and linked to a variety of deci-sions that the city and federal government had yet to make about which neigh-borhoods to rebuild and exactly how to rebuild them.

Migration scholars often remind us how immigrant assimilation may be dra-matically different for the same group of immigrants entering different social en-vironments (Portes and Rumbaut 2001). In contrast to the idea that assimilation is a linear process where immigrant groups become more incorporated into the American mainstream as time progresses, the assimilation process of immigrants is segmented, not linear, and varies with the human capital brought by the group of newcomers and with the context of the receiving community (Zhou 1997). One illustration is the incorporation of immigrants into small communities in southern Louisiana in the late 1990s (Donato, Stainback, and Bankston 2005). Despite similarities in the economic and social makeup, the early incorporation experiences of immigrants substantially varied across these communities.

Our early fieldwork in New Orleans also pointed to complexity in the in-corporation experiences of migrant laborers. Rather than facing a labor de-mand that was consistently strong, we learned that migrant labor market op-portunities were much more diverse and chaotic than the descriptions presented in newspapers had suggested. This was a labor market into which people move in and out of quickly, where there is adequate labor supply one day and shortage the next and where what occurs in one neighborhood may be quite different than in another neighborhood. Even the most informed pre-dictions about labor supply and demand fell flat in the highly volatile and po-litically charged New Orleans post-Katrina.

Table 13.1 places our discussion about immigrants and their labor force ex-periences into a time line that attempts to describe, albeit broadly, the shifting conditions in the New Orleans labor market in the aftermath of the storm. We refer to this table to help us describe the immigrant experience. In the follow-ing sections, we rely on data from conversations with immigrant workers and employers to explain how varying contextual factors in the labor market shaped the immigrant experience we observed.

Table 13.1. Phases of Recovery in Post-Katrina New Orleans and Implications for the Local Labor Market

Phase 1: Immediately post-Katrina until November 2006: Demolition and cleanup
  Employers consist of large disaster reconstruction companies
  Work involves recovery of people and commercial structures
  Key tasks include cleanup, initial removal of debris, and demolition
  Worker skill level was largely unskilled, recruited from a broad area across the United
    States, including workers from California, Kansas, and Ohio
  Involves higher-than-usual occupational risks with little federal oversight
  Workers attracted to reports of high wages in New Orleans and by promise of papers
    by some employers
  Worker rights violations but no public knowledge
  Worker recruitment from all over the United States (and from Mexico)
  Housed in warehouses and large ballrooms of hurricane-damaged hotels
  Emergence of a few day labor sites

Phase 2: November 2005 to March 2006: Demolition, cleanup, and reconstruction
  Employers now diversify, large reconstruction companies, and large to medium-sized
    contractors, as some large companies begin to subcontract out work
  Work involves recovery of commercial and residential structures
  Key tasks largely include removal of debris and demolition, but new emphasis on
    rebuilding emerging
  Worker skill level is largely semiskilled
  Involves fewer occupational risks than in phase 1 but higher risks than for workers
    elsewhere
  Workers attracted to reports of high wages and promise of papers by some employers
  Public knowledge of worker rights violations emerges in migrant networks
  Worker recruitment is regional, from southeastern United States and Texas
  Housed in warehouses and large ballrooms of hurricane-damaged hotels and tent cities
  Number of day labor sites expands, many appear outside of large home supply chains
    and outside the city's center

Phase 3: March 2006 to present: Reconstruction
  Employer diversification continues, with many local contractors
  Work involves reconstruction
  Key tasks involve rebuilding
  Worker skill is semiskilled and skilled work
  Involves fewer occupational risks than phase 1 but higher risks than for workers
    elsewhere
  Workers attracted to high wages
  Extensive public knowledge of workers rights violations
  Worker recruitment is from southern Gulf states
  Housed in warehouses, ballrooms, and rooms in smaller motels
  Day labor sites now more established and institutionalized

Phase 1: Initial Period of Demolition and Cleanup

In many ways, the work available to immigrants immediately after the storm hit was quite different than elsewhere in the United States. Largely cleanup and demolition work, it demanded thousands of unskilled workers who were willing to work under very difficult conditions without the usual protections afforded to U.S. workers. Most workers were employed by large disaster reconstruction companies that were hired by the federal government to recover people and commercial structures. The work itself did not require high levels of skill; it involved cleanup, removal of debris, and demolition of unsafe structures. It also involved considerable health risks given the little, if any, federal oversight of the risks to migrant workers and how they could prevent them. Yet, despite the risks, immigrant workers in October 2005 described their initial work experience in New Orleans as their moneymaking phase; they expected "to make lots of money" and then return to their countries of origin.

As part of the recovery work, contractor activity was spurred on by the blue roofs program. Begun immediately after the storm, contractors were hired to secure temporary roofs, usually in the form of blue tarps, to homes and other buildings that had partially damaged roofs. To receive benefits, owners had to apply for the assistance and agree to occupy their homes within 30 days of the repair. Although most residents who qualified for the federally funded blue roof program applied in mid- to late fall, the Federal Emergency Management Agency (FEMA) reported that more than 80,000 roofs in Louisiana were temporarily repaired in this way.[6]

In this early stage, some employers found workers on day labor corners in areas outside New Orleans, and others recruited them from their established work crews in other cities. Of the two strategies, recruitment from outside the hurricane-affected area yielded many more workers. Labor recruiters encouraged workers to come to New Orleans and promised them high-paying jobs, housing, and food. Although they were promised adequate transportation, food, and housing, workers often found themselves highly dependent on employers for these items. Many immigrants reported that they were told they could not bring their own vehicle, and despite the employer promises, workers complained about inadequate food and housing. Recruitment from day labor sites was less successful because many who wanted to work were unable to get into the city of New Orleans immediately after the hurricane hit.

No matter where workers lived in this initial stage of recovery, immigrants were very visible as workers in New Orleans. They were initially concentrated in two types of housing arrangements: warehouses and trailers. Most workers who arrived in September and October were warehoused in hotel ballrooms and warehouses. Hundreds slept in large spaces that they described as tense because, in such dense living arrangements with little to do after work and frustration from many broken promises with employers, fights and allegations about stealing personal property were common. Workers who lived in trailers had better housing experiences; they enjoyed more stable housing and work arrangements with employers, although workers may have sacrificed higher salaries in return. Generally, workers arrived in a city that lacked adequate access to food, electricity, and public transportation. One consequence was that issues of transportation and housing took on unique importance. For example, one worker lived in his employer's trailer with three coworkers. He was recruited by his friend who had in turn been recruited directly in Ohio. Lacking transportation from the recruiter, they made their way to New Orleans in a car in mid-September. They made $10 an hour and claimed to be happy to work 10 hours a day, seven days a week. Although he knew other workers were making a higher salary, these workers were content with their pay in part because they had decent housing and a stable work arrangement. In contrast, another worker arrived in New Orleans from Miami at the end of September 2005. Recruited by an Atlanta roofing company, he was particularly motivated to come because the company offered $15 per hour and free food and housing. He boarded one of the vans that the company sent every day with 19 other men. When he arrived, he joined other employees in tents located in a warehouse his employer shared with another affiliated roofing company, but he quickly found the company did not fulfill its promises. Rather than three meals a day, he was given only breakfast and lunch. For dinner he went to the Red Cross because there was no other way to obtain food. Moreover, although his employer did fulfill the promise of $15 per hour for 10 hours per day for the first week, after that the number of work hours dropped down to six hours per day. After just 15 days of work, his employer terminated his contract.

Although many workers were happy about the pay they could earn working six to seven days a week for 10 to 12 hours per day, some complained that they grew tired and weak from inadequate food. Many workers claimed that their lives consisted of working and sleeping with little or no access to other areas of the city for recreation. Male workers found that living and working in a tense environment stimulated physical disputes, particularly where alcohol had been involved. In cases where they had not directly been involved in a physical altercation with another male worker, workers complained that these troubles kept them awake and affected their performance on subsequent days.

Therefore, workers' dependency on employers for housing meant that employers also exerted a high degree of control over migrant labor. Workers began to complain that the terms on which they had been recruited were not met. For example, some found they were paid less or not at all for their work. One explained that the large work crew he was a part of required him to pay his employer for fraudulent papers so that their paychecks could be processed (rather than being paid cash). This worker paid a $600 fee for the papers, although he never received them. Others complained about the housing conditions they had to endure and claimed they were not what had been promised when they were recruited, and these complaints were particularly common where workers had gone unpaid. For instance, one worker explained that a work crew of 15 persons slept in a school bus every night. He explained that this would not have been a problem had the employer paid them, but he claimed "they brainwashed us" by paying him smaller amounts each week than what he was owed and promising to pay the next week. Many workers complained they were not fully paid and/or went unpaid for several weeks of work. Furthermore, most of the city's businesses were still closed. As a result, workers were unable to buy their own food, and they depended on their employers to provide food and/or transportation to restaurants and stores.

Together with the difficult nature of the work, these factors led many workers to feel they had made significant sacrifices to work in New Orleans. Clearly one was the health risks they experienced on the job. Most workers lacked dust masks, gloves, and respirators, even though they spoke about the strong smell of the debris around them (Fletcher and Pham 2006). Without transportation and knowledge of the city, migrant workers could not secure such equipment on their own. Given these very difficult conditions, we were not surprised to hear that some workers left early—before completing their contracts—because of the higher risks of disease and injury they confronted.

During fieldwork in October 2005, we saw no signs of federal occupational health standards and practices enforcement. Although documents were translated into Spanish, they were available only via the Internet until mid-October, when the CDC began to distribute statements describing the standards at the Hispanic Chamber of Commerce. Furthermore, our conversations with representatives from the CDC and the Occupational Safety and Health Administration (OSHA) suggest that few, if any, federal controls were in place to protect these workers immediately after this disaster. At that time, OSHA decided to suspend enforcement and act only in an advisory capacity, and the CDC claimed that it could not investigate standard health and safety issues for immigrant workers given its complex subcontracting arrangements.

Phase 2: From November 2005 to March 2006—Reconstruction Begins, albeit Slowly

Eventually, the initial strong demand for unskilled labor waned after November 2005 for several months, despite the need for reconstruction in the city. The slowing down of the demand for immigrant labor reflected large-scale uncertainty over whether and how to invest in rebuilding because FEMA had not released its revised flood zones for the state. With these maps, insurance companies and banks would determine where to rebuild and how to rebuild, such as what building specifications and elevations were necessary for owners to follow. Jobs were certainly available given the rise in building permits (from 6,250 to 16,000) between January and February, but this activity was not nearly what was needed to rebuild the majority of the city. The Brookings Institution noted that more than 50,000 homes had severe damage (Liu, Fellowes, and Mabanta 2006).

During this period, employers began to diversify. Large reconstruction companies began to subcontract increasing amounts of work out to large to medium-sized contractors who entered the New Orleans labor market looking for workers. Subcontractor relationships with workers became increasingly complex and informal; some were labor recruiters, but others subcontracted work to particular workers who, in turn, later became labor recruiters. Moreover, sometimes subcontractors designated a particular worker a supervisor because he spoke at least some English and then paid that supervisor the salaries for all workers and expected him to distribute them. These practices created suspicion, conflict, and uncertainty among workers. As a result of the spontaneity embedded in this emerging labor market and the rising informality embedded in subcontractor–worker relationships, an "every worker for himself" attitude developed, and individuals took advantage of opportunities as they received them.

Despite the decline in labor demand, workers continued to migrate to New Orleans. Many came because they followed word of mouth (*corridas de voz*) stories about plentiful work and high-paying jobs and rumors of employers' promises of legal papers. Workers from areas within the region were particularly effective at stimulating more migration among friends and acquaintances, creating a largely regional rather than national migration flow, and the momentum helped fuel further informal recruitment of workers. Nonetheless, workers' rights violations also expanded, and eventually (later in phase 2) they made the headlines and reached potential migrants through their social networks. Furthermore, the degree of uncertainty faced by workers in this labor market rose, as larger contracts ended and smaller subcontractors usually could not guarantee work for a long duration.

By late fall, day labor sites had begun to expand. Although some had developed immediately after the hurricane hit, only now did they become an important source of labor recruitment. Employers found workers every day on day labor corners inside New Orleans, but they also found workers at day labor sites in neighboring cities such as Houston. In these cities, day laborers also began recruiting each other and pooling their resources to share transportation costs to New Orleans and employer and housing contacts. Day labor sites in New Orleans offered workers more independence from employers, and they were places where workers could share information about adequate housing and employment. Therefore, gradually workers grew less dependent on employers.

Housing conditions also shifted during this period. By November, an increasing number of migrants led to the growth of what became known as tent cities. Although still housed largely in warehouses and some in trailers, many migrants also lived in tents across the city. This gave workers some freedom from employers and offered them social opportunities to either participate in cooking food or go out to the few restaurants that began to open in the city. On the one hand, these housing conditions raised additional problems for workers because they were exposed to rain and, at least in City Park, had to pay

"$300 a month, plus five dollars per shower every time they wanted to bathe" (Aguilar 2005). On the other hand, some workers found camaraderie in sharing the difficulties of limited housing options. For instance, one worker claimed that working together to prepare meals in the tent cities felt like a brotherhood, and he described the unwritten rule that whoever woke first in the morning started preparing coffee and food—just like brothers in a family would. Other housing options also emerged in this phase. For example, workers shared their vehicles as an alternate and temporary housing option. Home owners and builders also offered workers housing in homes while they repaired them in exchange for reduced rent. The conditions were difficult, however, as housing became increasingly crowded. For example, a one-bedroom unit that lacked appliances and basic services such as water and electricity was used to house more than 15 people.

Phase 3: March 2006 to Present—Reconstruction

This phase is different than the earlier two because of its emphasis on reconstruction and because it remains ongoing. Although these phases vary from one area of the city to the next and some parts of Orleans Parish may still remain in the demolition and cleanup stage, in much of the city and its inner suburban ring, by March in some areas, work had begun to shift from unskilled and semiskilled removal of sheetrock and patching roofs to skilled and semiskilled work in flooring and cabinetmaking. This shift resulted in greater opportunities for smaller independent contractors, especially for self-employed immigrant workers.

Generally, the roles of employers and workers were more clearly defined in this phase. The work itself in this third phase is more predictable than earlier phases, it includes migrants in construction trades as well as those doing service work, and employers now attract migrant workers using H2B visas.[7] Consistent with other work (see Donato, Stainback, and Bankston 2005), however, field reports suggest that migrant workers with visas were worse off then those without them. Temporary visas mean that workers live in employer-negotiated housing. Workers were also less able to identify who is responsible for a rights violation, such as not paying salaries, and to vote with their feet than workers without visas. Employers have greater power to return the migrants they do not want, bring in replacement workers, and blame foreign recruiters for the lies they may have told workers.

Housing conditions also made migrant workers less visible. With at least some hotel rooms now cleaned, some employers moved workers into them. Workers lived in these hotels until their contracts ended, and, at that time, they were often left to find alternate arrangements—assuming they wanted to remain in New Orleans. In an attempt to clean up the city for Mardi Gras, the city also removed most tent cities by mid-March and reduced the use of vehicles as an alternate housing option. Together with federal marshals, the city also rounded up undocumented migrants from day labor sites and other places visible to tourists. Finally, other workers continued to live in smaller hotels and some shared apartments, although this type of housing left some migrants homeless when they could not pay rising rents.

With more predictable employment and housing, migrants began to bifurcate into two groups: those more and those less settled. This is consistent with reports from employers who described growth in a permanent, institutionalized Latino workforce as a major consequence of the hurricane. Now with more semiskilled and skilled migrant workers in the city, the likelihood of settlement was higher than in earlier phases that attracted unskilled workers. Field reports suggested that intentions to remain in New Orleans were highest among those skilled workers. The more settled migrants live south of the center and in Kenner; they have more stable employment and live in more stable households than migrants who are less settled. Importantly, their households include family members, such as women and children, who may supplement income by selling food. The less settled live as close as possible to job/labor pickup sites, usually in temporary and group housing. They are the most economically and physically vulnerable, fear being robbed by others, and have few social ties to the area. This bifurcation will have important implications, a topic we address in our final thoughts.

FINAL THOUGHTS

In this chapter, we have attempted to describe how immigrants entered the New Orleans labor market after Hurricane Katrina hit. We began by setting the historical context and documenting the ways in which immigration to the Gulf Coast states became less particularistic and included a substantial presence of Mexicans by 2000. We then examined immigration to the city of New Orleans post-Katrina, using field observations as our key data source because recent quantitative data sets underestimate the foreign born.

From our fieldwork, our findings illustrate how an immigrant labor market emerges in New Orleans after Hurricane Katrina hit. Although initially brought in for assistance in building recovery, we found that quickly more and more immigrants arrived through formal and informal routes attracted to employment in New Orleans. Shifts in the conditions of the migrant labor market meant that migrant workers moved from strong reliance on their employers for work as well as living conditions, including food, into a time of uncertainty and diversification when many more migrants and smaller subcontractors entered the labor market. One key consequence was the emergence of the present period; it contains signs of two clearly distinct migrant populations: those who are settling and appear to be becoming long-term residents of New Orleans and those less settled who continue to live in very difficult conditions and may be subject to exploitation. Together the findings illustrate the institutionalization of an immigrant labor market in a postdisaster economy of New Orleans.

Only time will tell how this story ends and what immigrants will have meant to the city's revitalization over the long run. But several items are now clear. First, Latino immigrants have secured a strong presence in the city, and given the signs of settlement, they are likely to become an important voice in the future. Second, the role immigrants play can be understood only within the larger context of existing immigration to the region and to other parts of the United States. Finally, although the labor market responses to Hurricane Katrina described here are historically unique, the immigrant labor market that has emerged in New Orleans after this disaster followed a pattern of early increase and then stabilization, and more recently it is showing signs of institutionalization. Only future research will tell us how comparable this case of immigrant labor market emergence is to others yet to occur in the twenty-first century.

NOTES

We are grateful for the generous support we received from the American Sociological Association's Fund for the Advancement of the Discipline in support of this research. We are also grateful to Shirin Hakimzadeh, who, together with the first author, published an expanded version of the history section in this paper as "The Changing Face of the Gulf Coast: Immigration to Louisiana, Mississippi and Alabama," in *Migration Information Source* (January 2006). Please direct all correspondence to this author at the Department of Sociology, Vanderbilt University, Garland Hall 201, VU Station 37235-1811, Nashville, TN 37235 (katharine.donato@vanderbilt.edu).

1. Nicole Trujillo Pagán was in the field in New Orleans for two weeks in October 2005; she returned to New Orleans in March and April 2006 for three weeks and again in late May for three months. During this time, she went to day labor sites around the city and conducted a series of guided conversations with immigrants. Carl Bankston spoke to as many employers as possible during the summer of 2006, and Donato and Singer visited New Orleans several times after Katrina hit. All conversations were guided by an open-ended set of questions that are available on request from the authors.

2. As of February 2006, the Port of New Orleans reported to have "regained 100 percent of cargo ship calls" they reported before Hurricane Katrina struck the Gulf Coast (http://www.portno .com/message.htm).

3. Signs of Cuban refugee settlement first appeared in New Orleans in the 1960s (see Carballo 1970).

4. Estimates from the American Community Survey for 2005 are comparable to the data presented here. In Louisiana, 11.2 percent of the foreign-born were born in Mexico; in Mississippi, 27.5 percent were born in Mexico and in Alabama 30.4 percent.

5. Again, data from the 2005 American Community Survey are consistent with increased concentration of the foreign population in metropolitan areas. In New Orleans, 16,347 foreign-born persons made up approximately 3.7 percent of the population, compared to 2.8 percent in Louisiana. In Gulfport–Biloxi, 7,747 foreign-born persons represented 3.2 percent of the population, relative to 1.5 percent in Mississippi. In Mobile County, the 12,775 foreign-born represented 3.2 percent of the population compared to 2.7 percent for the entire state of Alabama.

6. The program formally ended January 7, 2006.

7. These visas permit the temporary entry of unskilled and semiskilled workers. Companies apply to the federal government for the visas on the basis of labor demand unmet by the local population and then attract workers to meet the demand for labor.

Postscript

Considering Katrina

Lee Clarke

Disaster, risk, and danger are in the air. In 2005, it was Katrina. In 2004, it was a tsunami that started in the Indian Ocean. In 2003, it was SARS. In 2002, nearly 2,000 people died in a ferry accident off the coast of Gambia. In 2001, it was the World Trade Center collapse. Social science has something important to say about all those events.

But we will struggle to understand the meaning of Katrina for a long time. This volume is an example of that struggle, and there is a considerable amount of illumination herein. The editors of *The Sociology of Katrina* have called what I've written here a "postscript," and while it comes at the end of the volume, I don't summarize or analyze the foregoing chapters. Certainly, it is not possible to write a postscript to Katrina because the disaster is ongoing. Rather, I shall use this occasion to ruminate on the event and on social science.

Katrina initiated two disasters. One disaster happened along the Mississippi coast, and one disaster happened in New Orleans. I do not in any way believe that the suffering in Mississippi was less important or intense. But there are two things that distinguish that place from New Orleans: it has been destroyed before, and there are strong institutional forces that will profit enormously from its reconstruction. That the Mississippi coast has been destroyed before means there are mental models available that will tell people when they are recovering and when they have recovered. No such signposts are available for New Orleans. The enormous profits that gambling generates for business and government in Mississippi means that redevelopment there will be expedited. In New Orleans there are fewer profit centers, fewer revenue streams, and thus fewer concentrated interests to drive recovery. It's hard to imagine a worse recipe for recovery than having no idea what it looks like and few commercial interests in seeing it happen.

SOME RUMINATIONS ON DISASTER AND SOCIAL SCIENCE

Whenever big events happen, social scientists respond. When big disasters happen, all our skills and instincts come to the fore. Journalists turn to us for sound bites and analysis. We rush to the scene for insight and data. The grant-writing and grant-making apparatus churns. More people in the social sciences try to run projects on disaster and trauma. Thus we do profit from other people's suffering.

Although I bear no responsibility, I have my own guilt from such profiteering. As Katrina's fury was ruining New Orleans and the Mississippi coast, my book *Worst Cases: Terror and Catastrophe in the Popular Imagination* (Clarke 2006) was in production at the University of Chicago Press with an expected release date of December 2005. Katrina pushed my publisher to produce the book more quickly. As it happened, I have a paragraph in the final chapter of *Worst Cases* in which I talk about a big hurricane drowning 80 percent of New Orleans under 20 feet of water. This was seen by many as prophetic, although I've always thought it was about as prophetic as predicting that tomorrow the sun will rise in the east. In any case, Katrina couldn't have come at a more propitious time for my book. My publisher calls *Worst Cases* "evergreen," meaning that the next big disaster will vault it back in to high demand, as will the one after that and the one after that.

I have and will continue to refer to the disaster known as Katrina in the conventional way: "Katrina." There are other ways of naming the disaster, and we know that labels matter for how people think about that which has been labeled. I have tried, in various speeches and talks that I've given, to use the word "Katrita" because Hurricane Rita brought considerable damage of her own. But no one likes the term. I'll call it Katrina, but we are wise to remember that there is no necessary or natural reason to do so.

It is only immediately obvious that we should consider Katrina a pivotal event. On closer inspection, the usual reasons don't seem special. We've lost cities before and larger ones too: Dresden, Nagasaki, and Hiroshima, for instance. In addition, as appalling as the death toll in New Orleans was—and it *was* appalling because nearly all the deaths were preventable—it was still a small number compared to the carnage that comes from tobacco or automobiles every day. I do not understand why people say New Orleans reminded Americans that there's a race problem in our country. I know of no evidence and of no person who does not know this.

Extreme events like Katrina pose an interesting problem for social scientists, one that might be profitable to explore deeply. It is a rare, even singular, event, but most of our conceptual apparatus and nearly all our measurement tools are best suited for recurring events. Even if we take a random sample of, say, survivors, thus enabling true things to be said about the population of New Orleans survivors, we still have not answered the question of generalizability. If, for instance, we find a continued sense of trauma among survivors, do the conclusions we draw from such a study apply to all disasters? There are good reasons to think that they do, but there are also good reasons to be circumspect about such conclusions.

One of social science's responsibilities is to dispel myths, particularly those stories that people tell themselves about how and why groups and organizations work as they do. With disasters, we are particularly well equipped to fulfill this responsibility because we've been researching disasters for half a century. Some of the most robust, myth-dispelling "findings" in the social sciences concern disaster. These include research that shows that panic and paralyzing fear are rare, that looting is not very important, that there is usually a lack of incivility, and that there is no "cry wolf" problem regarding warnings. Particularly pernicious is the myth that the proper response to disorder is centralization, the most extreme manifestation of which is "militarizing" everything, from the distribution of scarce goods and services to keeping order at the point of an automatic weapon.

When we try to analyze Katrina, we might divide our work into questions of what happened before the storm, what happened during, what happened immediately after, and what will happen in the future. The chapters in this volume concentrate mostly on what happened during and immediately after, so there is a large research agenda that we might develop.

I'll say just a few words on what happened before the storm, which is important not only for understanding the setup for big disasters but also for what will happen in the future. There is a lesson to be learned, to use a hackneyed phrase, that, if heeded carefully, would change how academics think and write about disaster even as it changes nonexpert understandings of disaster. The latter, in turn, could have profound implications for policy regarding disaster. The lesson is that there is *no such thing as a natural disaster*. If Katrina revealed anything, it was that institutional failures put people in harm's way. The flood controls were inadequate. Subsidence of the ground beneath New Orleans was caused by human activities. Poverty is entirely the result of institutional arrangements. The ruination of the wetlands was not caused by nature. There is no good reason to use the phrase "natural disaster" regarding Katrina or any other disaster. It does not meaningfully discriminate among types of disasters. If people's responses to calamity vary reliably with the origins of the hazard, that itself is because of anthropogenic "causes." The label "natural disaster" carries risks of its own, especially that it deflects attention and responsibility from the institutions that actually put people at risk.

Of course, there has been work on "vulnerabilities," but it may be that we've overconcentrated on how people, groups, and organizations respond to hazards. We need a lot more attention on what creates the conditions that lead to calamity in the first place. One of those conditions is population concentration. In *Worst Cases*, I identified population concentration as a major contributor that puts us at risk of extreme events, even as we live longer—and better— in rich, modern societies. More than one-half of America's population now lives close to a coastline. More than 80 percent of Florida's population now lives within 20 miles of saltwater.

Population concentration is an instance of a more general category. In *The Next Catastrophe*, Charles Perrow (2007) argues that the single most important action we could take to avert big disasters is to "shrink the target." Perrow's argument is that by making large, concentrated targets, the damage increases when the target is hit (whether it is hit by, to use his subtitle, "natural, industrial, [or] terrorist disasters"). We need more attention on creation of the target. In New Orleans, this entails investigating the incentives to ignore risk, barriers to policies and actions that would have mitigated the risk, building an inadequate flood control system, and facilitating people building homes in the most vulnerable parts of the city. There were many failures of response to Katrina, as it approached and after it left, but the most important failure— most important in the sense of creating great risk for people—was what happened *before* the levees broke.

SOME RUMINATIONS ABOUT NEW ORLEANS

Asked about why the Federal Emergency Management Agency (FEMA) was so ineffective in preparing for and responding to Katrina, Michael Brown famously denigrated Louisiana as being "dysfunctional." His charge elicited snickers and even outrage at the time. But Brown was right, and it's hard to imagine a persuasive argument to the contrary. I wrote, less than two weeks after the event, an article for the Social Science Research Council (Clarke 2005) in which I not only assigned the lion's share of responsibility for the failures to the federal government but also neglected the responsibilities of the local and state governments. That wasn't wrong, but it wasn't right enough, either. Imagine conducting a study of the political economy of New Orleans and Louisiana before Katrina, asking about how well the social system worked to protect the vulnerable, to ensure fairness, and to advance the well-being of its denizens. Concretely, this would mean looking at Louisiana's schools, its housing, and its medical care systems. It would mean looking at how well democracy was working there and how much progress was being made in ameliorating ills such as poverty, racism, and environmental degradation. Any such study would surely have come to Brown's conclusion. I dare say that the political economic system did not take care of poor people or black people *before* Katrina. I see no compelling reason to have expected otherwise once the levees broke.

The media are crucial, we all know. But in what ways? We learn in *The Sociology of Katrina* that media portrayals of Katrina survivors, victims, and villains were inaccurate. We might add that stylized ideas about the South were used as an overlay for the other inflammatory, ignorant, and racist images we were subjected to. Yet we also learn that the response in New Orleans was at least somewhat different from what we see in other disasters. There does seem to have been some nontrivial amount of looting and asocial behavior in New Orleans, although, as you see in this volume, there are contradictory expert opinions regarding the matter. To the extent that there was asocial behavior and to the extent that we regard this as anomalous, there is something new to explain.

The images we saw were horrible and shocking: bodies floating and reports of rape, pillage, and murder. Much of what we were being told was wrong in the usual way that media representations are wrong. By using the most sensational, alarmist, and violent images while pretending they were the core of reality, the media contributed to mythmaking and inaccurate portrayals of what was happening to and by people. The irony is that the real horror hardly needed sensationalizing—a system (or nonsystem) of paralyzed organizations and ineffective politicians acting as if someone else were responsible. Kanye West mischaracterized the problem as one of President Bush's personal orientation toward "black people." The problem with that telling is that "the problem," after the levees broke, was more general. With a few significant exceptions, the failure was systemwide: organizations failed, politicians failed, and individuals—black and white—failed.

There are a number of important issues for which we do not yet have adequate answers. I shall mention a few of the most obvious ones.

Why did such a large proportion of the city stay put?

From rescue data, we know that the U.S. Coast Guard and Louisiana's Department of Wildlife and Fisheries saved perhaps as many as 100,000 people (these are the big success stories). This was nearly a quarter of the population of New Orleans. We also know, from work in this volume, that perhaps half of those who did not evacuate failed to leave because they did not believe the disaster would be as bad as it was. We explain why most poor people didn't evacuate by saying that evacuation is expensive, that they had no place to go, or that they had insufficient access to transportation. But if we're going to hold emergency and disaster-related organizations to account for failing to prepare adequately, we must also wonder about the misperception of risk among those who could have left but did not.

Properly, FEMA took a lot of heat for the failed response. *However, given that most of the rest of the response system was in disarray, what could FEMA have done that would have made a difference?*

Relatedly, FEMA seems to have responded well in the previous year in Florida when *four* hurricanes screamed through there. I do not believe the comparative explanation is that Florida is a red state whose governor was the president's brother while Louisiana was a blue state, although that is a hypothesis worth investigating. As a system, Florida was better prepared for disaster, but that is a descriptive statement rather than an explanatory one. We learn in this volume that leadership was absent from Washington, D.C. and that communications were destroyed and there was great uncertainty about the extent of the damage. Doesn't this suggest that it is reasonable to conclude that everyone was simply overwhelmed, that the event was so large that it would have been impossible to respond much better?

Why was the body count not higher?

Early in the disaster, Mayor Ray Nagin estimated that perhaps 10,000 people had died. At the time, that number did not seem all that unlikely. The heat was sweltering, many people were probably in poor health to begin with, and highly vulnerable people were swimming around in a toxic concoction of oil, chemicals, and excrement—all would suggest a much higher mortality rate.

How shall we characterize the response of the private sector?

Most of the research I've read, including what's reported in this volume, is about nonprivate actors: churches, government agencies, the Red Cross, the military, and so on. This tight focus is probably the result of looking at rescue more than looking at the conditions that lead to the disaster, all the human actions that created and concentrated the target in the first place. If we more closely investigate the private sector, what might we learn about vulnerability?

Why is the death of New Orleans not seen, outside of the area or among social scientists, as losing a piece of the United States of America?

My sense is that New Orleans is seen by most of the country as just another disaster, and most disasters bring recovery in their wake, so people presume the same is happening there. But this is different. Why isn't there more urgency about this terror, as compared, say, with the terror wrought on 9/11?

I can only say the following in writing rather than speech, and I'm embarrassed to say it at all when I'm around my friends and colleagues from New Orleans. New Orleans is gone. It will not be "back" as it was. We learn in this volume that the vast majority of rental units were wiped out, as were nearly 40 percent of housing units that owners lived in. The most precious thing lost in the drowning of New Orleans was cultural value. Culture lives in the interaction between people and their architecture. Large proportions of both are gone from New Orleans and won't be back.

But let us be forthright and not overvalorize the old New Orleans. If music and a strong sense of place attachment defined New Orleans, so did corruption, dire poverty, blatant racism, and pervasive substance abuse. Of course, it is also true that just because there is a new New Orleans does not in any way mean that those deplorable conditions will not define it once again.

In rich, modern societies, we've come to have high expectations for safety and protection. The people of New Orleans expected their governments to take care of them. One reason for such expectations is that our leaders claim that they will indeed protect us. Another reason is simply that as we live longer and better, we come to take longevity and a high standard of living for granted (Freudenburg 1993). But when the world falls apart, when for whatever reason our expectations are not met, the result can be what I've called "social liquefaction." Liquefaction is what happens when an earthquake causes liquid-saturated ground to become unstable. Social liquefaction is when institutional trust becomes similarly unstable. Perhaps we saw social liquefaction in New Orleans.

There is an inflation of expectations in modern societies. The general issue here concerns *proportionality*, an idea that is invoked in studies of panic (action out of proportion to reality), environmental justice (risk out of proportion to benefit), economic development (reward out of proportion to investment), and so on. Perhaps if social science attends more carefully to issues of proportionality, it can come to a better understanding of how expectations are created, maintained, and frustrated.

There may be a silver lining in people calling into question the trustworthiness of leaders and organizations. What if people led their lives assuming that they are not protected? Perhaps they would be prompted to shore up civil society, or perhaps they would learn how to foster resilience by more effectively using social networks and families. There is a contradiction for which I have no good resolution: organizations and their putative masters create massive dangers for us, but we tend to look to organizations for rescue and even salvation. Yet a consistent message from research on disaster and community, such as that reported in this volume, is that less centralized social actors are those most deserving of our trust.

Appendixes

Table A1. Multinomial Logistic Regression Coefficients Predicting Type of Evacuation Response

	Evacuated in Unison (ref.)		Evacuated by Division		Stayed by Division		Stayed in Unison	
	b	SE	b	SE	b	SE	b	SE
R-1: Risk								
New Orleans resident	—	—	-0.17	0.15	0.25	0.19	-1.49***	0.25
Other Gulf Coast area (ref.)	—	—	—	—	—	—	—	—
R-2: Roles and responsibilities								
Mother (ref.)	—	—	—	—	—	—	—	—
Childless female	—	—	-0.02	0.16	-0.33	0.23	0.11	0.21
Father	—	—	0.04	0.18	0.68**	0.23	0.29	0.23
Childless male	—	—	0.22	0.19	0.78***	0.24	0.50*	0.24
Employed before hurricane	—	—	0.25*	0.15	0.45*	0.20	0.16	0.18
R-3: Resources								
Age 18–64 (ref.)	—	—	—	—	—	—	—	—
Age 65+	—	—	-0.40	0.24	-0.37	0.34	0.08	0.27
Ln(household income)	—	—	-0.16	0.08	-0.58***	0.11	-0.22*	0.11
R-4: Race/ethnicity								
White (ref.)	—	—	—	—	—	—	—	—
Black	—	—	0.34*	0.14	0.42*	0.20	0.45*	0.18
Hispanic	—	—	0.23	0.30	0.27	0.41	-0.84	0.56
Asian	—	—	0.10	0.44	-1.27	1.06	-0.73	0.79
R-5: Religious faith								
Depended on religious faith	—	—	-0.07	0.15	0.48**	0.18	0.22	0.18
Constant	—	—	1.38	0.87	4.15***	1.06	1.28	1.09
Log ratio (d.f.)					172.6 (33)			
Pseudo-R^2					.043			
N					1,510			

Note: * $p < .05$; ** $p < .01$; *** $p < .001$.

Table A2. Ordinary Least Squares Coefficients Predicting Current and Short- and Long-Term Stress

| | Model 1 | | Model 2 | | Model 3 | |
| | Current Stress | | Short-Term Stress | | Long-Term Stress | |
	b	SE	b	SE	b	SE
Type of evacuation response						
Stayed in unison (ref.)	—	—	—	—	—	—
Stayed by division	0.39***	0.10	0.45***	0.09	0.36***	0.09
Evacuated by division	0.45***	0.09	0.54***	0.08	0.33***	0.08
Evacuated in unison	0.02	0.09	0.24*	0.08	0.14	0.08
R-1: Risk						
New Orleans resident	0.36***	0.07	0.31***	0.06	-0.05	0.06
Other Gulf Coast area (ref.)	—	—	—	—	—	—
R-2: Roles and responsibilities						
Female, mother (ref.)	—	—	—	—	—	—
Female, not mother	-0.06	0.08	-0.10	0.07	-0.06	0.07
Male, father	-0.36***	0.08	-0.22**	0.07	-0.19**	0.07
Male, not father	-0.40***	0.09	-0.32***	0.08	-0.25**	0.08
Employed before hurricane	-0.05	0.06	-0.03	0.06	-0.13*	0.06

(continued)

Table A2. *Continued*

	Model 1		Model 2		Model 3	
	Current Stress		Short-Term Stress		Long-Term Stress	
	b	*SE*	*b*	*SE*	*b*	*SE*
R-3: Resources						
Age 18–64 (ref.)	—		—		—	
Age 65+	0.09	0.11	-0.17	0.10	-0.12	0.10
Ln(household income)	-0.05	0.04	-0.06	0.03	-0.03	0.03
R-4: Race/ethnicity						
White (ref.)	—		—		—	
Black	0.16*	0.07	0.22***	0.06	0.22***	0.06
Hispanic	0.11	0.15	0.32*	0.13	0.16	0.13
Asian	0.22	0.24	0.65***	0.20	0.46*	0.21
R-5: Religious faith						
Depended on religious faith	-0.03	0.07	-0.18**	0.06	-0.15*	0.06
Constant	0.34***	0.40	2.15***	0.35	1.90***	0.36
F ratio (14)	10.8***		13.7***		5.3***	
R^2	0.09		0.11		0.05	
N	1,475		1,503		1,469	

Note: * p < .05; ** p < .01; *** p < .001.

References

Aberbach, Joel D., and Jack L. Walker. 1970. "Political Trust and Racial Ideology." *American Political Science Review* 64: 1199–219.

Acker-Hocevar, M., and D. Touchton. 2002. "How Principals Level the Playing Field of Accountability in Florida's High-Poverty/Low Performing Schools-Part I: The Intersection of High-Stakes Testing and Effects of Poverty on Teaching and Learning." *International Journal of Educational Reform* 11: 106–24.

Aflatooni, A., and M. P. Allen. 1991. "Government Sanctions and Collective Political Protest in Periphery and Semiperiphery States: A Time-Series Analysis." *Journal of Political and Military Sociology* 19: 29–45.

Aguilar, John. 2005. "All in the Family." *Rocky Mountain News*, September 3.

Aguirre, B. A., D. Wenger, T. A. Glass, M. Diaz-Murillo, and G. Vigo. 1995. "The Social Organization of Search and Rescue: Evidence from the Guadalajara Gas Explosion." *International Journal of Mass Emergencies and Disasters* 13: 93–106.

Aldridge, Stephen, and David Halpern with Sarah Fitzpatrick. 2002. "Social Capital: A Discussion Paper." Performance and Innovation Unit, http://www.strategy.gov.uk/downloads/seminars/social_capital/socialcapital.pdf (accessed October 15, 2006).

Altman, I., and S. M. Low. 1992. *Place Attachment*. New York: Plenum Press.

American Bar Association. 2006. *Hurricane Katrina Task Force Subcommittee Report*. Washington, D.C.: American Bar Association.

American Federation of Teachers. 2005. "In the Wake of Katrina, Higher Education Community Steps Forward." http://www.aft.org/higher_ed/news/2005/katrina.htm (accessed September 14, 2005).

American Geriatrics Society. 2006. "Lessons from Hurricane Katrina: *AGS News* talks to Charles Cefalu, MD." *AGS Newsletter* 37, no. 1: 11, 15.

American Society of Civil Engineers. 2006. *Hurricane Katrina: One Year Later, What Must We Do Next?* Reston, Va.: American Society of Civil Engineers.

American Sociological Association. 2005. Annual Conference Program.

———. 2006. Annual Conference Program.

Amrhein, S. 2005. "In Big Easy Cleanup, 'Us' vs. 'Them.'" *St. Petersburg Times*, October 23.

Anonymous. 1996. "Child Poverty Reduces Lifetime Worker Output." *Challenge* 39, no. 5: 39–41.

———. 2005. "Strom Victims Cope through Writing." *News for You* 53, no. 46: 2.

Apuzzo, M. 2005. "Officials Say Pace of Finding Bodies in Miss. Is Slowing." *Associated Press*, September 12.

Arata, Catalina M., J. Steven Picou, G. David Johnson, and T. Scott McNally. 2000. "Coping with Technological Disaster: An Application of the Conversation of Resources Model to the Exxon Valdez Oil Spill." *Journal of Traumatic Stress* 13, no. 1: 23–39.

Associated Press. 2005a. "Portable Military Headquarters Sees First Action in New Orleans." *Associated Press*, September 20.

———. 2005b. "States Oppose Greater Role for Military in Disasters." *Associated Press*, November 4.

Baker, Joel K. 2003. *Landscapes: Nature, Culture and the Production of Space*. Pittsburgh, Pa.: University of Pittsburgh Press.

Baker, Richard. 2005. "Points of View August 29, 2005." Cited in Reagan, Michael, Gina Webb, Caroline Harkleroad, Carley Brown, Lisa Reagan, and Deb Murphy. *Katrina State of Emergency*. Kansas City, Mo.: Lionheart Books.

Banks, W. 2005. "Mold, Mildew, and the Military Role in Disaster Response." Forum posting for the *Jurist*, http://jurist.law.pitt.edu/forumy/2005/10/mold-mildew-and-military-role-in.php (accessed April 1, 2007).

Barnshaw, John. 2005. "The Continuing Significance of Race and Class among Houston Hurricane Katrina Evacuees." *Natural Hazards Observer* 30: 11–13.

———. 2006a. "Beyond Disaster: Locating Hurricane Katrina within an Inequality Context." Paper presented at the 101st Annual Meeting of American Sociological Association annual meetings, Montreal, August 13.

———. 2006b. "Beyond Disaster: Locating Katrina within an Inequality Context." Pp. in *Learning from Catastrophe: Quick Response Research in the Aftermath of Hurricane Katrina*, edited by G. Guibert. Boulder, Colo.: Natural Hazards Applications and Information Center, 47–70.

Bartkowski, John P., and Helen A. Regis. 2001. "Faith-Based Food Assistance in the Rural South." Mississippi State, Miss.: Southern Rural Development Center.

Barton, Allen. 1969. *Communities in Disaster: A Sociological Analysis of Collective Stress Situations*. Garden City, N.Y.: Doubleday.

Basso, Keith H. 1996. *Wisdom Sits in Places*. Albuquerque: University of New Mexico Press.

Bates, Frederick, et al. 1963. *The Social and Psychological Consequences of a Natural Disaster: A Longitudinal Study of Hurricane Audrey*. Study No. 18. Washington, D.C.: Disaster Research Group.

Baum, Andrew, and India Fleming. 1993. "Implications of Psychological Research on Stress and Technological Accidents." *American Psychologist* 48, no. 6: 665–72.

Baumgartner, M. P. 1988. *The Moral Order of a Suburb*. New York: Oxford University Press.

Beck, Ulrich. 1992. *The Risk Society*. Newbury Park, Calif.: Sage.

———. 2006. "Living in the World Risk Society" *Economy and Society* 35, no. 3: 329–45.

Berggren, Ruth E., and Tyler J. Curiel. 2006. "After the Storm—Health Care Infrastructure in Post-Katrina New Orleans." *New England Journal of Medicine* 354: 1549–52.

Berry, Brian J. L., and John D. Karsarda. 1977. *Contemporary Urban Ecology*. New York: Macmillan.

Biemiller, Lawrence. 2006. "Forging Tomorrow's Artisans." *Chronicle of Higher Education*, http://chronicle.com/weekly/v52/i18/18a06401.htm (accessed January 6, 2006).

Birkland, T. A. 1997. *After Disaster: Agenda Setting, Public Policy, and Focusing Events*. Washington, D.C.: Georgetown University Press.

Blaikie, P., T. Cannon, I. Davis, and B. Wisner. 1994. *At Risk: Natural Hazards, People's Vulnerability, and Disasters*. New York: Routledge.

Blanchard, W. 2003. *Outlines of Competencies to Develop Successful 21st Century Hazard or Disaster or Emergency or Hazard Risk Managers*. Emmetsburg, Md.: Higher Education Project, Emergency Management Institute, National Emergency Training Center.

Block, R., and A. Schatz. 2005. "Local and Federal Authorities Battle to Control Disaster Relief." *Wall Street Journal*, December 8, A1, A13.

Bluestein, G. 2006. "Katrina's 'John Wayne' general keeps tabs on home state." *Associated Press*, September 7.

Bolin, Robert. 1985. "Disasters and Social Support." In *Disasters and Mental Health Selected Contemporary Perspectives*, edited by B. Sowder. Washington, D.C.: U.S. Government Printing Office, 97–106.

Bolin, Robert, and P. Bolton. 1986. *Race, Religion and Ethnicity in Disaster Recovery*. Boulder: Institute of Behavioral Sciences, University of Colorado.

Bolin, Robert, and L. Stanford. 1998. "The Northridge Earthquake: Community-Based Approaches to Unmet Recovery Needs." *Disasters* 22, no. 1: 21–38.

Bolton, Derek, Jonathan Hill, Dominic O'Ryan, and Orlee Udwin. 2004. "Long Term Effects of Psychological Trauma on Psychosocial Functioning." *Journal of Child Psychology and Psychiatry* 45, no. 5: 1007.

Bonilla-Silva, Eduardo. 2001. *White Supremacy and Racism in the Post–Civil Rights Era*. Boulder, Colo.: Lynne Rienner.

Bonnes, M., and G. Secchiaroli. 2003. "Lecture Four: Place Attachment and Place Identity." In *Introduction to Environmental Psychology*, http://sss-student-tees.ac.uk/psychology/modules/year2/environmental_psych/lect4.doc.

Bourdieu, Pierre. 1986. "The Forms of Capital." In *Handbook of Theory and Research for the Sociology of Education*, edited by J. Richardson. New York: Greenwood Press, 241–58.

Bow, Valmai, and Laurie Buys. 2003. "Sense of Community and Place Attachment: The Natural Environment Plays a Vital Role in Developing a Sense of Community." Paper presented at the Social Change in the 21st Century Conference, Brisbane, Australia, November 21.

Brainard, Jeffrey. 2006. "FEMA Money May Go to Private Colleges." *Chronicle of Higher Education*, http://chronicle.com/weekly/v53/i08/08a03402.htm (accessed October 13, 2006).

Brodie, Mollyann, Erin Weltzien, Drew Altman, Robert Blendon, and John Benson. 2006. "Experiences of Hurricane Katrina Evacuees in Houston Shelters: Implications for Future Planning." *American Journal of Public Health* 96: 1402–8.

Brookings Institution. 2005. "New Orleans after the Storm: Lessons from the Past and a Plan for the Future." Metropolitan Policy Program Report. Washington, D.C.: Brookings Institution.

Brown, D. 2005. "Military Police Head to New Orleans." *Chattanooga Times Free Press*, September 2.

BRRRC (Biloxi Relief, Recovery, and Revitalization Center). 2006. *East Biloxi Community Plan*, http://www.warnkecc.com/wp-content/uploads/BRC_Plan_6.29.06.pdf (accessed April 1, 2007).

Bryant, Salatheia, and Cynthia Garza. 2005. "School Bus Comandeered by Renegade Refugees First to Arrive at Astrodome." *Houston Chronicle*, September 1.

Bullard, Robert D. 1983. "Solid Waste Sites and the Houston Black Community." *Sociological Inquiry* 53: 273–88.

Bureau of Labor Statistics. 1994. "Orleans Parish Unemployment Statistics for 1994." http://data.bls.gov/map/servlet/map.servlet.MapToolServlet?state=22&datatype=unemployment&year=1994&period=M13&survey=la&map=county&seasonal=u (accessed April 1, 2007).

———. 2005. "Orleans Parish Unemployment Statistics for August, 2005." http://data.bls.gov/map/servlet/map.servlet.MapToolServlet?state=22&datatype=unemployment&year=2005&period=M08&survey=la&map=county&seasonal=u (accessed April 1, 2007).

Burns, R. 2005. "Historic Changes Possible in Military's Role in Emergencies." *Associated Press*, September 17.

Burt, Ronald S. 1992. *Structural Holes: The Social Structure of Competition*. Cambridge, Mass.: Harvard University Press.

———. 2004. "Structural Holes and Good Ideas." *American Journal of Sociology* 110, no. 2: 349–99.

Campo-Flores, Arian. 2005. "A New Spice in the Gumbo: Will Latino Day Laborers Locating in New Orleans Change its Complexion?" *Newsweek*, December 5.

———. 2006. "Katrina's Latest Damage." *Newsweek*, March 13.

Caplow, T., L. Hicks, and B. J. Wattenberg. 2000. *The First Measured Century: An Illustrated Guide to Trends in America, 1900–2000*. Washington, D.C.: AEI Press.

Carballo, M. 1970. "A Socio-Psychological Study of Acculturation/Assimilation: Cubans in New Orleans." Ph.D. diss., Tulane University.

Cardozo, Barbara Lopes, Oleg O. Bilukha, Carol A. Gotway Crawford, Irshad Shaikh, Mitchell I. Wolfe, Michael L. Gerber, and Mark Anderson. 2004. "Mental Health, Social Functioning and Disability in Postwar Afghanistan." *Journal of the American Medical Association* 292: 575–84.

Carnevale, Dan. 2006a. "Hurricane Katrina: A Professor, and His University, Count on Distance Education." *Chronicle of Higher Education*, September 1, 12.

———. 2006b. "Students Designed Databases to Help Red Cross Coordinate Hurricane Volunteers." *Chronicle of Higher Education*, May 12.

"Catholic Agencies Mobilize for Relief." 2005. *America* 192, no. 2.

Cavendish, James C. 2000. "Church-Based Community Activism: A Comparison of Black and White Catholic Congregations." *Journal for the Scientific Study of Religion* 39: 371.

Centers for Disease Control. 2005. "Surveillance for Illness and Injury after Hurricane Katrina—New Orleans, Louisiana, September 8–25, 2005." *Morbidity and Mortality Weekly Report* 54: 1018–21.

———. 2006a. "Assessment of Health-Related Needs after Hurricanes Katrina and Rita—Orleans and Jefferson Parishes, New Orleans Area, Louisiana, October 17–22, 2005." *Morbidity and Mortality Weekly Report* 55, no. 2 (January 20): 38–41.

———. 2006b. "Mortality Associated with Hurricane Katrina—Florida and Alabama, August–October 2005." *Morbidity and Mortality Weekly Report* 55, no. 9 (March 10): 239–42.

Chamlee-Wright, Emily. 2006. "After the Storm: Social Capital Regrouping in the Wake of Hurricane Katrina." Global Prosperity Initiative Working Paper. Arlington, Va.: Mercatus Center, George Mason University.

Chaves, Mark, and Lynn M. Higgins. 1992. "Comparing the Community Involvement of Black and White Congregations." *Journal for the Scientific Study of Religion* 31: 425.

Chen, D. W. 2002. "More Get 9/11 Aid, but Distrust of U.S. Efforts Lingers." *New York Times*, August 27.

Chronicle of Higher Education. 2005. "Southern U. Will Shut Down 19 Academic Programs on New Orleans Campus as Part of Hurricane Recovery." *Chronicle of Higher Education*, December 12.

Chung, Man Cheung, Ian Dennis, Yvette Eassthope, Steven Farmer, and Julie Werret. 2005. "Differentiating Posttraumatic Stress between Elderly and Younger Residents." *Psychiatry* 68, no. 2: 164–73.

Claritas. 2006. "Claritas Announces Release of Hurricane Katrina-Adjusted Population Estimates." http://www.claritas.com/claritas/Default.jsp?ci=5&si=1&pn=katrina_pop_estimates (accessed April 1, 2007).

Clarke, Lee. 2005. "Worse Case Katrina." In *Understanding Katrina: Perspectives from the Social Sciences*, http://www.understandingkatrina.ssrc.org/Clarke (accessed April 1, 2007).

———. 2006. *Worst Cases: Terror and Catastrophe in the Popular Imagination.* Chicago: University of Chicago Press.

Clarke, Lee, and J. F. Short. 1993. "Social Organization and Risk: Some Current Controversies." *Annual Review of Sociology* 19: 375–99.

Clemons, Gina. 2006. "A Matter of Time? Learn from the Past, Prepare for the Future." Paper presented at National Disaster Coalition: Preparedness and Response for the ESRD Community, Washington, D.C., January 19.

CNN.com. 2005. "Lt. Gen. Honoré a 'John Wayne Dude'." http://www.cnn.com/2005/US/09/02/honore.profile (accessed September 3, 2005).

Coastal Women for Change. 2006. http://cwcbiloxi.com.

Cochrane, Harold. 1975. *Natural Hazards and Their Distributive Effect.* Boulder: University of Colorado Press.

Coleman, James S. 1988. "Social Capital in the Creation of Human Capital." *American Journal of Sociology* 94: 95–120.

Coleman, James S., Elihu Katz, and Herbert Menzel. 1966. *Medical Innovation: A Diffusion Study.* New York: Bobbs-Merrill.

Collins, Randall. 1998. *The Sociology of Philosophies.* Cambridge, Mass.: Harvard University Press.

———. 2004. *Interaction Ritual Chains.* Princeton, N.J.: Princeton University Press.

Comfort, L. K., Y. Sungu, D. Johnson, and M. Dunn. 2001. "Complex Systems in Crisis: Anticipation and Resilience in Dynamic Environments." *Journal of Contingencies and Crisis Management* 9, no. 3: 144–58.

Connolly, Ceci. 2005. "New Orleans Health Care Another Katrina Casualty." *Washington Post*, November 25.

Cooperman, Alan, and Elizabeth Williamson. 2005. "FEMA Will Reimburse Faith Groups." *Washington Post*, September 27.

Coser, Ruth. 1975. "The Complexity of Roles as Seedbed of Individual Autonomy." In *The Idea of Social Structure: Essays in Honor of Robert Merton*, edited by Lewis Coser. New York: Harcourt Brace Jovanovich, 237–264.

Couch, Stephen R. 1996. "Environmental Contamination, Community Transformation and the Centralia Mine Fire." In *The Long Road to Recovery: Community Response to Industrial Disaster*, edited by James K. Mitchell. Tokyo: United Nations University Press, 60–84.

Couch, Stephen, and J. Stephen Kroll-Smith. 1985. "The Chronic Technical Disaster: Toward a Social Scientific Perspective." *Social Science Quarterly* 66: 564–75.

Crossett, Kristen, Thomas J. Culliton, Peter Wiley, and Timothy R. Goodspeed. 2004. *Population Trends along the Coastal United States, 1980–2008*. National Oceanic and Atmospheric Administration Coastal Trends Report Series. Washington, D.C.: National Oceanic and Atmospheric Administration.

Crowley, Shelia. 2006. "Where Is Home? Housing for Low-Income People after the 2005 Hurricanes." In *There Is No Such Thing as a Natural Disaster: Race, Class and Hurricane Katrina*, edited by Chester Hatman and Gregory D. Squires. New York: Routledge, 121–66.

Cunningham, K. 2004. "Permanent War? The Domestic Hegemony of the New American Militarism." *New Political Science* 26, no. 4: 551–67.

Cuthbertson, Beverly H., and Joanne M. Nigg. 1987. "Technological Disaster and the Nontherapeutic Community: A Question of True Victimization." *Environment and Behavior* 19: 462–83.

Cutter, Susan L. 2005. "The Geography of Social Vulnerability: Race, Class, and Catastrophe." Social Science Research Council, http://understandingkatrina.ssrc.org/Cutter (accessed November 5, 2005).

Cutter, Susan L., Bryan J. Boruff, and W. Lynn Shirley. 2003. "Social Vulnerability to Environmental Hazards." *Social Science Quarterly* 84, no. 1: 242–61.

Davila, M., J. W. Marquart, and J. L. Mullings. 2005. "Beyond Mother Nature: Contractor Fraud in the Wake of Natural Disasters." *Deviant Behavior* 26: 271–93.

Day, Christopher. 2002. *Spirit and Place: Healing Our Environment*. Oxford: Architectural Press.

DeBose, Brian. 2005. "Blacks Fault Lack of Local Leadership." *Washington Times*, http://washington times.com/national/20050909-113107-3180r.htm (accessed September 10, 2005).

Delgado Community College. 2006. "Hurricane Katrina Chronicles." http://www.dcc.edu/katrina_chronicles/overview.htm (accessed April 1, 2007).

Democratic Party. 2006. "Six Questions." http://www.democrats.org/a/2006/07/six_questions_f.php (accessed April 1, 2007).

Department of Homeland Security. 2004. *Final Draft: National Response Plan*. Washington, D.C.: U.S. Government Printing Office.

Deshler, D., and M. Ewert. 1996. "Participatory Action Research: Traditions and Major Assumptions." Cornell Participatory Action Research Network, http://www.parnet.org/tools/Tools_1.cfn.

Dewan, Shaila. 2006. "Evacuee Study Finds Declining Health." *New York Times*, http://www.nytimes.com/2006/04/18/us/nationalspecial/18health.htm (accessed April 18, 2006).

DiMaggio, Paul J. 1998. "The Relevance of Organization Theory to the Study of Religion." In *Sacred Companies*, edited by N. J. Demerath III, Peter Dobkin Hall, Terry Schmitt, and Rhys H. Williams. New York: Oxford University Press, 7–23.

DiMaggio, Paul J., and Walter W. Powell. 1983. "The Iron Cage Revisited: Institutional Isomorphism and Collective Rationality in Organizational Fields." *American Sociological Review* 48: 147–60.

Division of Business and Economic Research, College of Business Administration, Louisiana State University in New Orleans. 1967. *Statistical Abstract of Louisiana*. New Orleans: Louisiana State University in New Orleans.

Dominguez, Virginia R. 2005. "Seeing and Not Seeing: Complicity in Surprise." In *Understanding Katrina: Perspectives from the Social Sciences*, http://www.understandingkatrina.ssrc.org/Dominguez (accessed April 1, 2007).

Donato, K. M., and C. L. Bankston III. 2007. "The Origins of Employer Demand for Immigrants in a New Destination: The Salience of Soft Skills in a Volatile Economy." In *New Faces in New Places: The Changing Geography of American Immigration*, edited by Douglas S. Massey. New York: Russell Sage Foundation.

Donato, K. M., and S. Hakimzadeh. 2006. "The Changing Face of the Gulf Coast: Immigration to Louisiana, Mississippi, and Alabama." Feature story in *Migration Information Source*, Migration Policy Institute, http://www.migrationinformation.org/Feature/display.cfm?id=368 (accessed April 1, 2007).

Donato, K., M. Stainback, and C. L. Bankston III. 2005. "The Economic Incorporation of Mexican Immigrants in Southern Louisiana: A Tale of Two Cities." In *New Destinations of Mexican Immigration in the United States: Community Formation, Local Responses and Inter-Group Relations*, edited by Victor Zuniga and Ruben Hernandez-Leon. New York: Russell Sage Foundation, 76–102.

Drabek, T. E. 1986. *Human System Responses to Disaster: An Inventory of Sociological Findings*. New York: Springer-Verlag.

———. 1991. "The Evolution of Emergency Management." In *Emergency Management: Principles and Practice for Local Government*, edited by T. E. Drabek and G. J. Hoetmer. Washington, D.C.: International City and County Management Association, 3–29.

Drabek, Thomas E., William H. Key, Patricia E. Erickson, and Juanita L. Crowe. 1975. "The Impact of Disaster on Kin Relationships." *Journal of Marriage and the Family* 37, no. 3: 481–94.

Dunlap, C. J., Jr. 1999. "The Police-ization of the Military." *Journal of Political and Military Sociology* 27, no. 2: 217–33.

Dunne, Mike. 2005. "State Officials Urge Phase 1 Evacuations for Low-Lying Areas." *The Advocate*, http://www.ohsep.louisiana.gov/newsrelated/StateUrgePhase1.htm (accessed July 8, 2005).

Durkheim, Émile. 1960. *The Division of Labor in Society*. New York: Free Press (orig. 1893).

Durkin, Maureen S., Naila Khan, Leslie L. Davidson, Sultana S. Zaman, and Zena A. Stein. 1993. "The Effects of a Natural Disaster on Child Behavior: Evidence of Posttraumatic Stress." *American Journal of Public Health* 83, no. 11: 1549.

Dwyer, J., and C. Drew. 2005. "Fear Exceeded Crime's Reality in New Orleans." *New York Times*, September 29.

Dynes, Russell. 1970. *Organized Behavior in Disaster*. Lexington, Mass.: Heath Lexington Books.

———. 1978. "Interorganizational Relations in Communities under Stress." In *Disasters: Theory and Research*, edited by E. L. Quarantelli. Thousand Oaks, Calif.: Sage, 49–64.

———. 1993. "Social Science Research: Relevance for Policy and Practice." In *Improving Earthquake Mitigation: Report to Congress*. Washington, D.C.: Federal Emergency Management Agency, Office of Earthquakes and Natural Hazards, 67–89.

———. 1998. "Coming to Terms with Community Disaster," Pp 109-126 in *What Is a Disaster? Perspectives on the Question*, edited by E. L. Quarantelli. New York: Routledge, 109–26.

———. 2002. "The Importance of Social Capital in Disaster Response." Preliminary Paper No. 327. Newark, DE: Disaster Research Center.

———. 2006. "Social Capital: Dealing with Community Emergencies." *Homeland Securities Affairs* 2, no. 2 (July): 1–26.

Dynes, Russell, and Benigno Aguirre. 1978. "Organizational Adaptation to Crises." *Disasters* 3: 71–73.

Dynes, Russell, and E. L. Quarantelli. 1968. "What Looting in Civil Disturbances Really Means." *Trans-action* 5, no. 6: 9–14.

Dynes, Russell, and Havidán Rodríguez. 2005. "Finding and Framing Katrina: The Social Construction of Disaster." In *Understanding Katrina: Perspectives from the Social Sciences*, http://www.understandingkatrina.ssrc.org/Dynes_Rodriguez (accessed April 1, 2007).

Dyson, Michael Eric. 2006. *Come Hell or High Water: Hurricane Katrina and the Color of Disaster.* New York: Basic Civitas.

Eaton, L. 2005. "In Louisiana, Worker Influx Causes Ill Will." *New York Times,* November 4.

Ebaugh, Helen Rose, Paula F. Pipes, Janet Saltzman Chafetz, and Martha Daniels. 2003. "Where's the Religion? Distinguishing Faith-Based from Secular Social Service Agencies." *Journal for the Scientific Study of Religion* 42: 411–26.

Edelstein, Michael. 1988. *Contaminated Communities: The Social and Psychological Impacts of Residential Toxic Exposure.* Boulder, Colo.: Westview Press.

———. 2000. "Outsiders Just Don't Understand." In *Risk in The Modern Age: Social Theory, Science and Environmental Decision-Making,* edited by M. J. Cohen. New York: St. Martin's Press, 123–42.

Edsall, T. B. 2005. "Bush Suspends Pay Act in Areas Hit by Storm." *Washington Post,* September 9.

Ehrenreich, John, and Sharon McQuaide. 2001. *Coping with Disasters: A Guide to Psychosocial Intervention.* Center for Psychology and Society, State University of New York, http://www.inhwwb.org (accessed April 1, 2007).

Ehrenreich, N. 2002. "Masculinity and American Militarism." *Tikkun* 17, no. 6: 45–48.

Elliott, James R., and Marcel Ionescu. 2003. "Post-War Immigration to the Deep South Triad: What Can a Peripheral Region Tell Us about Immigrant Settlement and Employment?" *Sociological Spectrum* 23: 159–80.

Elliott, James R., and Jeremy Pais. 2006. "Race, Class, and Hurricane Katrina: Social Differences in Responses to Disaster." *Social Science Research* 35, no. 2: 295–321.

Enarson, Elaine, and Joseph Scanlon. 1999. "Gender Patterns in Flood Evacuation: A Case Study in Canada's Red River Valley." *Applied Behavioral Science Review* 7, no. 2: 103–24.

Endleman, Robert. 1952. "An Approach to the Study of Disasters." Unpublished manuscript.

Erikson, Kai T. 1976. *Everything in Its Path: Destruction of Community in the Buffalo Creek Flood.* New York: Simon and Schuster.

———. 1994. *A New Species of Trouble.* New York: Norton.

Evelyn, Jamilah. 2005. "Retooling after the Storm: Delgado Community College Will Focus More on Job Training as New Orleans Rebuilds." *Chronicle of Higher Education,* December 9, A22–A24.

Falk, William W., M. O. Hunt, and L. O. Hunt. 2006. "Hurricane Katrina and New Orleanians' Sense of Place: Returning and Reconstruction or 'Gone with the Wind'?" *Du Bois Review* 3 (August): 115–28.

Farnam, T. W. 2006. "9/11 Responders Seek Options for Care." *Newsday,* November 15.

Feagin, Joe, Hernan Vera, and Pinar Batur. 2001. *White Racism.* 2nd ed. New York: Routledge.

Federal Bureau of Investigation. 1994. *Uniform Crime Reports.* Washington, D.C.: U.S. Government Printing Office.

Federal Emergency Management Agency. 2006. "2005 FEMA Disaster Declarations." http://www.fema.gov/news/disasters.fema?year=2005#em (accessed April 1, 2007).

Field, Kelly. 2006. "Damaged Colleges Get $50-Million." *Chronicle of Higher Education,* September 29, 29.

Fischer, Henry W., III. 1994. *Response to Disaster.* New York: University Press of America.

———. 1998. *Response to Disaster.* 2nd ed. Lanham, Md.: University Press of America.

Fletcher, L. E., and P. Pham. 2006. "Rebuilding after Katrina: A Population-Based Study of Labor and Human Rights in New Orleans." http://www.law.berkeley.edu/news/pr/2006/katrina060706.html (accessed April 1, 2007).

Flynn, James, Paul Slovic, and C. K. Mertz. 1994. "Gender, Race and Perception of Environmental Health Risks." *Risk Analysis* 14, no. 6: 1101–8.

Fogg, Piper. 2006a. "New Orleans College Presidents Decline to Meet with AAUP over Layoffs." *Chronicle of Higher Education,* September 1, 19.

———. 2006b. "New Orleans Homecoming—One Professor's Overload." *Chronicle of Higher Education,* January 20, A1–A17.

———. 2006c. "New Orleans Homecoming: At Tulane, Living on a Cruise Ship Is No Luxury Vacation." *Chronicle of Higher Education,* January 20, A14.

Foote, Kenneth E. 1988. "Object as Memory: The Material Foundations of Human Semiosis." *Semiotica* 69: 259–63.

———. 1997. *Shadowed Ground*. Austin: University of Texas Press.

Ford, Glen, and Peter Gamble. 2006. "A Hurricane of Differences." AlterNet: Hurricane Katrina, http://www.alternet.org/katrina/30605 (accessed April 1, 2007).

Fothergill, Alice. 2003. "The Stigma of Charity: Gender, Class, and Disaster Assistance." *Sociological Quarterly* 44, no. 4: 659–80.

Freedy, John R., Michael E. Saladin, Dean G. Kilpatrick, Heidi S. Resnick, and Benjamin E. Saunders. 1994. "Understanding Acute Psychological Distress following a Natural Disaster." *Journal of Traumatic Stress* 7: 257–73.

Freeman, R. B. 1983. "Crime and Unemployment." In *Crime and Public Policy*, edited by James Q. Wilson. San Francisco: Institute for Contemporary Studies Press, 89–106.

———. 1996. "Why Do So Many Young American Men Commit Crimes and What Might We Do about It?" *Journal of Economic Perspectives* 10, no. 1: 25–42.

Freudenburg, William R. 1993. "Risk and Recreancy: Weber, the Division of Labor, and the Rationality of Risk Perceptions." *Social Forces* 71: 909–32.

———. 1997. "Contamination, Corrosion and the Social Order: An Overview." *Current Sociology* 45, no. 3: 19–39.

———. 2000. "The Risk Society Reconsidered: Recreancy, the Division of Labor, and Risk to the Social Fabric." In *Risk in the Modern Age: Social Theory, Science and Environmental Decision-Making*, edited by M. J. Cohen. New York: St. Martin's Press, 107–20.

Freudenburg, William R., and T. R. Jones. 1991. "Attitudes and Stress in the Presence of Technological Risk: A Test of the Supreme Court Hypothesis." *Social Forces* 69, no. 4: 1143–68.

Frey, W. H., and A. Singer. 2006. *Katrina and Rita Impacts on Gulf Coast Populations: First Census Findings*. Washington, D.C.: Brookings Institution.

Frickel, Scott. 2005. "Our Toxic Gumbo: Recipe for a Politics of Environmental Knowledge." Social Science Research Council, http://understandingkatrina.ssrc.org/Frickel (accessed April 1, 2007).

Fritz, Charles E. 1961. "Disasters." In *Contemporary Social Problems*, edited by R. Merton and R. Nisbet. New York: Harcourt, 651–94.

Fussell, Elizabeth. 2005. "Leaving New Orleans: Social Stratification, Networks, and Hurricane Evacuation." Social Science Research Council, http://understandingkatrina.ssrc.org (accessed April 1, 2007).

Gabe, Thomas, Gene Falk, Maggie McCarty, et al. 2005. *Hurricane Katrina: Social-Demographic Characteristics of Impacted Areas*. Washington, D.C.: Congressional Research Service, Library of Congress.

Gallagher, Charles A. 2003. "Color-Blind Privilege: The Social and Political Functions of Erasing the Color Line in Post Race America." *Race, Gender and Class* 10, no. 4, 22–37.

Gately, Susan E. 2005. "Help Your Students Deal with Tragedy." *Intervention in School and Clinic* 41, no. 1: 5–8.

Giddens, A. 1984. *The Construction of Society: Outline of Theory of Structuration*. Berkeley: University of California Press.

———. 1989. "A Reply to My Critics." In *Social Theory of Modern Societies: Anthony Giddens and His Critics*, edited by D. Held, and J. B. Thompson. Cambridge: Cambridge University Press, 249–301.

Gill, Duane A., and J. Steven Picou. 1991. "The Social Psychological Impacts of a Technological Accident: Collective Stress and Perceived Health Risks." *Journal of Hazardous Materials* 27: 77–89.

———. 1998. "Technological Disaster and Chronic Community Stress." *Society and Natural Resources* 11: 795–816.

Gilman Nils. 2005. "What Katrina Teaches about the Meaning of Racism." In *Understanding Katrina: Perspectives from the Social Sciences*, http://www.understandingkatrina.ssrc.org/Gilman/pf (April 4, 2007).

Glaser, E. L., and B. Sacerdote. 1999. "Why Is There More Crime in Cities?" *Journal of Political Economy* 107, no. 6: S225–S258.

Global Disaster Information Network. 1997. *Harnessing Information and Technology for Disaster Management: The Global Disaster Information Network.* Disaster Information Task Force Report. Washington, D.C.: Global Disaster Information Network.

Goenjian, Amen K., et al. 1994. "Possttraumatic Stress Disorder in Elderly and Younger Adults after the 1988 Earthquake in Armenia." *American Journal of Psychiatry* 151, no. 6: 895–901.

Goffman, Erving. 1959. *Presentation of Self in Everyday Life.* New York: Anchor.

———. 1967. *Interaction Ritual.* New York: Doubleday.

Gould, E. D., B. A. Weinberg, and D. B. Mustard. 2002. "Crime Rates and Local Labor Market Opportunities in the United States: 1979–1997." *Review of Economics and Statistics* 84, no. 1: 45–61.

Government Accountability Office. 2006. *Hurricane Katrina: Better Plans and Exercises Needed to Guide the Military's Response to Catastrophic Natural Disasters.* Report to the Congressional Committees. Report No. GAO-06-643. Washington, D.C.: Government Accountability Office.

Granovetter, Mark. 1973. "The Strength of Weak Ties." *American Journal of Sociology* 81: 1287–303.

———. 1974. *Getting a Job: A Study of Contacts and Careers.* Cambridge, Mass.: Harvard University Press.

———. 1983. "The Strength of Weak Ties: A Network Theory Revisited." *Sociological Theory* 1: 201–33.

Gravois, John. 2005. "After Katrina, Neighboring Universities Suffer Different Fates." *Chronicle of Higher Education*, October 7, A29–A30.

Green, B. L. 1996. "Traumatic Stress and Disaster: Mental Health Effects and Factors Influencing Adaptation." In *International Review of Psychiatry*, vol. 2, edited by F. L. Mak and C. C. Nadelson. Washington, D.C.: American Psychiatric Press, 177–210.

Green, J. J., A. Jones, and C. Pope. 2004. "Underemployment and Workforce Development in the Mississippi Delta: Community-Based Action Research for Program Planning to Increase Livelihood Security." *Southern Rural Sociology* 20, no. 1: 80–106.

Green, J. J., A. M. Kleiner, J. Montgomery, and I. S. Bayer. 2006. "Working the Frontlines of Relief, Recovery, and Redevelopment: Exploring the Views of Service Providers in the Wake of Disaster." Paper presented at the annual meeting of the Rural Sociological Society, Louisville, Ky., August 10–13.

Grinage, Bradley D. 2003. "What You Should Know about Post-Traumatic Stress Disorder." *American Family Physician* 68, no. 12: 2409.

Gunter, Valerie J., Marilyn Aronoff, and Susan Joel. 1999. "Toxic Contamination and Communities: Using an Ecological–Symbolic Perspective to Theorize Response Contingencies." *Sociological Quarterly* 40, no. 4: 623–40.

Hacker, Andrew. 2003. *Two Nations: Black and White; Separate, Hostile, Unequal.* New York: Scribner.

Haddow, G. D., and J. A. Bullock. 2003. *Introduction to Emergency Management.* Boston: Butterworth-Heinemann.

Hagan, Joseph F., Jr., Jane M. Foy, William L. Coleman, and Edward Goldson. 2005. "Psychosocial Implications of Disaster or Terrorism on Children: A Guide for the Pediatrician." *Pediatrics* 116, no. 3: 787–96.

Hanifan, L. J. 1920. *The Community Centre.* Boston: Silver Burdette.

Hansen, Jane O. 2006. "Through Hell and High Water." *Atlanta Journal and Constitution*, May 5–26.

Harden, Blaine, and Shankar Vedantam. 2005. "Many Displaced by Katrina Turn to Relatives for Shelter." *Washington Post*, September 8.

Harper, D. W., L. Voigt, and W. E. Thornton. 2003. "Structural Covariates of Murder in New Orleans." Paper presented at the meeting of the European Society of Criminology, Helsinki, August 27–30.

Harrington, S. E. 2005. "Rethinking Disaster Policy after Hurricane Katrina." In *On Risk and Disaster: Lessons from Hurricane Katrina*, edited by R. J. Daniels, D. F. Kettl, and H. Kunreuther. Philadelphia: University of Pennsylvania Press, 203–21.

Harris County Joint Information Center. 2005a. "The Astrodome Site Is Not Turning Away Evacuees." Press release, http://www.hcjic.org/news_release.asp?intRelease_ID=1950&intAcc_ID=62 (accessed September 2, 2005).

256 *References*

———. 2005b. "Number of Citizens." Press release, http://www.hcjic.org/default.asp (accessed September 20, 2005).

———. 2005c. "Press Briefing Regarding the Transfer of Superdome Evacuees to the Houston Astrodome." Press release, http://www.hcjic.org/news_release.asp?intRelease_ID=1948&intAcc_ID=62 (accessed August 31, 2005).

Hartman, Chester and Gregory D. Squires, eds. 2006. *There Is No Such Thing as a Natural Disaster: Race, Class and Hurricane Katrina.* New York: Routledge.

Hashimoto, M. 1987. "The Minimum Wage Law and Youth Crimes: Time-Series Evidence." *Journal of Law and Economics* 30: 443–64.

Haughey, Margaret, Fern Start, and Jose Da Costa. 2001. "Literacy Achievement in Small Grade 1 Classes in High Poverty Environments." *Canadian Journal of Education* 26, no. 3: 301–20.

Healey, G. 2003. *Deployed in the USA: The Creeping Militarization of the Home Front.* Policy Analysis No. 303. Washington, D.C.: Cato Institute.

Hebel, Sarah. 2006. "Hurricane Katrina: A Trauma Expert Helps a Campus Cope." *Chronicle of Higher Education,* http://chronicle.com/weekly/v53/i02/02a01602.htm (accessed September 1, 2006).

Henry, J. M., and C. L. Bankston III. 2002. *Blue Collar Bayou: Louisiana Cajuns in the New Economy of Ethnicity.* New York: Praeger.

Herring, Cedric. 2006. "Hurricane Katrina and the Racial Gulf: A Du Boisian Analysis of Victims' Experiences." *DuBois Review* 3 (March): 129–44.

Hewitt, Kenneth. 1983. *Interpretations of Calamity from the Viewpoint of Human Ecology.* London: Allen and Unwin.

Hill, Anne M., and June O Neill. 1994. "Family Endowments and the Achievement of Young Children with Special Reference to the Underclass." *Journal of Human Resources* 29, no. 4: 1064–201.

Hirsch, William B. 1997. "Justice Delayed: Seven Years and No End in Sight." In the *Exxon Valdez Disaster: Readings on a Modern Social Problem,* edited by J. S. Picou, D. A. Gill, and M. J. Cohen. Dubuque, Iowa: Kendall/Hunt, 271–307.

Hispanic Business. 2005. "USHCC Deplores Remarks by New Orleans Mayor Ray Nagin regarding Mexican Workers and the Rebuilding of New Orleans." http://www.hispanicprwire.com/news.php?l=in&id=5044&cha=11 (accessed October 28, 2005).

Hobfoll, Stevan E. 1989. *The Ecology of Stress.* New York: Hemisphere.

Holzer, Harry J., and Robert I. Lerman. 2006. "Employment Issues and Challenges in Post-Katrina New Orleans." In *After Katrina: Rebuilding Opportunity and Equity into the New New Orleans,* edited by Margery Austin Turner and Sheila R. Zedlewski. Washington, D.C.: Urban Institute Press, 9–16.

Horowitz, Mardi J. 2001. *Stress Response Syndromes.* 4th ed. Lanham, Md.: Rowman & Littlefield.

Horowitz, Mardi J., Charles Stinson, and Nigel Field. 1991. "Natural Disasters and Stress Response Syndromes." *Psychiatric Annals* 21: 556–62.

House, E., M. Patton, M. Scriven, and N. Uphoff. 1996. "The PAR Tool Box: Traditions and Major Assumptions." Cornell Participatory Action Research Network, http//:www.parnet.org/tools/Tools_1.cfn.

House, James S. 2002. "Understanding Social Factors and Inequalities in Health: 20th Century Progress and 21st Century Prospects." *Journal of Health and Social Behavior* 43: 125–42.

Houston Joint Information Center. 2005. http://www.hcjic.org (accessed April 2, 2007).

Hunter, Albert J. 1985. "Private, Parochial, and Public Social Orders: The Problem of Crime and Incivility in Urban Communities." In *The Challenge of Social Control: Citizenship and Institution Building in Modern Society,* edited by Gerald D. Suttles and Mayer N. Zald. Norwood, N.J.: Ablex.

Hurlbert, Jeanne S., Valerie Haines, and John J. Beggs. 2000. "Core Networks and Tie Activation: What Kinds of Routine Networks Allocate Resources in Nonroutine Situations?" *American Sociological Review* 65: 598–618.

Hurlbert, Jeanne, John Beggs, and Valerie Haines. 2001. "Social Networks and Social Capital in Extreme Environments." In *Social Capital: Theory and Research,* edited by N. Lin, K. Cook, and R. Burt. New York: Aldine de Gruyter, 209–31.

InfoPlease. 2005. "Quick Facts from the U.S. Census Bureau: Homestead, Florida." http://www
.infoplease.com/us/census/data/florida/homestead (accessed April 3, 2007).

Ishiguro, Y. 1998. "A Japanese National Crime: The Korean Massacre after the Great Kanto Earthquake of 1923." *Korea Journal* 38, no. 4: 331–55.

Jackson, Maria-Rosario. 2006. "Rebuilding the Cultural Vitality of New Orleans." In *After Katrina: Rebuilding Opportunity and Equity into the New New Orleans*, edited by Margery Austin Turner, and Sheila R. Zedlewski. Washington, D.C.: Urban Institute Press, 55–62.

Jacobson, Louis, Robert LaLonde, and Daniel Sullivan. 1993. "Earnings Losses of Displaced Workers." *American Economic Review* 83, no. 4: 685–709.

——. 2005. "What Are the Long-Term Returns to Training Dislocated and Disadvantaged Adults, What Works Best for Diverse Populations, and Can Short-Term Measures Assess Long-Term Benefits and Hold Programs Accountable?" Paper presented at the annual research conference of the Association for Public Policy and Management, Washington, D.C., November 4.

Jafari, S. 2005. "Back from Iraq, Alabama Guardsmen Take on Anarchy at Home." *Associated Press*, September 2.

Janowitz, M. 1960. *The Professional Soldier: A Social and Political Portrait*. Glencoe, Ill.: Free Press.

Johnson, C. 2004. *The Sorrows of Empire: The Military Secrecy, and the End of the Republic*. New York: Henry Holt.

Johnson, James H., Jr. 1985. "A Model of Evacuation—Decision Making in a Nuclear Reactor Emergency." *Geographical Review* 75, no. 4: 405–18.

Jonsson, Patrik. 2006. "In New Orleans, an Industrious Kind of Spring Break." *Christian Science Monitor*. http://www.csmonitor.com/2006/0317/p01s02-ussc.html (accessed April 1, 2007).

Journal of Blacks in Higher Education. 1999. "Money and Higher Education: Blacks Continue to Have a Steeper Hill to Climb." *Journal of Blacks in Higher Education* 26, no. 13: 13–14, 16.

Juhn, C. 1992. "Decline of Male Labor Market Participation: The Role of Declining Market Opportunities." *Quarterly Journal of Economics* 107: 79–121.

Kaczor, B. "Navy rescuers: Toughest part not getting all Katrina victims." *Associated Press*, (1 Sep. 2005).

Kaiser Family Foundation. 2005. "The Washington Post/Kaiser Family Foundation/Harvard University Survey of Hurricane Katrina Evacuees." http://www.kff.org/newsmedia/upload/7401.pdf (accessed April 1, 2007).

Kasperson, Roger, and K. David Pijawka. "Societal Response to Hazards and Major Hazard Events: Comparing Natural and Technological Hazards." *Public Administration Review* 45 (1985): 7–19.

Kates, R. W., C. E. Colton, S. Laska, and S. P. Leatherman. 2006. "Reconstruction of New Orleans after Hurricane Katrina: A Research Perspective." *Proceedings of the National Academy of Sciences of the United States of America* 103, no. 40: 14653–60.

Katz, L. F., and K. M. Murphy. 1992. "Changes in Relative Wages, 1963–1987: Supply and Demand Factors." *Quarterly Journal of Economics* 107: 35–78.

Kawachi, Ichiro, Bruce Kennedy, Lochner Kimberly, and Deborah Prothrow-Smith. 1997. "Social Capital, Income Inequality and Morality." *American Journal of Public Health* 87, no. 9: 1491–98.

Kellner, D. 2002. "September 11, Social Theory, and Democratic Politics." *Theory, Culture and Society* 19, no. 4: 147–59.

Kessler, Ronald C., and Jane D. McLeod. 1984. "Sex Differences in Vulnerability to Undesirable Life Events." *American Sociological Review* 49, no. 5: 620–31.

Kilic, Emine, Halise Devrimci Ozguven, and Iaik Sayil. 2003. "The Psychological Effects of Parental Mental Health on Children Experiencing Disaster: The Experience of Bolu Earthquake in Turkey." *Family Process* 42, no. 4: 485–96.

Killian, Charles, Walter Peacock, and Frederick Bates. 1983. "The Impact of the 1976 Guatemalan Earthquake on Inequality of Household Domestic Assets." Paper presented at the annual meeting of the Midwest Sociological Society, Kansas City, Mo., April 13.

Kletzer, Richard. 1998. "Job Displacement." *Journal of Economic Perspectives* 12, no. 1: 115–36.

Klinenberg, Eric. 2002. *Heat Wave: A Social Autopsy of Disaster in Chicago*. Chicago: University of Chicago Press.

258 References

Klocke, B. V. 2004. "Framing the World: U.S. Elites and Media Discourses of the War on Terrorism." Doctoral diss., University of Colorado.

Kniss, Fred, and David Todd Campbell. 1997. "The Effect of Religious Orientation on International Relief and Development Organizations." *Journal for the Scientific Study of Religion* 36, no. 1: 93–193.

Koenig, Harold G. 2006. *In the Wake of Disaster: Religious Response to Terrorism and Catastrophe.* Philadelphia: Templeton Foundation Press.

Konigsmark, A. R. 2006. "Crime Takes Hold of New New Orleans." *USA Today*, December 1, 1A, 4A.

Kreps, Gary A. 1978. "The Organization of Disaster Response: Some Fundamental Theoretical Issues." In *Disasters: Theory and Research*, edited by E. L. Quarantelli. Thousand Oaks, Calif.: Sage, 65–85.

———. 1984. "Sociological Inquiry and Disaster Research." *Annual Review of Sociology* 10: 309–30.

———. 1989. *Social Structure and Disaster.* Newark: University of Delaware Press.

Kreps, Gary, and Thomas Drabek. 1996. "Disasters are Nonroutine Social Problems." *International Journal of Mass Emergencies and Disasters* 14:129–53.

Kroll-Smith, J. Steven, and Steven Robert Couch. 1987. "A Chronic Technical Disaster and the Irrelevance of Religious Meaning: The Case of Centralia, Pennsylvania." *Journal for the Scientific Study of Religion* 26, no. 1: 25–37.

———. 1991. "What Is a Disaster? An Ecological Symbolic Approach to Resolving the Definitional Debate." *International Journal of Mass Emergencies and Disasters* 9: 355–66.

———. 1993. "Symbols, Ecology, and Contamination: Case Studies in the Ecological-Symbolic Approach to Disaster." *Research in Social Problems and Public Policy* 5: 47–73.

———. 1994. "Environmental Controversies, Interactional Resources, and Rural Communities: Siting versus Exposure Disputes." *Rural Sociology* 59: 25–44.

Ladd, Helen F., and Jens Ludwig. 1997. "Federal Housing Assistance, Residential Relocation, and Educational Opportunities: Evidence from Baltimore." *American Economic Review* 87, no. 2: 272–77.

Lamberg, Lynne. 2006. "Katrina Survivors Strive to Reclaim Their Lives." *Journal of the American Medical Association* 296: 499–500, 502.

Lambrew, Jeanne M., and Donna E. Shalala. 2006. "Federal Health Policy Response to Hurricane Katrina: What It Was and What It Could Have Been." *Journal of the American Medical Association* 296:1394–97.

Laska, Shirley. 2004. "What if Hurricane Ivan Had Not Missed New Orleans?" *Natural Hazards Observer* 39, no. 2: 5–6.

Leventhal, Emily A., and Daniel P. Mears. 2002. "Will Churches Respond to the Call? Religion, Civil Responsibility, and Social Service." *Journal of Sociology and Social Welfare* 29, no. 2: 53.

Lichbach, Mark A. 1985. "Protest in America: Univariate ARIMA Models of the Postwar Era." *Western Political Quarterly* 38, no. 3: 388–412.

Light, Donald W. 2004. "Ironies of Success: A New History of the American Health Care 'System.'" *Journal of Health and Social Behavior* 45 (extra issue): 1–24.

Link, Bruce G., and Jo Phelan. 1995. "Social Conditions as Fundamental Causes of Disease." *Journal of Health and Social Behavior* (extra issue): 80–94.

Liu, A., M. Fellowes, and M. Mabanta. 2006. *Katrina Index: Tracking Variables of Post-Katrina Recovery,* http://www.brookings.edu/metro/pubs/200607_KatrinaIndex.pdf (accessed April 1, 2007).

Liu, A., M. Mabanta, and M. Fellowes. 2006. *Katrina Index: Tracking Variables of Post-Katrina Recovery,* http://www.brookings.edu/metro/pubs/200512_katrinaindex.pdf (accessed April 1, 2007).

Living Cities.2006. *Moving Forward: Recommendations for Rebuilding East Biloxi,* http://www.living cities.org/pdf/Biloxi_Final_Report.pdf (accessed April 1, 2007).

Lopes Cardozo, Barbara, Leisel Talley, Ann Burton, and Carol Crawford. 2004. "Karenni Refugees Living in Thai-Burmese Border Camps: Traumatic Experiences, Mental Health Outcomes and Social Functioning." *Social Science and Medicine* 58: 2637–44.

Los Angeles Department of Health and Hospitals, Los Angeles Recovery Authority. 2006. *2006 Louisiana Health and Population Survey, Expanded Preliminary Results, October 6, 2006: Orleans*

Parish, http://popest.org/files/PopEst_ExpanPrelim_Report_Orleans_100606.pdf (accessed April 1, 2007).

Lotke, Eric, and Robert L. Borosage. 2006. *Hurricane Katrina: Natural Disaster, Human Catastrophe.* Washington, D.C.: Campaign for America's Future.

Lou, Michael, and Campbell Robertson. 2005. "A New Meaning for 'Organized Religion': It Helps the Needy Quickly." *New York Times,* September 9.

Louisiana Department of Health and Hospitals. *Reports of Missing and Deceased,* http://www.dhh.louisiana.gov/offices/page.asp?ID=192&Detail=5248 (accessed April 1, 2007).

Lowenthal, David. 1985. *The Past Is a Foreign Country.* New York: Cambridge University Press.

Lush, Tamara. 2005. "For Forecasting Chief, No Joy in Being Right." *Saint Petersburg Times,* August 30. http://www.sptimes.com/2005/08/30/State/For_forecasting_chief.shtml (accessed November 12, 2005).

Magill, J. T. 2005–2006. "On Perilous Ground." *Louisiana Cultural Vistas,* winter, 32–43.

Mangan, Katherine. 2005. "Tech Revival: Program Helps Dillard U. Professors Rebuild Course Materials and Raise Spirits." *Chronicle of Higher Education,* December 16, A29.

——. 2006a. "Colleges to Share Katrina Money." *Chronicle of Higher Education,* September 8, 35.

——. 2006b. "Ex-Presidents Join UNCF Katrina Fund." *Chronicle of Higher Education,* September 1, A46.

——. 2006c. "Hands-On Course in New Orleans Gives Students from across the Country an Education in Disaster." *Chronicle of Higher Education,* January 12, A10–A11.

——. 2006d. "Katrina Blog at Tulane U. Provides a Venue for Reflection and Memory." *Chronicle of Higher Education,* January 23.

——. 2006e. "Louisiana Tries to Lure Students Back." *Chronicle of Higher Education,* May 12, A33.

——. 2006f. "In New Orleans, Young Journalists Learn the Ropes." *Chronicle of Higher Education,* June 9, A48.

——. 2006g. "Schooled in Disaster: Public-Health Students in New Orleans Get Lessons in Crisis Relief First Hand." *Chronicle of Higher Education,* March 10, A33–A34.

——. 2006h. "Tulane U. Faces Lawsuit over Merger." *Chronicle of Higher Education,* March 31, A33.

——. 2006i. "2 Heirs Sue Tulane U." *Chronicle of Higher Education,* May 26, A34.

——. 2006j. "Xavier Sues Insurers for Katrina Payments." *Chronicle of Higher Education,* September 15.

Mangan, Katherine, and Jeffrey Selingo.2006. "College Presidents Seek More Hurricane Relief." *Chronicle of Higher Education,* May 5.

Marshall, Brent K., and J. Steven Picou. In press. "Post-Normal Science, the Precautionary Approach, and Worst Cases: The Challenge of 21st Century Disasters." *Sociological Inquiry.*

Marshall, Brent K., J. Steven Picou, and Duane Gill. 2003. "Terrorism as Disaster: Selected Commonalities and Long-Term Recovery for 9/11 Survivors." *Research in Social Problems and Public Policy* 11: 73–96.

Marshall, Brent K., J. Steven Picou, and Jan Schlichtmann. 2004. "Technological Disasters, Litigation Stress and the Use of Alternative Dispute Resolution Mechanisms." *Law and Policy* 26, no. 2: 289–307.

Martinez, Loreto M. 2000. *Neighborhood Context and the Development of African American Children: Children of Poverty, Studies on the Effects of Single Parenthood, the Feminization of Poverty, and Homelessness.* New York: Garland.

Martinez, M. 2005. "Big Easy Uneasy about Migrant Wave." *Chicago Tribune,* November 3.

Massey, Douglas S., and Nancy Denton. 1993. *American Apartheid: Segregation and the Making of the Underclass.* London: Harvard University Press.

Mawson, Anthony R. 2005. "Understanding Mass Panic and Other Collective Responses to Disaster." *Psychiatry* 68, no. 2: 95–113.

May, P J., and W. Williams. 1986. *Disaster Policy Implementation: Managing Programs under Shared Governance.* New York: Plenum Press.

Mayer, Susan E., and Christopher Jenkins. 1989. "Growing Up in Poor Neighborhoods: How Much Does It Matter." *Science* 243: 1441.

Maynes, Bill, and Rosemary Foster. 2000. "Educating Canada's Urban Poor Children." *Canadian Journal of Education* 25, no. 2: 56.

McCabe, Robert. 2000. "Measuring Up: The State-by-State Report Card for Higher Education, Underprepared Students," http://measuringup.highereducation.org/2000/articles/Underprepared Students.cfm (accessed April 1, 2007).

McCarthy, D., D. J. Peterson, N. Sastry, and M. Pollard. 2006. *Repopulation of New Orleans after Hurricane Katrina*. Santa Monica, Calif.: RAND, Gulf States Policy Institute.

McDaniel, J., and V. Casanova. 2003. "Pines in Lines: Tree Planting, H2B Guest Workers, and Rural Poverty in Alabama." *Southern Rural Sociology* 19, no. 1: 73–96.

McFarlane, Alexander C., and Peter Papay. 1992. "Multiple Diagnoses in Posttraumatic Stress Disorder in the Victims of a Natural Disaster." *Journal of Nervous and Mental Disease* 180: 498–504.

McIntosh, Peggy. 1989. "White Privilege: Unpacking the Invisible Knapsack." *Peace and Freedom*, July/August, 89.

McPherson, Miller. 1982. "Hypernetwork Sampling: Duality and Differentiation among Voluntary Organizations." *Social Networks* 3: 225–49.

McPherson, Miller, Lynn Smith-Lovin, and James M. Cook. 2001. "Birds of a Feather: Homophily in Social Networks." *Annual Review of Sociology* 27: 415–44.

Mercuri, Anne, and Holly L. Angelique. 2004. "Children's Responses to Natural, Technological, and Na-Tech Disasters." *Community Mental Health Journal* 40, no. 2: 167.

Meyer, John W., and Brian Rowan. 1977. "Institutional Organizations: Formal Structure as Myth and Ceremony." *American Journal of Sociology* 83, no. 2: 340–63.

Mileti, Dennis. 1999. *Disasters by Design: A Reassessment of Natural Hazards in the United States*. Washington, D.C.: John Henry Press.

Mileti, D. S., T. E. Drabek, and J. E. Haas. 1975. *Human Systems in Extreme Environments: A Sociological Perspective*. Boulder: Institute for Behavioral Science, University of Colorado.

Milgram, Stanley. 1967. "The Small World Problem." *Psychology Today* 2: 60–67.

Miller, DeMond S. 2006. "Visualizing the Corrosive Community: Looting in the Aftermath of Hurricane Katrina." *Space and Culture* 9, no. 1: 71–73.

Miller, DeMond S., and Jason D. Rivera. 2006. "Guiding Principles: Rebuilding Trust in Government and Public Policy in the Aftermath of Hurricane Katrina." *Journal of Public Management and Social Policy* 12, no. 1: 37–47.

———. In press. "Setting the Stage: Roots of Social Inequality and the Human Tragedy of Hurricane Katrina." In *Through the Eye of Katrina: Social Justice in the United States*, edited by Richelle S. Swan and Kristin A. Bates.

Miller, George. 2006. "Reverse the Raid on Student Aid Act of 2006." House Education and the Workforce Committee. http://www.govtrack.us/congress/bill.xpd?bill=h109-5150 (accessed April 1, 2007).

Miller, H. I. 2005. "Fighting a Second Gulf War." *Washington Times*, September 3.

Milligan, Melinda J. 1998. "Interactional Past and Potential: The Social Construction of Place Attachment." *Symbolic Interaction* 21, no. 1: 1–33.

Milliman, J., J. Grosskopf, and O. E. Paez. "An Exploratory Study of Local Emergency Managers' Views of Military Assistance/Defense Support to Civil Authorities (MACA/DSCA)." *Journal of Homeland Security and Emergency Management* 3, no. 1(2006):1-17.

Minkler, Meredith, Esme Fuller-Thompson, and Jack M. Guralnik. 2006. "Gradient of Disability across the Socioeconomic Spectrum in the United States." *New England Journal of Medicine* 355: 695–703.

Mississippi Renewal Forum. 2006. *Mississippi Renewal Forum: A Reconstruction Plan for Biloxi, Mississippi*, http://www.mississippirenewal.com/documents/Rep_Biloxi.pdf (accessed April 1, 2007).

Molaison, Elaine Fontenot. 2006. "Katrina: Experiences and Education." *Journal of Renal Nutrition* 16: 1–2.

Molotch, Harvey. 2005. "Death on the Roof: Race and Bureaucratic Failure." Social Science Research Council, http://understandingkatrina.ssrc.org (accessed April 1, 2007).

Morgan, M. J. 2006. "American Empire and the American Military." *Armed Forces and Society* 32, no. 2: 202–18.

Morris, C. 2002. *The San Francisco Calamity.* Champaign: University of Illinois Press.

Morrow, B. H. 1999. "Identifying and Mapping Community Vulnerability." *Disasters* 23, no. 1: 1–18.

Morrow, B. H., and E. Enarson. 1996. "Hurricane Andrew through Women's Eyes: Issues and Recommendations." *International Journal of Mass Emergencies and Disasters* 14, no. 1: 5–22.

Mulcahy, M. 2005. "Hurricanes, Poverty and Vulnerability: An Historical Perspective." In *Understanding Katrina: Perspectives from the Social Sciences,* http://understandingkatrina.ssrc.org/Mulcahy (accessed April 1, 2007).

Musselman, Dominique L., and Charles B. Nemeroff. 2000. "Depression Really Does Hurt Your Heart: Stress, Depression, and Cardiovascular Disease." *Progress in Brain Research* 122: 43–59.

Myers, Samuel L., Hyeoneui Kim, and Cheryl Mandala. 2004. "The Effect of School Poverty on Racial Gaps in Test Scores: The Case of the Minnesota Basic Standards Tests." *Journal of Negro Education* 73, no. 1: 81.

National Governors Association. 1979. *Emergency Preparedness Project: Final Report.* Washington, D.C.: National Governors Association.

NBC Nightly News. 2005. November 12.

Nesmith, Jeff. 2006. "Disaster Role Urged for Health Centers." *Atlanta Journal and Constitution,* August 8, A5.

Neumeister, L. 2005. "A General Becomes the Face of Control Following Katrina." *Associated Press,* September 11.

Newman, Mark, Albert-László Barabási, and Duncan J. Watts. 2006. *The Structure and Dynamics of Networks.* Princeton, N.J.: Princeton University Press.

Nichols, Laura, and Barbara Gault. 2003. "The Implications of Welfare Reform for Housing and School Instability." *Journal of Negro Education* 72, no. 1: 104.

Nigg, Joanne, John Barnshaw, and Manuel Torres. 2006. "Hurricane Katrina and the Flooding of New Orleans: Emergent Issues in Sheltering and Temporary Housing." *Annals of the American Academy of Political and Social Science* 604: 113–28.

Nolan, Bruce. 2005. "Katrina Takes Aim." *New Orleans Times-Picayune,* August 28.

Norris, F., C. M. Byrne, E. Diaz, and K. Kaniasty. 2001. "The Range, Magnitude, and Duration of Effects of Natural and Human-Caused Disasters: A Review of the Empirical Literature." National Center for PTSD, http://www.ncptsd.org/facts/disasters/fs_range.html (accessed April 1, 2007).

Nyhan, Paul. 2005. "College Divide Threatens to Keep the Poor in Poverty." *Seattle Post-Intelligencer,* September 27.

O'Brien, Soledad. 2005. "FEMA under Fire." *CNN Video,* September 2.

O'Harrow, R., Jr. 2005. *No Place to Hide.* New York: Free Press.

Office of Emergency Preparedness. 2005. "State of Louisiana Emergency Operations Plan," http://upload.wikimedia.org/wikipedia/en/3/3c/EOPSupplement1a.pdf (accessed April 1, 2007).

Oliver-Smith, Anthony. 1986. *The Martyred City: Death and Rebirth in the Andes.* Albuquerque: University of New Mexico Press.

———. 1989. "Post-Disaster Housing Reconstruction and Social Inequality: A Challenge to Policy and Practice." *Disasters* 14: 7–19.

———. 1996. "Anthropological Research on Hazards and Disasters." *Annual Review of Anthropology* 25: 303–28.

Ott, Riki. 2005. *Sound Truth and Corporate Myths: The Legacy of the Exxon Valdez Oil Spill.* Cordova, Alaska: Dragonfly Sisters Press.

Palacio, Grace G. 2004. "Adolescent Narrative Responses to September 11th: A Qualitative Investigation into Meaning Making, Trauma, and Themes Revealed in Parent and Young Adult Narratives." Dissertation, Long Island University.

Pan American Health Organization. 2004. *Management of Dead Bodies in Disaster Situations.* Washington, D.C.: Pan American Health Organization.

Parslow, Ruth A., Anthony F. Jorm, and Helen Christensen. 2006. "Associations of Pre-Trauma Attributes and Trauma Exposure with Screening Positive for PTSD: Analysis of a Community-Based Study of 2085 Young Adults." *Psychological Medicine* 36, no. 3: 387.

Paxton, Pamela. 1999. "Is Social Capital Declining in the United States? A Multiple Indicator Assessment." *American Journal of Sociology* 105: 88–127.

Payne, January W. 2005. "At Risk before the Storm Struck: Prior Health Disparities Due to Race, Poverty Multiply Death, Disease." *Washington Post*, September 13.

Peacock, Walter, and Frederick Bates. 1982. "An Assessment of Impact and Recovery at the Household Level." In *Recovery, Change and Development: A Longitudinal Study of the 1976 Guatemalan Earthquake*, edited by F. Bates. New York: Bantam.

Peacock, Walter, Betty Morrow, and Hugh Gladwin. 1997. *Hurricane Andrew: Ethnicity, Gender, and the Sociology of Disasters*. Miami, Fla.: International Hurricane Center.

Pelling, Mark. 2003. *The Vulnerability of Cities: Natural Disasters and Social Resilience*. London: Earthscan.

Pérez-Lugo, M. 2001. "The Mass Media and Disaster Awareness in Puerto Rico: A Case Study of the Floods in Barrio Tortugo." *Organization and Environment* 14, no. 1: 55–73.

Perrow, Charles. 2007. *The Next Catastrophe: Reducing Our Vulnerabilities to Natural, Industrial, and Terrorist Disasters*. Princeton, N.J.: Princeton University Press.

Perry, Ronald W., Marjorie Green, and Alvin H. Mushkatel. 1983. *American Minority Citizens in Disaster*. Tempe: Arizona State University Center for Public Affairs.

Perry, R. W., and M. K. Lindell. 2003. "Preparedness for Emergency Response: Guidelines for the Emergency Planning Process." *Disasters* 27, no. 4: 336–50.

Perry, Ronald W., Michael K. Lindell, and Marjorie Green. 1981. *Evacuation Planning and Emergency Management*. Lexington, Mass.: Heath.

Phillips, Brenda. 2002. "Qualitative Methods and Disaster Research." In *Methods of Disaster Research*, edited by R. Stallings. Philadelphia: Xlibris, 194–211.

Pickel, M. L. 2005. "Immigrant Workers Rile New Orleans; Rules Shelved, Crews Labor for Meager Pay." *Atlanta Journal-Constitution*, October 19.

Picou, J. Steven. 1996a. "Compelled Disclosure of Scholarly Research: Some Comments on 'High Stakes' Litigation." *Law and Contemporary Problems* 3, no. 59: 149–57.

———. 1996b. "Sociology and Compelled Disclosure: Protecting Respondent Confidentially." *Sociological Spectrum* 16, no. 3: 207–38.

———. 1996c. "Toxins in the Environment, Damage to the Community: Sociology and the Toxic Tort." In *Witnessing for Sociology: Sociologists in Court*, edited by P. Jenkins and S. Kroll-Smith. Westport, Conn.: Greenwood Press, 210–23.

———. 2000. "The Talking Circle as Sociological Practice: Cultural Transformation of Chronic Disaster Impacts." *Sociological Practice: A Journal of Clinical and Applied Sociology* 2, no. 2: 77–97.

Picou, J. Steven, and Duane A. Gill. 1997. "The Exxon Valdez Oil Spill and Chronic Psychological Stress." In *Proceedings of the Exxon Valdez Oil Spill Symposium*, edited by S. D. Rice, R. B. Spies, D. A. Wolfe, and B.A. Wright. Bethesda, Md.: American Fisheries Society, 879–93.

———. 2000. "The Exxon Valdez Disaster as Localized Environmental Catastrophe: Dissimilarities to Risk Society Theory." In *Risk in the Modern World*, edited by M. Cohen. London: Macmillan, 143–70.

Picou, J. Steven, Duane A. Gill, and Maurie J. Cohen, eds. 1997. *The Exxon Valdez Disaster: Readings on a Modern Social Problem*. Dubuque, Iowa: Kendall/Hunt.

Picou, J. Steven, and Brent K. Marshall. 2006. "Katrina as a Na-Tech Disaster." Paper presented at the Southern Sociological Society meetings, New Orleans, March.

Picou, J. Steven, Brent K. Marshall, and Duane A. Gill. 2004. "Disaster, Litigation and the Corrosive Community." *Social Forces* 82, no. 4: 1448–82.

Picou, J. Steven, and Donald R. Rosebrook. 1993. "Technological Accident, Community Class Action Litigation and Scientific Damage Assessment: A Case Study of Court Ordered Research." *Sociological Spectrum* 13: 117–38.

Pilisuk, Marc, Susan Hillier Parks, and Glenn Hawkes. 1987. "Public Perception of Technological Risk." *Social Science Journal* 24, no. 4: 403–13.

Pine, John C. 2006. "Hurricane Katrina and Oil Spills: Impact on Coastal and Ocean Environments." *Oceanography*, 19, no. 2: 37–39.

Plocek, K. 2006. "Shortchanged." *Houston Press*, February 9.

Pool, I., and M. Kochen. 1978. "Contacts and Influence." *Social Networks* 1: 1–48.

Popkin, Susan J., Margery Austin Turner, and Martha Burt. 2006. "Rebuilding Affordable Housing in New Orleans: The Challenge of Creating Inclusive Communities." In *After Katrina: Rebuilding Opportunity and Equity into the New New Orleans*, edited by Margery Austin Turner and Sheila R. Zedlewski. Washington, D.C.: Urban Institute Press, 1–13.

Port of New Orleans. 2003. [Informational booklet].

Portes, Alejandro, and Reuben Rumbaut. 2001. *Legacies: The Story of the Immigrant Second Generation*. Berkeley: University of California Press.

Prewitt Diaz, Joseph O. 1999. "Stressors on Puerto Rican Children as a Result of Hurricane Georges." *Education* 119, no. 4: 658–63.

Prinstein, Mitchell J., Annette M. La Greca, Eric M. Vernberg, and Wendy K. Silverman. 1996. "Children's Coping Assistance: How Parents, Teachers, and Friends Help Children Cope after a Natural Disaster." *Journal of Clinical Child Psychology* 25, no. 4: 463–75.

Proshansky, H. M., A. K. Fabian, and R. Kaminoff. 1983. "Place-Identity: Physical World Socialization of the Self." *Journal of Environmental Psychology* 3: 57–83.

Provenzo, Eugene F., and Asterie Baker Provenzo. 2002. *In the Eye of Hurricane Andrew*. Gainesville: University Press of Florida.

Purpura, P. 2005. "1,000 National Guard Troops Arrive; 'We're Getting the Troops in as Fast as We Can.'" *New Orleans Times-Picayune*, September 3.

Quarantelli, Enrico. 1978. "Some Basic Themes in Sociological Studies of Disasters." In *Disasters: Theory and Research*, edited by E. L. Quarantelli. Thousand Oaks, Calif.: Sage, 2–14.

———. 1982a. "General and Particular Observations on Sheltering and Housing in American Disasters." *Disasters* 6: 277–81.

———. 1982b. "Sheltering and Housing after Major Community Disasters: Case Studies and General Observations." Final Project Report No. 29. Columbus, Ohio: Disaster Research Center.

———. 1985. "An Assessment of Conflicting Views on Mental Health: The Consequences of Traumatic Events." In *Trauma and Its Wake: The Treatment of Post-Traumatic Stress Disorder*, edited by Charles Figley. New York: Brunner/Mazel, 173–215.

———. 1987. "What Should We Study: Questions and Suggestions for Researchers about the Concept of Disasters." *International Journal of Mass Emergencies and Disasters* 5: 7–32.

———. 1995. "What Is a Disaster?" *International Journal of Mass Emergencies and Disasters* 13: 361–64.

———. 1998. *What Is Disaster? Perspectives on the Question*. London: Routledge.

———. 2002. "The Role of the Mass Communication System in Natural and Technological Disasters and Possible Extrapolation to Terrorist Situations." *Risk Management: An International Journal* 4, no. 4: 7–21.

———. 2005. "Catastrophes Are Different from Disasters: Some Implications for Crisis Planning and Management Drawn from Katrina." In *Understanding Katrina: Perspectives from the Social Sciences*, http://understandingkatrina.ssrc.org/Quarantelli (accessed April 1, 2007).

Quarantelli, E. L., and Russell R. Dynes. 1970. "Property Norms and Looting: Their Patterns in Community Crises." *Phylon: The Atlanta University Review of Race and Culture* 31, no. 2: 168–82.

———. 1977. "Response to Social Crisis and Disaster." *Annual Review of Sociology* 3: 23–49.

Raphael, S., and R. Winter-Ebmer. 2001. "Identifying the Effect of Unemployment on Crime." *Journal of Law and Economics* 44: 259–83.

Reagan, Michael, Gina Webb, Caroline Harkleroad, Carley Brown, Lisa Reagan, and Deb Murphy. 2005. *Katrina State of Emergency*. Kansas City, Mo.: Lionheart Books.

Reason, P., and H. Bradbury, eds. 2001. *Handbook of Action Research: Participative Inquiry and Practice*. London: Sage.

Reckdahl, K. 2006. "The Myths of New Orleans." *Tucson Weekly*, August 24.

Reed, B. J., and D. R. Segal. 2000. "The Impact of Multiple Deployments on Soldiers' Peacekeeping Attitudes, Morale, and Retention." *Armed Forces and Society* 27, no. 1: 57–78.

Relph, E. 1976. *Place and Placelessness*. London: Pion, 1976.

Renne, John. 2005. "Car-Less in the Eye of Katrina." *Planetizen*, September 6.

Reviving the Renaissance. 2006. *The City of Biloxi: Reviving the Renaissance*, http://biloxi.ms.us/Reviving_the_Renaissance/index.html (accessed April 1, 2007).

Reynolds, Paul David. 1971. *A Primer in Theory Construction*. New York: Macmillan.

Ritchie, Liesel. 2004. "Voices of Cordova: Social Capital in the Wake of the Exxon Valdez Oil Spill." Ph.D. diss., Mississippi State University.

Robinson, Walter. 2005. "Hurricane Katrina and the Arts," http://www.artnet.com/magazineus/news/robinson/robinson9-15-05.asp (accessed April 1, 2007).

Rodríguez, G. 2005. "La Nueva Orleans," *Los Angeles Times*, September 25.

Rodríguez, H., and Aguirre, B. E. 2006. "Hurricane Katrina and the Healthcare Infrastructure: A Focus on Disaster Preparedness, Response, and Resiliency." *Frontiers of Health Services Management* 23, no. 1: 13–24.

Rodríguez, H., W. Diaz, J. Santos, and B. Aguirre. 2006. "Communicating Risk and Uncertainty: Science, Technology, and Disasters at the Crossroads." In *Handbook of Disaster Research*, edited by H. Rodríguez, E. L. Quarantelli, and R. Dynes. New York: Springer, 476–88.

Rodríguez, H., J. Trainor, and E. L. Quarantelli. 2006. "Rising to the Challenges of a Catastrophe: The Emergent and Pro-Social Behavior Following Hurricane Katrina." *The Annals of the American Academy of Political and Social Science* 604 (special issue): 82–101.

Roig-Franzia, M. 2005. "In New Orleans, No Easy Work for Willing Latinos." *Washington Post*, December 18.

Root, J., and A. Davis. 2005. "Undocumented Immigrants Flock to Jobs on Gulf Coast." *Duluth News Tribune*, October 12.

Rosenbaum, Sara. 2006. "U.S. Health Policy in the Aftermath of Hurricane Katrina." *Journal of the American Medical Association* 295: 437–40.

Ruscio, Kenneth P. 1996. "Trust, Democracy, and Public Management: A Theoretical Argument." *Journal of Public Administration Research and Theory* 6, no. 3: 461–77.

Russell, Gordon. 2005. "Nagin Orders First-Ever Mandatory Evacuation of New Orleans." *New Orleans Times-Picayune*, August 28.

Sabine, George. 1952. "The Two Democratic Traditions." *Philosophical Review* 61: 451–74.

Sampson, Robert J. 1995. "The Community." In *Crime*, edited by James Q. Wilson and Joan Petersilia. Oakland, Calif.: ICS Press, 225.

Sanchez, M. 2005. "Illegal Workers Eyeing the Gulf Coast." *San Diego Tribune*, September 24.

Saulny, Susan. 2006a. "A Legacy of the Storm: Depression and Suicide." *New York Times*, June 21, A1, A15.

———. 2006b. "New Orleans Details Steps to Repair Its Legal System." *New York Times*, August 7.

Scanlon, Joseph. 2006. "Unwelcome Irritant or Useful Ally: The Mass Media in Emergencies." In *Handbook of Disaster Research*, edited by H. Rodríguez, E. L. Quarantelli, and R. R. Dynes. New York: Springer, 413–29.

Schleifstein, Mark. 2005. "Mayor Urges Storm Preparations." *New Orleans Times-Picayune*, August 27.

Schlesing, A. 2005. "Armed for Trouble, Arkansas Soldiers Enter City in Crisis." *Arkansas Democrat-Gazette*, September 3.

Scott, Loren C. 2006. *Advancing in the Aftermath III: Tracking the Recovery from Katrina and Rita*. Baton Rouge, La.: Loren C. Scott and Associates, Inc.

Selener, D. 1997. *Participatory Action Research and Social Change*. Ithaca, N.Y.: Cornell University Press.

Selingo, Jeffrey. 2005. "Tulane Slashes Departments and Lays Off Professors." *Chronicle of Higher Education*, December 16, A1–A30.

Sellnow, T. L., M. W. Seeger, and R. R. Ulmer. 2002. "Chaos Theory, Informational Needs, and Natural Disasters." *Journal of Applied Communication Research* 30, no. 4: 269–92.

Selznick, Philip. 1996. "Institutionalism 'Old' and 'New.'" *Administrative Science Quarterly* 41: 270–77.

Showalter, P. S., and M. F. Meyers. 1994. "Natural Disasters in the United States as Release Agents of Oil, Chemicals or Radiologic Materials between 1980–1989: Analysis and Recommendations." *Risk Analysis* 14: 169–82.

Silove, Derrick, and Richard Bryant. 2006. "Rapid Assessments of Mental Health Needs after Disasters." *Journal of the American Medical Association* 296: 576–78.

Siman, B. A. 1977. *Crime during disaster*. Dissertation. Ann Arbor, Mich.: University Microfilms International.

Simmel, Georg. 1971. "Group Expansions and the Development of Individuality." In *George Simmel*, edited by Donald Levine. Chicago: University of Chicago Press, 251–93.

———. 1978. *The Philosophy of Money*. Edited and translated by Tom Bottomore and David Frisby. Routledge and Kegan Paul (orig. 1907).

Social Science Research Center. 2006. "Post-Katrina Guiding Principles of Disaster Social Science Research," http://www.ssrc.msstate.edu/Katrina/Publications/Guiding%20Principles.pdf (accessed April 1, 2007).

Solomonoff, R., and A. Rappoport. 1951. "Connectivity of Random Nets." *Bulletin of Mathematical Biophysics* 13: 107–17.

Southern University at New Orleans. 2006. http://www.suno.edu/faq.htm.

Stallings, Robert. 1998. "Disaster and the Theory of Social Order." In *What Is a Disaster? Perspectives on the Question*, edited by E. Quarantelli. London: Routledge, 127–45.

———, ed. 2002. *Methods of Disaster Research*. Philadelphia: Xlibris.

Stallings, R. A., and E. L. Quarantelli. 1985. "Emergent Citizen Groups and Emergency Management." *Public Administration Review* 45 (special issue): 93–100.

Stanton-Chapman, Tina L., Derek A Chapman, Ann P. Kaiser, and Terry B. Hancock. 2004. "Cumulative Risk and Low-Income Children's Language Development." *Topics in Early Childhood Special Education* 24, no. 4: 227–38.

Stein, A. A. 2006. *Mississippian Moundbuilders and Their Artifacts*, http://www.mississippian-artifacts.com (accessed April 1, 2007).

Steinberg, Ted. 2006. *Acts of God: The Unnatural History of Natural Disaster in America*. New York: Oxford University Press.

Stempel, C. 2006. "Televised Sports, Masculinist Moral Capital, and Support for the U.S. Invasion of Iraq." *Journal of Sport and Social Issues* 30, no. 1: 79–106.

STEPS (Steps Alliance for South Mississippi). 2006. http://www.stepsouthms.org (accessed April 1, 2007).

Stoecker, R. 2005. *Research Methods for Community Change: A Project-Based Approach*. Thousand Oaks, Calif.: Sage.

Strauss, Abraham L. 1978. *Negotiations: Varieties, Contexts, Processes, and Social Order*. San Francisco: Jossey-Bass.

Stringer, E. T. 1999. *Action Research*. Thousand Oaks, Calif.: Sage.

Swerczek, Mary, and Allen Powell II. 2005. "2000 Kids Still Separated from Parents; Officials Tracking Cases for Reunion." *New Orleans Times-Picayune*, September 17.

Sylves, R. T. 2006. "President Bush and Hurricane Katrina: A Presidential Leadership Study." *Annals of the American Academy of Political and Social Science* 604: 26–56.

Tabor, Kim. 2005. "Library Services Helping Students Cope with Disaster." *Teacher Librarian* 33: 65.

Taub, Richard, Garth Taylor, and Jan D. Dunham. 1984. *Paths of Neighborhood Change: Race and Crime in America*. Chicago: University of Chicago Press.

Taylor, Ralph, Stephen Gottfredson, and Sidney Brower. 1984. "Block Crime and Fear: Defensible Space, Local Ties, and Territorial Functioning." *Journal of Research in Crime and Delinquency* 21: 303–31.

Thienkrua, Warunee, Barbara Lopes Cardozo, M. L. Somchai Chakkraband, Thomas E. Guadamuz, Wachira Pengjuntr, Prawate Tantipiwatanaskul, Suchada Sakornsatian, Suparat Ekassawin, Benjaporn Panyayong, Anchalee Varangrat, Jordan W. Tappero, Merritt Schreiber, and Frits van Griensven for the Thailand Post-Tsunami Mental Health Study Group. 2006. "Symptoms of Posttraumatic Stress Disorder and Depression among Children in Tsunami-Affected Areas in Southern Thailand." *Journal of the American Medical Association* 296: 549–59.

Thoits, Peggy A. 1987. "Gender and Marital Status Differences in Control and Distress: Common Stress versus Unique Stress Explanations." *Journal of Health and Social Behavior* 28, no. 1: 7–22.

Thomas, D., and D. Mileti. 2003. *Designing Educational Opportunities for the Hazards Manager of the 21st Century.* Report of a workshop funded by the National Science Foundation and the FEMA Higher Education Project. Boulder: Institute of Behavioral Science, Natural Hazards Center, University of Colorado.

Thomas-Long, Roslyn. 2005. "Lessons to Learn: Voices from the Front Lines of Teachers for America." *Canadian Journal of Education* 28: 210–13.

Thompson, Dennis F. 2004. *Restoring Responsibility: Ethics in Government, Business, and Healthcare.* New York: Cambridge University Press.

Tierney, Kathleen. 2003. "Disaster Beliefs and Institutional Interests: Recycling Disaster Myths in the Aftermath of 9-11." In *Research in Social Problems and Public Policy, Vol. 11: Terrorism and Disaster: New Threats, New Ideas,* edited by L. Clarke. New York: Elsevier Science, 33–51.

———. 2005. "The Red Pill." In *Understanding Katrina: Perspectives from the Social Sciences,* http:// understandingkatrina.ssrc.org/Tierney (accessed April 1, 2007).

———. 2006. "Recent Developments in U.S. Homeland Security Policies and Their Implications for the Management of Extreme Events." In *Handbook of Disaster Research,* edited by H. Rodríguez, E. L. Quarantelli, and R. R. Dynes. New York: Springer.

Tierney, K., C. Bevc, and E. Kuligowski. 2006. "Metaphors Matter: Disaster Myths, Media Frames, and Their Consequences in Hurricane Katrina." *Annals of the American Academy of Political and Social Science* 604: 57–81.

Tierney, Kathleen, Michael Lindell, and Ronald Perry. 2001. *Facing the Unexpected: Disaster Preparedness and Response in the United States.* Washington, D.C.: John Henry Press.

Trainor, Joseph E., William Donner, and Manuel Torres. 2006. "There for the Storm: Warning, Response, and Rescue among Non-Evacuees in Hurricane Katrina." In *Learning from Catastrophe: Quick Response Research in the Wake of Hurricane Katrina.* Boulder, Colo.: Natural Hazards Center.

Travers, J., and Stanley Milgram. 1969. "An Experimental Study of the Small World Problem." *Sociometry* 32: 425–43.

Treaster, Joseph B. 2006. "Judge: Insurers Must Pay for Water Damage." *Mobile Press-Register,* November 29, 1A, 4A.

Tulane University. 2005. "Tulane University—A Plan for Renewal," http://renewal.tulane.edu/ renewalplan.pdf (accessed April 1, 2007).

Turner, R. H., Joanne M. Nigg, and Denise Heller Paz. 1986. *Waiting for Disaster: Earthquake Watch in California.* Berkeley: University of California Press.

Twigger-Ross, C., and D. L. Uzzell. 1996. "Place and Identity Process." *Journal of Environmental Psychology* 16, no. 3: 205–20.

Tyson, A. S. 2005. "Strain of Iraq War Means the Relief Burden Will Have to Be Shared." *Washington Post,* August 31, A14.

University of Michigan School of Public Health. 2005. http://phastbreak.blogspot.com/2006/02/ welcome.html (accessed April 1, 2007).

U.S. Bureau of the Census. 1940, 1950, 1960, 1970, 1980, 1990, 2000. Washington, D.C.: U.S. Government Printing Office.

———. 2000a. *American Community Survey,* http://www.census.gov/acs/www.

———. 2000b. *Census Brief: The Foreign-Born Population,* http://www.census.gov/population/www/ cen2000/briefs.html.

———. 2004. *American Community Survey Hurricane Data*, http://www.census.gov/Press-Release/www/2005/katrina.htm.

———. 2005a. *American Community Survey, 2005*, http://www.factfinder.census.gov.

———. 2005b. *Census Bureau Estimates Nearly 10 Million Residents along Gulf Coast Hit by Hurricane Katrina*, http://www.census.gov/Press-Release/www/releases/archives/hurricanes_tropical _storms/005673.html.

———. 2005c. *Quick Facts*, http://quickfacts.census.gov/qfd/states/12/1232275.html.

U.S. Conference of Mayors. 2005. *2005 National Action Plan on Safety and Security in America's Cities*. Washington, D.C.: U.S. Conference of Mayors.

U.S. Department of Justice. 2006. *Hurricane Katrina Fraud Task Force home page with links to the HK-FTF Progress Reports*, http://www.usdoj.gov/katrina/Katrina_Fraud (accessed April 1, 2007).

University of Virginia. 2006. *Geostat Collections, Historical Census Browser*, http://fisher.lib.virginia .edu/collections/stats/histcensus (accessed April 1, 2007).

van Griensven, Frits, M. L. Somchai Chakkraband, Warunee Thienkrua, Wachira Pengjuntr, Barbara Lopes Cardozo, Prawate Tantipiwatanaskul, Philip A. Mock, Suparat Ekassawin, Anchalee Varangrat, Carol Gotway, Miriam Sabin, and Jordan W. Tappero for the Thailand Post-Tsunami Mental Health Study Group. 2006. "Mental Health Problems among Adults in Tsunami-Affected Areas in Southern Thailand." *Journal of the American Medical Association* 296: 537–48.

Van Tuyll, H. P. 1994. "Militarism, the United States, and the Cold War." *Armed Forces and Society* 20, no. 4: 519–30.

Voelker, Rebecca. 2006a. "In Post-Katrina New Orleans, Efforts Under Way to Build Better Health Care." *Journal of the American Medical Association* 296: 1333–34.

———. 2006b. "Post-Katrina Mental Health Needs Prompt Group to Compile Disaster Medicine Guide." *Journal of the American Medical Association* 295: 259–60.

Voth, D. E. 1979. "Social Action Research in Community Development." In *Community Development Research: Concepts, Issues, and Strategies*, edited by E. J. Blakely. New York: Human Sciences Press, 67–81.

Waller, M. 2006. "In the Wake of Katrina, Thousands of Spanish-Speaking People Are Migrating to New Orleans, Drawn by the Dream of a Better Life." *Times-Picayune*, October 8.

Warren, Roland. 1984. *Community in America*. 2nd ed. New York: McGraw-Hill.

Wasserman, Stanley, and Katherine Faust. 1994. *Social Network Analysis: Methods and Applications*. Cambridge: Cambridge University Press.

Watts, M. 1992. "Capitalisms, Crises, and Cultures I: Notes toward a Totality of Fragments." In *Reworking Modernity: Capitalism and Symbolic Discontent*, edited by A. Pred and M. Watts. New Brunswick, N.J.: Rutgers University Press, 1–20.

Waugh, W. L., Jr. 2000. *Living with Hazards, Dealing with Disasters: An Introduction to Emergency Management*. Armonk, N.Y.: M. E. Sharpe.

Webb, Gary R. 2002. "Sociology, Disasters and Terrorism: Understanding Threats of the New Millennium." *Sociological Focus* 35: 87–95.

Weine, Stevan, Nerina Muzurovic, Yasmina Kulauzovic, et al. 2004. "Family Consequences of Refugee Trauma." *Family Process* 43, no. 2: 147–59.

Weisler, Richard H., James G. Barbee IV, and Mark H. Townsend. 2006. "Mental Health and Recovery in the Gulf Coast after Hurricanes Katrina and Rita." *Journal of the American Medical Association* 296: 585–88.

Wellman, Barry, and Barry Leighton. 1979. "Networks, Neighborhoods, and Communities: Approaches to the Study of the Community Question." *Urban Affairs Quarterly* 14: 363–90.

Wenger, Dennis, and E. L. Quarantelli. 1989. *Mass Media Systems and Community Hazards and Disasters*. Final Project Report no. 36. Newark: Disaster Research Center, University of Delaware.

White House. 2006. *The Federal Response to Hurricane Katrina: Lessons Learned*. Washington, D.C.: White House.

Williams, D. R., M. E. Patterson, and J. W. Roggenbuck. 1992. "Beyond the Commodity Metaphor: Examining Emotional and Symbolic Attachment to Place." *Leisure Science* 14: 29–46.

Williams, D. R., and J. J. Vaske. 2002. "The Measurement of Place Attachment: Validity and Gereralizability of a Psychometric Approach." Paper written and prepared by U.S. Department of Agriculture Forest Service, Rocky Mountain Research Station, Fort Collins, Colorado.

Wilson, William Julius. 1996. *When Work Disappears.* New York: Knopf.

Winship, Christopher, and Larry Radbill. 1994. "Sampling Weights and Regression Analysis." *Sociological Methods and Research* 23, no. 2: 230–57.

Wisner, Ben, Piers Blaikie, Terry Cannon, and Ian Davis. 2004. *At Risk: Natural Hazards, People's Vulnerability and Disasters.* 2nd ed. London: Routledge (orig. 1994).

Wynia, Matthew K., and Lawrence O. Gostin. 2004. "Ethical Challenges in Preparing for Bioterrorism: Barriers within the Health Care System." *American Journal of Public Health* 94: 1096–102.

Yin, Robert K. 2003. *Case Study Research: Design and Methods.* 3rd ed. Applied Social Research Methods. Thousand Oaks, Calif.: Sage.

Young, Stacy, Lina Balluz, and Josephine Malilay. 2004. "Natural and Technological Hazardous Material Releases during and after Natural Disasters: A Review." *Science of the Total Environment* 322: 3–20.

Zedlewski, Sheila R. 2006. "Pre-Katrina New Orleans: The Backdrop." In *After Katrina: Rebuilding Opportunity and Equity into the New New Orleans,* edited by Margery Austin Turner and Sheila R. Zedlewski. Washington, D.C.: Urban Institute Press, 1–8.

Zeigler, Donald J., Stanley D. Brunn, and James H. Johnson Jr. 1981. "Evacuation from a Nuclear Technological Disaster." *Geographical Review* 71, no. 1: 1–16.

Zhou, D. 1997. *Disaster, Disorganization and Crime.* Dissertation. Ann Arbor, Mich.: University Microfilms International.

Zhou, Min, and Carl L. Bankston III. 1998. *Growing Up American: How Vietnamese Children Adapt to Life in the United States.* New York: Russell Sage Foundation.

Index

About the Editors
and Contributors

Carl L. Bankston III is professor and chair in the Department of Sociology and codirector of the Asian Studies Program at Tulane University. His research interests include international migration, race and ethnicity, and sociology of education. He is author of over 100 journal articles and book chapters, and he is author or editor of 14 books. These include *Growing Up American: How Vietnamese Children Adapt to Life in the United States* (with Min Zhou, 1998), *A Troubled Dream: The Promise and Failure of School Desegregation in Louisiana* (with Stephen J. Caldas, 2002), and *Blue Collar Bayou: Louisiana Cajuns in the New Economy of Ethnicity* (with Jacques Henry). His books have received the Thomas and Znaniecki Award for outstanding book in international migration, the Mid-South Sociological Association Distinguished Book Award, the Louisiana Library Association Book Award, and the Stanford Lyman Distinguished Book Award.

John Barnshaw is research projects coordinator at Disaster Research Center and a doctoral student in the Department of Sociology and Criminal Justice at the University of Delaware. As projects coordinator, Barnshaw works with colleagues on a variety of research projects ranging from the evacuation of lower Manhattan during the September 11, 2001, World Trade Center attacks to the more recent evacuation of New Orleans in the aftermath of Hurricane Katrina. His research interests include stratification and inequality in a variety of social contexts, ranging from disasters to educational tracking to infectious epidemiology. For the past two years, Barnshaw has been a summer scholar in the Modern Methods in Epidemiology and Biostatistics Program through Harvard University and Karolinska Institutet. He has given lectures and presentations across the United States as well as several in international meetings. In addition to his international presentations, Barnshaw has also been involved in assisting local villagers in sustainable development projects in Mbita and Mfangano, Kenya. His current disaster research focuses on inequality in social networks and communities in the aftermath of Hurricane Katrina.

Christine Bevc is a Ph.D. student in the Department of Sociology at the University of Colorado at Boulder. She is also a graduate research assistant with the Natural Hazards Center, the mission of which is to advance and communicate knowledge on hazards mitigation and disaster preparedness, response, and recovery. Before she began working on her doctoral degree, she earned her master of arts degree in applied sociology from the University of Central Florida. Her research on the military's role in disasters has also been included in a special issue of the *Annals of the American Academy of Political and Social Sciences* on Hurricane Katrina. Her article "Metaphors Matter: Disaster Myths, Media Frames, and Their Consequences" is coauthored with Kathleen Tierney and Erica Kuligowski (2006).

David L. Brunsma is associate professor of sociology at the University of Missouri at Columbia. He was the program chair and organizer of the 2006 annual meetings of the Southern Sociological Society held in New Orleans shortly after Hurricane Katrina. He is editor of the recent *Mixed Messages: Multiracial Identities in the "Color-Blind" Era* (2006) and author or editor of six books and numerous articles. He is a member of Sociologists Without Borders and is the Race and Ethnicity Section editor at *Sociology Compass*, and his work focuses on critical sociological inquiries into race, racism, racial identities, epistemologies, and sociologies of knowledge.

George E. Capowich earned his Ph.D. at the University of Maryland at College Park and currently is an associate professor of sociology and criminology at Loyola University in New Orleans. His research interests include quantitative methods, testing criminological theories of crime causation, examining the composition and effects of neighborhood social networks, and program evaluation. His publications include several chapters in edited books and articles in journals such as *Youth and Society, Journal of Criminal Justice, Criminal Justice and Behavior, Sociological Quarterly,* and *Journal of Research in Crime and Delinquency.*

Lee Clarke is author of *Mission Improbable* and *Worst Cases.* He is often invited to speak about leadership, culture, disaster, and organizational and technological failures; he consults with corporations, government agencies, and research foundations. Dr. Clarke has written for or been featured in the *Atlantic Monthly,* the *Boston Globe,* National Public Radio, the *Washington Post,* and the *New York Daily News,* among others. He has been featured in the *New York*

Times and the *Harvard Business Review*. His edited volume *Terrorism and Disaster: New Threats, New Ideas* was published in 2003. Clarke was awarded the Rutgers Graduate School Award for Excellence in Teaching and Graduate Research (1996–1997) and the Northeastern Association of Graduate Schools' 1998 Graduate Mentoring Award. In August 2005, he was honored with the Fred Buttel Distinguished Scholarship Award by the Environment and Technology Section of the American Sociological Association.

Shyamal Das is currently an assistant professor of sociology at Minot State University, North Dakota. His areas of expertise are in areas of the sociology of development, gender, and sociological theories. His current research focuses on the sociology of education, corruption in developing countries, perceptions of sexual orientation in relation to regional and religious distinctiveness, and sex trafficking.

Katharine M. Donato is currently a professor of sociology at Vanderbilt University. Her broad interests focus on topics related to social stratification and demography, specifically international migration between Mexico and the United States. Her research has addressed questions related to the impact of U.S. immigration policy on the labor market incorporation of migrants, the process of immigrant incorporation in new U.S. destinations, and the ways in which social networks affect the health of Mexican families (see http://www.mexmah.com). With funding from the National Science Foundation and the Russell Sage Foundation, she has just begun a new tricity project that examines immigrant parent school involvement. Her publications have appeared in *Social Forces, International Migration, International Migration Review, Population Research and Policy Review*, and *Social Science and Medicine*.

Russell R. Dynes is founding director of the Disaster Research Center at the University of Delaware. He received his B.A. and M.A. from the University of Tennessee and his Ph.D. from Ohio State University. He served as chair of the Department of Sociology at Ohio State University and the University of Delaware. From 1977 to 1982, he was executive officer of the American Sociological Association in Washington, D.C. From 1976 to 1979, he chaired the Committee on International Disaster Assistance of the National Academy of Sciences/National Research Council, and in 1979, he served as head of the Task Force on Emergency Preparedness and Response for the President's Commission on the Accident at Three Mile Island. From 1986 to 1990, he served as president of the Research Committee on Disasters of the International Sociological Association. He has been a Fulbright lecturer in Egypt, India, and Thailand as well as a visiting professor at University College, Cardiff. He is author or editor of 11 books, including *Organized Behavior in Disaster, Sociology of Disaster, Disasters, Collective Behavior and Social Organization*, and *Handbook of Disaster Research*, as well as over 100 articles, many on disaster-related topics.

Lisa A. Eargle is an associate professor of sociology at Francis Marion University. She teaches a wide variety of courses in stratification and inequality, population dynamics, and research methods. Her research interests include the factors influencing local economic development patterns, consequences of local development patterns for populations and social institutions, and transnational crime.

James R. Elliott is an associate professor of sociology at the University of Oregon. His scholarship focuses on urban development and social inequalities in the United States, ranging from research on native- and foreign-born migration, racial and gender inequalities in the labor market, struggles over public housing, and social vulnerabilities to environmental hazards. His projects have received funding from a variety of sources, including the U.S. Department of Housing and Urban Development and the National Science Foundation. With assistance from colleagues at Tulane, Loyola, and Xavier universities, Dr. Elliott is currently heading a study of sociodemographic change in post-Katrina New Orleans. He was in New Orleans when Katrina hit, taking refuge and volunteering at a local hospital.

Kai Erikson is William R. Kenan Jr. Professor Emeritus of Sociology and American Studies at Yale University. He is past president of the American Sociological Association (ASA), the Society for the Study of Social Problems, and the Eastern Sociological Society. He has been a fellow of the Center for Advanced Study in the Behavioral Sciences and a visiting scholar of the Russell Sage Foundation. He is the author of *Wayward Puritans: A Study in the Sociology of Deviance*, which won the MacIver Award of the ASA, and of *Everything in Its Path*, which won the Sorokin Award of the ASA. He is the only sociologist to ever twice win the top award of the ASA for the best book of the year. His latest book is titled *A New Species of Trouble: Explorations in Disaster, Trauma, and Community*. His research and teaching interests include American communities, human disasters, and ethnonational conflict. He has been master of Trumbull College, chair of the American Studies program at Yale, editor of *The Yale Review*, and chair of the Department of Sociology.

Ashraf Esmail is currently a faculty member at Delgado Community College in sociology and criminal justice. He currently serves as coeditor of the *Journal of Urban Education*. His research interests include urban/multicultural/peace education, family, cultural diversity, political sociology, criminology, social problems, and deviance. He has published in various book chapters and journal articles.

Kelly Frailing is currently a master's student in criminal justice at Loyola University in New Orleans. She was previously a foster care worker, adult group home supervisor, and children's mental health program evaluator. She has a variety of research interests, including mental health and corrections, disasters and crime, and applications of conflict theory. She is a member of Alpha Phi Sigma and plans to pursue her Ph.D. in criminology beginning in the fall of 2007. Her contribution to this volume was expanded from a presentation given at the 2006 Southern Sociological Society meeting in New Orleans.

Elizabeth Fussell has been assistant professor of sociology at Tulane University since 2001. She received her Ph.D. from the University of Wisconsin at Madison in 1998. From 1998 to 2001, she had a postdoctoral fellowship at the Population Studies Center at the University of Pennsylvania. She has two main areas of research: international migration, specifically from Mexico to the United States, and the young adult life course. She has published research on these topics in *Social Forces, Demography, International Migration,* and *Advances in Life Course Research* as well as several edited volumes. Currently she is studying the arrival of Latino migrants in New Orleans after Hurricane Katrina. In addition, she is working with Mary Waters, interviewing young women community college students in New Orleans about their lives since Hurricane Katrina.

John J. Green is assistant professor and graduate coordinator for community development in the Division of Social Sciences at Delta State University. Additionally, he is founding director of the Institute for Community-Based Research. A collaborative partnership with the Center for Community and Economic Development, the institute works with students, faculty, and community organizations to engage in applied research. His research and teaching interests include participatory methods, food and agriculture, rural poverty, health and development connections, globalization, and the social dimensions of disaster. He received a B.A. degree in political science and M.S. degree in sociology from Mississippi State University and a Ph.D. in rural sociology from the University of Missouri at Columbia. His disaster-related research with Anna M. Kleiner and Albert B. Nylander III continues, with particular focus on learning from service providers working with nonprofit organizations.

Timothy J. Haney is a graduate teaching fellow and Ph.D. student in the Department of Sociology at the University of Oregon at Eugene. From 2003 to 2006, he was a graduate student in sociology at Tulane University and a resident of New Orleans. His research agenda centers on "neighborhood effects," or the influence of residential location and neighborhood characteristics on individual outcomes, as well as the social and demographic transformation of post-Katrina New Orleans. He has a forthcoming publication in *Social Science Research* that unpacks the relationship between neighborhood poverty, perceived neighborhood disorder, and self-esteem. He is currently collecting original survey data for a research project on post-Katrina New Orleans that focuses on housing, social networks, and employment (funded by the National Science Foundation, principal investigator James R. Elliott).

Dee Wood Harper is professor of sociology and coordinator of graduate studies in Criminal Justice, Loyola University in New Orleans. He earned a B.A. from George Peabody College of Vanderbilt University and an M.A. and Ph.D. from Louisiana State University. He was a National Institute of Mental Health postdoctoral fellow (1973–1974) in social psychiatry at the Tulane University School of Medicine, Department of Psychiatry and Neurology, Social Psychiatry Unit. His scholarly research, spanning over 40 years, has been wide ranging, addressing issues in gerontology, the sociology of education, the epidemiology of addiction, the sociology of tourism and crime, and, more recently, the death penalty and violent crime and deviance. His research has appeared in the *American Journal of Sociology, Sociological Symposium, Annals of Tourism Research, International Journal of Law and Information Technology, Artificial Intelligence and Applications, Proceeding: Artificial Intelligence Applications Conference,* and *Criminal Justice Review* with work currently under review with *Homicide Studies* and *Police Practice and Research: An International Journal.*

Emily Holcombe is currently a research assistant at Child Trends in Washington, D.C. She has a B.A. from Rice University in sociology and policy studies, where she was studying while conducting research on the response of the religious community to the evacuees of Hurricane Katrina. Her current research interests include fertility, family formation, public policy, and social service provision.

Anna M. Kleiner is assistant professor in the Department of Sociology and Criminal Justice at Southeastern Louisiana University. She completed her Ph.D. in rural sociology at the University of Missouri at Columbia. As an applied sociology researcher and former economic development specialist and community planner, Dr. Kleiner has extensive experience developing and implementing strategies to enhance collaborative efforts assisting community groups with identifying and answering questions impacting their quality of life. She has promoted the use of community-based research methodologies to explore and address the social implications of disasters and the local impacts of the globalization of agriculture and food. Dr. Kleiner continues her research collaboration with John J. Green, Albert B. Nylander III, and community-based partners relative to the social impacts of Hurricane Katrina on communities in Louisiana and Mississippi.

Marcus M. Kondkar is an associate professor of sociology at Loyola University in New Orleans. He received his doctoral degree in sociology from the University of Virginia. His research interests include criminology, sociology of law, and sociological theory. He is currently conducting research on patterns of domestic violence and intimate partner homicide in the United States and serves on Mayor Nagin's Domestic Violence Advisory Board in New Orleans. He has published articles in *Social Justice, American Journal of Public Health,* and *Legal Systems of the World: A Political, Social, and Cultural Encyclopedia.*

Nancy Kutner is professor of rehabilitation medicine, Emory University School of Medicine, and adjunct professor of sociology at Emory University. Her research, supported by the National Institutes of Health, focuses on quality of life, rehabilitation, and psychosocial aspects of chronic kidney disease. This work includes a collaborative study with epidemiologists at Tulane University of the impact of Hurricane Katrina on the health of dialysis patients. She has an ongoing research interest in functioning and well-being outcomes in aging and chronic health conditions, especially the association of race, gender, and socioeconomic status with these outcomes. Her publications include chapters in *21st Century Sociology: A Reference Handbook* (2006), *The Sociology of Health and Illness: Critical Perspectives* (2004), and *Research in the Sociology of Health Care* (2003, 2000, 1994, 1987).

Kris Macomber is a doctoral student at North Carolina State University. Her specializations include social inequality, social psychology, teaching sociology, and critical pedagogy. Other interests include visual sociology and qualitative methodology. Her current research focuses on the reproduction of patriarchy in material culture, intimate partner violence, and the social construction of masculinity.

Brent K. Marshall is an associate professor in the Department of Sociology and a research associate in the Institute for Social and Behavioral Sciences at the University of Central Florida. He has published numerous theoretical and empirical articles in the areas of disasters, environmental justice, environmental risk, and natural resource management. He is also a member of the American Sociological Association's Gulf Coast Disaster Research Team.

DeMond Shondell Miller is an associate professor of sociology and director of the Liberal Arts and Sciences Institute for Research and Community Service at Rowan University in Glassboro, New Jersey. He has worked as an evaluator for alcohol and tobacco social norms projects and as principal investigator to facilitate research projects involving environmental issues and community satisfaction. His primary area of specialization is environmental sociology, disaster studies, the study of the social construction of place, community development, and social impact assessment. Dr. Miller has presented and published several professional papers; recent examples of such work can be found in *The Researcher, The Qualitative Report, Journal of Emotional Abuse, Space and Culture: An International Journal of Social Spaces, International Journal of the Humanities,*

Journal of Black Studies, Journal of Public Management and Social Policy, and *Southeastern Sociological Review.*

Albert B. Nylander III is the chair of social sciences and associate professor of sociology and community development at Delta State University. His research and teaching interests include sociology of education, sociology of leadership, community studies and health care. He has published several articles in the *Journal of the Community Development Society.* He received a B.S.E. degree in secondary education and an M.S. degree in sociology from the University of Mississippi and obtained the Ph.D. in sociology from Mississippi State University.

David Overfelt is a graduate of sociology at the University of Missouri at Columbia. As a radical public sociologist, he tries to merge his academic work with his activism. In this, he is a member of Sociologists Without Borders, and his work focuses on critical inquiries into place, urban planning and development, globalization, politics, and the inequalities generated through the policies formed in these arenas of life.

J. Steven Picou is professor of sociology and chair of the Department of Sociology, Anthropology, and Social Work at the University of South Alabama in Mobile. He has held academic and research appointments at Louisiana State University, Ohio State University, and Texas A&M University. Professor Picou's teaching and research interests include environmental sociology, disasters, the sociology of risk, and applied sociology. He has published numerous articles in these areas, the most recent appearing in *Social Forces, Environment and Behavior, Social Science Research, Law and Policy,* and the *Sociological Inquiry.* In 2001, Professor Picou was awarded the Distinguished Contribution Award by the Environment and Technology Section of the American Sociological Association for his basic and applied research activities in Alaskan fishing communities and Native villages impacted by the *Exxon Valdez* oil spill. Over the years, his research has been funded by agencies such as the National Science Foundation, the Environmental Protection Agency, the U.S. Department of Commerce, and the Alabama Department of Environmental Management. At present, he is directing several projects on the health risks associated with seafood consumption and the long-term social impacts of Hurricane Katrina.

Jason David Rivera is a research associate at Rowan University in the Liberal Arts and Sciences Institute for Research and Community Service. He has recently worked on research dealing with public policy in reference to disaster mitigation and relief, social justice in the face of disasters, and the reconfiguration of landscapes and their effect on local and global politics as well as research pertaining to improving university and community relations. Examples of his research can be found in the *Journal of Public Management and Social*

Policy, Space and Culture: An International Journal of Social Spaces, Journal of Black Studies, and *International Journal of the Humanities.*

Havidán Rodríguez is a core faculty member and former director of the Disaster Research Center and professor in the Department of Sociology and Criminal Justice at the University of Delaware. He is currently working on research focusing on population composition, geographic distribution, natural hazards, and vulnerability in the coastal regions of Puerto Rico. He is a lead social science researcher for the Engineering Research Center for Collaborative Adaptive Sensing of the Atmosphere (funded by the National Science Foundation), and he is a member of the social science research team of the Mid-America Earthquake Center funded by the National Science Foundation. Rodríguez is the coeditor (with E. L. Quarantelli and R. R. Dynes) of the *Handbook of Disaster Research* (2006).

Sarah E. Rusche is a doctoral student in sociology at North Carolina State University. Her areas of specialization include social inequality, social psychology, and teaching excellence. Sarah's current research interests include antiblack discrimination by restaurant servers and critical pedagogy.

Audrey Singer is immigration fellow at the Metropolitan Policy Program at the Brookings Institution. Her areas of expertise include demography, international migration, immigration policy, and urban and metropolitan change. She has written extensively on U.S. immigration trends, including the new metropolitan geography of immigration, naturalization and citizenship, undocumented migration, and the changing racial and ethnic composition of the United States. She is currently coediting a book on the fastest-growing immigrant populations among second-tier metropolitan areas, including Atlanta, Washington, D.C., Dallas, Minneapolis–St. Paul, Charlotte, and Austin. She received her Ph.D. in sociology from the University of Texas at Austin and conducted postdoctoral research at the University of Chicago.

Kathleen Tierney is a professor in the Department of Sociology and the Institute of Behavioral Science at the University of Colorado. She is also the director of the Natural Hazards Center, which since 1976 has served as a clearinghouse for research findings in the fields of hazards, disasters, and risk. Before her move to Colorado in 2003, she was the director of the University of Delaware's Disaster Research Center. For more than 25 years, Professor Tierney has conducted research on the social aspects and impacts of natural and technological disasters, civil unrest, and, more recently, large-scale acts of terrorism. Her publications include *Disasters, Collective Behavior, and Social Organizations* (coedited with Russell R. Dynes, 1994), *Facing the Unexpected: Disaster Preparedness and Response in the United States* (coauthored with Michael Lindell and Ronald Perry, 2001), and dozens of journal articles, book chapters, and technical reports dealing with the societal dimensions of hazards and disasters. From 2004 to 2006, Professor Tierney served on the National Academy of Sciences Committee on Disaster Research in the Social Sciences. Her work on Hurricane Katrina also appears in the edited volume *On Risk and Disaster: Lessons from Hurricane Katrina* (2005), in the *Annals of the American Academy of Political and Social Science*, and in the Katrina online forum of the Social Science Research Council (http://www.ssrc.org).

Joseph Trainor is a professional staff researcher at the University of Delaware Disaster Research Center (DRC) and an ABD doctoral candidate in the Department of Sociology and Criminal Justice at the University of Delaware. Trainor has been involved in a number of funded research projects focusing on issues related to the social and organizational aspects of disasters and emergency management. He was the principal analyst in a network analytic study of multiorganizational coordination after the September 11, 2001, World Trade Center attacks and was the lead graduate researcher on a project to examine the organizational and institutional development and operation of ESF#9/USAR in the United States. Trainor also has had field research experiences as part of a reconnaissance team that traveled to India and Sri Lanka immediately following the December 2004 Indian Ocean tsunami and as the lead field researcher for DRC's reconnaissance effort to examine the social aspects of Hurricane Katrina. Trainor's foci include the impact of organizational design on disaster response (including NIMS), issues related to multiorganizational vertical and horizontal coordination, the integration of research and practice, and the general sociobehavioral response to disasters.

Nicole Trujillo-Pagán is assistant professor of sociology and Chicano-Boricua studies at Wayne State University, where she teaches and researches in several areas, including colonialism, modernization, medicine, gender, and ethnic issues. Her scholarship has focused on the relationship between colonialism and the practice of medicine in Puerto Rico's modernization experience during the twentieth century. Her other interests include urban institutions, gender issues, the Asian diaspora, and health reconstruction efforts in post-Katrina New Orleans.

Delmar Wright is doctoral student at North Carolina State University. Much of his previous research has been in the areas of racial inequality within the workplace. His research interests include racial and gender inequality along with the study of formal organizations and work processes. He is a member of the American Sociological Association and the Southern Sociological Society.